Tastes from Valley to Bluff

THE
FEATHERSTONE FARM
COOKBOOK

Tastes from Valley to Bluff

THE FEATHERSTONE FARM COOKBOOK

MI AE LIPE

Cover and book design by Mi Ae Lipe
What Now Design
www.whatnowdesign.com

Front Cover: Background photo by Featherstone Farm. Clockwise from far left: Stir-fry by Paul Cowan, represented by Dreamstime.com; stuffed peppers by Pawel Strykowski, represented by Dreamstime.com; strawberries, lettuce seedlings, and squash seedlings by Featherstone Farm; and salad by Ingrid Balabanova, represented by Dreamstime.com.

Back Cover: Background photo by Featherstone Farm. Clockwise from far left: Tomatoes by Irina Ponomarenko, represented by Dreamstime.com; shrimp pasta by David Smith, represented by Dreamstime.com; cabbage by Featherstone Farm; melon balls by Olga Lyubkina, represented by Dreamstime.com; and lettuce washing by Featherstone Farm.

Printed and bound in Canada by Hignell Book Printing.

To order additional copies of this book, inquire about discounts, or offer your comments and suggestions,
please contact the author by email:
miae@whatnowdesign.com

To contact Featherstone Farm:

Featherstone Fruits and Vegetables
30997 Zephyr Valley Lane
Rushford, Minnesota 55971
507-452-4244
www.featherstonefarm.com
info@featherstonefarm.com

First Edition
ISBN: 978-1-4276-2205-1
Library of Congress Control Number: 2007932837

To Stefan and Ryan,
who never needed any encouragement
to eat their vegetables

and to Ron,
who could sum up Brussels sprouts in two words:
Why bother?

Contents

Acknowledgements

No book is ever the work of a single author. Just as it takes a village to raise a child, a cookbook, in particular, represents the culmination of many talented and dedicated contributors.

First and foremost, I thank Jack Hedin and Rhys Williams of Featherstone Farm for their incredible, unflagging support and patience during the five years it took to bring this project to reality. A huge thanks go to others at Featherstone for letting me use their excerpts and recipes from farm newsletters, especially past CSA managers Sarah Libertus and Sarah Stone, and volunteers Margaret Trott and Margaret Houston. Of course, the seeds of the book began with the recipes so generously donated by Featherstone Farm's own CSA members, especially Pam Garetto (her enthusiasm for the project from the start was truly infectious!). I remain especially grateful to Featherstone's current CSA manager, Mary Benson, and bookkeeper, Larisa Walk, for their assistance with the cookbook's promotion, distribution, photos, and food preservation information.

In gathering material for this book, I was honored to receive the warm support, generous advice, and permission to use recipes from some of the most respected names in the American culinary field today, including Greg Atkinson, celebrated Pacific Northwest chef and culinary consultant; Elizabeth Schneider, a prominent authority on fruits and vegetables; Paige Brady, director of publications for Whole Foods Market; Peter Reinhart, internationally recognized bread baker; Tarre Beach, former managing editor of *Saveur* magazine; Mollie Katzen, author of the legendary *The Enchanted Broccoli Forest* and *The Moosewood Cookbook;* Julie Ridlon, chef and owner of Chanterelle Catering and Clayton Farmers Market of St. Louis, Missouri; *Food & Wine* magazine; and Joel Patraker, former manager of New York City's famous Union Square Greenmarket and buyer for The Four Seasons Restaurant. (More detailed permissions acknowledgments appear in the back of this book.) To all of these contributors, I am forever grateful. I also thank each and every one of the publishers and other individuals, named and unnamed, whose recipes appear in this book.

I also heartily thank program coordinator Doug Wubben at the Madison Area Community Supported Agriculture Coalition (MACSAC) for his willingness to not only let me reprint several recipes from their outstanding cookbook, *From Asparagus to Zucchini: A Guide to Cooking Farm-Fresh, Seasonal Produce*, but also for his constructive advice and generous support. MACSAC's incredible book in no small part inspired this volume.

Nelda Danz and Melinda McBride are fellow editors who generously agreed to help look over the manuscript under nearly impossible deadlines. Last but not least, I thank my father, Dewey, who instilled in me a lifelong love for vegetable gardening when he handed me a packet of parsley seeds when I was seven, and a dearly loved family friend, Kitty, whose dog-eared volume of M. F. K. Fisher's *The Art of Eating* forever changed my culinary outlook at a tender age.

This cookbook is the product of a wonderful collaboration between Featherstone Farm and members of our ten-year-old community-supported agriculture (CSA) program, principally Mi Ae Lipe. I believe that it will bring you not only great recipes and produce preparation ideas, but also information about the seasonality of fresh fruits and vegetables in the upper Midwest. This is its primary purpose, and I believe it succeeds admirably. My great thanks go to Mi Ae for all her work in bringing it to fruition.

In a larger sense, however, this book represents an answer to many questions that come to my mind during contemplative periods while working on the farm. These are questions about vocation, community, and my commitment to transforming American agriculture at its roots. Of course, I will be seeking these answers for as long as I am a farmer, but writing for this cookbook provides a good opportunity to take stock in my progress to date.

Growing vegetables means far more to me (and I suspect to many farmers) than merely planting, cultivating, and harvesting crops. Farmers are literally caretakers of ecosystems, custodians of generations' worth of agricultural knowledge of the land that sustains us. And we have the privilege to spend our lives feeding people. Yet many people have little or no understanding of what it is we do, or how our craft impacts the environment and now our culture that inhabits it.

To walk into any supermarket in modern-day America is to see many things that are right in American agriculture. The great variety of fresh fruits and vegetables on the shelves, their availability and generally high quality for most of the year, their affordability for most people—these are all successes that would have been almost unimaginable even two or three generations ago. The recent growth of the organic food industry promises to make even more healthful, environmentally responsible food available to many more people.

And yet, when we look beyond the breathtaking colors and vitality of this produce, how much do we really know about the origins of these various crops? What can we say about how their production has impacted the environment, labor fairness, and land use and sustainability, to name just a few? We all want to feel good about what we eat, to know not only that it is free of pesticides and pathogens but also that the farms that produce these crops are held to a high standard of ecological and humane stewardship.

The U.S. Department of Agriculture and Federal Food and Drug Administration are charged with monitoring and ensuring the quality of the nation's food system. But recent news reports (from *E. coli* contamination in spinach to mad cow disease) suggest how difficult it is to ensure this absolutely. And what about the larger issues—soil erosion, groundwater contamination, and greenhouse gas emissions? What do we know about how we contribute to such problems merely by shopping at the grocery store?

The answer to all these questions lies in both knowledge and transparency. If farmers and consumers can come together to talk about food, both will be empowered to pursue their needs and ideals with greater confidence. Consumers can learn directly how the crops that feed them are produced. If they don't like what they hear, they can appeal directly to producers for something better. Farmers can learn what values consumers place on food other than low price, and how agricultural practices can be adapted to reflect those values.

This cookbook is part of a solution to the anonymity in the modern industrial food system. It offers information about how we grow, harvest, and handle fresh fruits and vegetables on our farm, as well as our history and agricultural philosophy. Moreover, it is an invitation to you, as consumers of our farm's produce, to think more about what you eat and to ask more questions if you don't find the answers here in these pages. This cookbook is certainly a great collection of recipes. I hope it will be more for you as well, providing a starting point for dialogue between the farmer and consumer that will enrich us all.

Thank you for purchasing this book, and for your support of local, organic agriculture.

Jack Hedin
Rushford, Minnesota
October 2007

One of my earliest childhood memories growing up in the San Francisco Bay Area was sitting in the backseat of my parent's 1964 Plymouth as we headed home and looking out the window just in time to see corn. Not a big cornfield, mind you, but a scant two-acre, rectangular plot full of tall, exotic-looking plants with wavy leaves, their emerald lushness contrasting with the arid brown dirt and surrounding golden hills. At a certain time in the summer, the little produce stand next to it would throw open its doors and overflow with vegetables, melons, berries, and, of course, fresh sweet corn. Later in the fall, pumpkins abounded, their late-ripening siblings lying in the fields behind the yellowing corn.

In all of the years and thousands of times we drove past this produce stand, we never once stopped there, and why we did not mystifies me to this day, other than we were not in the habit of getting our food anywhere but from a supermarket. It all seemed so foreign to me, this quaint harvest out in the open air, unprotected, unrefrigerated, to a child heavily sheltered and who knew vegetables only as civilized bundles in chilled grocery display cases.

Fifteen years later, I moved to Wisconsin, and for the first time, driving through Minnesota, I saw more corn than I ever imagined could possibly exist. It is perhaps fitting that while I grew up only a couple hundred miles from one of the largest-scale agricultural operations in the world, California's improbably productive Central Valley, that I would finally get to taste genuine vegetable bounty from a small organic farm in Minnesota almost by pure chance. Once I did, I was hooked, and for several years I was a CSA (community-supported agriculture) member of Featherstone Farm, receiving some of the most delicious produce I had ever eaten.

I have always considered myself a far more dedicated eater than a cook of any merit. However, my lifelong passions of food, culture, and gardening, coupled with being a book editor and designer, inspired me to create a cookbook for Featherstone. Initially I conceived it as a place for CSAers to share their recipes and to get ideas on what to do with that eggplant or kale lurking in the basket. Certainly, I myself often had plenty of questions and little inspiration when I lugged my own lavish CSA boxes home, often to a hungry family begging for dinner in a hurry.

Five years since those first germinating thoughts, the cookbook has flourished. It has evolved from a mere seedling repository of recipes and serving ideas to a truly comprehensive resource for preparing and enjoying more than fifty different fruits and vegetables, whether they appear in a weekly CSA basket, in the supermarket, or at your local farmers market.

It is my hope that you will not only learn how to make the most of these fruits and vegetables, but you will get a behind-the-scenes look at how your CSA membership impacts the farmer, the environment, your health, and ultimately the well-being of this earth. May you enjoy this journey, every delicious bite at a time.

Mi Ae Lipe
October 2007
Seattle, Washington

About Featherstone and Zephyr

Featherstone Fruits and Vegetables is located on a 550-acre property in Winona County in southeastern Minnesota, owned by the Zephyr Valley Community Land Co-op (ZVCC). The Co-op was established in 1994 by six individuals who were interested in making a living close to the land within a community of like-minded people.

Through the first ten years of its existence, ZVCC grew into a lively cooperative of fourteen adults and as many children. ZVCC members have constructed their own homes on the farm; collectively reroofed and renovated two historic barns on the property; constructed a new "common" house, community swimming pond, and sauna; and begun the long process of restoring the property's woodlots, wetlands, and pastures, which have suffered from years of overgrazing. Although only Jack Hedin (and formerly Rhys Williams) make their living from Featherstone Fruits and Vegetables, several members have gardens and keep small livestock on community land.

Of the 550 acres that make up the Zephyr property, only about fifty are suitable for cultivating annual crops. That farmland is now rented by Featherstone on a long-term basis. Featherstone has significantly improved the fields by amending soils, installing buried irrigation, and building permanent deer fencing. Featherstone has also constructed and remodeled a number of buildings on the property, including three greenhouses and a machine shop.

Featherstone employs about a dozen seasonal workers every year, and many of them live on the Zephyr property. This has been a mutually beneficial arrangement for years; the farm workers enjoy many of the co-op's amenities during the summer, and the co-op residents grow and learn from having a truly multicultural community right on the property.

Featherstone now rents as much farmland in the bluffs surrounding Zephyr as it does at ZVCC itself. Eventually Featherstone may purchase a neighboring farm as a home for a new packing and crop storage shed. But even as this small farm business expands, it will always remain rooted at the Zephyr Co-op.

Featherstone's History

The history of Featherstone Fruits and Vegetables began in the late 1980s, when Jack Hedin and his partner Jenni McHugh embarked on a series of farm internships that took them from New England to Pennsylvania to California. During this period they acquired the practical knowledge of vegetable production, as well as the love of agriculture that would be the foundation of their work in Minnesota. It was also when Jack's vision for Featherstone began to take shape.

A primary element of this vision that Jenni and Jack shared from the outset was the desire for an organic farm to be the center of a rural community. As a young couple, they had lived and worked in two such communities, Full Belly Farm near Davis, California, and the Wiscoy Community Co-op in Winona County, Minnesota, not far from the present Featherstone site. In 1994, they became the founding members of the Zephyr Valley Land Community Co-op (see page XIII), where they have lived and farmed ever since.

In their first seasons as certified organic producers (1997 to 1999), Jack and Jenni were joined by Jack's brother, Ed. The farm's scale was quite small—one greenhouse, five acres on a single site, one tractor, and a small number of part-time employees. The main outlets for their crop were the Rochester farmers market and a twenty-member community-supported agriculture (CSA) group in Winona. Many mistakes were made in those early days, because applying knowledge gained in other parts of the country to the unique microclimates of this Minnesota bluff country proved far more daunting than expected. Humility and a sense of humor were essential to survive these early days.

As the farm grew in complexity and scale, Jenni turned her attention to other work (midwifery and infant and maternal health), and Ed began to think of a future beyond farming. Rhys and Tracy Williams, old friends of Jenni's from her days at an upstate New York orchard, moved to the area in 1998. While Rhys searched for a nearby orchard to purchase and convert to organic management, he and his family began spending more time at Featherstone and visiting the Zephyr Co-op. When Ed finally moved on after the 1999 season, Rhys joined Jack in forming a farm partnership in 2000.

The years from 2000 to 2006 saw rapid growth in all aspects of Featherstone's operations. The acreage under cultivation rose from ten to forty and then to eighty acres, as new farm sites were rented to ensure a more predictable, quality crop. Tractors, equipment, and greenhouses were added to support production. More full-time employees were hired. The Minnesota CSA grew to two hundred shares in Winona, Rochester, and Minneapolis-St. Paul. Then a wholesale business supplying food co-ops and natural food stores from Minneapolis to Chicago opened up, as more places called for Featherstone produce. By and large, the farm succeeded in growing enough quality crops to fill most of the demand.

In March 2006, Rhys underwent an emergency surgery that left him with a significant disability. Although his love of agriculture and commitment to Featherstone remained undiminished, the summer's work in 2006 convinced him that he would not be able to continue a life in farming. Reluctantly, in the winter of 2007, he withdrew from the partnership.

Featherstone continues to manage about one hundred acres of fruit and vegetable crops on five sites on and near the original home farm at the Zephyr Co-op. Although the farm's business model has evolved significantly as the farm's scale has grown, the fundamental vision that Jack and Jenni brought with them to the land remains unchanged—a commitment to true organic practices, with the help of a diverse, ethically managed farm crew, and with a healthy relationship to the broader community, near and wide. Above all else, agriculture remains a labor of love at Featherstone Fruits and Vegetables.

The Featherstone Farm crew of 2007.

Featherstone's founders and owners Jenni McHugh and Jack Hedin are seated, third and second from the right, along with their sons Emmet, Jasper, and Oscar.

Featherstone for the Future

But this rough magic / I here abjure. …
The Tempest
Act V, Scene I, 50 to 51

Featherstone Fruits and Vegetables has grown and matured in every conceivable fashion over the past decade, to the point that I can say we are good practitioners of the modern paradigm of organic vegetable production: long monocultures of hybrid plants, maintained by fossil fuel-hungry machines, packed and shipped to relatively distant markets.

I am proud of what we've achieved. We are providing very good food to many people, in a way that is lighter on the land than our conventional farming neighbors. Moreover, we have developed relationships with customers, local businesses, and rural neighbors that have hopefully helped spread the word about organic, local, and regional food production. We are part of a movement that is, I believe, advancing in the right direction.

Nevertheless, I am convinced that we can and should be doing more to pursue sustainability. Not the kind of marketing-driven sustainability that some farmers have promoted of late, as a kind of half-hearted move toward being certified organic. I'm talking about the kind of sustainability I studied in anthropology courses on pre-industrial societies: Peruvian and Indonesian and other farmers who have grown crops on terraces or paddies for thousands of years without depleting the soil, without hybrid and genetically modified organism (GMO) technology and, most importantly, without fossil fuels and their attendant pollution.

I am not proposing to return our farm to the Stone Age. I am proposing to use our successful organic farm as a platform from which to launch something qualitatively different: a "farm within a farm" that is a true model of sustainability, incorporating the best technologies from the pre- to post-industrial world. This land would be eight or ten acres within our larger organic farm, operated according to this completely different paradigm.

What will this Featherstone Farm for the Future (FFF) look like? For one thing, it will emphasize livestock as a source of fertility (on-farm compost), animal traction (oxen and horses plowing annual crops), and year-round income (sales of meat, eggs, and animal products). To support the livestock, FFF will devote much of its land to perennial grasses for grazing, with the added benefits of soil building that this brings. The new Featherstone "farm within a farm" will endeavor to be self-sustaining in everything from seed varieties (no hybrids) to crop storage (earth-sheltered root cellars).

FFF will need to incorporate appropriate modern technologies to support aspects of its work. Photovoltaic cells will be used to generate electricity for refrigeration, shop power, and to charge battery-equipped vehicles (small tractors as well as light trucks). Current geothermal technology will be harnessed to heat greenhouses for early and late season production. Every aspect of the future farm's energy, fertility, and horticultural needs will be assessed with an eye for sustainability.

This FFF "farm within a farm" is still a number of years from coming to fruition. For me, it represents a life's work that must develop slowly to ensure its success. But I am thinking through all of the current issues with an eye as to how they will ultimately impact the FFF idea.

It may be years until we plow our first furrow with some sustainably derived energy source, or raise our first vegetable crop with seeds harvested on the farm. Yet there is no time like the present to begin the planning, the organization, and the fundraising that will ultimately make it all possible. We will be looking to current customers—particularly within our CSA and the Twin Cities co-ops—for advice and support. We will be applying for grants to assist with all aspects of the financial plan. And we will be taking baby steps in the direction of sustainability as part of our day-to-day operation.

FFF is not intended as a replacement for our current farm. I imagine that we will continue to use diesel-powered tractors on most of our acreage, for example, until the oil runs out or I am in my grave (whichever comes first!). Rather, this "farm within a farm" represents an experiment for the future, the success of which will ultimately be determined by future generations.

I got into agriculture twenty years ago with an idealistic vision—to create something positive and life-affirming in a world where most of the news we hear is discouraging. Featherstone for the Future is ultimately an effort to expand that vision, as an experiment in true sustainability.

Please feel free to contact me with questions or suggestions of any kind.

Jack Hedin
June 2007

How To Use This Book

One of my many goals in creating this book was to assemble a truly useful and enjoyable reference for cooking the more than fifty fruits, vegetables, and herbs grown by Featherstone Farm. As a former Featherstone CSA subscriber myself, I was often faced with that eternal question of what to do with all that luscious produce in my box or basket. Home cooks inherently realize that they are blessed with a gold mine of the freshest, tastiest fruits and vegetables around when their weekly share arrives, but they may be at a loss at how to take advantage of that bounty. (Or, how do you get that stubborn family member to try kohlrabi? What on earth is that thing, anyway?)

This book is arranged by season, to reflect the farm's growing cycle and to emphasize seasonality, a concept that sadly, in this age of year-round supermarket availability, is nearly unknown to many home cooks. Each season brings a unique appreciation of the present jewels flowing out of the fields and greenhouses, and keen anticipation of future garden treats, made all the more precious by their fleeting presence. The crops listed within each season may be available across more than one season; for instance, radishes appear in the CSA boxes both in the spring and fall, but they are listed in the book under the Fall section, when they are far sweeter and less fibrous.

Within each season, every crop is listed alphabetically for easy reference. Each entry covers history, nutrition, selection, storage, trimming and cleaning, and an array of cooking techniques, including steaming and boiling, stir-frying and sautéing, baking and roasting, blanching and freezing, and microwaving. Some crops contain additional instructions for grilling or simple drying techniques. All of the entries contain handy information on measurements, equivalents, and, where appropriate, substitutions (especially in the case of herbs). Perhaps one of the most useful parts of the book are the listings of complementary foods, herbs, and seasonings, as well as extensive serving suggestions, which are sure to spark even more cooking and preparation ideas.

The recipes that appear in this book range from traditional, Midwestern comfort-food dishes to the more eclectic and international. The recently burgeoning interest in regional and ethnic cuisines has happily resulted in people becoming more knowledgeable about different ingredients, and we are unbelievably fortunate to be cooking in an age when we have so many choices. Many of this book's recipes can be easily adapted to fit dietary preferences, with either the addition or omission of meat, fowl, fish, eggs, and dairy. Some recipes are simple and quick to prepare, while others are more complex. Hopefully some of the more unusual ones or serving suggestions will encourage you to try some unexpected combinations.

Some notes: This book does not extensively cover certain techniques, such as canning, making jams and jellies, baking, deep-fat frying, and drying. Countless books and copious Internet resources cover these topics much more effectively than space allows here; I trust that if the reader has a specific interest, they can pursue that information on their own. This book is meant to provide a comprehensive overview on everyday preparation.

Another item worth noting is that this book covers only the fruits, vegetables, and herbs that Featherstone Farm grows as of late 2006. Thus, some common vegetables such as carrots, which the farm did not raise in prior years, are not included.

This book assumes that you already know many of the basics of cooking, food preparation, and related terminology. I highly recommend books such as *Cookwise* by Shirley O.

Corriher and *Brilliant Food Tips and Cooking Tricks* by David Joachim for terrific information on cooking techniques and the science behind them.

Many strong opinions abound about cooking times, particularly with vegetables. One person may feel that broccoli is just right when it has been steamed for three minutes and still retains a bright green color; others think that this same vegetable is still raw at this stage and requires a half hour (or more) of rapid boiling to make it edible. Many of the boiling, steaming, and sautéing times listed in this book err on the side of al dente rather than overcooking. If you prefer your veggies more tender, please adjust your cooking times accordingly.

I personally find that cooking is an organic process. Certainly, we all have occasion to strictly follow certain recipes, especially for particular dishes that call for exact proportions or techniques, like baking and deep-frying. But frequently, when we come home tired after a long workday or have a hungry family becoming more cranky by the minute, we are used to cooking intuitively, throwing in a bunch of this and a pinch of that, according to whim and preference. I strongly encourage you to do this with many of this book's recipes, and be creative with various combinations of herbs, spices, sauces, and condiments.

Sprinkled throughout are dozens of related tidbits, which range from a glimpse into a typical summer day on the farm to how to cool the burn of chile peppers, as well as fascinating trivia, cooking tips, ingredient sources, and further references. Also included are pieces from Featherstone's newsletters over the years, written by its staff, CSA members, and volunteers, which offer thought-provoking insight into the farm's philosophy and methods.

I hope you find this book a fun, valuable resource that you will want to turn to again and again. I heartily welcome your thoughts and feedback; please feel free to email me at miae@whatnowdesign.com.

Happy cooking and eating!

Making salsa in Zephyr's Common House.

Crops and Seasons

CROP	VARIETIES	SEASON
Arugula		Spring, October
Asparagus		Spring
Basil (Italian)		Spring through fall
Beans (String)	*Green Snap, Haricots Verts, Royal Burgundy, Yellow Wax*	Spring through fall
Beets	*Chioggia, Detroit Red*	Spring greens, best roots in fall
Bok Choy		Spring, best in fall
Braising Mix		Spring, fall
Broccoli	*Green, Purple*	Spring, fall
Cabbage	*Green & Red Head, Red Napa, Savoy*	Spring, best in winter
Cantaloupe		August
Cauliflower		Fall
Chives		Spring
Cilantro		Summer through fall
Collards	*Flash, Top Bunch*	Spring and fall
Corn	*Bi-Color & White Supersweets*	July 20 to September 1
Cucumbers	*Burpless Slicing*	Summer
Dill		Summer
Eggplant	*Asian, Globe*	Mid-summer
Garlic (Green)		Spring
Garlic (Mature)	*German Red, Porcelain White (Asian)*	Summer, fall, winter (cured)
Honeydew Melon		Summer
Kale	*Green (Winterbor), Red (Redbor), Toscano (Lacinato or Dinosaur)*	Fall through winter
Kohlrabi	*White Vienna*	Spring, but mainly fall
Leeks		October
Lemongrass		Summer
Lettuce	*Green & Red Butter (Bibb), Green & Red Leaf, Oakleaf, Romaine*	Spring through summer

Mizuna		Spring, fall
Mustard Greens	*Green, Red*	Fall
Onions	*Green Bunching*	Spring through summer
	Mars (Red), Copra (Yellow)	Fall
	Walla Walla Sweet	Summer (bunched with tops in July)
Peas	*Snow, Sugar Snap*	Spring, summer (June 20 to July 10)
Peppers (Sweet)	*Green & Red Bell, Lipstick, Red & Gold (ripened), Sweet Chocolate*	July to September
Peppers (Hot)	*Jalapeño, Long Red Cayenne, Serrano*	Summer
Potatoes (New and Mature)	*All Blue, Bintje (Gold), Desiree Pink, Langlade White, Red Norland, Romance (Red-gold), Russian Fingerling, Yukon Gold*	All "new" during July to August; cured for use September to January
Pumpkin		Fall
Radishes	*Champion Red, Easter Egg*	June, September through October
Raspberries	*Autumn Bliss, Autumn Briton*	September
Rosemary		Summer
Rhubarb		May through early June
Salad Mix		June
Savory		Summer
Squash (Summer)	*Patty Pan, Yellow Straightneck, Zucchini*	Summer
Squash (Winter)	*Acorn, Butternut, Carnival, Heart of Gold, Kabocha/Buttercup, Pie Pumpkin, Red Kuri, Spaghetti, Sweet Dumpling*	Fall, Winter
Spinach	*Baby salad (bagged)*	Spring
	Overwintered (bunched)	Fall
Swiss Chard	*Bright Lights, Ruby Red*	Spring, summer
Strawberries	*Winona*	June
Tarragon		Summer
Tatsoi		Spring, fall
Thyme		Summer
Tomatoes	Red Slicer (Hothouse)	July
	Cherry *(Red Grape, Sungold)*	August through September

Tomatoes (continued)	Heirlooms & Romas *(Amish Paste, Brandywine, Cherokee Purple, German Stripe, Green Zebra, Red Zebra, Aunt Ruby Green, San Marzano, Yellow Roma)*	August through September
Turnips		October
Watermelon	*Mickey Lee, Sugar Baby, Yellow Doll*	Summer
Zucchini	*Ambassador, Elite*	Summer

Spring

❀ IN SOUTHERN MINNESOTA, SPRING CROPS ARE CONSIDERED
ANYTHING HARVESTED FROM THE END OF WINTER UP THROUGH THE
END OF JUNE. THEY INCLUDE PERENNIAL CROPS (ASPARAGUS, RHUBARB, AND
STRAWBERRIES), ANNUAL CROPS SEEDED IN THE SPRING (SALAD CROPS, GREENS,
AND PEAS), AND OTHERS PLANTED IN THE FALL AND OVERWINTERED IN
THE GROUND FOR AN EARLY SPRING HARVEST (SPINACH AND GARLIC).

OUR SPRING PERENNIAL CROPS ARE WELL-KNOWN AND MUCH-LOVED.
WE GROW THEM ALL AT FEATHERSTONE FARM, AND THEY FORM A SUBSTANTIAL
PART OF OUR CSA BOXES IN MAY AND JUNE. THE SPRING ANNUAL CROP
PLANTINGS, BY CONTRAST, CAN BE MUCH MORE DIFFICULT TO MANAGE.
BUT WHEN THEY DO SUCCEED, THE RESULTS ARE WONDERFUL.

Spring Crops Featured

Arugula
Asparagus
Basil (Italian)
Bok Choy
Chives
Green Garlic
Lettuce
Peas
Salad & Braising Mixes
Spinach
Strawberries
Swiss Chard
Rhubarb

Weather plays more of a role in the production of annual spring crops than at any other time of the year. The rate at which our topsoil sheds its winter frost, dries, and warms to a suitable planting temperature varies widely year to year. Spring weather can speed or delay this process dramatically. Since the ground must be sufficiently dry to permit tillage with a heavy tractor, the months of April and May are often an uneven rhythm of rain delays followed by periods of frenetic planting activity.

If all goes well, sometime in the middle of May we begin to harvest the first spring-planted salad mix, which is often the best of the year. Lettuces and Asian greens like cool soil and will remain sweet and tender as long as they grow slowly. As the days lengthen and the soil becomes warmer, they are at greater risk of turning bitter.

Meanwhile, the spinach and garlic that were planted the previous fall detect the first warmth of spring. These tiny spinach plants have waited patiently under the snow for months, and now they sprout new leaves and grow dramatically in April. By early May they are often full-grown and ready to harvest for bunching. In contrast to spring-seeded spinach, which is picked young and tender for salads, "overwintered" spinach is much better for cooking. It has a heartiness and richness of flavor that make it a wonderful, short-lived treat. By the first of June anything remaining in this planting has gone to seed.

In May, green garlic shoots are another early delight. Like a young onion (scallion), the garlic plant makes a tall shaft capped by deep blue-green foliage before it begins to form a bulb after the solstice. The portion of this shaft buried in the ground is pure white and has a wonderfully bright, spring-garlic flavor. Even the green shaft and parts of the leaves can be eaten fresh at this stage.

Our greenhouses are invaluable assets in producing spring crops. Transplants produced in the greenhouse in March—lettuces, cabbage, broccoli, and even beets, kohlrabis, and cilantro—can be put out in the field as early as the first week in April. They are covered with a light spun fabric to warm them day and night, and are foliar fed (sprayed directly on the leaves) with organic fertilizers when the weather is too cool for their roots to absorb nutrients from the soil. With a little luck (and lots of hard work!) they can begin to yield harvests in early June.

Leaf lettuce, in particular, is at its best at this time of year. The cool, moist spring mornings are perfect for this crop. However, it grows remarkably quickly in the long days of June, and as long as the soil remains cool and moist, lettuce leaves remain crunchy and sweet. Likewise, transplanted beets have a window of high quality in June, before the heat of summer makes them tough and bitter.

One way of envisioning spring crops is that, before peas and broccoli ripen in late June, one is eating almost exclusively the stems and foliage of various crops. And these parts of the plants tend to thrive best before the solstice's peak day length directs many crops to put their energy into seed or fruit production, depriving the foliage of the energy (read: sugar!) that makes them particularly sweet and delicious.

Sugar snap peas, for example, are the pinnacle of spring crops. Planted in the field the very first week of April, they finally begin producing seed pods toward the end of June, foreshadowing similar crops, such as green beans, that will appear within a couple of weeks.

Nothing is more quintessentially spring in the Minnesota garden than a fat sugar snap pea, freshly picked on a cool morning in June, when the last chill of winter has finally melted away into the warm breezes.

FARMER'S TABLE MENU — SPRING
— UP TO JUNE 15 —

BY JACK HEDIN

APPETIZER
Fresh Sugar Snap Peas and Radishes on Ice

GRILL
Asparagus Spears with Balsamic Vinegar
Hamburgers

ON THE SIDE
Steamed Beets

SALAD
Salad Mix

DESSERT
Rhubarb Shortcake

I am a minimalist in the kitchen, and particularly during this time of the year, I prefer fresh produce with as little preparation as possible. After months of spicing up storage crops from the root cellar, I'm ready for the clear, unadulterated zip of spring on the tongue.

For the hamburgers, I chop up lots of green garlic—shoots, leaves, and all—and work it into the beef in advance to give the burgers a spectacular flavor. The steamed beets are the highlight of this meal for me, because they are the first harvest of the season and so tender and flavorful. I steam the thinly sliced roots first, then the stems and greens, so they do not overcook. I also find that the leaves in the salad mix at this time of the year are so delicate that they do not require much dressing.

We do eat meat on the farm, because we have good access to free-range poultry, pork, and lamb, and grass-fed beef. In addition to the host of ethical and ecological reasons to support such farming practices, I believe that the eating quality of each is vastly higher than its industrial counterpart, and well worth looking for at the farmers market.

Arugula
Asparagus
Basil (Italian)
Beans (String)
  Royal Burgundy, Green Snap,
  Yellow Wax
Beets (greens and baby roots)
  Chioggia, Detroit Red
Bok Choy
Broccoli
  Green
Cabbage
  Green & Red Head, Savoy
Chives
Collards
  Flash, Top Bunch
Green Garlic
Green Onions
Kale
  Green, Toscano
Kohlrabi (spring transplant)
  White Vienna
Lettuce
  Green & Red Butter (Bibb),
  Green & Red Leaf, Oakleaf,
  Romaine
Peas (June 20 to July 10)
  Snow, Sugar Snap
Radishes
Salad & Braising Mixes
Spinach (baby salad; overwintered
  and bunched)
Strawberries
  Winona
Swiss Chard (spring to summer)
  Bright Lights, Ruby Red, Swiss
Rhubarb

Arugula

ERUCA SATIVA

Arugula is a relative newcomer to the American gastronomic scene. Often mistaken for lettuce, this peppery green is actually a member of the mustard family. Arugula is also known as garden rocket, rocket, rocket salad, rugola, rucola, or roquette. Arugula prefers cool weather, and although it is available in supermarkets year-round, it is best either in the spring or fall.

HISTORY

Arugula has been a favorite since Roman times in Mediterranean countries, where both the leaves and seeds are used in salads and in cooking. It was even favored as an aphrodisiac, dating back to the first century C.E.

NUTRITION

Arugula is high in vitamins A and C, iron, and calcium. A half-cup serving contains only two calories.

SELECTION

Arugula should be fresh-looking, with no wilted or limp leaves or stems. Avoid discolored, yellowed specimens, which indicate advanced age or improper storage.

STORAGE

Store fresh arugula unwashed in a tightly wrapped bag in the refrigerator vegetable crisper. Unlike some other greens, arugula does not keep well; use within 2 to 3 days.

TRIMMING AND CLEANING

Like spinach and leeks, arugula often harbors sand or other unpleasant grit. Unless you enjoy a little crunch with your greens, wash the leaves by submerging in water and swishing about thoroughly. Rinse under running water, then pat or spin-dry.

STEAMING & BOILING

Arugula responds well to a gentle, brief steaming. To prepare, wash arugula well but do not dry. Place in a steamer basket, cover, and steam in its own moisture for about 2 to 3 minutes. Boiling is not recommended for this delicate green, for overcooking will destroy its peppery, characteristic flavor.

STIR-FRYING & SAUTÉING

Add arugula leaves near the end of cooking time of stir-fries and sautés, and cook until just wilted, usually about 1 or 2 minutes. Be careful not to overcook, or arugula's delicate flavor will dissipate.

MICROWAVING

Wash arugula but do not dry. Place in a microwave-safe dish and cook on High power for about 2 to 4 minutes, or until the greens are tender.

BLANCHING AND FREEZING

Freezing arugula is not recommended because of its high water content and delicate flavor. However, if you want to persist, try shredding it into ½-inch ribbons; sautéing in olive oil, salt, and pepper; and packaging 1-cup portions tightly in zipper-lock freezer or vacuum food sealer-type bags, or freezer containers. Alternatively, you can freeze arugula as pesto (see the Pesto sidebar under Basil on pages 16–17).

COMPLEMENTARY HERBS, SEASONINGS & FOODS

Apples, avocado, bacon, basil, blue cheese, butter, citrus, dill, eggs, fennel, fish, garlic, goat cheese, ham, lemon balm, lemon juice, marjoram, olive oil, onions, oregano, Parmesan cheese, pasta, pears, pecans, pine nuts, poultry, seafood, tarragon, thyme, walnuts.

SERVING SUGGESTIONS

- Liberally sprinkle arugula in any tossed lettuce salad to add zip and interest.
- Add arugula to stir-fries near the end of the cooking time.
- Try arugula instead of lettuce in a surprise BLT; the pepperiness of arugula pairs beautifully with a good-quality, thick-cut, maple-cured bacon.
- Try using arugula sprouts in salads or sandwiches instead of alfalfa sprouts.
- Combine arugula with thinly shaved Parmesan cheese, good-quality olive oil, white wine vinegar, salt, and freshly ground black pepper.
- Substitute arugula for part or all of the basil to make a zippy, unusual pesto. (Unlike basil, arugula keeps its vibrant green color!)
- Add to pizzas after baking.
- Arugula makes a great "mixing" green; combine with different lettuces, chicory, endive, spinach, herbs, and flowers for a dynamic salad.
- Arugula goes wonderfully with fennel, apples, mandarin oranges, red onions, and pomegranates in salads. Fruity flavors help to offset its assertive pungency.
- If arugula is not available, you can substitute watercress for a similar spicy flavor, or vice versa.
- Lightly sauté arugula as a green and serve with pastas, robust meats, or a good roasted chicken.

PASTA WITH ARUGULA   SERVES 4

2½ cups chopped tomatoes
¼ cup chopped kalamata olives
2 tablespoons olive oil
2 cloves garlic, crushed
Salt and pepper
8 ounces uncooked gemelli pasta
3 cups arugula, torn and trimmed

½ cup Asiago cheese, grated

1. Combine the tomatoes, olives, olive oil, garlic, salt, and pepper in a bowl; set aside.

2. Cook and drain the pasta. Add the hot pasta and arugula to the bowl.

3. Toss everything together, sprinkle with the cheese, and serve promptly.

— *Ruth Charles, Featherstone Farm CSA member*

SAUTÉED MUSHROOMS ON TRICOLORE SALAD SERVES 4

1 endive, leaves separated
2 small bunches arugula, well-washed
1 medium-sized head radicchio, cored and pulled apart
½ cup extra-virgin olive oil
1 clove garlic, thinly sliced
1 pound assorted fresh mushrooms, such as cremini, shiitake,
  portobello, chanterelle, and white button, sliced ½-inch thick
1 teaspoon chopped fresh rosemary leaves
¼ cup balsamic vinegar
Salt and freshly ground black pepper
8 large shavings of Parmesan cheese

1. In a bowl, toss together the endive, arugula, and radicchio leaves. Cover with a damp towel and set aside.

2. In a large skillet, heat the olive oil over medium-high heat. Add the garlic and cook, stirring until it turns golden, about 3 minutes. Add the mushrooms, then decrease the heat to low, and cook, stirring occasionally, until the mushrooms are soft. Add the rosemary, balsamic vinegar, salt, and pepper to taste. Simmer until thickened, about 2 minutes.

3. Meanwhile, divide the greens on 4 serving plates. While the mushrooms are still hot, spoon them over the greens. Top with Parmesan cheese and serve immediately.

— *www.cooksrecipes.com*

ARUGULA AND GRILLED GOAT CHEESE SALAD SERVES 4

Goat cheese can be bought in many different forms. For this recipe, look for cylinder-shaped goat cheese from a delicatessen or for small rolls that can be cut into pieces weighing about 2 ounces.

CROUTONS
About 1 tablespoon olive oil
About 1 tablespoon vegetable oil
4 slices Italian bread

Books

The United States of Arugula: The Sun-Dried, Cold-Pressed, Dark-Roasted, Extra Virgin Story of the American Food Revolution
David Kamp; Broadway, 2007.

Greens Glorious Greens: More Than 140 Ways to Prepare All Those Great-Tasting, Super-Healthy, Beautiful Leafy Greens
Johnna Albi and Catherine Walthers; St. Martin's Griffin, 1996.

SAUCE

3 tablespoons apricot jam
4 tablespoons white wine
2 teaspoons Dijon mustard

DRESSING

3 tablespoons walnut oil
1 tablespoon lemon juice
Salt and pepper

1 (8-ounce) cylinder-shape goat cheese
Generous handful of arugula
About 4 ounces frisée (curly endive)

1. Heat the olive and vegetable oils in a frying pan and fry the slices of Italian bread on one side only, until lightly golden brown. Transfer to a plate lined with paper towels.

2. To make the sauce, heat the jam in a small saucepan until warm but not boiling. Push through a strainer into a clean pan, to remove the pieces of fruit, and then stir in the white wine and mustard. Heat gently and then keep warm until ready to serve.

3. Blend the walnut oil and lemon juice and season with a little salt and pepper.

4. Preheat the broiler a few minutes before serving the salad. Cut the goat cheese into 2-ounce rounds and place each piece on a crouton, untoasted side up. Place under the broiler and cook for 3 to 4 minutes until the cheese melts.

5. Toss the arugula and frisée in the walnut oil dressing and arrange attractively on four individual serving plates. When the croutons are ready, arrange on each plate and pour over a little of the apricot sauce.

— *Christine Ingram,* The Cook's Encyclopedia of Vegetables

Rows of arugula in the fields.

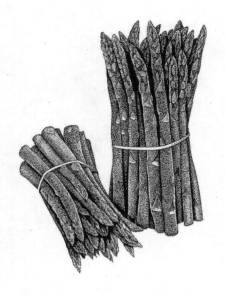

Asparagus

ASPARAGUS OFFICINALIS

Few vegetables represent spring as much as asparagus, with its tender shoots poking out of the moist, dark earth to meet the warm sun and lengthening days. This perennial garden favorite is a member of the lily family, with edible shoots that are harvested in an all-too-brief season. Featherstone cultivates green asparagus, but in Europe white asparagus (created by piling soil high around the emerging shoots) is a highly prized delicacy.

HISTORY

Humans have eaten asparagus since ancient times, cultivating it 2,000 years ago in the Mediterranean and Asia Minor. The ancient Greeks and Romans were particularly fond of it; the latter even froze it! Asparagus was eaten fresh in season and dried for consumption in other times of the year. Asparagus was prized not only as a food plant but also as medicine, used to treat an array of symptoms from heart trouble to toothaches.

NUTRITION

Asparagus is high in vitamins A, B-complex (especially folic acid), and C, as well as potassium and zinc. Like most veggies, asparagus has no fat; four spears contain only 15 calories.

SELECTION

Good asparagus should feel firm, not limp or shriveled (especially its tips), with an attractive green color (except for white asparagus, which is deliberately kept pale yellow to keep the stalks tender). Stalks that are large at the base may be tough or woody; such specimens should be trimmed or peeled before cooking.

STORAGE

Wrap unwashed asparagus in a plastic bag and place in the refrigerator vegetable crisper. Use as soon as possible, within one or two days, before all of the sugars turn to starches. If you cannot use asparagus for more than a day, either wrap the ends in a damp paper towel or bundle the spears with a rubber band and stand them upright in a container in an inch of water.

TRIMMING & CLEANING

Wash and thoroughly drain the spears in cool running water. (Watch out for grit trapped under the scales.) The tougher bottom ends can be either snapped or sliced off. If your asparagus spears are thicker and older, you may need to peel them first. Thin or very fresh stalks do not need peeling.

STEAMING & BOILING

A perennial dilemma with asparagus is that the thicker bottom ends take longer to cook, while the tender tips become mushy. Steaming asparagus upright in a deep steamer, double boiler, or percolator solves this prob-

lem, but then the spears lose their bright green color. Boiling asparagus uncovered in lots of salted water keeps it nice and green, but you will have to monitor for that exact moment when the spears go from being deliciously crisp-tender to mushy. Boil rapidly for 4 to 5 minutes, testing by piercing them with a fork; when they are tender, drain and plunge them immediately into cold water to stop them from cooking further.

STIR-FRYING & SAUTÉING

Cut the spears diagonally into ½-inch pieces, leaving the tips whole. Stir-fry the pieces in butter or hot oil in a skillet or wok at medium-high heat. Stir constantly until tender-crisp, 3 to 5 minutes.

BAKING & ROASTING

Baking or roasting asparagus in the oven brings out its natural sweetness and makes a sophisticated dish that is very easy to prepare. Roast spears at 500°F for about 8 to 10 minutes, depending on their thickness, or until they can be pricked easily with a knife.

MICROWAVING

Microwave fresh asparagus by placing 1 pound in a shallow, microwave-safe baking dish or serving bowl. If you are cooking whole spears, arrange with the tips in the center. Add about ¼ cup water and cover tightly. Microwave on High power for 4 to 7 minutes for spears, 3 to 5 minutes for cuts and tips. Stir or turn half way through the cooking time.

- 1 cup = 2 to 3 minutes
- 2 cups = 3 to 4 minutes
- 1 pound = 8 to 10 minutes

BLANCHING & FREEZING

To blanch asparagus, thoroughly wash it and trim the stem ends as necessary. Sort into piles, according to stalk thickness: small, medium, and large. You may either leave the spears whole or cut them into 2-inch lengths. Blanch in boiling water for 1½ minutes for small stalks, 2 minutes for medium, or 3 minutes for large. Plunge into an ice-water bath to stop the cooking, drain, and pack in zipper-lock freezer or vacuum food sealer-type bags, or freezer containers. Squeeze out excess air and leave ½ inch of headspace (unless you are using the vacuum sealing method). Use within 8 months for best quality.

EQUIVALENTS, MEASURES & SERVINGS

- 16 to 20 spears = 1 pound = 2⅔ to 3 cups cut into 1- to 1½-inch pieces
- ½ pound per person (6 to 8 spears)

COMPLEMENTARY HERBS, SEASONINGS & FOODS

Bacon, butter, chicken, chives, crab, garlic, halibut, ham, hollandaise sauce, leeks, lemon, lobster, mushrooms, nutmeg, Parmesan cheese, pasta, potatoes.

SERVING SUGGESTIONS

- Serve cooked asparagus warm with hollandaise sauce or topped with butter and Parmesan cheese.

Spears on the Water

Roman emperors were so fond of asparagus that they kept special boats for the purpose of fetching the vegetable, calling them the "Asparagus Fleet."

- Serve cooked asparagus cold with a simple vinaigrette, or olive oil, lemon juice, and sea salt.
- Asparagus is the ultimate finger food. Believe it or not, proper etiquette calls for eating asparagus with your fingers, not utensils! Kids love dipping spears in a little dish of melted butter, salad dressing, or mayonnaise.
- Slice into 1-inch pieces and stir-fry with other vegetables in a wok with a little corn, peanut, or sesame oil.
- Substitute asparagus for leeks in a leek tart or quiche recipe, or combine the two vegetables.
- Top pizza with very thin spears or tips of parboiled or steamed asparagus.
- Sauté asparagus in chicken broth for more flavor.
- Place parboiled asparagus spears, tomatoes, mushrooms, and shredded mozzarella cheese on top of focaccia bread for an elegant garden pizza.
- French-fry asparagus just like potato fries for a delicious and unusual dish, or try as a tempura vegetable.
- Asparagus and morel mushrooms, lightly sautéed in butter, are a magical combination, with happily synchronized farmers market appearances.
- Add cooked asparagus to your favorite omelet or scrambled eggs.
- If you are lucky enough to encounter young, tender asparagus the width of a pencil, try serving it raw with carrot and celery sticks and a favorite dip.
- Grill asparagus brushed with olive oil, vinaigrette, or your favorite dressing.

ROASTED BACON-WRAPPED ASPARAGUS   SERVES 4

1 bunch asparagus (about 15 to 20 spears)
1 small white onion, thinly sliced
2 tablespoons olive oil
10 slices of raw, thick-cut bacon, cut into half-strips
Freshly ground pepper and salt

1. Preheat the oven to 370°F.

2. Wash and trim the asparagus. Line a 9 × 12-inch pan with aluminum foil, and brush it with 1 tablespoon of the oil to keep the asparagus from sticking. Wrap each spear with a half-strip of bacon, tucking the ends under the asparagus, and place it in the pan. Place the onion rings over the asparagus, drizzle with the remaining oil, and sprinkle with salt and pepper.

3. Cover and bake for 45 minutes, or until the spears are tender and the bacon is crisp on the edges.

— *Mi Ae Lipe, Featherstone Farm CSA member*

ASPARAGUS AND SHRIMP SALAD   SERVES 4

This is a wonderful spring-summer salad.

1½ pounds asparagus, washed, trimmed, and peeled

Asparagus Eating Champ

The central California city of Stockton is home to the three-day Asparagus Festival, celebrated in the last full weekend in April.

Among the much-anticipated entertainment is the annual World Deep-Fried Asparagus Eating Competition. In 2007, competitive eater Joey Chestnut took first place and the $1,500 cash prize by consuming 8.6 pounds of the tempura-style fried stalks in 10 minutes.

½ cup water
1 slice lemon
1 sprig parsley
5 peppercorns
½ teaspoon salt
16 to 20 small shrimp, raw, unshelled
½ cup mayonnaise
½ cup sour cream
½ teaspoon lemon juice
¼ teaspoon dry mustard
½ teaspoon prepared horseradish (optional)
1 tablespoon gin
Salt and freshly ground black pepper
Lettuce leaves

1. Blanch the asparagus for a few minutes in boiling water and drain it on paper towels. Cut off the tips; cut the stems diagonally into 2-inch pieces. Place tips and stem pieces in a large bowl and set aside.

2. Combine the water, lemon slice, parsley, peppercorns, and salt in a medium-sized saucepan. Heat to boiling; then decrease the heat. Add the shrimp and simmer, uncovered, until they turn pink, about 4 minutes. Drain, cool slightly, shell and devein, and add them to the asparagus.

3. Combine the mayonnaise with the sour cream in a medium-sized bowl. Beat in the lemon juice, mustard, horseradish, gin, and salt and pepper to taste. Spoon this dressing over the asparagus and shrimp, and toss well. Serve on lettuce leaves, at room temperature or slightly chilled.

— *Bert Greene,* Greene on Greens

. . . .

ASPARAGUS AND SPINACH SOUP   SERVES 6 TO 8

This is wonderful hot, but it is also excellent chilled.

1 pound asparagus, washed, trimmed, and peeled
3 cups chicken stock
1 cup chopped fresh spinach leaves, washed
2 tablespoons unsalted butter
10 whole scallions, bulbs and green tops, roughly chopped
Pinch of ground cloves
3 tablespoons cornstarch
1 cup heavy or whipping cream
Salt and freshly ground black pepper
Sour cream (optional)

1. Place the asparagus in a medium-sized saucepan and cover with the chicken stock. Heat to boiling over high heat; decrease the heat.

Books

The Asparagus Festival Cookbook
Jan Moore, Barbara Hafly,
and Glenda Hushaw;
Celestial Arts, 2003.

From Asparagus to Zucchini:
A Guide to Cooking
Farm-Fresh Seasonal Produce
Madison Area Community
Supported Agriculture Coalition
(MACSAC); Jones Books, 2004.

Simmer, covered, 3 minutes. Remove the asparagus from the stock and set aside. Add the spinach to the saucepan and cook 3 minutes. Drain; reserve the stock.

2. Cut the tips off the asparagus; reserve. Chop the stems into 1-inch pieces; reserve.

3. Melt the butter in a medium-sized saucepan over low heat. Add the scallions; cook until wilted. Stir in the cloves, cooked spinach, and asparagus stems. Cook, covered, over low heat for 10 minutes.

4. Remove the cover; add the reserved stock.

5. Place the cornstarch in a small bowl. Slowly beat in the cream until the mixture is smooth. Stir this into the vegetable mixture in the saucepan. Heat to boiling; remove from heat.

6. Cool the mixture slightly and purée it in the blender or processor in two batches (be careful—the hot liquid will expand). Return the purée to the saucepan and reheat over low heat. Season with salt and pepper to taste; stir in the asparagus tips. Serve garnished with dabs of sour cream, if desired.

— *Bert Greene,* Greene on Greens

. . . .

SPAGHETTI WITH SPRING VEGETABLES   SERVES 6

5 medium-sized tomatoes
¼ pound small asparagus
1 medium-sized zucchini
¼ pound small white mushrooms
1 large red or green bell pepper
5 tablespoons olive oil
1 medium-sized onion, thinly sliced
Salt and pepper
3 tablespoons parsley, chopped
2 cloves garlic, finely chopped
1 pound spaghetti

1. Peel, seed, and dice the tomatoes. Wash the asparagus and cut the tips off the stalks; cut both the stalks and tips into 1-inch-long pieces, but keep them separate. Wash and dry the zucchini and mushrooms; cut into thin slices. Wash the pepper and cut into short, thin strips.

2. Heat the oil in a large skillet. Add the pepper strips and asparagus stalks and sauté over medium heat for 5 to 6 minutes. Add the onion, zucchini, asparagus tips, and mushrooms. Sauté 4 to 5 minutes. Add the diced tomatoes, salt, and pepper. Cook uncovered over medium heat for 10 minutes, stirring frequently. Stir in the parsley and garlic. Taste and adjust for seasoning.

3. Cook the spaghetti; drain and place in a warm deep dish or bowl. Pour the sauce over the spaghetti, and serve immediately.

— *Jeanette Mettler Cappello; Fruits and Veggies—More Matters; Centers for Disease Control & Prevention*

. . . .

ASPARAGUS AND MORELS   SERVES 6

1 stick (8 tablespoons) unsalted butter
2 medium-sized shallots, finely chopped
2 large cloves garlic, minced
1 teaspoon chopped fresh thyme, plus 6 sprigs, for garnish
1 pound morels, cleaned and halved or quartered lengthwise
1 cup dry white wine
1 cup vegetable or chicken stock
Salt and freshly ground pepper
1 pound asparagus, trimmed to 6 inches long

1. In a large skillet over medium heat, melt 6 tablespoons of the butter. When the butter is hot but not browned, add the shallots and garlic, then sprinkle the thyme on top. Add the morels and cook until lightly browned, about 5 minutes, taking care not to burn the butter.

2. Pour in the wine and boil until it is almost evaporated, about 5 minutes. Add the stock, stir well, and simmer until the liquid is reduced and has thickened slightly. Season lightly with salt and pepper and swirl in the remaining 2 tablespoons butter. (You should now have about 3 cups.)

3. Meanwhile, prepare the asparagus. If the spears are thicker than ½ inch in diameter, peel the bottom half of each with a vegetable peeler.

4. In a large skillet with a tight-fitting lid, bring ½ inch of water to a boil. Lay the asparagus in the pan, cover, and cook vigorously just until the bottom of a stalk can be pierced easily with a sharp knife, about 4 minutes. Drain on paper towels.

5. Divide the asparagus among 6 dinner plates and spoon the morels across the middle of the asparagus, making sure that each serving includes 1 or 2 spoonfuls of the pan juices. Garnish each plate with a sprig of thyme and serve immediately.

— *Joel Patraker,* The Greenmarket Cookbook

one-pound bundles. (Also, any stalks that are "deformed" (grown crooked) are discarded into the "dinner for Sarah" pile. (However, if that pile grows too large, I can be persuaded to share.)

Next, the ends are cleanly cut so that the stalks in each bunch are semi-uniform in length. Then the finished bunches are carried to our coolers. There they wait to be packed in your produce boxes or dropped off at your pick-up site, and carried into your home. Finally, when you open your box and eat it up, the journey of an asparagus stalk has come to an end.

Incredibly, the journey of an asparagus stalk is significantly shorter than the sagas many other vegetables endure. I find it all quite amazing. The intense individual care and gentle handling each piece of produce sees before you pluck it from your box or supermarket shelf is mind-boggling. (Think about cherry tomatoes, each fruit individually picked and placed in your pint.)

Witnessing firsthand a vegetable's journey has made me more appreciative of a perfectly formed fruit, and more forgiving of the small dings and bruises that inevitably mark a road-weary traveler. It has also opened up a soft place in my heart for the deformed, and helps me remember that the asparagus with a crooked neck tastes the same as its beautiful brother.

Basil

A beloved herb that is related to mint, basil is popular in Mediterranean and Asian (especially Thai) dishes. It thrives in hot, humid weather, disliking even the coolness of spring and early summer. In northern climates, basil acts as an annual, but in its native tropical climate, it grows year-round. Featherstone cultivates an Italian green largeleaf variety that has a robust, terrific flavor.

Numerous types of basil grow around the world, including lemon basil, African blue basil (which smells like camphor), and licorice basil. In fact, some basils are so sensitive to regional microclimates that plants of the same species grown in different locales produce distinctly different-tasting pestos.

HISTORY

Basil originated in India, where it was revered and used in religious occasions and funerals. The herb later migrated to the Mediterranean through the spice routes. Used as a kitchen herb since at least 400 B.C.E., the ancient Greeks and Romans associated the plant with death and love, respectively. It was favored in England in the sixteenth century for a time, its popularity eventually died out there, although it is still an essential ingredient in that country's turtle soup.

NUTRITION

Basil is noted to have many medicinal properties. It is well-known as a remedy for digestive upsets, and basil tea is said to dispel flatulence. It is often used for headaches and anxiety, and its aroma alone is reputed to have calming properties. Basil is an exceptionally rich source of vitamin K.

SELECTION

If possible, basil should be purchased as fresh bunches (usually these are plentiful in season, at farmers markets, or in larger natural foods supermarkets). This way you can see the condition of the leaves. Try to avoid getting basil in those tiny, flat plastic boxes; these scanty sprigs tend to be well past their prime and outrageously expensive. Avoid basil that is wilted or wearing large brown patches on its leaves.

STORAGE

Store unwashed basil in a plastic bag in the refrigerator vegetable crisper, but for no longer than a few days. Fresh basil will turn brown rather quickly if it is kept in the refrigerator, although this does not affect its flavor. To avoid this discoloration, you can purée the basil in a blender or a food processor and top it with a protective layer of olive oil.

TRIMMING & CLEANING

Strip the leaves off the tough stems and wash thoroughly to rinse away any grit or sand.

FREEZING

You can freeze basil, either puréed with olive oil and garlic scapes, or in leaf form (just be forewarned that the leaves will turn brown). If you don't think you will use it all before it goes bad, chop up the leaves and freeze them into ice cubes with a little water or olive oil. To thaw, simply drop a few in a strainer and let the ice melt away, or just drop them frozen into sauces and soups.

DRYING

Fresh basil is far superior to the dried version, which contains only a fraction of its distinctive flavor and fragrance. Even basil frozen in the manner described above is better than the dried herb.

If you want to oven-dry the herb, spread a layer of leaves on a cookie sheet and place the herbs in a warm (up to 180°F) oven for 3 to 4 hours, stirring the herbs periodically until they are thoroughly dry. Or remove the best leaves from the stems and arrange on a paper towel so the leaves do not touch. This layer is covered with a towel and another layer of leaves is added. Five layers may be dried at one time using this method.

A microwave oven can also be used for small quantities of herbs. Place 4 or 5 herb branches in the microwave between paper towels. Heat for 2 to 3 minutes on High power. If the herbs are not brittle and dry when removed, repeat the microwave drying for 30 seconds more. Note: The heat generated during microwaving not only removes moisture but also some of the oils, so these herbs may not have as intense a flavor as herbs dried by other methods.

EQUIVALENTS, MEASURES & SERVINGS

- 1 tablespoon chopped fresh basil = 1 teaspoon dried basil

COMPLEMENTARY HERBS, SEASONINGS & FOODS

Cheese, chicken, duck, eggplant, eggs, fish, lamb, liver, majoram, olive oil, onions, oregano, pasta, pesto, pizza, pork, potatoes, rabbit, rosemary, sage, salads, shellfish, soups, summer savory, sweet peppers, tomato sauce, tomatoes, veal, vegetables, vinegars, zucchini.

SERVING SUGGESTIONS

- Basil has a famous affinity for tomatoes and cheese; a favorite Italian summer salad combines basil, olive oil, rounds of fresh mozzarella cheese, and vine-ripened tomatoes.
- Substitute basil for parsley in meatloaf; it adds a marvelously savory, perfumed flavor.
- If you are a huge basil fan, tear off the leaves from the stems and add liberal quantities to tossed salads, just like any other green. This is especially good with fresh mint and thin shreds of fresh ginger.
- Substitute fresh basil for spinach.
- Use pesto to add flavor to a salmon loaf.
- Chop a few leaves into egg and cheese dishes to add flavor and color.
- Substitute basil for parsley in the filling for deviled eggs.
- Place a few leaves in sandwiches.
- The uses of pesto are numerous: for spreading on ham sandwiches, mix-

"As made in Genoa it is certainly one of the best sauces yet invented for pasta, and one tablespoonful of pesto stirred in at the last minute gives a delicious flavor to a minestrone."

— *Elizabeth David,*
food writer and cookbook author

"If the definition of poetry allowed that it could be composed with the products of the field as well as with words, pesto would be in every anthology."

— *Marcella Hazan,*
Italian cooking authority

ing into mashed potatoes, stirring into tomato or bean soup, dabbing on salmon, marinading meat kebabs, saucing pizza, adding to stuffed eggs, mixing with salad oil and using as a dressing …

SUBSTITUTIONS

If you do not have basil on hand, use oregano or thyme.

....

DEVILED EGGS WITH SALMON AND BASIL   MAKES 24 DEVILED EGG HALVES

The salmon and basil gives a delicious, unexpected twist to these deviled eggs. Make plenty, for these never last long at parties or potlucks.

1 dozen eggs
1 (15½-ounce) can pink or red salmon, juice reserved
3 tablespoons mayonnaise
½ cup onion, finely chopped
1 large clove garlic, finely chopped
1 cup loosely packed basil, finely chopped
Salt and freshly ground pepper
Chopped fresh parsley or paprika, for garnish (optional)

1. Hard-boil the eggs, peel off their shells, and cut them in half lengthwise. Scoop out the yolks, place them in a small bowl, and mash them lightly. Set aside the egg white halves.

2. Add the salmon and reserved juice, mayonnaise, onion, garlic, basil, and pepper to the mashed yolks. (Additional salt is usually not necessary with the salmon and its juice, but taste and adjust the seasoning if necessary.) Mix thoroughly, and place heaping scoopfuls back into the egg whites.

3. Garnish with parsley or paprika, if desired. For best results, chill several hours before serving to let the flavors mingle.

— *Mi Ae Lipe, Featherstone Farm CSA member*

....

PESTO   MAKES ABOUT 1 CUP

¾ cup extra-virgin olive oil
1 clove garlic
1 tablespoon pine nuts or walnut pieces
¼ teaspoon salt
⅓ cup freshly grated Parmesan cheese
4 cups fresh basil leaves

Place all of the ingredients except the basil in a blender or food processor. Blend until smooth, then add the basil, a handful at a time, blending until all of the basil is incorporated and the pesto is somewhat smooth.

Variations

- Substitute cilantro for basil and add a little lemon or lime juice.
- Substitute tarragon for basil.
- Substitute 1 cup of rosemary and 2 cups of parsley for basil.
- Substitute mint for basil.

Suggestions for Use

- Mix with cold or hot pasta, rice, or other grains.
- Use as a sauce for fish, chicken, or pork.
- Top a baked potato or fill an omelet.
- Use to flavor pizza or tomato sauce, dressings, yogurt, etc.

— *MACSAC, From Asparagus to Zucchini*

few green herbs.

A slightly different version of the sauce exists in Provence, France, known as pistou, which is usually made with only olive oil, basil, and garlic. Cheese is optional but pistou generally does not contain nuts.

Pesto is a sauce best eaten as soon as possible, although it will keep a few days if it is covered with a layer of olive oil (this also preserves its green color). It also freezes well; try filling an ice-cube tray and pop out the cubes as needed for winter pasta dishes or soups.

REAL BASIL CHEESECAKE
MAKES 10 SERVINGS

2 large eggs
1 cup sour cream
¾ cup granulated sugar
1 cup basil leaves, destemmed
2 tablespoons cornstarch
2 tablespoons lemon juice
1 teaspoon vanilla
2 pounds cream cheese, at room temperature
2 tablespoons butter, softened
1 cup crushed vanilla wafers or graham crackers

1. Preheat the oven to 450°F.

2. In a food processor or mixer, lightly beat the eggs. Add the sour cream, sugar, basil, cornstarch, lemon juice, and vanilla. Process until smooth. Add the cream cheese, ½ pound at a time, and process to incorporate.

3. Spread softened butter on the bottom and half way up the sides of a 9- or 10-inch springform pan. Cover the buttered area with the wafer or cracker crumbs, pressing to be sure they stick.

4. Pour in the cheesecake batter and bake 35 to 40 minutes, or until a toothpick or knife inserted in the center comes out clean. Run a knife around the edges of cake as soon as it comes out of oven.

5. Cool on a wire rack for 5 minutes, then remove the side of the pan. Finish cooling. Cut with dental floss into thin wedges.

— *MACSAC, From Asparagus to Zucchini*

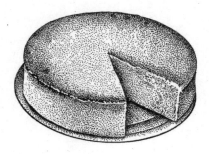

CHICKEN STIR-FRY WITH BASIL
SERVES 4

A stir-fry is always a quick and easy dinner option, and chicken with vegetables are especially delicious when simply flavored with basil and dried orange zest. Jazz it up even more with a bit of mirin (rice cooking wine), if desired.

2 tablespoons high-heat (high-oleic) sunflower or safflower oil, divided
½ large red onion, cut in half and thinly sliced
3 large shiitake mushrooms, destemmed, halved, and thinly sliced
¼ to ½ teaspoon dried ground or 1 teaspoon grated fresh orange peel
2 cups small broccoli florets
2 small carrots, peeled and cut into matchstick pieces
1 pound chicken tenders, cut into ¾-inch cubes
2 tablespoons slivered fresh basil
Bragg's Liquid Aminos, to taste

Ingredient options: Use tamari instead of liquid aminos if you do not require a gluten-free recipe.

1. Heat 1 tablespoon of the oil over medium-high heat. Add the onion, mushrooms, and orange peel and stir-fry for 5 minutes.

2. Add broccoli and carrots and stir-fry another 5 minutes or until broccoli is bright green and just tender. Transfer to a bowl and set aside.

3. Heat the remaining tablespoon of oil in the same pan. Add the chicken cubes and stir-fry for 5 minutes or until completely cooked. Return the vegetables back to the skillet with the chicken. Add the basil and stir-fry 1 more minute. Season to taste with the liquid aminos or tamari.

— *Whole Foods Market*

Basil seedlings in the greenhouse.

Bok Choy

BRASSICA RAPA,
CHINENSIS GROUP

Bok choy by any other name may or may not be the same. Confusion reigns over the many varieties of this traditional Asian stir-fry vegetable, their interchangeable labels, and regional differences (think Chinese cabbage, Shanghai bok choy, Taiwan bok choy, pac choi, bok choi, and bak choy, to name just a few). The bok choy referred to here (and grown by Featherstone) looks like a miniature Swiss chard, with broad, dark green leaves, satiny white stalks, and a delicate cabbage flavor. Both the stems and leaves are edible, ideal as a lightly cooked vegetable.

HISTORY

Bok choy is native to China, where it makes a frequent appearance in the wok. Although bok choy and hundreds of other closely related Asian Brassica cultivars have been a part of the Asian diet for centuries, they did not find their way into Europe and North America until the 1800s, and they are still not widely used outside of ethnic restaurants and cuisines in those regions. Bok choy is very popular in the Phillipines, where it was introduced by immigrant Chinese who settled there after Spain's conquest of the islands in the 1500s.

NUTRITION

Like other members of the cabbage family, bok choy packs a nutritional wallop, with significant vitamin C, folic acid, iron, and dietary fiber, with only 24 calories per cup.

SELECTION

Choose bunches with firm stems and fresh-looking leaves. Very large stems may be somewhat tougher; the general rule is that the smaller the vegetable, the more tender and sweet it will be. Very small bunches may be cooked whole.

STORAGE

Fresh bok choy will keep tightly wrapped, unwashed, in a plastic bag in the refrigerator vegetable crisper for up to a week, although it may start to yellow after 3 days.

TRIMMING & CLEANING

Bok choy tends to collect sand and grit at the base of the stalks, so a thorough cleaning or at least inspection is in order. Separate the stalks from the central stem and rinse under running water, or if they are particularly dirty, scrub gently with a vegetable brush.

STEAMING & BOILING

With its high water content, bok choy tends to collapse and go limp very quickly when cooked. Overcooking makes it quite watery. The leaves cook much more quickly than the stalks, so if you want both of them to be present in the finished dish, put the stems in first, then add the leaves a minute or two later. Steam bok choy stalks for about 6 minutes, or until tender, and leaves for about 4 minutes. As for boiling, cook stems in salted water for 4 minutes and leaves for 2 to 3 minutes.

STIR-FRYING & SAUTÉING

Stir-frying and sautéing bring out the best in bok choy, which responds best to cooking over high heat. Cut stalks into ½-inch pieces and stir-fry or sauté for about 6 minutes and the leaves for 3 minutes, or until just wilted.

MICROWAVING

Rinse and coarsely chop greens; place slightly wet leaves in a microwave-safe dish; cover and cook on High power.

- 2 cups = 2 minutes
- 1¼ pounds = 7 to 10 minutes

BLANCHING & FREEZING

Freezing is not recommended for bok choy because of its high water content.

EQUIVALENTS, MEASURES & SERVINGS

- 2 cups leaves = ½ cup cooked greens

COMPLEMENTARY HERBS, SEASONINGS & FOODS

Bacon, beef, chicken, fish, garlic, ginger, hot peppers, mushrooms, onion, pork, sesame oil, soy sauce, sweet and sour seasonings, tofu.

SERVING SUGGESTIONS

- Swirl leaves and stems into stir-fries.
- Bok choy's watery texture and mild flavor best complements savory seasonings and rich meats, such as roast pork. Try braising it with duck legs or fish.
- Bok choy can be used in any recipe calling for Swiss chard.
- The tender stalks lend themselves quite well to dip, as an alternative or complement to carrot and celery sticks.
- Try substituting bok choy stems for celery; chop into egg and chicken salads, or spread peanut butter in them.
- Stir-fry with asparagus and garlic, or sugar snap peas and ginger.
- Bok choy's delicate flavor combines well with mushrooms. Braise or stir-fry with porcinis, oyster mushrooms, thinly sliced portobellos, shiitakes, or morels.
- Stir-fry with shrimp or crab for a quick, delicious meal.
- Try wilting bok choy as you would spinach, adorned with hot bacon dressing.
- Use bok choy in the filling for eggrolls and spring rolls.
- Shred bok choy for a crunchy Asian salad with ramen noodles and slivered almonds.
- Bok choy blends well with cheese and eggs. Use it in gratins, omelettes, fritattas, scrambled eggs, and casseroles.

Books

Beyond Bok Choy:
A Cook's Guide to Asian Vegetables
Rosa Lo San Ross and Martin Jacobs;
Artisan, 1996.

The Asian Grocery Store Demystified
Linda Bladholm; Renaissance Books,
1999.

The Breath of a Wok:
Unlocking the Spirit of Chinese Wok
Cooking Through Recipes and Lore
Grace Young; Simon & Schuster,
2004.

BOK CHOY PROVENÇALE

SERVES 4

1 head bok choy, chopped
1 clove garlic
1 large onion
Olive oil
2 eggs
1 cup mozzarella cheese, shredded
2 tablespoons fresh mint, chopped
Salt and pepper to taste

1. Preheat the oven to 375°F.

2. Sauté the bok choy, garlic, and onion in the olive oil just until the garlic and onions are tender and the bok choy is wilted.

3. Beat together the eggs and cheese in a baking dish, and then blend in the sautéed bok choy mixture. Add the mint, salt, and pepper.

4. Bake in the oven for 15 minutes, or until the eggs are firm. Serve immediately.

— *Ruth Charles, Featherstone Farm CSA member*

STIR-FRIED DUNGENESS CRAB WITH SWEET CHILI SAUCE AND BOK CHOY

SERVES 4

2 Dungeness crabs, 1½ pounds each
¼ cup peanut oil
3 cloves garlic, chopped
1-inch piece fresh ginger, grated
2 fresh red chiles, sliced
4 heads baby bok choy, halved
1 cup water
¼ cup dark brown sugar
¼ cup low-sodium soy sauce
½ lemon, juiced
¼ cup sake
1 tablespoon cornstarch mixed with 2 tablespoons water
Butter lettuce
2 chopped green onions, white and green parts
¼ cup chopped, unsalted, roasted peanuts
White rice, for serving

1. First "dismantle" the crabs before you wok-fry them. Toss the crabs into salted boiling water for 2 minutes. Next, place the crabs top-side up, stick your thumb under the edge of the top shell, pull forward, and lift the shell up and off. Reserve the whole shells for serving presentation. Scrape out the gills that are found on top of the body. Now,

turn the crabs over and on the underbelly you will find the "apron," a slightly lifted triangular flap; pull this off too. Finally, rinse the crabs of all of the grey or green spongy stuff (the soft yellow matter is fat or "crab butter" and considered desirable by many; keep it if you wish.) Divide the crabs into quarters with a big knife, leaving the legs attached to the 4 sections.

2. Heat the peanut oil in a wok over high heat until almost smoking. Add the garlic, ginger, chiles, and bok choy. Stir-fry for 1 minute, then remove to a side platter. Toss in the crab pieces, including the top shells. Take the top shells out after 1 minute and continue to stir-fry the crab for 3 minutes. With a big spoon or spatula, remove the crab pieces to the side platter.

3. To prepare the sauce, pour the water into the wok, along with the brown sugar, soy sauce, lemon juice, and sake. Stir for 2 minutes to dissolve the sugar. Stir in the cornstarch slurry and cook another minute until the sauce thickens.

4. Return the crabs and bok choy to the pan, and toss everything together to coat. Cover, and cook for 3 minutes.

5. To serve, line a large platter with butter lettuce leaves, and arrange the crabs with the top shell back on top so it looks roughly like a whole crab again. Place the bok choy around the crab and pour the sauce all over the top. Garnish with the green onions and peanuts. You'll need crab crackers, mini forks, a side bowl for the shells, a stack of napkins, and bowls of warm lemon water to clean your hands. Serve with steamed white rice.

— *Tyler Florence, Foodnetwork.com*

BALLISTIC BABY BOK CHOY AND FRIED TOFU   SERVES 4

Because tofu soaks up so many flavors and seasonings, it is ideal to use in many dishes that have a strong flavor base. If you have been eating tofu, consider yourself lucky—it is now touted as a food that reduces some risks of cancer as well as lowering cholesterol levels. If it is used and cooked properly, even your most carnivorous friends can be persuaded to try it. Seduce them with this recipe.

16 ounces firm tofu
3 tablespoons chile oil, or 3 tablespoons corn oil mixed with
      1 teaspoon crushed and dried santaka or Thai chile,
      or 2 teaspoons New Mexican red chile
1½ pounds baby bok choy, washed and coarsely chopped
4 cloves garlic, minced, or several stalks of chopped green garlic
6 scallions, sliced
1 red bell pepper, julienned
4 tablespoons water
4 tablespoons soy sauce

2 dried shiitake mushrooms, rehydrated and sliced

¾ cup water chestnuts or jicama, coarsely chopped

3 teaspoons sugar

2 teaspoons crushed and dried santaka or Thai or New Mexican
    red chile, or to taste

1½ teaspoons cornstarch or arrowroot mixed with 2 tablespoons water

4 cups cooked rice

1. Cut the tofu into 1-inch slices and place them on paper or linen towels; cover with more towels. Place a cookie sheet on top of the tofu and place several weights (such as canned goods) on top to help squeeze the excess liquid out of the tofu. Drain for 15 to 20 minutes. Cut the tofu into 1-inch cubes.

2. Heat the pepper oil in a large sauté pan or wok on medium-high heat. Sauté the tofu cubes, turning them when necessary, until they become golden brown. Drain the tofu cubes on paper towels and set aside.

3. In a large skillet with a cover, add the bok choy, garlic, scallions, bell pepper, and water. Cover and steam until the bok choy is tender, about 5 minutes. Add the soy sauce, tofu, mushrooms, water chestnuts or jicama, sugar, crushed red chile, and the cornstarch mixture and toss to mix. Stir lightly until the sauce boils, decrease the heat, and allow it to simmer for 1 minute. Serve the mixture immediately over hot, cooked rice.

— *www.fooddownunder.com*

WILTED GREENS WITH COCONUT   SERVES 4

I lived in Australia for a couple of years, and my palate has never been the same. I grew to enjoy the intermingling of sweet, sour, and salty flavors as well as the mix of slightly bitter with sweet in a savory dish. If you do not have access to a coconut tree to make your own fresh coconut (and how many of us do?), head to any Indian or Southeast Asian market or natural food store to find unsweetened coconut.

What greens you decide to use will determine the cooking time. Spinach takes about 3 minutes, whereas Chinese broccoli will take at least 5 minutes.

2 tablespoons sesame oil

2 pounds greens, such as spinach, bok choy, or Chinese broccoli

¼ cup unsweetened shredded coconut

Salt and black pepper

Heat a 12-inch sauté pan or wok until hot, and add the oil. Cook the greens until just wilted, then add the coconut and toss to combine. Season with salt and pepper. Serve immediately.

— *Richard Ruben,* The Farmer's Market Cookbook

Chives

Chives is the smallest species of the much beloved Allium, or onion, family. Perennial chives grow from bulbs in dense clumps (hence the plural name) that sprout grasslike, hollow, tubular leaves. Later, in midsummer, chives bear delicate, globe-shaped pink or purple blossoms that are also edible.

The flavor of chives is among the most delicate of the onion family, and they are better used raw or barely cooked. They constitute one of the fines herbes of French cooking, along with tarragon, chervil, and parsley. Their leaves are easier to snip with scissors than to cut with a knife.

HISTORY

Chives are thought to be native to Britain, although it also grows wild in Greece and Italy. Europeans have grown chives since the Middle Ages, although both regular chives and the closely related garlic chive *(Allium tuberosum)* have been used in Asian cuisines for centuries.

NUTRITION

Although they are not typically used in large enough quantities to be a significant source of nutrients, chives do contain vitamins A and K, potassium, phosphorus, magnesium, and calcium.

SELECTION

Choose chives that look fresh and plump, with no signs of wilting, yellowing, or other discoloration. Thicker-tubed leaves tend to be more fibrous than smaller ones.

STORAGE

Chives that are unwashed and tightly wrapped in a plastic bag will keep for up to a week in the refrigerator vegetable crisper.

TRIMMING & CLEANING

Rinse quickly and pat gently dry (avoid bruising the tender leaves). The easiest way to chop them finely is to gather up a whole bunch of stems, slightly twist them together horizontally, and snip them with a pair of kitchen scissors.

FREEZING

You can freeze chives by snipping them into small lengths and freezing them in a single layer on a baking sheet. Then they can be placed in zipper-lock freezer or vacuum food sealer-type bags. No thawing is necessary before using.

DRYING

Chives can be dried, although they lose much of their flavor this way (if you really crave fresh chives in the winter, better keep a pot growing indoors!). To dry, spread chives in a thin layer on a baking sheet or tray and dry them in the oven at no hotter than 100°F for 4 to 6 hours, or until crisp.

COMPLEMENTARY HERBS, SEASONINGS & FOODS

Chervil, eggs, fish, parsley, potatoes, salads, shellfish, soft cheeses, sole, soups, tarragon, vegetables.

SERVING SUGGESTIONS

- Sprinkle a tablespoon of chopped chives over an omelet or into eggs about to be scrambled.
- Add a tablespoon into each cup of milk when making a white sauce, to add color and flavor.
- Snip a fresh spoonful over hot soups.
- Stir chopped chives into softened butter, which can then be spread over thick bread and baked like garlic bread.
- Tie up chive leaves into spears, then use as a garnish on puff pastry parcels, dumplings, deviled eggs, or open-faced crackers adorned with dabs of savory spread.
- To add a gentle oniony flavor, sprinkle a few tablespoons of chives at the last minute of cooking stir-fries.
- Give soft cheeses extra character with finely chopped chives.
- Sprinkle on tomato and cucumber salads.
- Dress up cottage cheese with fresh chives and other herbs.
- An Alpine treat is black rye bread spread with butter and chopped chives.
- Lightly chopped or whole chive flowers make a lovely, edible garnish for summer salads and chilled soups.

SUBSTITUTIONS

Use green onion, finely chopped leek, or mild sweet onion.

. . . .

HERB BUTTER   MAKES ABOUT ½ CUP

1 stick (½ cup) butter, softened
½ cup chives, finely chopped
2 teaspoons lemon juice
Salt and garlic powder, or crushed fresh garlic, to taste

Combine all of the ingredients in a mixer bowl and beat until blended, about 2 minutes.

— *Emily, Featherstone Farm CSA member*

. . . .

BABY POTATOES WITH LEMON AND CHIVES   SERVES 4

1 pound baby potatoes

Books

Onion: The Essential Cook's Guide to Onions, Garlic, Leeks, Spring Onions, Shallots and Chives
Brian Glover; Lorenz Books, 2001.

In Celebration of Chives
Guy Cooper and Gordon Taylor; The Herb Society, 1981.

1 ounce butter
1 teaspoon chives, coarsely chopped
½ teaspoon grated lemon rind

1. Wash and steam the potatoes for 12 to 15 minutes until tender. (If preferred, they can be cut in half before cooking.)

2. In a separate pan heat the butter, and add the chopped chives and lemon rind. Toss to release the flavors, then pour over the potatoes and serve.

— *www.fooddownunder.com*

CHIVE AND PARMESAN POPCORN   SERVES 1

⅔ cup popcorn
⅓ cup butter
Pepper
½ cup fresh chives, finely chopped
1 cup Parmesan cheese, finely grated
Salt

Pop the popcorn. Melt the butter. Grind as much pepper as you want into the butter. Sprinkle the chives over the popcorn along with the grated cheese. Drizzle the butter mixture over the popcorn, and salt to taste.

— *www.fooddownunder.com*

BOURSIN DIP   MAKES 1 CUP

Add other fresh herbs to taste—rosemary, thyme, basil, oregano, summer savory, sage—any or all, it's all good. If necessary, thin with sour cream or yogurt to the desired dipping consistency.

8 ounces cream cheese
1 tablespoon lemon juice
1 clove garlic, minced
½ teaspoon Worcestershire sauce
½ teaspoon dry mustard
1 tablespoon fresh parsley
1 tablespoon chives

Mix and refrigerate, but serve at room temperature. You may need to thin this a bit with yogurt or sour cream for a dipping consistency. I make this dip at least a day ahead to let the flavors mingle. Enjoy!

— *Maureen Cooney,* The Bluff Country Co-op Cookbook

Green Garlic 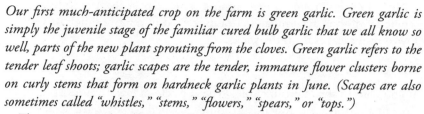 ALLIUM SATIVUM

Our first much-anticipated crop on the farm is green garlic. Green garlic is simply the juvenile stage of the familiar cured bulb garlic that we all know so well, parts of the new plant sprouting from the cloves. Green garlic refers to the tender leaf shoots; garlic scapes are the tender, immature flower clusters borne on curly stems that form on hardneck garlic plants in June. (Scapes are also sometimes called "whistles," "stems," "flowers," "spears," or "tops.")

These young, curling flower stalks are delicious, with a broad spectrum of uses from soups to salads to garnishes. Stronger in flavor than chives, green garlic's pungency is milder than its cured siblings. Use it any way that you would use shallots or regular garlic. (Jack claims that you have only to fill your roasting pan with meat and green garlic and cook slowly to taste the richest roast ever made.) Garlic scapes are highly prized delicacies in European and Korean cuisine because of their subtle garlic flavor, tender-crisp texture, and nutraceutical potency.

Garlic is a heavy feeder that enjoys rich, organic, heavily composted soil. In October the cloves are placed in the ground and mulched, so the ground does not freeze and thaw continually in the winter. There they rest all winter until around the first of April, when we rake the mulch off the beds to allow the sun to warm the soil. By mid-April the garlic shoots stand four to five inches tall, often growing almost an inch a day. This succulent, tender growth has a great spring garlic flavor, and the first shorties make their appearance in the CSA baskets in May.

Like most spring crops, green garlic's season is fleeting. By early June the stems and leaves start getting woody, as the plant's moisture is drawn out of the above-ground shoot and into the now-forming bulb. Their next reincarnation appears in the fall, as cured garlic in October.

HISTORY

See Garlic on page 306.

NUTRITION

See Garlic on page 306.

SELECTION

You are unlikely to find this springtime treat in the grocery store, but you may be lucky enough to run across it at farmers markets during that brief window in late spring or very early summer. Choose shoots and scapes that look fresh, not wilted. Older, larger scapes and shoots (especially toward the end of the season or in the summer) tend to be fibrous.

STORAGE

Some vegetables do not store well after being washed, getting slimy if not used immediately; green garlic is one of these. To keep the garlic crisp, forgo a quick rinse and instead store the scapes in a brown paper bag in the refrigerator, where they will last for weeks. Wash the garlic right before using.

TRIMMING & CLEANING

Like small children, green garlic tends to be grubby. Scrub the scapes slightly and rinse them under running water, especially at their bases, where sand often accumulates. You may need to remove tough or yellowed outer leaves from the stalks.

STEAMING & BOILING

If you plan to steam green garlic, keep it brief—a few minutes at most. To add a subtle garlic touch, add some chopped scapes to the steamer basket in which other vegetables are cooking during the last couple minutes of steaming. Boiling tends to leach out its delicate flavor.

STIR-FRYING & SAUTÉING

Add green garlic to a stir-fry during the last several minutes of preparation. To sauté green garlic, slice 6 to 8 stalks into thin rounds and sauté in a couple of tablespoons of butter or olive oil for at least 10 minutes.

MICROWAVING

Microwave green garlic like you would green onions. Chop into 1- or 2-inch pieces, place in a microwave-safe container containing ½ inch of water, cover, and microwave on High power for 3 to 5 minutes. Drain, and they are ready to use in cooked dishes.

BLANCHING & FREEZING

If you cannot use your green garlic right away, chop up the scapes into 1-inch pieces, place them in zipper-lock freezer or vacuum food sealer-type bags or freezer containers, and squeeze out the excess air. They will keep for about 6 to 8 months, if you can resist using them for that long.

EQUIVALENTS, MEASURES & SERVINGS

- 1 stalk green garlic = 1 or 2 regular garlic cloves

COMPLEMENTARY HERBS, SEASONINGS & FOODS

Beans, beef, beets, cabbage, chicken, eggplant, eggs, fish, lamb, lentils, mushrooms, pasta, pork, potatoes, poultry, rice, shellfish, spinach, tomatoes, vegetables, zucchini.

SERVING SUGGESTIONS

- Steam rice until it is about 80 percent cooked; take three green garlic shoots and place right on top of the rice; the garlic will wilt, releasing its aromatic juices down into rice.
- Finely chop a tablespoon or two of green garlic and add to your tuna fish salad. Delicious on sandwiches!
- Combine green garlic (cut into 1-inch lengths), basil, pine nuts, olive oil, Parmesan cheese, and lemon juice in a food processor or blender to make a delicious pesto.
- Throw sautéed green garlic into pasta salads and salad dressings.

- Chop up garlic shoots and mix with ground beef for the best grilled hamburgers you've ever tasted.
- Use green garlic in stir-fries.
- Sauté green garlic and add to frittatas, omelets, or scrambled eggs.
- Top potato soup with finely chopped scapes for a stronger kick than chives.
- Sprinkle chopped green garlic over pizza or Italian grinders.

··

GARLIC SCAPE PIZZA   MAKES 1 12-INCH PIZZA

6 to 8 green garlic scapes with stems
½ medium-sized onion
½ fresh red bell pepper
½ fresh yellow bell pepper
1 tablespoon butter
3 to 4 cloves garlic, chopped
3 to 4 ounces tomato paste
1 (12-inch) baked pizza crust
½ cup mozzarella cheese
3 ounces fresh spinach
½ cup Cheddar cheese
5-inch stick of sliced pepperoni
10 fresh cherry tomatoes, sliced in half
¾ cup Parmesan cheese

1. Preheat the oven to 350°F.
2. Slice the garlic scapes, onions, and peppers into small pieces. Sauté in the butter and garlic until tender, and set aside to cool.
3. Spread the tomato paste over the pizza crust, and sprinkle with mozzarella cheese.
4. Make a bed of spinach over the mozzarella cheese. Cover the spinach with the sautéed vegetables, and sprinkle on the Cheddar cheese. Add the sliced pepperoni and cover with fresh tomatoes. Sprinkle the Parmesan cheese over the top of the pizza.
5. Bake in the oven for 20 to 25 minutes.

Suggestions, substitutions, and additions:

- Buy prepared pizza crust or make your own. If you prepare your own dough, bake ahead of time and use fresh, or freeze for later use.
- Use garlic scapes that are as young as possible and include some of the stems.
- Add hot pepper seeds while sautéing the vegetables.
- Use about a pound of hot Italian sausage cooked to a crisp in a skillet in place of pepperoni, or go meatless.
- Any of the ingredients may be increased or decreased, depending on taste.

— *David Sutton, The Garlic Store*

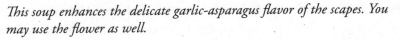

GARLIC SCAPE SOUP

SERVES 4

This soup enhances the delicate garlic-asparagus flavor of the scapes. You may use the flower as well.

3 cups garlic scapes, cut into 2-inch pieces
1 medium-sized onion, chopped
1 tablespoon olive oil
1 teaspoon fresh thyme leaves or ½ teaspoon dried thyme
3 cups chicken broth
1 cup cream
Salt and pepper

1. Sauté the garlic scapes and onion in the olive oil over medium heat until the vegetables become soft. Add the thyme at the end.

2. In a food processor, purée the vegetables and add chicken broth as needed to make a smooth paste.

3. In a saucepan, heat the vegetable mixture and add the remaining broth. Bring to a simmer and add the cream. Adjust the seasoning with salt and pepper.

— *The Garlic Store*

BABY GREEN GARLIC MASHED POTATOES

SERVES 6

1½ pounds russet potatoes, peeled
4 tablespoons butter
2 bunches baby green garlic, green leaves only
½ cup milk
½ cup cream
Salt and freshly ground pepper

1. Leave the potatoes whole if small, or cut in half if large. Place them in a large saucepan with enough salted water to cover them by several inches. Bring to a simmer, cover partially, and adjust the heat to maintain a gentle simmer. Cook until a knife slips in easily, about 30 minutes. Drain, then return the potatoes to the warm pot. Return the pot to the stove and shake until any moisture evaporates.

2. While the potatoes cook, melt the butter in a small saucepan over moderate heat. Add the baby green garlic and sauté until softened, 3 to 5 minutes. Add the milk and cream. Season with salt and pepper.

3. Put the boiled potatoes through a food mill or ricer. Add the hot milk mixture and stir with a wooden spoon until smooth.

— *The Garlic Store*

1 pound beets
2 large leeks
1 large onion
3 celery ribs
1 carrot
½ pound turnips
3 small russet potatoes, peeled
3 cups shredded cabbage
Handful of chopped green garlic scapes
2 tablespoons butter
½ tablespoon salt
1 cup canned diced tomatoes
3 bay leaves
1 tablespoon sugar
Water
Salt and pepper
3 tablespoons white or red wine vinegar
½ cup sour cream mixed with 1 tablespoon prepared horseradish
Finely chopped fresh dill

1. Julienne the beets. Wash, peel, and dice all of the remaining vegetables.

2. Cook the leeks, onion, celery, carrot, turnips, potatoes, cabbage, and scapes in melted butter. Toss with the salt and cook for 20 minutes, or until the vegetables are tender.

3. Add the beets, tomatoes, bay leaves, and sugar. Add 8 cups of water and simmer for 25 minutes, or until the beets are tender.

4. Add salt and pepper as necessary. Stir in the vinegar. Serve hot or cold with a spoonful of sour cream-horseradish mixture and a sprinkling of fresh dill.

— *Featherstone Farm*

Lettuce

LACTUCA SATIVA

Time was when lettuce in America meant only the anemic, tightly headed iceberg, wrapped in lattice-woven clear plastic, sitting huddled in the supermarket produce section. Thankfully, those days are a distant memory as we stroll through those same aisles or in farmers markets and encounter a bounty of different lettuces and other greens from which to choose for the evening's salads or cookpot.

Lettuce is eaten mostly as a raw salad green in the United States, but in some countries such as France and China, it is also cooked as a vegetable in its own right. (Stir-fried iceberg is an incredibly popular dish in Hong Kong.) Besides the familiar crisphead variety, the iceberg, there are now butterhead lettuces (like Boston and Bibb), romaine (famous in Caesar salad), looseleaf types (which include frilly varieties and oak leaf), and stem lettuces, which are more likely to be seen in Asian markets. Lettuces dislike summer heat, and are at their best either in the spring or fall.

Featherstone grows several varieties of lettuce:

Red Leaf Lettuce
This is a new variety of Red Oak lettuce. It has a much darker red color and is very sweet. It makes a wonderful salad.

Green Romaine
Romaine is a hardy head lettuce that keeps well and stands up to the toughest of additions (e.g., salty croutons, fishy Caesar dressing, or grated strands of robust cheese).

Green Butter Lettuce
Rich and buttery, this lettuce is perfect for delicate citrus vinaigrettes. The butter lettuces are slow growers that never form overly large heads. Be careful when handling them, as their soft leaves bruise easily.

Red Butter Lettuce
This is our most delicate lettuce. The Red Butter is just as it sounds: a smooth-tasting lettuce with a beautiful red hue. As with other red lettuces, this lettuce will spoil faster than the sturdy romaine, so enjoy this lettuce while it is fresh.

HISTORY

The exact homeland of lettuce remains lost to the ages, although many authorities believe that its wild cousin originated in Europe or Southwest Asia. Lettuce was recorded as growing in Babylonian gardens as early as 800 B.C.E., and lettuce seeds have been found in ancient Egyptian tombs. The earliest lettuces did not form heads but instead grew leaves from a tall, central stalk, which our modern lettuces mimic when they bolt, or go to seed, in hot weather. Lettuce did not reach East Asia until after 30 C.E., and it was slow to find favor with the French, who pre-

"I don't think America will have really made it until we have our own salad dressing. Until then we're stuck behind the French, Italians, Russians, and Caesarians."

— *Pat McNelis*

ferred watercress instead during the Middle Ages. Columbus probably introduced the plant to America, where Thomas Jefferson had it grown in his gardens at Monticello.

NUTRITION

The nutrient content of lettuce varies widely depending on the type. The chlorophyll-deprived iceberg is less nutritious than romaine, and all lettuces have an extremely high water content. A 2-cup serving of romaine contains 143 percent of your daily requirement for vitamin K, 60 percent of your vitamin A, nearly half of your vitamin C, and over a third of your folate. Lettuce is also a good source of manganese.

SELECTION

Look for fresh, crisp heads, with no signs of withering, sliminess, or discoloration. Contrary to popular belief, a brownish color on the underside of the cut stem end is not necessarily a sign of bad or old lettuce; the milky sap of cut lettuce naturally oxidizes when exposed to air.

STORAGE

To keep lettuce fresher longer, wash and dry romaine and leaf lettuce thoroughly before storing. Wrap the greens in paper towels or a clean kitchen towel, then place in plastic bags. Seal the bags tightly and keep in the refrigerator vegetable crisper. Periodically check the bags and replace any damp towels. Butter lettuces, on the other hand, should not be washed before storing.

If you find yourself preparing a lot of lettuce or other salad greens, a salad spinner can be quite useful in removing excess moisture before serving. (If you do not have a salad spinner, placing greens in an empty pillowcase bound with a rubber band and running it in the laundry dryer for 5 minutes on low heat can be quite effective.) Salad greens should always be thoroughly dry before being dressed, otherwise the salad risks becoming a watery mess.

Lettuce and other salad greens should not be stored next to apples or other fruits that emit ethylene gas, which will hasten spoilage and cause brown spots.

TRIMMING & CLEANING

Lettuces, especially those from a farmers market or fresh from a field, can harbor more than their fair share of dirt. To clean, remove the outer leaves and rinse them thoroughly under either running water or by submerging and swishing them in a sinkful of water. Keep rinsing the inner leaves as well until all traces of dirt are gone. Then cut off the base where the leaves attach to the stem, as this tends to be bitter.

STEAMING & BOILING

Steamed lettuce may sound strange to Americans, but the Chinese, who rarely eat their vegetables raw, prefer their lettuce braised and steamed. Shredded lettuce can be briefly steamed for 2 to 3 minutes and topped with butter, or add lettuce toward the very end of preparation of slow-cooked meats and vegetables. Boiling tends to be too harsh for this delicate green.

June 10, 2006:
A Day in the Life of a Farmer

by Jack Hedin,
Featherstone Farm Owner

5:30 A.M.

It's already light out by the time I come down to the shop office to open things up. This is my best chance to get my thoughts together for the day, and to check over affairs in the office—I won't be back here much today. Checking on lettuce orders for the day, phoning in a compost order (two semi-trailer loads to be delivered tomorrow), noting a few phone calls to be returned later, and, above all, prioritizing the various projects of the day ... I have to be ready for the crew by 6.

5:58 A.M.

Everyone is in early as usual. I give a quick outline of the day's work for everyone in a mixture of English and Spanish (hopefully the Hmong speakers have understood!). I set a number of people to preparing the field wagons for the lettuce harvest (120 cases for the food co-ops). Then I outline jobs for a number of others: one guy will be chisel plowing and making beds at the Lacher farm on the ridge. Two others will be cultivating winter squash with the Regi weeder all morning. I tell these two I'll be by to check on progress if I can; if they finish the field before I get there, they can start laying out tomato trellis stakes in a nearby field. I hear several motors starting up as I dash back up to the office to call home and let my family know where I'll be if they want to find me.

6:35 A.M.

Ten people are now out picking lettuce. It is an experienced crew, but this is only our third cutting of the season and I want to make sure

---

STIR-FRYING & SAUTÉING

Although uncommon in America, stir-fried lettuce is a favorite dish in some Asian countries. Simply place washed, dried lettuce leaves in a wok or skillet in which vegetable oil and seasoning have been heated, and stir-fry for about 1 minute, or until the lettuce just wilts. Add a bit of soy or oyster sauce, and cook for 1 more minute, or until the lettuce is tender but still bright green.

MICROWAVING

Microwaving is not lettuce's favorite treatment, although it is acceptable if the lettuce is shredded and combined with other ingredients that contain a bit of cooking liquid or sauce. Microwave on High power for about 2 minutes, or until the lettuce is tender but not shriveled.

BLANCHING & FREEZING

Freezing is not recommended for lettuce because of its high water content,

EQUIVALENTS, MEASURES & SERVINGS

- *Leaf and Romaine Lettuce*   1 medium-sized head = 8 cups leaves
- *Bibb & Butter Lettuce*   1 medium-sized head = 4 cups leaves
- 1 pound raw lettuce = 4 to 5 2-cup servings
- 5 cups raw lettuce (about ½ pound) = about 1 cup cooked
- Allow ½ cup cooked lettuce per person
- 1 whole braised lettuce = 1 serving

COMPLEMENTARY HERBS, SEASONINGS & FOODS

Anchovies, apples, avocados, bacon, cheese, croutons, eggs (poached and hardcooked), garlic, goat cheese, herbs, Parmesan cheese, lemon juice, mayonnaise, greens, mustard, nuts, oils (walnut and olive), onions, oranges, peanut, pepper, raisins, sea salt, sesame, vinaigrette, vinegar (balsamic and rice wine).

SERVING SUGGESTIONS

- Try a truly lush taco, with plenty of shredded green leaf or Bibb lettuce.
- For fun, try substituting a sturdy lettuce leaf for the seaweed wrapper in sushi.
- Cut tightly headed lettuce into wedges and serve with salad dressing as a dip.
- Stir-fry lettuce in a little sesame oil, ginger, and soy sauce just like you would spinach or other tender greens.
- Lettuce is tasty wilted with onion and bacon dressing.
- One popular French dish combines green peas, shallots, butter, sugar, water or stock, and shredded lettuce, covered and cooked on low heat for 15 minutes or until tender.
- Put out romaine leaves along with other raw vegetables on the crudite tray and your favorite dips.
- The old standby: a truly good bacon, lettuce, and tomato sandwich, made with only the finest quality bread, a thick-cut bacon, farm-fresh lettuce, and vine-ripened tomatoes.
- Pickle lettuce with sugar, salt, and vinegar in the refrigerator the same way as cucumbers.
- Stuff romaine or Bibb lettuce leaves with blue cheese, walnuts, and bacon.

CITRUS BUTTER SALAD

SERVES 2 TO 4

This is a terrific beginning-of-summer salad.

CITRUS VINAIGRETTE

2 tablespoons grapefruit juice

½ tablespoon Champagne vinegar

¼ teaspoon salt

2½ tablespoons olive oil

1 finely chopped 12-inch stalk green garlic

½ tablespoon olive oil

1 head green butter lettuce

¼ cup toasted pine nuts

1. Mix all of the vinaigrette ingredients together thoroughly.

2. Sauté the green garlic in a hot pan with ½ tablespoon of the olive oil. Cook for 1 to 2 minutes, or until it turns barely brown.

3. Toss all of the ingredients and top with Citrus Vinaigrette (recipe above).

— *Featherstone Farm*

BRAISED LETTUCES

SERVES 8

1 head escarole

2 Belgian endives

1 Boston lettuce

¼ cup olive oil

2 tablespoons minced garlic

1 tablespoon ground coriander

½ teaspoon thyme

½ teaspoon rosemary

1 cup water

---

farm. He stops and reports that the transmission's power shift has been slipping more and more recently. This will require evaluation by a mechanic in town—we discuss the options for a farm call or taking the tractor to Rushford on the trailer (which would take it out of commission at a busy time). We decide to have the tractor finish chisel plowing at Lacher's, then to substitute the new McCormick for making planting beds later in the day, so Evan can take the John Deere into Hammel's in the afternoon. Tractor troubles at this time of year are stressful.

9:24 A.M.

Back in the shop, everything is quiet. I call Jim to make sure he can look at the 4020 if we get it to him in the afternoon. The lettuce crew will be finished before long. I've got only a few minutes to sneak home to get breakfast and to check on the kids. I pedal up to the house and have a quick bite and catch up on the news with a three-day-old Star Tribune that's lying around. Then the boys interrupt me with a request to throw the baseball a bit. I indulge myself for a few minutes in a game of catch, feeling guilty that I should be in the shop getting ready for the lettuce crew.

9:55 A.M.

In the shop, the wagons stacked with boxed lettuces are just rolling in. I check with the pickers about quality issues and their ideas about the next harvest volume. We agree that work on the fence must happen today—two guys want to go after it right away and start looking for supplies. The beds for transplanting cabbage will not be ready until later in the day, so I send the remaining crew out to hoe garlic until lunch. I then zip up to the office to talk with Larisa about lettuce availability for later in the week, so she can update her faxes to the co-ops in the Twin Cities. Larisa has

11:00 A.M.

I've forgotten about the squash crew at the Lacher farm, so I get in the truck and drive up on the ridge to check in as I'd promised. The squash cultivating is done, and the two guys have moved over to caging tomatoes. The squash looks magnificent in the early summer sun, and I take a moment to walk through and admire their work. My reverie is interrupted by bad news—cucumber beetles are attacking the buttercups (the most susceptible of the squashes) in force. I know from experience that this is the crop's most vulnerable time—if we can use an organic spray to control the beetles for a week and follow it up with foliar feed to rejuvenate the damaged leaves, the crop will be fine. I will have to communicate this plan to Salvador, the spray manager.

I decide to check on Hugo and the 4020. Walking over the ridge, this takes me past the field of tomatoes. This too looks beautiful—no disease or weeds. I'm surprised at how much progress crew has made on trellising the cherry tomatoes in the last week. I remind myself that this year we need to irrigate the toms before they show heat stress … it won't be long now.

Hugo is doing well on the chisel plowing, so I don't interrupt him. Walking out into the field to see if the quack grass is under control, I happily find few white succulent roots being turned up. This old hay field has come around nicely in three seasons. Next I spend 20 minutes mounting the bedmaker on the McCormick—luckily both were left up here last week—so it will be ready for Hugo after lunch. I call Evan on his cell phone and ask him to get the 4020 loaded on the trailer and down to Rushford after lunch.

2 tablespoons white wine vinegar
¼ cup whipping cream

1. Preheat the oven to 350°F.

2. Trim and discard the outer leaves from the escarole, leaving the lighter green center. Cut in half from root to tip. Trim and discard any discolored outer leaves from the endive and Boston lettuce, and cut them in half from root to tip.

3. In a large skillet with a lid, heat the olive oil over medium heat and add the escarole, endives, and lettuce. (If they do not fit in the skillet, perform this operation in batches as they cook down.) Cook the lettuce until it turns golden on both sides. Add the garlic, coriander, thyme, rosemary, water, and vinegar. Cover, place the skillet in the oven, and cook 15 minutes.

4. Transfer the skillet to the stovetop and remove the lettuces to a plate. Let them cool. Using a spatula, press down on the lettuces to squeeze out any braising liquid, and add it to the skillet. Add the cream to the braising liquid, and cook until the mixture becomes saucelike. Pour into a bowl and let cool.

5. To serve, arrange all of the lettuces, endive, and escarole on a platter and pour the sauce over the top.

— *www.recipelu.com*

. . . .

ASIAN TURKEY LETTUCE WRAPS   SERVES 8

1 red bell pepper, diced
1 teaspoon vegetable oil
1 pound ground turkey breast
½ cup green onions, sliced
1½ tablespoons fresh ginger, finely grated
½ teaspoon red pepper flakes
3 cloves garlic, minced
1 tablespoon soy sauce
⅓ cup hoisin sauce
8 lettuce leaves, washed, dried, chilled
¼ cup sliced almonds, toasted

1. Sauté the bell pepper in the vegetable oil for 2 minutes. Add the turkey, green onions, ginger, red pepper flakes, and garlic. Stir while cooking for 5 minutes, or until the turkey is no longer pink.

2. Add the soy sauce and hoisin sauce. Heat thoroughly for one minute.

3. Spoon the turkey mixture into each lettuce leaf. Sprinkle with the toasted sliced almonds, roll up tightly, and serve immediately.

— *Honeysuckle White, CooksRecipes.com*

JONNO'S CAESAR DRESSING

MAKES 1 CUP

Contributed by a CSA member, this variation of the classic Caesar dressing substitutes store-bought mayonnaise for the raw egg, providing creaminess without the safety concerns of uncooked egg.

1½ tablespoons anchovy paste
1 teaspoon freshly ground pepper
Juice of ½ lemon
1 tablespoon mayonnaise
¼ teaspoon salt
¼ cup olive oil
⅓ cup of the best finely grated Parmesan cheese you can find

Mix together the anchovy paste, pepper, lemon juice, mayonnaise, and salt. Then slowly mix in the olive oil and Parmesan cheese.

— *Featherstone Farm CSA member*

WRIGLEY-MARCO'S CAESAR SALAD

SERVES 1

This is the Caesar salad that was served for decades at the restaurant in the world-famous Wrigley Building in Chicago, home to the chewing gum company and one of the Windy City's most beautiful architectural landmarks.

DRESSING

¼ teaspoon salt
½ clove garlic
2 to 3 anchovy filets
5 turns of the pepper mill
¼ teaspoon vinegar
½ lemon
1 egg yolk
½ teaspoon soy sauce
2 drops Tabasco
¼ cup olive oil
½ teaspoon spicy mustard

Romaine lettuce, washed, dried, and chilled
Parmesan cheese
1 to 2 tablespoons croutons

Whisk together all of the dressing ingredients in a bowl or blender. Coarsely tear the romaine lettuce and place in a bowl. Add the dressing and toss well. Just before serving, grate Parmesan cheese over the top and sprinkle with croutons.

— *Maureen Cooney*

12:25 P.M.

I look up to realize that everyone has returned to the home farm but me. I take this opportunity to visit with Henry and Violette Lacher, the retired owners of this farm, at their home across the road. I ask Henry about truck access through his farmyard for compost delivery. I spend a few minutes with Violette, admiring her fabulous perennial flower garden, and I'm reminded of how much I enjoy senior farmers like the Lachers, and how important their support and advice is for our farm.

1:15 P.M.

I'm startled once again when I check my watch—I've got to get back to the home farm and make sure everything is on track. On the way back down the valley I pass first one truckful of guys on the way back to the tomatoes—they've determined that the tom cages should be finished today, and that they need five people to do it. Great—this crew runs itself with few snags! I mention to Salvador that he will have to spray the buttercup squash in the evening, when the beetles are more active. Then I pass Evan in the big truck and trailer, on his way to get the John Deere. Things are taking care of themselves.

Back in the shop, I try to catch up on a couple of phone calls and emails. I work on the plan to transplant broccoli over the next few weeks—numbers of beds, varieties, and timing—before being interrupted by the CSA crew, who have finished their planting. We discuss the next generations of salad crops, but they don't have the beds ready to plant yet. So I ask them to set up the irrigation in the lettuce for running overnight. This reminds me that we need new pipe gaskets. I drop twenty minutes calling around to find them at an irrigation supplier.

GREEK SALAD   SERVES 8

1 large or 2 small heads fresh lettuce, such as romaine, green leaf, red leaf, or any combination, or mesclun
4 tomatoes, each cut into 8 wedges
½ red onion, thinly sliced
32 Greek olives, preferably kalamata
1 pound Greek feta cheese, crumbled
1 cucumber, peeled and cut into 32 slices
16 pepperoncini (pickled peppers)
Greek Salad Dressing (recipe below)
8 pinches of dried oregano (or minced fresh oregano or majoram)

Assemble the ingredients as described above or create your own pat-tern. Like most other salads, this can be mixed as one large salad, then tossed, but my preference is to arrange it on individual plates. Drizzle the dressing over the top and sprinkle the oregano over all.

GREEK SALAD DRESSING   MAKES 3 CUPS, ABOUT 8 SERVINGS

1 cup extra-virgin olive oil (kalamata if available, otherwise any variety)
⅓ cup red wine vinegar
⅓ cup lemon juice
¼ cup Greek kalamata olive brine
14 pitted Greek kalamata olives
3 large cloves fresh garlic
¾ cup crumbled feta cheese
¼ medium-sized onion
¼ teaspoon whole peppercorns
¼ teaspoon dried oregano

Purée all of the ingredients except the oregano in a blender or food processor until smooth. Stir in the oregano. Store unused dressing, covered, in the refrigerator. It will keep for up to 2 weeks.

— *Peter Reinhart*, Sacramental Magic in a Small-Town Café

SIMPLE ROMAINE SALAD   SERVES 1

Break off a good-sized leaf from a head of romaine lettuce. Squeeze on lemon or lime juice, salt, and pepper to taste and arrange on your plate with the rest of your meal (perhaps a salmon fillet) alongside a dab of garlic mayonnaise. Dip your lettuce as you eat it.

— *Margaret Houston*, Featherstone Farm CSA member

MYLAR'S LETTUCE WRAPS

These Asian-inspired appetizers make fun, interactive hors d'oeuvres for kids and adults alike and are great at parties. Choices of fillings and seasonings are limited only by your imagination.

LETTUCE

Wash and thoroughly dry large lettuce leaves. Butterhead lettuces work extremely well for these wraps, but any lettuce with large, pliable leaves is suitable. Arrange on a large serving platter.

FILLING SUGGESTIONS

- Strips of chicken, turkey, steak, barbecued beef, corned beef, ground beef, pastrami, deli meats, pepperoni, savory pork
- Smoked salmon, carp, tuna packed in oil, anchovies, kippers
- Chunks of hardboiled egg
- Shredded or sliced cheese
- Green and red bell pepper slices, onion rings, tomato pieces, bean sprouts, and other vegetables
- Shredded lettuce
- Baked or fried tofu
- Sprigs of fresh herbs like cilantro, parsley, mint, basil, shiso
- Your favorite stir-fry recipe
- Fruit, such as apples, pears, mandarin oranges, strawberries, blueberries, raspberries
- Roasted nuts or ground peanuts
- Tuna, ham, chicken, or egg salad
- Whole shrimp, crab, or lobster pieces

CONDIMENT SUGGESTIONS

- Chili sauce
- Mayonnaise
- Mustard
- Hummus
- Tapenade
- Ketchup
- Hoisin sauce
- Nuoc mam (Vietnamese fish sauce)
- Soy sauce
- Plum sauce
- Pickled ginger
- Salsas
- Whipped cream or honey (for fruit wraps).

Arrange the filling ingredients on serving platters, set out the condiments and lettuce leaves, and let the fun begin.

— *Mi Ae Lipe, Featherstone Farm CSA member*

to be opened up. I talk with Mike about renting another fieldwork tractor while this one is laid up … we need equipment in the field this time of year. We agree that Evan can bring a big Case back to the farm this afternoon, but it will be a full load even for the fifth-wheel. It will be expensive, but it will keep us going in the field.

5:20 P.M.
I realize that I haven't thought about my family once in hours. I call home to see if I can bring anything home from town when I return. I drop by the IGA grocery for a few things, including a 12-pack of Pepsi (their favorite) for the crew. They're getting a lot done, working long hours, and it's hot. I depend on and appreciate them immensely. Driving home, I realize that I haven't eaten anything myself since 10 this morning. I've been so busy that I've completely forgotten about lunch. I see Salvador leaving the farm to spray the cucumber beetles as I come in. I hand him a cold Pepsi as we pass in the driveway…

Salad Tonight, My Dear?

Ancient Egyptians believed lettuce was an aphrodisiac.

Books

Fields of Greens
Annie Somerville; Bantam, 1993.

The Harrowsmith Salad Garden
Turid Forsyth and Merilyn Simond Mohr; Camden House, 1992.

Salads
Leonard Schwartz;
HarperCollins, 1992.

The Best 50 Salad Dressings
Stacey Printz, Bristol Publishing Enterprises, 1999.

FRENCH CREAM OF LETTUCE SOUP SERVES 6

This soup sounds bland, but isn't. This savory and attractive French first-course soup has a wonderful consistency and is distinctive enough to set up strongly flavored courses. It is silken enough in texture to make you champ at the bit to eat more.

4 tablespoons butter
2 cloves garlic, finely minced
2 tablespoons parsley, minced
1 tablespoon fresh tarragon, minced
1 cup onion, chopped
2 cups romaine lettuce, finely shredded
1 cup watercress, finely chopped
4 cups beef or vegetable stock
2 egg yolks
2 cups light cream
Salt and freshly ground black pepper

1. Heat the butter in a large saucepan, then sauté the garlic, parsley, tarragon, and onion until the onion is transparent. Add the lettuce and watercress, and stir over low heat for 5 minutes. Stir in the stock and simmer, uncovered, for 30 minutes.

2. When ready to serve, beat the egg yolks and cream together with several tablespoons of the hot soup. Then pour the mixture into a saucepan, stirring constantly over low heat until the soup thickens slightly. (Do not allow it to boil!) Stir in salt and pepper and serve immediately.

— *www.fooddownunder.com*

Spring lettuce seedlings awaiting planting in the valley.

Pea   PISUM SATIVUM, MACROCARPON GROUP

Peas grown on a farm like Featherstone and delivered to the consumer within hours of picking are truly gems of the garden. Once you taste such fresh peas, their sweetness and sheer vegetable flavor will spoil you for anything less.

These legume siblings of beans come in several forms. There is the common garden pea with which we are most familiar, with peas suitable for shelling, and two subspecies of edible-podded peas, the snow pea and the sugar snap. Featherstone grows these "sugar peas," as they are also known, but not shell peas.

The flat pods of snow peas have a terrific pea flavor without the hassle of shelling, and they are extremely popular in stir-fries. Sugar snaps, with their juicy fleshy pods and full-size peas, combine the best attributes of regular shell and snow peas. Both of these pea varieties are at their most succulent and sweet in late spring or early summer.

HISTORY

The garden pea is one of the oldest foods eaten by humans, and its precise origins remain so ancient that they are unknown. Popularly the pea is attributed to central Asia; indeed the oldest carbon-dated peas were found between Burma and Thailand, and are believed to be from 9750 B.C.E. The ancient Egyptians, Greeks, and Romans all enjoyed peas, as did Charlemagne, who ordered them planted in his gardens in about 800 C.E.

Until the time of the Italian Renaissance, however, peas were generally consumed mature and dried, and it was not until Catherine de' Medici introduced them to her court when she married Henry II of France that the fresh, young *piselli novelli* became fashionable. Subsequently they became all the rage during Louis XIV's time, so much so that both he and the ladies of his court were notoriously obsessed with them.

Snow peas and sugar snaps have existed at least since the 16th century. Sometimes called Chinese snow peas, these flat-podded legumes are neither from China nor do they have any obvious connection with snow; instead they may have been developed in Holland in the 1500s.

Varieties of the fleshy-podded sugar snap pea have been around for at least 300 years, but it was not until plant breeder Calvin Lamborn created an All-American Selection-winning hybrid in the early 1970s by crossing snow peas with a thick-walled rogue he found in his test plants that this vegetable suddenly became popular.

NUTRITION

Peas are rich in vitamin K, a nutrient essential for proper blood clotting and bone maintenance. They are also an excellent source of manganese, vitamin C, thiamine, folate, vitamin A, phosphorus, vitamin B6, niacin, iron, copper, tryptophan, and dietary fiber.

SELECTION

Choose fresh-looking peas with firm, uniformly bright-green pods. Avoid flabby, overly large or discolored pods—all signs of old, tired, starchy peas.

STORAGE

Like all peas, use snows and sugar snaps as soon as possible, because their sugars start turning into starch at the moment of picking. If you must store them, put them in a perforated plastic bag and refrigerate them in the vegetable crisper for no more than 2 or 3 days.

TRIMMING & CLEANING

Snow and sugar snap peas usually need only to be gently rinsed. Not all sugar peas have strings; if they do, snap off the stalk end and pull down on the thicker side of the pod to remove the central string. Test to see if the other side requires stringing as well.

STEAMING & BOILING

Overcooking is an anathema to both snows and sugar snaps. Steam peas over rapidly boiling water for 3 to 5 minutes, or until the pods are crisp-tender and still bright green. Boiling should be kept to an absolute minimum: about 2 to 3 minutes.

STIR-FRYING & SAUTÉING

Sugar snaps and snow peas are delicious stir-fried or sautéed for 2 to 4 minutes in a little water, stock, or sesame oil in a wok until they are just crisp-tender, before they turn limp.

MICROWAVING

Place peas in a microwave-safe dish, add 2 to 3 tablespoons water, cover, and cook on High power.

- 1 pound = 4 to 6 minutes

BLANCHING & FREEZING

To blanch snows and sugar snaps, wash, and, if necessary, string. Blanch the pods in rapidly boiling water for 2½ to 3 minutes. Drain and plunge them in ice water to stop cooking, then pack them in zipper-lock freezer or vacuum food sealer-type bags, or freezer containers. Squeeze out excess air and leave ½ inch of headspace (unless you are using the vacuum sealing method). Frozen peas should last up to 1 year at 32°F or below.

EQUIVALENTS, MEASURES & SERVINGS

- 3 ounces = 1 cup
- 1 pound sugar snaps = 4 to 5 cups strung peas = 4 to 5 servings
- 1 pound snow peas = 3 servings

COMPLEMENTARY HERBS, SEASONINGS & FOODS

Almonds, bacon, balsamic vinegar, butter, carrots, chicken, chives, citrus, cream, fennel, garlic, ginger, ham, leeks, lemon, lettuce, majoram, mint, mushrooms, new potatoes, nutmeg, olive oil, onion, orange juice, parsley, peanuts, prosciutto, rice, risotto, rosemary, sage, salmon, shallots, tofu.

SERVING SUGGESTIONS

- Snow peas and sugar snaps can be tossed whole into the wok for stir-fries.
- Serve raw or lightly steamed on a plate with a variety of dipping sauces:

mayonnaise, melted butter, salad dressing. A favorite with children.

- A traditional New England Fourth of July meal is salmon, peas, and new potatoes. Serve with freshly made lemonade and strawberries for dessert.
- Lightly sauté sugar snaps in a little butter and salt, and serve.
- Chop herbs like tarragon, dill, mint, basil, and parsley, and combine with chopped scallions and steamed peas.
- Pickle and can snap peas just like small cucumbers, using bread-and-butter pickle recipes.
- Toss a few snow peas in with fresh pastas to add crunch, flavor, and nutrition.
- Combine snow pea pods or snapped sections of sugar peas with shredded chicken, green onion, mayonnaise, almonds, raisins, and chopped apple for a most unordinary chicken salad.
- Stir-fry snow or sugar snaps with mushrooms.
- Try raw snow peas julienned in salads.
- For an unusual hors d'oeuvre, stuff blanched sugar snap peas with cream cheese combined with chopped fresh spring radish and green garlic.
- Throw sugar snaps or snows into the soup pot during the last few minutes of cooking.

MUSHROOM, SNOW PEA, AND SPINACH SALAD SERVES 6

¼ cup olive oil
¼ cup vegetable oil
¼ cup tarragon vinegar
1 teaspoon minced fresh tarragon or ½ teaspoon dried tarragon
½ teaspoon Dijon mustard
Salt and pepper
1¼ pounds snow peas, strings removed
1 bunch spinach, destemmed, washed, dried, and chilled
8 ounces fresh mushrooms, sliced
4 large radishes, thinly sliced

1. Whisk the oils, vinegar, tarragon, and mustard in a small bowl. Add salt and pepper to taste. (This dressing can be prepared 2 days ahead and stored at room temperature.)

2. Bring a large pot of salted water to boil. Add the snow peas; cook 45 seconds. Drain, run the peas under cold water, and drain again.

3. Combine the peas, spinach, mushrooms, and radishes in a large bowl. (This can be prepared 4 hours ahead. Cover and refrigerate.)

4. Toss the salad with enough dressing to lightly coat. Pass the remaining dressing separately.

— *MACSAC,* From Asparagus to Zucchini

PAMELA'S FRESH PEA SOUP   MAKES ABOUT 7 CUPS

1 tablespoon butter

1 tablespoon olive oil
1 clove garlic
1 large onion, chopped
1 small head lettuce, shredded
15 leaves fresh spinach
1 tablespoon chopped parsley
3 cups fresh sugar snap peas, or 5 cups young shell peas
5 cups chicken stock
¼ cup uncooked white rice
2 teaspoons sugar
Salt and freshly ground pepper
¼ cup finely chopped fresh mint
About 1 cup milk
Fresh mint sprigs

1. Heat the butter and oil in a large pot, add the garlic and onion, and sauté until softened.

2. Add the lettuce, spinach, and parsley; cook, stirring, until the vegetables wilt. Add the peas and 3 cups of the stock. Cover the pot, bring to a boil, then decrease the heat to a simmer, and cook until the peas become soft, about 5 minutes. Remove from heat.

3. In a food processor or blender, process in batches until coarsely blended. Return to the pot. Add the remaining 2 cups stock. Bring to a boil, add the rice, decrease the heat, and cook 15 minutes. Add the sugar, salt, pepper, and mint; stir in enough milk to reach the desired consistency. Heat slowly, stirring, until the soup is hot. Do not boil.

4. Garnish each serving with a sprig of mint.

— *MACSAC,* From Asparagus to Zucchini

Sugar Snap Peas with Orange

SERVES 4

1 pound fresh sugar snap peas
1 teaspoon grated orange rind
3 tablespoons fresh orange juice
2 tablespoons (¼ stick) very cold unsalted butter, cut into small pieces
Salt and pepper

1. Trim and destring the peas.

2. Steam the peas for 2 to 3 minutes, or until they just begin to become tender. Transfer them to a saucepan.

3. Over low heat, toss the peas with orange rind, orange juice, butter, and salt and pepper to taste until the butter melts. Serve immediately.

— *Ann Hodgman,* One Bite Won't Kill You

Grilled Summer Corn and Sugar Snap Pea Salad

Buying a bag of sugar snap peas for me is like walking home with a fresh loaf of bread—I need a spare. I cannot resist crunching away on those sugary, tender green pods.

4 ears of corn, as fresh as possible
1 tablespoon olive oil
1 small red onion, diced
1 chile, diced (very hot, such as serrano, habañero, or jalapeño)
2 teaspoons cumin seed, ground
½ pound sugar snap peas, cut into thirds
⅛ cup red wine vinegar
¼ cup Italian parsley leaves, chopped
Salt and black pepper

1. Peel the husks from the corn and remove the silk. On a very hot grill, cook the corn to blister and lightly char. Carefully cut the corn kernels from the cob and set aside.

2. Heat a 2-quart saucepan over medium heat and add the olive oil. Add the onion and chile, cooking until the onion becomes translucent, about 3 to 5 minutes. Add the cumin and cook for 30 seconds.

3. Add the sugar snap peas and cook for about 3 minutes to "off" the rawness the peas. Remove from heat, mix in the corn, the red wine vinegar, and parsley, then season with salt and pepper. Serve warm or cold.

— *Richard Ruben,* The Farmer's Market Cookbook

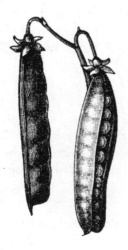

Salad and Braising Mixes

A riotous combination of young, tender greens makes up salad mix, while somewhat older, more hearty types of leaves constitutes braising mix. The former is best served raw as a delicate salad, whereas the latter is usually too coarse and strong-flavored for salad but is better suited for cooking.

Featherstone cultivates a variety of lettuces that it harvests early for its salad mixes. Usually salad mix is planted only in the spring and fall because the cooler weather suits it better. The resulting greens taste more sweet and flavorful than those maturing in the hotter summer months.

The braising mix consists of young leaves cut, washed, and dried from three different types of kale, chard, mizuna, spinach, and sometimes cultivated dandelions. These greens taste better lightly cooked rather than raw, and are wonderful steamed or braised. The braising mix is primarily available in the spring and occasionally in the fall.

HISTORY

Salad mix was virtually unknown in America before the late 1990s, when a taste for sophisticated foods and ethnic ingredients burgeoned, and "mesclun" was introduced to our palate and gastronomic consciousness. Mesclun originated in southern France and refers to a mix of assorted juvenile greens that can include chard, mustard greens, endive, lettuce, dandelion, chicory, mizuna, mâche, frisée, radicchio, sorrel, spinach, arugula, various herbs, and flowers. For Americans, the combination of precut, prewashed young lettuces, arugula, and other greens is now ubiquitous with the introduction of bagged grocery store salad mix.

NUTRITION

The nutritional content of salad mix varies widely depending on the types of greens included, but leafy greens tend to be powerhouses of nutrients, especially vitamins A and C, calcium, iron, potassium, and phosphorus.

SELECTION

When choosing either salad or braising mix in the supermarket or farmers market, look for greens that are fresh, not wilted-looking, with as few bruised leaves as possible. Slimy leaves tend to be spread decay quickly, so it is wise to pick through and discard these specimens before storing.

STORAGE

Featherstone's salad and braising mixes come prewashed and dried. If you prefer, you can rinse them one more time before serving, but the greens will keep far better dry until you are ready to use them. For mixes that seem too damp, slip a couple of paper towels in the bag among the greens. This will keep them drier and less susceptible to spoilage-inducing slime. (Conversely, if the greens seem to be on the dry side, use lightly dampened paper towels.) The greens should keep wrapped in a perforated plastic bag in the refrigerator crisper for up to a few days.

Salad greens should not be stored next to apples or other fruits that emit ethylene gas, which will hasten spoilage and cause brown spots.

TRIMMING & CLEANING

Other than an optional final rinse or picking through to discard wilted or decayed leaves, Featherstone's salad and braising mixes need no other preparation.

STEAMING & BOILING

Boiling is not recommended for salad mix, but a very quick steaming for 1 to 2 minutes renders the tender greens just wilted but still bright green and full of nutrients. Braising mixes, on the other hand, will need a bit longer cooking time. As their name suggests, braising greens can slowly simmer with meat or other vegetables until tender. They should be added during the last half to three-quarters of an hour before the end of cooking, depending on the toughness of the leaves and personal preference. Braising greens can be boiled for 8 to 10 minutes.

STIR-FRYING & SAUTÉING

Stir-fry salad mix in much the same way as lettuce: Simply toss salad mix in a wok or skillet in which vegetable oil and seasoning have been heated, and stir-fry for about 1 minute, or until the leaves just wilt. Add a bit of soy or oyster sauce, if desired, and cook for 1 more minute, or until the salad mix turns tender but is still bright green. Braised greens will take up to 3 to 4 minutes. They respond wonderfully to the wilted-greens treatment, with hot bacon dressing.

MICROWAVING

Salad mix can be cooked in the microwave if you do not want to bother with a steamer; place in a microwave-safe dish with a little water or cooking liquid and microwave on High power for about 2 minutes, or until the greens are tender but not shriveled. Braising mixes require about 4 to 5 minutes, or until tender.

BLANCHING & FREEZING

Freezing is not recommended for salad and braising mixes because of their high water content.

COMPLEMENTARY HERBS, SEASONINGS & FOODS

Anchovies, apples, avocados, bacon, cheese, croutons, eggs, garlic, goat cheese, herbs, Parmesan cheese, lemon juice, mayonnaise, greens, mustard, nuts, oils (walnut and olive), onions, oranges, peanut, pepper, raisins, sea salt, sesame, tofu, vinaigrette, vinegar (balsamic and rice wine).

SERVING SUGGESTIONS

- Fresh salad mix dressed with a light vinaigrette is hard to beat for a spring or an early summer salad.
- Toss a few handfuls in during the last minute or two of cooking a stir-fry, or sauté it on its own in a bit of butter or olive oil.

Salad mix is a relatively small crop for us in terms of volume, but it is a good example of the uniqueness of vegetable farming.

About two weeks ago, we were in the shop processing produce for the farmers market and our washing machine broke down, requiring us to dry all of the salad mix by hand. It then occurred to us that most folks don't know how their food is grown and processed. We offer Featherstone Farm CSA members opportunities to see the farm but rarely do they get to see how things are actually done. To give you an idea of how produce gets from our fields to your dinner table, here is the life cycle of salad mix.

First we order seed from a seed company, and then five or six varieties of lettuce are mixed together to form our own blend. Here at Featherstone, we use tractors for most field jobs, including direct seeding salad mix. A tractor with the seeder attachment drives over the already prepared soil bed, distributing the lettuce seed in three straight rows. Then the same process is followed to plant a bed of spinach, as well as another bed containing one row

- Throw in some salad mix into scrambled eggs, omelettes, or frittatas.
- Substitute salad mix for lettuce in sandwiches.
- Add variety to salad mix by adding fresh herbs, like basil leaves, dill sprigs, chervil, borage, or chopped chives. Edible flowers make beautiful, tasty decorations—try pansies, violets, nasturtiums, calendulas, daylily buds, or marigolds.
- Braising greens prepared southern-style, like collard greens, with ham hocks, bacon, or salt pork, are delicious.
- Boil braising greens in salted water, then drain the greens and prepare the pasta in the same cooking water to increase nutrition and flavor. Combine the greens and pasta along with anchovy filets, red pepper flakes, capers, tomatoes, garlic, and olives, for pasta puttanesca-style.
- Braising mix really shines when prepared simply—sautéed in olive oil with plenty of garlic. Serve it with a hearty meat, like rib roast or lamb, and sweet potatoes for a match made in heaven.

SEASONAL SALAD WITH HERB VINAIGRETTE

SERVES 6

Make the vinaigrette no more than a couple of hours before serving.

2 scant tablespoons red wine or sherry vinegar, or a combination
1 small clove garlic, peeled
Salt
6 tablespoons extra-virgin olive oil
Pepper
6 large handfuls salad greens, about ¾ pound

1. Measure the vinegar into a small bowl. Crush the garlic clove and add it to the vinegar, along with ½ teaspoon salt. After 10 minutes or so, whisk in the olive oil and a little freshly milled pepper. Taste and adjust the seasoning.

2. To serve, put the greens in a wide salad bowl and season with a small pinch of salt. Remove the garlic clove, whisk the vinaigrette, and toss the greens lightly with just enough dressing to make the leaves glisten. (Your clean hands make the best salad-tossing tools.) Serve immediately with garlic toast or croutons.

— *Featherstone Farm CSA member Pam Garetto (adapted from Alice Waters)*

TOSSED MESCLUN SALAD

SERVES 4

4 cups mesclun
2 cups romaine lettuce, torn into small pieces, washed, and dried
2 cups Boston lettuce, torn into small pieces, washed, and dried
½ cucumber, peeled, halved, and thinly sliced
½ yellow or red bell pepper, cut into very thin slivers
2 scallions, very thinly sliced
Your favorite dressing

Combine all of the ingredients except the dressing in a large salad bowl. Just before serving, toss with the dressing. Taste and add more if necessary, but be careful not to overdress the salad. Serve at once on 4 salad plates.

— *Jeanne Lemlin*, Vegetarian Classics

. . . .

BLACKBERRY-WALNUT MESCLUN SALAD   SERVES 4

    3 tablespoons balsamic vinegar
    1½ tablespoons olive oil
    2 teaspoons brown sugar
    1 clove garlic, minced
    Salt and freshly ground black pepper
    6 cups mesclun or other salad greens
    ¾ cup chopped yellow bell pepper
    ¼ cup chopped fresh mint
    1 cup fresh blackberries
    1 tablespoon toasted black walnuts (see Note)
    2 tablespoons crumbled blue cheese

In a large salad bowl, whisk together the vinegar, oil, sugar, and garlic; add salt and pepper. Toss with the remaining ingredients, and serve immediately.

Note

To toast the walnuts, heat a small, dry skillet over medium-high heat. Add the walnuts and toast, stirring often to prevent burning.

— *www.fooddownunder.com*

. . . .

MESCLUN WITH MAPLE MUSTARD TOFU POINTS   SERVES 4

    1 tablespoon soy sauce
    2 tablespoons Dijon mustard
    1 tablespoon sweet white miso
    1 tablespoon maple syrup
    1 tablespoon water
    1 teaspoon sesame oil
    Chili oil (optional)
    1 pound extra-firm low-fat tofu, frozen, defrosted, and drained
    ¼ pound mesclun or mixed salad greens
    Roasted red bell pepper strips (about 16)
    Seasoned rice vinegar

1. Preheat the broiler. Line a broiling pan with aluminum foil.

2. Mash and mix the soy sauce, mustard, miso, maple syrup, water, and

of arugula, one row of mizuna, and one row of tatsoi. Every time we change the seed, we need to adjust the size of the hole the seed is passing through on the planter so we can maintain the proper plant spacing. Once the seed is in the ground, we wait. If the weather is dry, sometimes we need to irrigate.

When the crop grows large enough to pick, the crew heads out with sharp knives and cuts the lettuce, spinach, and greens at ground level, placing them in plastic boxes for transport. We drive the boxes of greens back to the shop for cleaning. Dumping one box of salad mix into large tubs filled with cold water, we dunk the lettuce several times, pulling out any weeds in the process.

Gradually we add the rest of the greens and spinach to the tub and wash them with the lettuce. Then we scoop out the salad mix with laundry baskets lined with large fabric nets. After removing the nets full of salad mix, we place them in a household washing machine, where we process them for 30 to 60 seconds on the spin cycle. This removes most of the water, and then we can bag and weigh the salad mix for sale.

When our washing machine broke down, we became human salad spinners, twirling bags of mix over our heads to dry the lettuce! A dizzy but good workout.

Books

Fields of Greens
Annie Somerville; Bantam, 1993.

The Best 50 Salad Dressings
Stacey Printz; Bristol Publishing
Enterprises, 1999.

Simply Salads: More than 100
Delicious Creative Recipes Made
from Prepackaged Greens and a
Few Easy-to-Find Ingredients
Jennifer Chandler;
Thomas Nelson, 2007.

sesame and chili oils until thoroughly blended.

3. Press the tofu between 2 plates 4 or 5 times, until all of the water is released. Cut the tofu crosswise into 8 slices, about ½-inch thick. Cut each slice on the diagonal, creating triangles. Dip the triangles into the soy mixture and coat all sides.

4. Broil until lightly browned and slightly crusty on the first side, about 3 to 4 minutes. Turn the tofu over. Brush on any remaining soy mixture, and broil the second side until it is browned, about 3 minutes. (For a more barbecued taste, broil the tofu until slightly blackened around the edges.)

5. Serve either warm or at room temperature on top of the mesclun, red peppers, and rice vinegar, with crusty bread.

— *Lorna Sass,* The New Soy Cookbook: Tempting Recipes for Soybeans, Soy Milk, Tofu, Tempeh, Miso and Soy Sauce, *as appeared on* www.fooddownunder.com

POACHED EGGS WITH PANCETTA AND TOSSED MESCLUN

4 SERVINGS

8 large eggs
1 tablespoon extra-virgin olive oil
4 ounces thickly sliced pancetta, cut into ¼-inch dice
1 large shallot, minced
2 tablespoons white wine vinegar
2 tablespoons chopped tarragon
2 scallions, thinly sliced
10 cups mesclun (about 6 ounces)
Salt and freshly ground pepper
Toast points or steamed, sliced new potatoes, for serving

1. Bring a large, deep skillet filled with 2 inches of water to a simmer. Crack each egg into a cup and gently slide it into the water. Cook until the whites are solid but the yolks are still soft, 5 minutes. Using a slotted spoon, transfer the eggs to a paper towel-lined plate to drain.

2. Meanwhile, in a large skillet, heat the olive oil until shimmering. Add the pancetta and cook over moderately high heat until crisp, about 3 minutes. Add the shallot and cook until softened, 2 minutes. Remove from the heat and add the vinegar, tarragon, and scallions.

3. In a bowl, toss the mesclun with the dressing; season with salt and pepper. Transfer the salad to plates, top with the eggs, and serve with toast points.

—*Julie Ridlon, Chef/Owner, Chanterelle Catering and Clayton Farmer's Market, St. Louis, Missouri*

Spinach

SPINACIA OLERACEA

Succulent spinach is one of the most well-known vegetables in America, loved for its versatility in the kitchen but sometimes not so well-liked by juveniles. Belonging to the same family as beets, Swiss chard, and amaranth, spinach comes in several different forms: savoy, which has very crinkly leaves and is often the one available fresh in bunches; flat or smoothleaf, which has broader, smoother leaves; and semi-savoy, a hybrid type that combines the texture of savoy but is not nearly as difficult to clean.

Although spinach is available year-round in markets, it is a cool-weather crop that reaches its best in the spring (mid-May to June) and again in the fall (mid-September until frost). It is not to be confused with New Zealand spinach or water spinach, which are entirely different plants.

In recent times spinach has unfortunately been associated with E. coli outbreaks, the result of central California plants tainted by irrigation water contaminated with manure runoff. Although the chances that spinach grown locally on small-scale operations and available at farmer's markets would be similarly contaminated are extremely remote, similar outbreaks on lettuce, alfalfa sprouts, and certain fruits are a good reminder to thoroughly wash or cook our produce before using, whatever the source.

HISTORY

Spinach has a rich history as a favored vegetable. Its wild form originated in ancient Persia (now modern-day Iran), and the Arabs likely introduced the plant from Asia to Europeans. Interestingly, unlike many other modern vegetables, the ancient Italians and Greeks did not seem to know anything about it, even though spinach is common in many traditional Greek dishes. By the 1500s spinach was a favored Lenten food because of its early spring availability. When the Italian Catherine de' Medici married King Henry II of France, she introduced spinach to the French court, and to this day the phrase *à la florentine* still signifies a dish containing the vegetable (in France, but not in Florence).

Exactly how spinach got to America is a mystery, but it was growing in several American gardens by the early nineteenth century. In the late 1800s, a misplaced decimal point in a European publication pegged spinach's iron content as ten times too high, and it was not until 1937 that German chemists corrected the mistake. But by then the cartoon character Popeye was already extolling the muscle-building properties of this supposed wonder vegetable.

NUTRITION

A strong, muscular Popeye made the nutritional qualities of spinach famous, and indeed a 1-cup serving of spinach does contain almost 40 percent of your daily adult requirement for iron. Unfortunately, its naturally occurring oxalic acid binds with the iron, rendering much of this nutrient unusable. But spinach has plenty of other nutritional redemption, with

Books

Spinach and Beyond: Loving Life
and Dark Green Leafy Vegetables
Linda Diane Feldt;
Moon Field Press, 2003.

I Love Spinach Cookbook
Burgundy L. Olivier, 2003.
www.ilovespinach.com

Greene on Greens
Bert Greene;
Workman Publishing, 1984.

One Bite Won't Kill You
Ann Hodgman,
Houghton Mifflin, 1999.

Safety Tip

Some controversy exists as to
whether leftover spinach can
be safely reheated and eaten,
as bacteria can convert its
naturally occurring nitrates into
harmful compounds called nitrites.

Most of us have survived eating
spinach that has been reheated
at least once, but regardless, it
is probably best not to serve
such spinach to infants under six
months or very young children.

enormous amounts of vitamins K, A, and C, the B vitamins (especially folate), calcium, potassium, and manganese. Spinach is also one of the richest natural sources of lutein, a carotenoid that protects against degenerative diseases of the eye. It is also rather high in sodium for a vegetable, accounting for its slightly salty taste when cooked.

SELECTION

Both bunched and washed, bagged spinach should look fresh and bright green, free from yellowing or wilting leaves, bruises, slime, or decay.

STORAGE

Spinach should be stored unwashed and wrapped in a ventilated plastic bag in the refrigerator vegetable crisper until ready to use; depending on its condition, it will keep for 3 to 5 days. Before storing, inspect the bunch to make sure no slimy leaves are present, as rot will spread to other leaves quite quickly. Excess moisture also tends to promote sliminess; slipping in a paper towel among the leaves helps to keep things drier.

Spinach and other salad greens should not be stored next to apples or other fruits that emit ethylene gas, which will hasten spoilage and cause brown spots.

TRIMMING & CLEANING

Spinach loves sandy soil, and plenty of it often remains lodged in its leaves, sometimes even after several rinsings. The easiest way to wash spinach is to fill a big sink or bowl full of water, separate the leaves from the bunches, and completely submerge them, swishing vigorously. Inspect especially crinkly leaves and stems, where telltale brown grit may persist. Then rinse under cold running water, and repeat if necessary. To dry, use a salad spinner or gently pat the leaves dry between a couple of dishtowels.

STEAMING & BOILING

Steaming is an excellent way to cook spinach, which tends to be watery when boiled. About 1½ pounds of freshly washed (but not dried) raw spinach will steam in its own clinging water droplets if placed in a large pan, wok, or steamer basket, covered, and cooked for 5 to 8 minutes.

Or, if you prefer, boil spinach by dropping in into a large pot of boiling water and cook for 3 to 5 minutes. Be sure to drain it really well, even squeezing out some of the excess moisture, or the result will be a watery mush.

STIR-FRYING & SAUTÉING

Spinach is delicious in a stir-fry, especially when young leaves are tossed in during the last few minutes of cooking. To sauté spinach in quantity, use a little oil or stock, and start by placing in the pan about a quarter to a third of the total amount you plan to use. Cook these leaves down a bit, letting them wilt, then add the next third, and repeat the process until all of the spinach is used up.

Add more oil or stock as necessary. Toward the end of the cooking time, season with garlic, black pepper, nutmeg, salt, butter, or whatever seasoning you desire.

EQUIVALENTS, MEASURES & SERVINGS

- 1 pound raw spinach = 1 cup cooked
- ½ cup cooked = 1 serving

MICROWAVING

Wash and rinse, but do not dry. The water that clings to the leaves is enough moisture for it to cook in. Place leaves in a microwave-safe dish, cover, and cook on High power.

- 1 pound = 4 to 6 minutes

BLANCHING & FREEZING

To blanch, bring salted water to a boil. Drop the spinach into boiling water for 15 to 30 seconds until it turns bright green. Remove the spinach and immediately douse it with ice water to stop the cooking. Squeeze the excess water from the spinach, place it in zipper-lock freezer or vacuum food sealer-type bags, or freezer containers. Squeeze out excess air and leave ½ inch of headspace (unless you are using the vacuum sealing method). Frozen spinach will keep up to 6 months.

COMPLEMENTARY HERBS, SEASONINGS & FOODS

Almonds, anchovies, bacon, butter, cardamom, carrots, cheese, chiles, chives, cream, cumin, curry, eggs, fish, garlic, ginger, ham, hollandaise sauce, horseradish, hot peppers, leeks, lemon, lemongrass, mint, mushrooms, mustard, nutmeg, nuts, olive oil, olives, onions, oranges, pasta, pepper, pine nuts, raisins, raspberries, sesame, sour cream, soy, strawberries, sugar, tarragon, tomatoes, vinegar, walnuts, yogurt.

SERVING SUGGESTIONS

- Mix baby spinach with different lettuces, arugula, endive, dandelion greens, and fresh herbs for lush tossed salads bursting with flavorful greens.
- One of the classic spinach preparations is still the best: a wilted spinach salad made with hot bacon dressing, garnished with toasted almonds.
- Spinach combines wonderfully with pasta; toss in with cooked noodles, or use it in fillings for gnocchi and ravioli.
- Add a few spinach leaves in place of lettuce in your sandwiches, or add to tacos and burritos.
- Throw in a few handfuls of spinach leaves toward the end of cooking a stir-fry.
- Sprinkle some thinly sliced strawberries over your spinach salad, and serve with a balsamic vinegar dressing.
- Frittatas and crêpes benefit with the addition of some steamed spinach leaves to the mix.
- Substitute spinach for some of the basil and parsley in pesto.
- Make a creamy spinach soup, or add fresh spinach leaves to soups and stews.
- Layer spinach among the noodles and sauce in your favorite lasagna recipe.

GRANDMA'S SPINACH SOUFFLÉ   SERVES 4

Don't be put off by the word "soufflé"— this is very easy! Call it Baked Spinach if you feel more confident with that. The main trick here is to call

Eating Tip

Serve spinach with meats, vitamin C-rich fruits and vegetables, or white wine to help the body absorb more of its iron, which is bound in a less-accessible chemical form.

Cooking Tip

Spinach reacts adversely with certain metals, discoloring them. Use stainless steel knives (not carbon-steel blades), and avoid cooking it in aluminum pans or serving it in sterling silver dishes.

everyone to the table just before you take it out, so they can admire the puffy, golden top. My children, sadly, lack appreciation. They just see the green bits.

> 2 tablespoons flour
> 1 cup milk
> 3 eggs, whites and yolks separated
> 1 cup cooked spinach
> ½ to 1 cup grated or crumbled cheese (feta, sharp Cheddar, smoked anything, blue cheese, etc.)

1. Preheat the oven to 350°F.

2. In a microwave-safe dish, whisk the flour into the milk. Cook on Medium power in the microwave in 2-minute increments, stirring frequently, until it thickens and has a smooth consistency.

3. In a clean bowl, whip the egg whites and beat until soft peaks form.

4. In another dish, stir the egg yolks into the spinach and the milk-flour mixture. Using a rubber spatula, gently fold in the egg whites and pour into a 2-quart casserole dish.

5. Bake for 45 minutes, or until puffed and golden. Serve immediately.

— Margaret Houston, Featherstone Farm CSA member

"On the subject of spinach:
Divide into little piles.
Rearrange again into new piles.
After five or six maneuvers,
sit back and say you are full."

— Delia Ephron,
How To Eat Like a Child

SPINACH, NUTS, AND CHEESE   SERVES 2

This is a great savory dish. You can add hot chiles for added pizzazz.

> 2 slices minced thick-cut bacon (optional)
> 1 tablespoon olive oil
> ¼ cup minced onion (red or white)
> 2 green garlics, minced (or substitute 2 regular cloves garlic)
> ¼ cup walnuts
> 1 bunch spinach, coarsely chopped and washed
> ¼ cup cubed feta or fresh mozzarella cheese

1. Brown the bacon (if desired) and drain off the fat. Heat the olive oil in a skillet on medium-high heat, and sauté the onion, garlic, and walnuts until they soften.

2. Stir the spinach into the nut and oil mixture and cook down, about 5 minutes.

3. Add the bacon and cheese and cover until warmed, about 3 minutes.

— Judy, Featherstone Farm CSA member

GOMAE (SESAME SPINACH)   SERVES 2

This is a traditional Japanese dish of cooked spinach prepared with a

sesame paste, usually served at room temperature.

8 ounces spinach
2 tablespoons dark sesame oil
½ teaspoon soy sauce or tamari
1 teaspoon toasted sesame seeds

1. Bring a small pot of salted water to a boil. Drop the spinach into the boiling water for 1 to 2 minutes until it turns bright green. Immediately remove the spinach and plunge it into ice water for 1 minute to stop the cooking. Drain thoroughly, squeezing out excess water.

2. Mix the dark sesame oil and soy sauce or tamari together in bowl. Toss the oil mixture with the spinach and top with toasted sesame seeds. Serve warm or cold.

— *Featherstone Farm*

....

GARLIC SPINACH   SERVES 3 TO 4

This is a decidedly robust dish. After consuming it, don't have a job interview or plan to attend a cocktail social the next day, unless you're prepared to eat LOTS of parsley and breath mints.

1 tablespoon olive oil
3 to 8 cloves garlic, or 4 to 6 green garlic scapes
Many shakes of black pepper, or to taste
Several spritzes of Tabasco sauce, or to taste
2 pounds spinach leaves

1. Heat the olive oil in a skillet on medium heat. Mince or chop the garlic (I use a miniature food processor) and add to the oil. Sauté for 1 to 2 minutes, until the garlic begins to heavily perfume the kitchen (but be careful not to let it burn, or it will turn bitter).

2. Add the pepper and Tabasco sauce to the sizzling oil and garlic and let cook for about ½ minute. Then add enough spinach to fill the pan, stirring in more as it wilts and shrinks. Cook the spinach on medium-high heat for another 2 to 3 minutes, or until it wilts but is still a healthy green color.

3. Remove from the heat immediately and serve while piping hot.

— *Mi Ae Lipe, Featherstone Farm CSA member*

....

SPINACH SUPERBALLS   MAKES 3 DOZEN BALLS

This is a terrific dish for kids. If you don't feel like baking them all, you can freeze some of them unbaked.

2 pounds fresh spinach, lightly steamed, or 20 ounces frozen spinach

2 cups herb stuffing mix, crushed
1 cup grated Parmesan cheese (about 4 ounces)
8 tablespoons (1 stick) unsalted butter, melted
3 large eggs, beaten
1 to 2 large cloves garlic, crushed
¼ teaspoon pepper

1. Mush everything together with your hands in a large bowl. Chill the mixture, covered, for at least 2 hours, or overnight.

2. When you are ready to bake the spinach, preheat the oven to 350°F.

3. With wet hands, roll the mixture into 1-inch balls and place them on a cookie sheet. Bake them for 20 to 30 minutes, or until browned on the bottom and cooked through. You can't really judge the doneness by appearance, though; you will need to break open one of the balls and try it. Not a big problem.

— *Ann Hodgman,* One Bite Won't Kill You

CREAMY SPINACH SOUP   SERVES 4

5 ounces frozen spinach
1 large baking potato (8 ounces), peeled and thinly sliced
4 scallions, coarsely chopped
2 cloves garlic, chopped
1 cup low-sodium chicken broth diluted with 1¼ cups water
¼ teaspoon pepper
⅛ teaspoon salt
¾ cup low-fat milk
1 teaspoon unsalted butter
2 tablespoons grated Parmesan cheese

1. In a large saucepan, combine the spinach, potato, scallions, garlic, diluted broth, pepper, and salt. Cover and bring to a boil over high heat. Then decrease the heat to medium-low, and simmer until the potato is tender, about 15 minutes.

2. Transfer the solids to a food processor or blender and process to a smooth purée. Return the purée to the saucepan. Stir in the milk and butter, and warm the soup over medium heat, stirring frequently.

3. Ladle the soup into bowls and sprinkle with Parmesan cheese.

— *Fruits and Veggies—More Matters; Centers for Disease Control & Prevention*

Strawberry

FRAGARIA X ANANASSA

June spells summer weddings, the end of school, and delicious, sweetly fragrant strawberries. Although strawberries are commonly available now throughout the year, thanks to harvests from Chile and California, these big, beautiful, oversized berries often sadly disappoint. They lack the flavor and scent that their smaller, less perfect cousins deliver for a just a few rapturous weeks of the year. Wild strawberries carry the most intense flavor and perfume, but beating the birds and squirrels to them is a challenge.

A member of the vast rose family, strawberries are one of nature's oddities in that they are one of the few fruits with external seeds (the cashew is another). In fact, strawberries are actually not true berries at all but are considered "accessory fruits," meaning that its fleshy parts are not derived from the flower's ovaries, but from the peg at the bottom of a receptacle that contains the ovaries. Therefore, the seeds are the strawberry's true fruit, with that succulent, perfumed flesh merely a surrounding holder.

Strawberries come in a surprising number of forms. The strawberry with which we are most familiar is the garden strawberry, which spontaneously came into being when two Fragaria species crossed.

HISTORY

Diminutive but strongly flavored wild strawberries in their myriad variations have been treasured by humans for milennia. Strawberries appear to have originated in both the Old and New Worlds but were cultivated only relatively recently. Wild varieties (likely *Fragaria vesca*) were first documented appearing in gardens in the early 1300s, most likely as transplants. American or Virginia strawberries *(Fragaria virginiana)* shocked European explorers with their abundance and comparatively large fruit size.

Our modern strawberries resulted purely by accident in France in the early 1700s, when a French explorer brought back several specimens of a Chilean Fragaria species that bore enormous fruits with acceptable flavor. These all-female (unbeknownst to anyone) plants flourished but failed to set fruit until some male Virginian strawberries happened to be planted there. At last consummation took place, producing a fruit that has since become the world's leading strawberry. Still, many who know the intense flavor of the wild fruit still believe that any garden berry holds no candle to its untamed counterparts.

NUTRITION

A 1-cup serving of strawberries provides more than an adult's daily requirement for vitamin C, as well as 20 percent of manganese, all for just 43 calories. Strawberries also contain significant folate, potassium, iodine, dietary fiber, and antioxidants, including anthocyanin, which gives the fruit its scarlet color.

SELECTION

A bright, even shade of red with fresh green caps and an enticing scent promise ripeness. However, these characteristics do not always deliver the most rapturous fruit experience, as those gorgeous, huge California specimens sometimes prove. Locally grown strawberries are almost always a better bet, as truly ripe berries do not travel well. Avoid unripe berries that are greenish or yellow, and fruit with soft spots or wrinkled skins, which may signal mold or dehydration.

STORAGE

Before storing them in the refrigerator, check the fruit for signs of mold or overripeness. Remove any spoiling or soft berries immediately, so their malaise does not spread to their neighbors. Ripe berries should be eaten within 24 hours, and the remaining fruit should be kept unwashed until ready to use. Wrapping the container in plastic will reduce dehydration, and the berries should be used within a few days.

TRIMMING & CLEANING

Before using, wash fresh strawberries gently by floating them in a bowl of water or rinsing them briefly. Pat lightly dry with a paper towel.

BLANCHING & FREEZING

Thoroughly wash, dry, and hull strawberries before freezing. To freeze whole berries without sweetening, place them in a single layer on a cookie sheet in a freezer; once they are frozen, transfer them to zipper-lock freezer or vacuum food sealer-type bags, or freezer containers. Sliced berries should be sprinkled with a little lemon juice or ascorbic acid and water (the acid will help retain color).

Sugaring berries before freezing improves their color, flavor, and shape, and can be done either as a dry-pack (slice or halve the berries, sprinkle ⅓ to ¾ cup of sugar per each quart of fruit, then package, and freeze), or syrup-pack, which is especially good for whole berries. To make the syrup, dissolve 1 to 1¼ cups of sugar in each cup of water. Pack the berries in containers and cover with syrup, leaving ½ inch of headspace. Frozen berries should last about 10 months to a year.

MEASURES & EQUIVALENTS

- 6 or 7 strawberries = 1 cup
- 1 16-ounce clamshell container = 1 quart = 15 to 18 whole berries = 3 to 4 cups sliced or chopped
- 1 pint = 7 to 9 whole berries = 1½ or 2 cups sliced or chopped

COMPLEMENTARY HERBS, SEASONINGS & FOODS

Almonds, apricots, balsamic vinegar, bananas, basil, brown sugar, caramel, Champagne, chocolate, cinnamon, coconut, cognac, Cointreau, cinnamon, cream, cream cheese, crème fraîche, currant, figs, Grand Marnier, grapefruit, guavas, kirsch, kiwi, lemon, lime, maple syrup, mascarpone, nuts, oranges, passion fruit, peaches, pepper, pineapple, port, raspberries, rhubarb, sambuca, sherry, sour cream, sugar, vanilla, violets, wine, yogurt.

For More Information

Florida Strawberry Growers Association
www.straw-berry.org

California Strawberry Commission
www.calstrawberry.com

- Few pleasures in life beat ripe strawberries with thick Devonshire cream or whipped cream on a warm summer day.
- Pair strawberries with stir-fried scallops and sugar snap peas for a sumptuous, yet simple, light lunch or supper.
- Try warming a wedge or wheel of Brie cheese, then sprinkling with sugar and serving with fresh ripe strawberries for a luxurious treat.
- Slice a fresh, ripe papaya or cantaloupe in half, scoop out the seeds, and fill the hollows with sliced strawberries and grapes.
- Melt quality chocolate over very, very low heat or a fondue burner, serve with strawberries and champagne, and enjoy with friends.
- Add sliced strawberries to lettuce and fruit salads.
- Make fruit kebobs by skewering chunks of pineapple, bananas, strawberries, melon, grapes, other berries, and papaya. Great for kids and grownups alike, with or without whipped cream or maple syrup for dipping.
- Toss strawberries over cereal, pancakes, fruit salads, ice cream, oatmeal, and yogurt.

Freshly picked strawberries awaiting shipment.

SWEET-TART FRESH STRAWBERRIES   SERVES 12

The lightly acidic balsamic vinegar and the sweet brown sugar add refreshingly sweet, yet tangy flavor notes to enhance the berry flavor. You can also try adding a little freshly cracked black pepper.

2 quarts fresh strawberries, hulled
1 cup packed light brown sugar
¼ teaspoon salt
½ cup balsamic vinegar

About 1 to 2 hours before serving time, toss the strawberries with the brown sugar, salt, and vinegar in a large mixing bowl. Refrigerate and toss again. Drain and serve cold in a clear glass container.

— *Shirley Corriher,* CookWise

"Doubtless God could have made a better berry, but doubtless God never did."

— *William Butler on the wild strawberry*

High Turnover

Strawberries are treated as an annual crop in California, meaning that they are replaced every year to maintain optimal yields.

In other U.S. states such as Oregon, they are treated as perennial crops and allowed to bear for 4 to 5 years before being replaced.

A Lot of a Good Thing

California grows enough strawberries that if they were laid end to end, they would circle the world 15 times.

Florida, the next largest U.S. strawberry producer, grows nearly all of the country's winter crop.

Hope They Don't All Germinate

On average, each strawberry has 200 tiny seeds on its exterior.

FRUIT SHAKE   MAKES 1 SHAKE

Sugar or honey for sweetening
1 cup skim or soy milk
1 cup plain yogurt
1 tablespoon ground flaxseed or flaxseed oil
1 cup berries (strawberries, raspberries, or blueberries, etc.)
1 banana

Sweeten with sugar or honey, if needed, then place all of the ingredients in a blender and process well.

— *Kathy Delano,* The Bluff Country Co-op Cookbook

STRAWBERRY SHORTCAKE   SERVES 8

This is a real American classic—shortcake made with a rich biscuit base, lots of fresh strawberries, and a reasonably lavish hand with the whipped cream.

Shortcake
1¾ cups all-purpose flour
2 teaspoons baking powder
Pinch of salt
4 tablespoons (½ stick) lightly salted butter, cut into pieces
⅔ cup whipping cream

Topping
1 quart fresh strawberries, washed, dried, hulled, and halved
2 tablespoons sugar for sprinkling, plus 2 teaspoons for whipped cream
1½ cups whipping cream

1. Preheat the oven to 425°F. Butter an 8-inch round cake pan.

2. Mix the flour, baking powder, and salt in a bowl. Combine the butter pieces into the flour mixture with a pastry blender, two knives, or your fingers until the mixture resembles coarse meal. Add the cream and stir until the mixture just comes together. Shape into a flat disk and press lightly into the prepared pan, patting evenly to the edges. Bake on the center rack for about 20 minutes; the top should be lightly colored and feel firm to the touch. Turn out of the pan and right-side-up on a cake rack to cool.

3. When the shortcake is completely cool, slice in half horizontally with a long, thin knife. Slice the strawberries in half and sprinkle with 2 tablespoons of the sugar; set aside for about 30 minutes.

4. When ready to assemble, whip the cream with the remaining 2 teaspoons of sugar. Spread two-thirds of the strawberries with their juice

over the cut surface of the bottom half, cover with whipped cream, place the top half over the filling, press lightly, then spoon the berries on the center of the top layer only, and top with more whipped cream.

— *Rolce Redard Payne and Dorrit Speyer Senior,* Cooking with Fruit

STRAWBERRY BREAKFAST PIZZA   SERVES 5

1 (7½-ounce) package refrigerated biscuits (10 biscuits)
1 orange
2 (3-ounce) packages cream cheese, softened
4 teaspoons honey, divided
1 pint fresh strawberries, stemmed and halved
Mint sprigs, for garnish

1. Preheat the oven to 400°F.

2. Stack 2 biscuits; roll out to a circle about 6 inches in diameter, ⅛-inch thick. Place on an ungreased baking sheet. Prick all over with a fork. Repeat with the remaining biscuits to make a total of 5 circles. Bake until lightly browned, about 6 to 8 minutes. Loosen the biscuits and cool slightly.

3. Meanwhile, finely grate the peel from the orange. In a bowl, beat the cream cheese, orange peel, and 2 teaspoons of the honey to blend thoroughly; set aside. Juice the orange into another bowl. Add the strawberries and the remaining 2 teaspoons of honey. Toss, and place in a colander to drain.

4. Increase the oven temperature to 425°F. Spread the biscuits with the cheese mixture to within ½ inch of the edges, dividing equally. Bake just until the edges of the cheese brown lightly.

5. Top with the drained strawberries. Garnish with mint sprigs, and serve immediately.

— *California Strawberry Commission*

STRAWBERRY NACHOS   SERVES 6

3 cups sliced strawberries
⅓ cup sugar
¼ cup amaretto (almond-flavored liqueur)
½ cup nonfat sour cream
½ cup frozen reduced-calorie whipped topping, thawed
2 tablespoons sugar
⅛ teaspoon ground cinnamon
6 (7-inch) flour tortillas, cut into 8 wedges
Butter-flavored vegetable cooking spray
2 teaspoons cinnamon sugar

Books

Berries: A Country Garden Cookbook
Sharon Kramis;
Collins Publishers, 1994.

One Hundred One
Strawberry Recipes
Carole Eberly; Eberly Press, 1987.

Simply Strawberries
Sara Pitzer;
Storey Communications, 1985.

Grandma's Favorite
Strawberry Recipes
Lanette Coalson;
Father & Son Publishing, 2004.

2 tablespoons sliced almonds, toasted
2 teaspoons shaved semisweet chocolate

1. Combine the strawberries, ⅓ cup sugar, and amaretto in a bowl; stir well. Cover and chill 30 minutes. Drain, reserving juice for another use.

2. Preheat the oven to 400°F.

3. Combine the sour cream, whipped topping, sugar, and cinnamon in a bowl; stir well. Cover and chill.

4. Arrange the tortilla wedges on 2 baking sheets; lightly coat with cooking spray. Sprinkle evenly with the cinnamon sugar. Bake for 7 minutes or until crisp. Cool on a wire rack.

5. To serve, arrange the 8 tortilla wedges on a serving plate; top with about ⅓ cup of the strawberry mixture and 2½ tablespoons of the sour cream mixture. Sprinkle with almonds and chocolate.

— *Roz Kelmig, California Strawberry Commission*

Farm visitors and CSA members picking berries in the field during Featherstone's annual Strawberry Social.

Swiss Chard

BETA VULGARIS,
CICLA GROUP

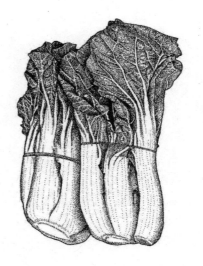

Chard is closely related to beets. Like its cousin, it consists of two edible parts: its meaty dark-green leaves, which are reminiscent of sturdy spinach, and its large, flat, celery-like stems or ribs, which can be cooked and served like asparagus. Young chard leaves are tender enough to eat raw, or they can be briefly steamed or blanched and used in most preparations that call for spinach. Rich, earthy, slightly salty, and yet bitter, it makes a delicious, nutritious addition to soups, quiches, and stir-fries.

Although it is available year-round, chard's prime season is summer, from June to August. Featherstone grows several varieties of chard: green with white stems; a variety with red stems called Ruby Red; and Bright Lights, whose brilliantly colored stems come in shades of orange, red, and yellow.

HISTORY

Paradoxically, Swiss chard does not have much to do with Switzerland; it is actually native to Sicily. The ancient Romans, Greeks, and Arabs ate chard and its beety cousins, but it was a Swiss botanist by the name of W. D. J. Koch who classified the plant in the 1800s; thus, the name of his homeland became part of the plant's common name.

NUTRITION

Chard is one of nature's nutritional powerhouses, an outstanding source of vitamins A, C, and K, as well as magnesium, potassium, iron, copper, and dietary fiber, all for only 35 calories per cup. Research studies have found that its phytonutrients, particularly anthocyanins and carotenoids, may significantly reduce one's risk of colon cancer.

SELECTION

Chard should be fresh, crisp, and unwilted. Avoid stems with cracked or brown ribs or leaves that are yellowing or drooping. For eating raw, choose chard with the smallest, tenderest greens. Larger leaves will be somewhat tougher and should be cooked.

STORAGE

Refrigerate unwashed chard in a perforated plastic bag in the vegetable crisper, where it will keep for several days.

TRIMMING & CLEANING

Chard's large, rumpled leaves make great hiding spots for dirt and resting insects, so a thorough wash in a sink or large bowl of water is a must. Grasp the stems and vigorously swish the leaves in the water several times. Grit will sink to the bottom, and a little extra help from fingers may be in order for the deeper crevasses. The stems, which often harbor sand, can be scrubbed lightly with a soft vegetable brush.

STEAMING & BOILING

The stems take longer to cook than the leaves, so trim and cook them separately. Colored chard stalks lose much of their color when boiled or steamed, so avoid overcooking them. To steam chard, use either a steamer or place freshly washed greens in a saucepan, tightly cover, and steam, using just the water clinging to them, for about 5 minutes. Stems will take a little longer, about 7 to 8 minutes, depending on their size. Chard can be boiled for about 8 to 15 minutes, depending on its size and condition, but take care to check it frequently for signs of overcooking and too much loss of color in its ribs.

STIR-FRYING & SAUTÉING

Chard responds well to being cooked briefly over high heat. Add freshly washed (but not dried), shredded chard leaves by the handful to the pan, stir, cover tightly, and cook for 5 to 8 minutes, or until they are wilted but still bright green. Chard stems, cut into 1-inch pieces, will take longer, about 13 to 20 minutes, but their time varies depending on their size and thickness.

BRAISING

Chard stems are delicious when braised in cooking liquid for about 20 to 25 minutes; leaves can be added during the last 10 minutes of cooking time.

MICROWAVING

Place sliced, freshly washed, shredded chard leaves with water still clinging to its leaves in a large bowl and cover tightly with plastic wrap. Microwave on High power for about 5 minutes. Stems cut into 1-inch pieces require a little longer time, about 8 minutes, but this will vary depending on their size and the microwave's wattage. Check the stems frequently and remember that they will continue to cook while they are standing.

BLANCHING & FREEZING

Unlike many greens, chard leaves do freeze acceptably well (but not the stems, as they will turn soggy). To prepare the leaves, trim them away from the stems and blanch briefly in boiling water for 2 minutes, then plunge into ice water for 2 minutes to halt the cooking. Drain and place in zipper-lock freezer or vacuum food sealer-type bags, or freezer containers. Squeeze out excess air but do not leave any headspace. Chard frozen at 0°F should keep for up to a year.

EQUIVALENTS, MEASURES & SERVINGS

- 1 pound = about ½ pound ribs and ½ pound leaves = 2 cups cooked
- 1 pound whole chard = 2 to 3 servings
- 1 pound leaves = 2 to 3 servings
- 1 pound ribs = 2 to 3 servings

COMPLEMENTARY HERBS, SEASONINGS & FOODS

Butter, cheese, cream, eggs, garlic, lemon, nutmeg, olive oil, onions, pasta, peppers, pine nuts, raisins, saffron, tomatoes, walnuts.

Cooking Tip

The oxalic acid in chard will react with aluminum and iron cookware, staining the greens a dark color and lending a metallic taste.

- Very young leaves can be eaten raw in salads, or used like lettuce in sandwiches. Try a BCT (bacon-chard-tomato sandwich).

- Use young, tender leaves raw in salads as a substitute for lettuce.

- If you love the taste of southern-style greens but don't have nearly enough time to leisurely boil the greens for hours, do a quicker version with chard, boiled for an hour with a ham hock, salt pork, several strips of bacon, even liquid smoke, along with a little vinegar, hot pepper sauce, salt, and sugar.

- Roasting the stems caramelizes them; drizzle with olive oil, garlic, salt, and pepper and roast for 20 minutes at 400°F.

- Boil chard leaves and stems separately and pat dry. Add diced bacon, pancetta, or proscuitto, and reheat.

- Wrap the big leaves around small fish for steaming or roasting on the grill.

- Use the leaves as a substitute for tortillas in tacos or fajitas.

- Try lightly steamed chard with a hot bacon dressing, like wilted spinach.

- The robust, substantial leaves of chard complement equally robust meats— ham, pork, pot roast, and lamb.

- Wrap lightly steamed chard leaves around your favorite vegetable or grain salad and roll into a package, like grape leaves in dolmas. Bake in a medium-heat oven and enjoy this nutrient-superstar alternative to stuffed cabbage.

CHARD WITH RAISINS AND ALMONDS SERVES 4 TO 6

A wonderful dish for kids, who love its sweetness and bright colors.

¼ cup slivered almonds
2 pounds rainbow chard
½ cup water
½ cup apple juice
½ cup raisins
2 tablespoons butter

1. Toast the almonds (an oven broiler is useful for this).

2. Wash the chard, but do not dry it. Cut the leaves away from the stems and roll into a chiffonade. Slice crosswise to shred the leaves. Then cut the stems into ½-inch pieces. In a large pan, sauté the chard stems in the water for about 4 minutes; then add the leaves and cook until they turn tender, about 5 to 8 minutes. Stir in the apple juice and raisins.

3. Then top with the butter and almonds, and toss lightly. Serve at once.

— *Ruth Charles, Featherstone Farm CSA member*

"You should eat it because Farmer Jack grew it."

— *Ruth Charles, Featherstone CSA Member*

SALMON POACHED WITH TOMATOES AND SWISS CHARD
SERVES 5 TO 6

1½ salmon fillets, skinless
Salt and freshly ground black pepper

12 ounces Swiss chard
4 tablespoons olive oil
1 large onion, thinly sliced
1½-inch cube fresh ginger, slivered
8 fresh or canned plum tomatoes, chopped
½ cup thick coconut milk
2 cups water

1. Cut the salmon fillets crossways into 6 pieces. Pull out the bones. Season with salt and pepper; allow to stand for 20 minutes.

2. Cut the chard's green leafy parts away from the central stems. Cut the greens into ¼-inch strips. Cut the stems into ⅛-inch strips.

3. Heat the oil in a very large frying pan over medium heat. Add the onion, ginger, and chard stems. Sauté for 5 minutes. Add the tomatoes and continue to sauté for another 4 to 5 minutes. Add the coconut milk and water, plus salt and pepper to taste. Simmer over low heat for 1 minute. Add the chard leaves.

4. Add the fish in a single layer on top of the sauce, spooning some of the sauce over the fish. Cover and simmer 5 minutes or until the fish is cooked through. Serve with the sauce and vegetables.

— Medford Mail Tribune, *May 3, 1994, as appeared on www.fooddownunder.com*

CHARD AND CHEDDAR OMELET   SERVES 4

Try this southern-style omelet with sautéed plum tomatoes and warm cornbread. Dessert can be butter pecan ice cream drizzled with bourbon.

4 tablespoons butter (¼ stick)
4 cloves garlic, minced
8 ounces red Swiss chard stemmed, chopped (about 6 cups packed)
1½ teaspoons hot pepper sauce
½ teaspoon salt
½ teaspoon freshly ground black pepper
10 large eggs
1½ cups grated sharp Cheddar cheese

1. Melt 1 tablespoon of the butter in an 8-inch nonstick skillet over medium-low heat. Add the garlic; sauté until soft, about 2 minutes.

2. Stir in the chard, and cover and cook until tender, about 4 minutes. Stir in the hot sauce. Season with salt and pepper. Transfer to a small bowl. Wipe the skillet clean.

3. Whisk the eggs, ¼ cup of the cheese, salt, and pepper in a medium-sized bowl to blend. Melt ½ tablespoon of the butter in the same skillet over medium-high heat. Add half of the egg mixture and cook until the eggs are just set in center, tilting the pan and lifting the edge of the omelet with a spatula to let the uncooked portion flow underneath, about 2 minutes. Scatter half of the chard mixture over half of

the omelet. Sprinkle ¼ cup cheese over the chard, then fold the omelet over the cheese; slide out onto a plate.

4. Repeat with the remaining butter, egg mixture, chard, and cheese.

— Bon Appétit, *February 2001, as adapted on www.fooddownunder.com*

. . . .

SWISS CHARD WONTON RAVIOLIS   SERVES 8

Wonton skins are such a versatile product. Outside of Asian markets, you can find them in the refrigerated section of the grocery store. If they are difficult to find, you may want to buy a small supply of them when you get the chance and freeze them. (The uncooked raviolis themselves freeze very well, although you must freeze them in a single layer before storing them in a plastic bag or container. Otherwise, they will stick to each other and you will find yourself serving very large raviolis.) Place the package of wontons in the refrigerator and let them defrost for about 2 hours.

1 bunch red or white Swiss chard (approximately 2 pounds)
2 tablespoons plus ½ cup olive oil
2 cloves garlic, finely minced
¾ cup Parmesan cheese
Salt and black pepper
1 package wonton wrappers (approximately 50 count)
¼ cup cornstarch

1. Remove the ribs from the leaves of the Swiss chard. Wash both, but keep them separate.

2. Bring a 4-quart pot of water to a boil and cook the leaves for 3 to 4 minutes. Drain. Roughly chop the leaves. Meanwhile, dice the ribs into small pieces and sauté in 2 tablespoons of olive oil with the garlic for 5 minutes. Drain the ribs through a fine sieve over a large bowl, collecting the liquid given off from the cooked ribs. Reserve the liquid.

3. Toss the Swiss chard leaves, ribs, and Parmesan cheese together. Taste and correct the seasoning with salt and pepper.

4. Place about a tablespoon's worth of the Swiss chard mixture in the center of a wonton skin. Lightly dampen the edges with water and lay another wonton skin on top. Carefully squeeze out any air from the ravioli and pinch the edges to seal. Place the completed raviolis on a tray lightly dusted with cornstarch (this helps prevent the raviolis from sticking to the surface). Continue with the rest.

5. Preheat the oven to 350°F.

6. Lightly oil a baking tray and lay the raviolis down in a single layer. Lightly brush the tops of the raviolis with olive oil. Place in the oven and bake for 10 minutes, or until golden brown.

7. Bring the reserved Swiss chard liquid to a boil, season with salt and pepper, and add the remaining oil to the liquid. Drizzle over each serving.

Reminiscences about Chard

by Margaret Houston, Featherstone Farm CSA Member & Newsletter Volunteer

September 4, 2002

I grew up in Saskatchewan; my mother's family farmed and had a huge kitchen garden. One vegetable that grows well in Saskatchewan is chard. So there was always lots of it.

We froze a lot of it right away. We washed, chopped, and blanched it, then packed it in pint freezer bags with twist ties, which fitted into tidy little cream-colored waxed paper boxes that stacked beautifully in the freezer.

We ate it just steamed in those days. Butter and salt do wonders, and I still eat it that way. Now I often sauté it with a little onion and garlic and olive oil—still with the salt and pepper. My mom also frequently made chard for lunch: toast on the bottom, chard, a poached egg, and cheese on top with a sprinkling of salt and pepper. Eggs Florentine for the Saskatchewan prairie!

I have enjoyed watching chard's reputation grow over the years, as well as its expansion into new color realms. The chard I first knew was white-stemmed; we always cut them off, but apparently Europeans think that is the best part of the vegetable.

I remember the first year Grandma grew ruby red chard. The combination of the red stem and the dark green leaf was stunning. Now we have the rainbow version, which is truly gorgeous. I would grow it in my yard as a foliage plant, but it requires more sun that I have to offer, so I have to rely on Rhys and Jack and crew!

Note

You may use any green leaf in this recipe. If you are using a thin-leafed green like spinach, blanch it in boiling water, drain, and squeeze out the excess water. Then proceed to assemble the raviolis.

— *Richard Ruben,* The Farmer's Market Cookbook

Seedlings in the greenhouse.

Rhubarb

RHEUM RHABARBARUM

Rhubarb is a curious phenomenon, for it is one of the few plants of which we consume just the thick stalks, or petioles. The assertive tartness of rhubarb is caused by the presence of large quantities of oxalic acid, which generally makes the leaves unpalatable and is toxic in high doses. The succulent, juicy stems are delicious, especially when sweetened with plenty of sugar, strawberries, or other fruits in pies, sauces, and jams.

In the Western hemisphere, rhubarb typically comes into season during April and May, making it one of the first fresh food plants to mature. It was much welcomed in times before produce was available year-round. Rhubarb is a perennial that grows from short, stubby rhizomes into rather large plants with huge leaves that resemble giant, red-stemmed Swiss chard. It is unusual in that it does not breed true from seed but rather must be propagated from cuttings of its rootstock.

HISTORY

Rhubarb is native to Asia, where the dried root has been used in traditional Chinese medicine for thousands of years. So revered was it for its healing qualities that rhubarb cost ten times as much as cinnamon in France during the mid-1500s. Although rhubarb was consumed as a food in the ancient Middle East, it did not exactly take the European or American culinary scene by storm. It remains a specialty food whose popularity waxes and wanes, depending on the public's attitude toward the vast amount of sweetener necessary to make it palatable.

Well-known for its laxative qualities since ancient times, rhubarb was once regarded as a medicinal plant rather than as food. It was not cultivated widely for the kitchen until the 1800s in Europe; apparently the unappetizing leaves rather than the stalks were generally sampled, which may have contributed to its delay in finding culinary enthusiasts.

NUTRITION

Rhubarb contains vitamins A, K, folate, calcium, magnesium, potassium, phosphorus, dietary fiber, and a fairly significant amount of lutein, a carotenoid that benefits eye health. A 1-cup serving contains just 25 calories.

SELECTION

Fresh rhubarb stalks should be firm, crisp, and brightly colored, with no signs of wilting and shriveling. Slender stalks are more tender than thicker stalks.

STORAGE

Wrap unwashed rhubarb stalks in a plastic bag and refrigerate in the vegetable crisper, where it will keep for up to 10 days.

Cooking Tip

The acidity of rhubarb reacts with aluminum, iron, and copper cookware, leading to discolored pans and possible leaching of the metals into the food. Use only anodized aluminum, stainless steel, or glass pans for cooking and baking rhubarb concoctions.

TRIMMING & CLEANING

Thoroughly wash the stalks under running water to remove all traces of dirt, and trim the very ends off and discard.

MICROWAVING

Rhubarb can be cooked by microwaving it on High power in a microwave-safe dish for about 12 to 14 minutes, or until the rhubarb is tender.

BLANCHING & FREEZING

Save a taste of spring by freezing rhubarb for later enjoyment. Simply cut the stalks into ¾-inch pieces, arrange them in a single layer on a baking pan, and place in the freezer. Once they are frozen, place them in zipper-lock freezer or vacuum food sealer-type bags, or freezer containers. Squeeze out excess air and leave ½ inch of headspace (unless you are using the vacuum sealing method).

   For more tender frozen rhubarb, you can blanch the stalks by boiling them for 1 minute and quickly plunging them in ice water. Then pack them for the freezer, leaving 1½ inches of headroom. Rhubarb may also be packed in a sugar syrup (see Strawberries on page 58). Frozen rhubarb should be used within 6 months.

EQUIVALENTS, MEASURES & SERVINGS

- 1 pound = 3 cups chopped = 2 cups cooked

COMPLEMENTARY HERBS, SEASONINGS & FOODS

Apples, berries, brandy, brown sugar, butter, cinnamon, cream, fruit, ginger, oranges, pepper, plums, sour cream, strawberries, sugar.

SERVING SUGGESTIONS

- Stewed rhubarb or rhubarb sauce or chutney makes a great counterpoint to hearty meats like duck, roast beef, corned beef, or Rock Cornish game hen.
- A light, tangy, and sweet rhubarb sauce makes a delectable topping for ice cream, pudding, custard, or pound cake.
- Top your breakfast cereal with sweetened rhubarb.
- Try English trifle with a twist, substituting the traditional strawberries with rhubarb prepared with cherries or raspberries.
- An early spring treat is a snack of washed, raw rhubarb stems and a bowl of sugar for dipping. As simple as can be, on a warm spring day.
- Add a sophisticated touch to stewed rhubarb or rhubarb sauces with the addition of fruit-flavored liqueurs (Grand Marnier, kirsch, Midori, or apple schnapps), brandy, port wine, or rosewater.
- Combine rhubarb with kumquats or oranges for a tasty chutney.
- Add very thin slices of rhubarb to spring soups or salads, or anywhere a bit of tartness is welcome.

RHUBARB CRISP   SERVES 6 TO 8

   6 to 8 cups rhubarb, thinly sliced and chopped (leave peel on)
   1½ cups granulated sugar
   2 tablespoons flour

1 tablespoon cinnamon
Pinch of salt

CRISP

1½ cups oatmeal
1 cup unbleached flour
½ cup whole wheat flour
1 cup brown sugar
1 cup chopped walnuts
3 tablespoons ground golden flaxseeds or wheat germ (optional)
½ teaspoon baking soda
½ teaspoon baking powder
½ cup melted butter

1. Preheat oven to 350°F.

2. Butter a 9 × 13-inch pan. In a large bowl, mix together the non-crisp ingredients (rhubarb, sugar, flour, cinnamon, and salt) and place the rhubarb mixture in the pan.

3. Combine the crisp ingredients in a small bowl, then add the butter. Spread the crisp mixture over the rhubarb. Bake for 35 to 40 minutes, until bubbling.

— *Robin Taylor, Featherstone Farm CSA member*

. . . .

BALSAMIC RHUBARB COMPOTE SERVES 4

3 tablespoons balsamic vinegar
⅔ cup sugar
¾ teaspoon fresh ginger, peeled and grated
2 fresh rhubarb stalks, leaves discarded, ends trimmed, and stalks cut crosswise into ¼-inch-thick slices, or 2 cups frozen sliced rhubarb, thawed, reserving liquid

1. In a saucepan, simmer the vinegar with the sugar and ginger, stirring until the sugar is dissolved.

2. Then stir in the rhubarb (with reserved liquid if using frozen). If you are using fresh rhubarb, simmer it until it is crisp-tender, about 1 minute, and transfer with a slotted spoon to a bowl, keeping the liquid behind in the pan. If you are using frozen rhubarb, transfer the rhubarb with a slotted spoon to a bowl as soon as the mixture returns to a simmer, keepng the liquid behind in the pan.

3. Simmer the liquid until it thickens slightly, about 5 minutes, and then remove the pan from heat. Stir in the rhubarb. Serve the compote warm or at room temperature.

— *Fruits and Veggies—More Matters; Centers for Disease Control & Prevention*

. . . .

Cooking Tip

If you prefer to not use large quantities of sugar in making rhubarb recipes, try preparing it with sweet fruits (strawberries, raspberries, or apples), apple juice concentrate, or small amounts of honey or stevia.

For More Information

The Rhubarb Compendium
www.rhubarbinfo.com

Rhubarb: Fruit or Vegetable?

Botanically and gastronomically, rhubarb is properly considered a vegetable, although it is often used like a fruit in recipes.

However, in 1947, the U.S. Customs court in Buffalo, New York, declared it a fruit, which allowed it to pass with a smaller import duty.

RHUBARB CHUTNEY

MAKES 3 PINTS

8 cups sliced rhubarb
2 cups white vinegar
2 cups white sugar
2 cups brown sugar, packed
2 cups golden raisins
2 cups finely chopped onions
½ teaspoon salt
½ teaspoon ground ginger
1 tablespoon mustard seed
1 cinnamon stick, broken up
1 teaspoon whole cloves

1. Mix the first 8 ingredients in a large, heavy-bottomed pot.

2. Tie the mustard seed, cinnamon stick, and cloves in a double layer of cheesecloth. Add to the pot.

3. Heat over medium heat, stirring often as the mixture comes to a boil and the sugar dissolves. Simmer, uncovered, for about 40 minutes until the chutney thickens, stirring occasionally. Discard the spice bag. Pour into hot sterilized jars to within ¼ inch of the top. Seal.

— *Shelly Black, www.epicurean.com*

....

RHUBARB PIE

MAKES 1 PIE

4 cups diced rhubarb stalks
¼ cup flour
1¼ cups sugar
1 tablespoon butter
4 tablespoons dry Jell-O tapioca mix
1 tablespoon lemon juice
Cinnamon
1 (9-inch) pie pan, lined with pie shell pastry (plus extra for top crust or lattice if desired) or graham cracker crust

1. Mix all of the ingredients together and let stand 15 minutes.

2. Preheat the oven to 450°F.

3. Pour the filling into the pie pan, and cover with a top crust or lattice, if desired. Sprinkle with cinnamon.

4. Bake 10 minutes at 450°F, then decrease the heat to 350°F and continue to bake for 40 to 45 minutes, or until the filling is bubbly.

— *Rich Hoyle*

Summer

WE OFTEN THINK OF THE RIPENING OF THE FIRST TOMATOES AND SWEET CORN IN THE GARDEN AS THE START OF THE SUMMER PRODUCE SEASON IN MINNESOTA. CERTAINLY, FEW OTHER CROPS ARE GREETED WITH SUCH ANTICIPATION. AND FROM THE FARMER'S VIEW, SPEEDING THE ARRIVAL OF THIS MOMENT EACH YEAR IS THE HIGHEST PRIORITY, WARRANTING TECHNIQUES THAT WOULD HAVE BEEN UNTHINKABLE A GENERATION AGO.

YET A SINGLE-MINDED FOCUS ON THE FRUITS OF HIGH SUMMER— TOMATOES AND MELONS IN PARTICULAR—OVERLOOKS SOME OF THE WONDERFUL CROPS OF EARLY SUMMER. BEGINNING IN EARLY JULY, A BROAD NEW ARRAY OF PRODUCE BECOMES AVAILABLE IN THE GARDEN.

Summer Crops Featured

Beans (String)
Cantaloupes
Cilantro
Corn
Cucumbers
Dill
Eggplant
Honeydew Melon
Lemongrass
Mizuna
Oregano
Peppers (Sweet)
Peppers (Hot)
Potatoes
Rosemary
Savory
Squash (Summer)
Tarragon
Thyme
Tomatoes
Watermelon
Zucchini

Summer Crops Available

Beans (String)
   *Green Snap, Haricots Verts,
   Royal Burgundy, Yellow Wax*
Cantaloupes
Cilantro
Corn (July 20 to September 1)
   Bi-color, White Supersweet
Cucumbers
   Burpless Slicing
Dill
Eggplant (mid-summer)
   Asian, Globe
Honeydew Melon
Lemongrass
Mizuna
Onions (Bunched bulbs with green
   tops)

Plants as unrelated as potatoes, green beans, and zucchini share one important attribute at this time of year: they move beyond the strictly foliar growth of spring and begin flowering (and subsequently fruiting) in the long days and heat of July.

At Featherstone Farm, the first day of summer always feels like the day we dig our first new potatoes—no matter how hot it's been in June! When purple and white flowers appear in the potato patch at the end of June, we know that the big day is just around the corner. But will it arrive in time for potato salad on the 4th of July? Most often it does, ushering in a few weeks of hand digging, to preserve the delicate skins and avoid bruising. By the time the tomatoes are ready in August, the spuds will be large and the skins tough enough to harvest with a mechanical digger.

To generate early harvests of summer squash, cucumbers, and basil, even green beans and sweet corn, we start early crops as transplants in the greenhouse in late April. These crops typically prefer the warm, dry conditions of the ridge fields that surround our home farm in the valley. As the threat of frost recedes in May, we transplant these crops into black plastic mulch in the field, and cover the rows with spun fabric supported by wire hoops. The enhanced growing environment under these "tunnels" contributes unbelievably to the growth and development of these crops. We plant the first generations of tomatoes, pepper, eggplants, and even melons in this way.

In July an explosion of new crops ripen for the CSA boxes. To complement the broccoli, cabbage, and kohlrabi of late June, we quickly add new potatoes, zucchini, and string beans. Herbs such as cilantro, basil, and parsley are developing enough to harvest. Asian eggplants ripen remarkably early if it is warm; cucumbers and peppers likewise will mature when it is hot enough.

Tomatoes at Featherstone come on in two waves. First is the greenhouse-grown hybrid fruit in July, followed by field-grown cherry and heirloom varieties. All are started as transplants in the greenhouse, often as early as the first day of March, but there the similarity ends.

Hybrid varieties developed for intensive greenhouse production are the first to be transplanted into the ground. They go into beds covered with plastic mulch and capped by row cover tunnels dug in the greenhouse floor in early April. These houses are minimally heated, but because they trap remarkable warmth as the sunlight hours lengthen during this time of the year, the rising soil temperature usually promotes rapid growth. Our greenhouse tomato plants are tied up on trellises and flower and fruit right in the houses. (Unlike commercial hothouse fruit, however, they are grown in composted organic soil, rather than hydroponically in water). The plastic greenhouse cover keeps them warm and dry enough that the fruit can be harvested at full ripeness for peak flavor, usually starting in the middle of July.

Heirloom and cherry tomatoes are generally transplanted out into the field in waves, starting in mid-May. The first generation only is covered with row tunnels, but all are supported, with the heirlooms in wire cages and the larger cherry plants tied with baling twine between steel posts. They begin to ripen for CSA boxes in early August.

By August many of us are becoming weary of heat on the farm. And yet we know that it is necessary to bring on that jewel of the summer produce crown, the melons. Cantaloupes and watermelons are both heat-loving crops. They are grown on the sandiest, hottest, driest soils on our Rushford farm, planted after all danger of frost in May. They develop thick mats of flower-drenched vines by the end of July, but they need more heat (particularly at night) to produce and ripen good fruit.

When we break a sweat by eight in the morning in August, we know we can look forward to snacking on chilled watermelon all day (as well as sweet corn and the best of the year's tomatoes for supper).

When the first chilly wind of early September arrives, we greet it with a huge sigh of relief, but some reluctance, too, as we say goodbye to the glory days of summer produce.

FARMER'S TABLE MENU — SUMMER
— UP TO SEPTEMBER 15 —

BY JACK HEDIN

APPETIZER
Baba Ghanoush

ENTRÉE
Stir-Fry

ON THE SIDE
Brown Rice
Steamed Sweet Corn

DESSERT
Fresh Raspberries

At this time of the year I am busier than ever. Planning bigger meals is difficult, which is ironic since this is also our season of greatest bounty. I often create stir-fries with whatever vegetables happen to be around, with little advance preparation or marinating; the intense flavors speak for themselves this time of year.

The baba ghanoush is, however, well worth the time to prepare in advance and leave in the refrigerator for snacking and appetizers all week. Roast the eggplants (no peeling or prep of any kind!) whole on the grill or directly over a gas flame on your stovetop. Turn them repeatedly until the skins are charred and the meats are completely wilted (8 to 15 minutes, depending on the size of the eggplants). At this point, your kitchen will smell remarkably like a village in Syria.

Copra, Mars Red, Walla Walla
Oregano
Peppers (Sweet)
　Green and Red Bell, Lipstick,
　Red & Gold (ripened), Sweet
　Chocolate
Peppers (Hot)
　Jalapeños, Long Red Cayenne,
　Serrano
Potatoes (all new in July)
　All Blue, Bintje, Desiree Pink,
　Langlade White, Red Norland,
　Romance, Russian Fingerling,
　Yukon Gold
Rosemary
Savory
Squash (Summer)
　Patty Pan, Yellow
　Straightneck, Zucchini
Strawberries (June)
　Winona
Swiss Chard
　Bright Lights, Ruby Red
Tarragon
Thyme
Tomatoes
　Cherry Tomatoes (August)
　　Red Grape, Sungold
　Hybrid Red Slicer (July)
　Heirlooms & Romas (August)
　　Amish Paste, Brandywine,
　　Cherokee Purple, German
　　Stripe, Green Zebra, Red
　　Zebra, Aunt Ruby's Green,
　　San Marzano, Yellow Roma
Watermelon
　Mickey Lee, Sugar Baby,
　Yellow Doll
Zucchini
　Ambassador, Elite

Attempt to scrape away most of the blackened skins without burning your fingers, then purée what is left with a bit of sesame tahini, garlic, lemon juice, and salt—but not too much—the standout here is the rich, roasted eggplant itself. I serve it with chopped tomatoes and whatever dipping veggies might be at hand.

The stir-fry is also a creation of spontaneity, using the vegetables that are at their succulent best, including bok choy, napa cabbage, carrots, leeks, peppers, broccoli, and kale, with lots of garlic. I also like to throw in some shrimp or chicken.

Squash seedlings enjoying the longer days in the valley.

Bean (String)

PHASEOLUS VULGARIS

Often called green beans or snap beans in America, string beans are one of the most common garden vegetables in the United States. String beans come in many forms, some 130 in all, ranging from the petite, delicately-flavored French variety, haricot verts, to the broader, meaty Italian specimens. String beans are divided into two categories: bush beans, which have a long, slender, rounded pod, and pole beans, which are usually large and quite flat.

Decades ago, string beans were named for the tough fibers that ran down from one tip to the other. While these "strings" have been bred out of most of the varieties, the moniker has stuck. The pods of these beans are green, yellow (referred to as wax beans), purple, red, or streaked.

String beans are actually immature seeds and pods; if left on the bush, the seeds swell and the pods become too fibrous to eat. However, they do not mature to become "shell" beans; string beans are bred specifically for their youthful succulence and tenderness.

Featherstone grows several types of string beans: Haricot verts (a skinny French bean); Jade (a traditional green bean); Royal Burgundy (a dark purple bean); and Indy Gold (a yellow wax bean that is very tender and much sweeter than its green counterpart).

HISTORY

Although soybeans and fava beans most likely originated in Asia and Europe, respectively, the haricot bean (which includes string beans) had long been a domesticated staple in American Indian diets by the time Columbus arrived. Precisely when humans began consuming the immature, green pods is impossible to know, but the modern, truly stringless varieties were bred only within the past 100 years.

NUTRITION

Like most vegetables, green beans are low in calories (43 per cup) but pack lots of fiber and nutrients. A cup's worth provides about 25 percent of your daily supply of vitamin K and 20 percent of vitamin C, as well as manganese, vitamin A, potassium, and folate.

SELECTION

Look for beans that are firm, crisp, velvety to touch, and not too swollen, which may indicate the beans inside are getting too mature to be at their tastiest. Supermarket green beans are often dehydrated; watch out for pods that are limp toward their ends, are starting to shrivel, or are easily bendable. Such beans often have little gustatory or nutritive value. Also beware of beans that are overly large, or worse yet, whose pods have a rough, spongy texture.

STORAGE

Refrigerate unwashed beans in a paper or perforated plastic bag in a

Green beans cooked in hard water can become very tough because the calcium in the water reacts with the pectic substances in the beans.

warmer section of the refrigerator. Use within 2 or 3 days. If they start to wilt, soaking in ice water may rehydrate them.

TRIMMING & CLEANING

Wash the beans in cool water. "Top and tail" them (snap off the top stem ends and bottom curved tips). With the modern varieties, no destringing is necessary.

STEAMING & BOILING

Boil green beans in several quarts of salted water until just tender and they have lost their raw taste, about 6 to 8 minutes. Steam green beans over rapidly boiling water for about 10 to 12 minutes, or until tender.

STIR-FRYING & SAUTÉING

Green beans are delicious stir-fried or sautéed for about 7 to 10 minutes on medium-high heat in a wok or large frying pan. Be sure to add some liquid, such as melted butter, olive oil, or even water to the pan, or they will stick. In the last couple minutes of cooking, toss with soy sauce or sesame oil.

BAKING & ROASTING

Green beans can be baked in a 350°F oven for 40 to 45 minutes, or until tender. For beans with an even richer flavor, drizzle them with a nut oil or dressing of your choice and roast for 20 to 25 minutes in a 425°F oven. When preparing green beans in the oven, make sure they are topped with or immersed in other ingredients, so they do not dry out.

MICROWAVING

Cut or snap beans into 1-inch pieces, then place in microwave-safe dish; add ¼ cup water; cover and cook on High power.

- 1 cup = 3 minutes
- 1 pounds = 7 to 12 minutes

BLANCHING & FREEZING

Blanch green beans in salted boiling water for 3 to 4 minutes, or until they are crisp-tender. Drain, then plunge them into an ice-water bath to stop their cooking. Then package them in zipper-lock freezer or vacuum food sealer-type bags, or freezer containers. Squeeze out excess air and leave ½ inch of headspace (unless you are using the vacuum sealing method). Green beans will keep about 9 to 14 months in the freezer. Rubbery green beans, when thawed, often mean they were past their prime to begin with, or they were cooked too long.

EQUIVALENTS, MEASURES & SERVINGS

- 1 pound = 3½ cups whole = 4 to 5 cups cut into 1-inch pieces = 3 to 4 servings

COMPLEMENTARY HERBS, SEASONINGS & FOODS

Almonds, bacon, basil, béchamel sauce, butter, cream, curry powder, dill, garlic, lemon, majoram, mint, mushrooms, mustard, nutmeg, nuts, olive oil, onions, orange, oregano, Parmesan cheese, parsley, pine nuts, rosemary, soy sauce, tarragon, tomatoes, vinegar, walnuts, Worcestershire sauce.

SERVING SUGGESTIONS

- Toss freshly boiled or steamed green beans with soy sauce, light vegetable oil, or Italian dressing.

- Munch raw beans with various dips. Kids like these as a finger food!

- Sprinkle chopped fresh herbs over steamed or boiled green beans; dill or mint are pleasant surprises with green beans.

- Stir-fry or sauté green beans with a mixture of peanut or sesame oil, soy sauce, scallions, garlic, ginger, chili paste, sugar, salt, and pepper for Szechuan-style beans.

- Drop a handful into stir-fries at the last minute to add flavor and crunch. (This works best with young, tender beans.)

- Treat your string beans as you would southern-style greens—cook them slowly with lots of water, a ham hock or piece of pork fatback, and finish off with a dose of vinegar and a dash of hot pepper sauce.

- Add interest to cooked green beans by tossing them with a light vinaigrette and slivered almonds or chopped hazelnuts.

- Create a colorful vegetable julienne with green and yellow string beans, carrot strips, golden beets, and red or orange bell pepper strips steamed or boiled briefly.

- Remember the old green-bean casserole standby? You know, green beans with a can of cream of mushroom soup poured over it, and crisp fried onions sprinkled on top? Don't be ashamed to admit you like it!

AVIYAL (MIXED VEGETABLES WITH COCONUT AND TAMARIND)

SERVES 6 TO 8

This is a classic Kerala Hindu dish. Tamarind is an extremely sour, tangy pulp extracted from the seed pods of the tamarind tree. Tamarind is available at Indian and Asian food stores. Curry leaves are not related to commercial curry powder, and when fried, release a flavor reminiscent of grapefruit and green peppers.

1-inch ball tamarind pulp
Warm water
1 cup finely grated fresh coconut or finely shredded, dried, unsweetened coconut
¼ cup peeled, chopped yellow onion
1¼ teaspoons ground cumin
½ teaspoon turmeric
¼ teaspoon cayenne
1 medium potato, peeled and cut into 2-inch-by-¼-inch sticks
2 small carrots, peeled, trimmed, and cut into 2-inch-by-¼-inch sticks
⅓ medium eggplant, trimmed and cut into 2-inch-by-¼-inch sticks
1 small zucchini, trimmed and cut into 2-inch-by-¼-inch sticks
¼ pound green beans, trimmed and cut crosswise into thirds
1 fresh hot green chile pepper (serrano or Thai), split lengthwise just

> "Ripe vegetables were magic to me. Unharvested, the garden bristled with possibility. I would quicken at the sight of a ripe tomato, sounding its redness from deep amidst the undifferentiated green. To lift a bean plant's hood of heart-shaped leaves and discover a clutch of long slender pods hiding underneath could make me catch my breath."
>
> — *Michael Pollan*

up to the stem
1¼ teaspoons salt
1 medium cucumber, peeled and cut into 2-inch-by-¼-inch sticks
½ cup shelled fresh or frozen peas
20 curry leaves
1 tablespoon coconut oil

1. Put the tamarind in a small bowl, add ½ cup warm water, and use your fingers to help dissolve some of it. Set aside for 5 minutes, then use your fingers to dissolve more of the softened tamarind. Strain through a fine sieve into a small bowl, pressing on any remaining tamarind. Set the tamarind juice aside, discarding the solids.

2. Grind the coconut, onion, cumin, ¼ teaspoon of the turmeric, ⅛ teaspoon of the cayenne, and about ½ cup water into a moist paste in an electric blender, then set aside.

3. Put the potato, carrots, eggplant, zucchini, green beans, chile, salt, the remaining ¼ teaspoon turmeric, remaining ⅛ teaspoon cayenne, and 1¼ cups water in a medium-sized pot. Bring to a boil over medium-high heat, and cook until the vegetables begin to soften, about 5 minutes. Add the cucumbers, peas, and reserved tamarind juice, and cook for 1 minute more.

4. Add the reserved coconut paste to the vegetables, decrease the heat to medium-low, and simmer until the sauce is thick, about 10 minutes. (Thin the sauce with water if it becomes too thick to simmer.) Add the curry leaves and coconut oil, and simmer for 1 minute longer.

— Saveur, *September–October 2000*

CREAMY GREEN BEAN AND MUSHROOM SOUP   SERVES 8

2½ cups finely chopped onion
⅓ cup butter
1 pound mushrooms, diced
⅓ cup flour
1 teaspoon paprika
6 cups vegetable stock
1 pound fresh green beans, cut into 1-inch pieces
1¼ cups heavy cream
Pinch of nutmeg
Salt and black pepper
Pinch of cayenne pepper

FRIED SHALLOTS

⅓ cup flour
½ teaspoon paprika
¼ teaspoon salt
Pinch of black pepper

1 cup shallots, thinly sliced and separated
1 cup canola oil

1. Sauté the onion and butter for 10 minutes over medium-low heat in a large stockpot. Add the mushrooms, flour, and paprika, and stir until the butter is absorbed.

2. Add the vegetable stock and green beans, and bring to a simmer, stirring occasionally. Simmer 10 minutes, or until the beans are tender.

3. Add the heavy cream, nutmeg, salt, and black and cayenne pepper. Heat through, and adjust the seasonings to taste.

4. Prepare the fried shallots: Toss the flour, paprika, salt, and black pepper with the shallots to coat. Remove the shallots from the mixture, shaking off excess flour. Fry in hot oil in a skillet until crisp and golden brown. Then drain the shallots on a paper towel.

5. Top the soup with the fried shallots, and serve.

— *Blue Heron Coffeehouse,* The Bluff Country Co-op Cookbook

ROASTED GREEN BEANS   SERVES 4

This recipe is good with strips of red bell pepper, although omit the water for the peppers because they are already so juicy. Kids love this dish.

1 pound fresh green beans, trimmed
1 teaspoon vegetable oil
1 teaspoon water
Salt and pepper

1. Preheat the oven to 500°F. Line a rimmed baking sheet with aluminum foil.

2. Stir the beans, oil, and water together in a bowl until the beans are coated—a task a child would like. (You can shake them all in a plastic bag too.)

3. Spread the beans out on the baking sheet and sprinkle them with salt and pepper. Bake for 8 minutes, or until cooked through. These are good hot or at room temperature.

— *Ann Hodgman,* One Bite Won't Kill You

LEMON-WALNUT GREEN BEANS   SERVES 8

8 cups small green beans
Cooking spray
2 cups sliced green onions
⅓ cup chopped walnuts
1½ tablespoons chopped fresh or ¾ tablespoon crushed

Growing Vegetables

by Jack Hedin,
Featherstone Farm Owner

June 15 , 2005

Growing up in suburbia (Louisville, Kentucky) and a small town (Red Wing, Minnesota), I had little experience with growing much of anything outside of a small flower garden.

I have always enjoyed good food, however, and since my first days in a college apartment, I've been an avid cook. I took a job in a natural food grocery with the first organic produce display in the state (Connecticut in 1987) and apprenticed on a small community-supported agriculture (CSA) farm in the Berkshires the following year.

I fell in love with growing vegetables at once. Jenni McHugh and I spent several years together working on farms from Pennsylvania to California before we married in the summer of 1994. We discovered the appeal of a cooperatively managed farm at Full Belly Farm near Sacramento, California, and we decided to find or create such an arrange-

dried rosemary
5 tablespoons fresh lemon juice
1½ tablespoons grated lemon rind

1. Arrange the green beans in a steamer basket over boiling water. Cover and steam 8 to 12 minutes or until crisp-tender. Plunge the beans into cold water to stop the cooking process; drain.

2. Spray a sauté pan with cooking spray. Over medium-high heat, add the green onions and sauté until tender. Add the green beans, walnuts, rosemary, and lemon juice; cook, stirring constantly, until thoroughly heated.

3. Sprinkle with lemon rind.

— *Fruits and Veggies—More Matters; Centers for Disease Control & Prevention*

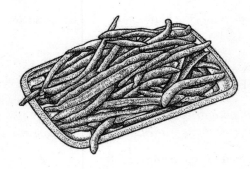

BASIC LO MEIN   SERVES 4

Lo mein doesn't take much effort, uses up loose odds and ends of vegetables in the refrigerator, and everyone loves it. It lends itself to many variations and can be made as a vegetarian dish with tofu.

MEAT OR TOFU AND MARINADE

1 pound boneless, skinless chicken, beef, or pork, sliced into
      matchsticks, or 1 pound extra-firm tofu, pressed and cubed
1 piece fresh ginger (1 inch long), peeled and minced
2 cloves garlic, minced
2 tablespoons soy sauce
1 tablespoon oyster sauce
1 tablespoon Chinese rice wine or dry sherry
1 teaspoon dark sesame oil
1 tablespoon cornstarch

NOODLES AND VEGETABLES

1 pound Chinese egg noodles or thin spaghetti
3 tablespoons peanut or canola oil
1 onion, halved and cut into slivers, or 1 leek, white and tender

green parts only, thinly sliced

2 cups chopped or julienned firm vegetables (asparagus, broccoli, baby corn, snap beans, snap peas, snow peas, or sugar snap peas, alone or in combination), corn kernels, or shelled peas

1 carrot, cut into matchsticks

2 tablespoons soy sauce, or to taste

4 cups slivered greens, such as bok choy, broccoli raab, cabbage, chard, escarole, or kale, alone or in any combination

⅓ cup oyster sauce, or to taste

1 cup mung bean sprouts

1. To marinate the meat or tofu, combine it in a bowl with the ginger, garlic, soy sauce, oyster sauce, wine, and sesame oil. Toss to mix well. Add the cornstarch and toss to mix. Set aside while you prepare the remaining ingredients.

2. Cook the noodles in plenty of boiling salted water until al dente. Drain well.

3. Heat a large wok over high heat. Add 2 tablespoons of the oil and heat. Add the meat or tofu and marinade, and stir-fry until the meat is cooked through (or the tofu is browned), 4 to 8 minutes. Use a heat- proof rubber spatula to scrape out the mixture from the wok and into a bowl, and keep warm.

4. Reheat the wok over high heat. Add the remaining 1 tablespoon of the oil and the onion, and stir-fry until tender, about 4 minutes. Push the onion to the sides of the wok and add the firm vegetables. Stir-fry until slightly tender, about 2 minutes. Add the carrot and 1 tablespoon of the soy sauce. Continue to stir-fry until the carrot is almost tender, about 3 minutes. Add the slivered greens and the remaining 1 tablespoon of soy sauce and stir-fry until all of the vegetables are tender, 3 to 6 minutes.

5. Add the noodles, meat or tofu and marinade, oyster sauce, and bean sprouts to the wok. Continue to toss and stir-fry until the ingredients are thoroughly mixed and heated through, 3 to 4 minutes. Taste and add more soy sauce and oyster sauce, if desired. Serve hot.

— *Andrea Chesman,* The Garden-Fresh Vegetable Cookbook

. . . .

SALAD NIÇOISE

SERVES 4

Do not toss this salad; it should look "arranged." This Riviera favorite goes best with vinaigrette dressing. You don't have to cook much—just boil the eggs and potatoes and steam the green beans (or pick them up at a salad bar for a no-cook meal). Then open a can and a couple of jars, chop, stir, assemble, and it's done. It's a fun finger-food meal for kids too!

Serve with good sliced French bread, warmed or toasted, and maybe even a chilled dry rosé wine.

ment closer to my family roots in southeast Minnesota. Jenni and I were founding members of the Zephyr community near Rushford, Minnesota, from its early meetings in 1992, and we moved to the farm in April of 1995. We have three sons, Emmet, Oscar, and Jasper.

I grow vegetables now for the same reasons I fell in love with farming as a young adult; it is simply the most life-affirming and fundamentally creative work I have ever done. Growing so many different crops without the aid of chemicals requires a huge range of skills, knowledge, and resources. Managing them all in concert is a great challenge, and when it all comes together at harvest time, the results are wonderful.

Certainly frustrations and disappointments lurk along the way, but these are learning opportunities for the next season. I love working with the earth; engaging my mind, body, and soul day-to-day in the field; and feeding people good food. It is my joy and privilege to be an organic farmer.

½ pound green string beans
4 small red or white potatoes
Salad Niçoise Vinaigrette (recipe below)
1 head Boston or red leaf lettuce
1 (6-ounce) can albacore or other high-quality tuna, drained
3 to 4 tomatoes, quartered, or 1 cup cherry tomatoes, halved
2 to 3 hard-boiled eggs, peeled and halved
1 green or yellow bell pepper, seeded and cut into thin rings
16 to 20 herbed black olives
2 tablespoons capers
8 anchovy filets (optional)

SALAD NIÇOISE VINAIGRETTE

1 tablespoon white-wine vinegar
1 tablespoon lemon juice
½ teaspoon Dijon mustard
1 clove garlic, minced
1 pinch of fresh or dried tarragon or basil
Salt and freshly ground black pepper
½ cup extra-virgin olive oil

1. Steam the string beans until just crisp-tender. Cool, then trim.

2. Bring a medium saucepan of lightly salted water to a boil. Add the potatoes and cook 6 minutes, or until fork-tender.

3. Meanwhile, prepare the vinaigrette. In a small bowl, stir together the white-wine vinegar, lemon juice, Dijon mustard, garlic, tarragon or basil, and salt and pepper to taste. Slowly add the olive oil, whisking until the mixture is well-blended.

4. Peel the cooked potatoes, if desired, and cut into ¼-inch slices while still very warm. Douse with 2 tablespoons of the vinaigrette and allow to cool.

5. Thoroughly wash and spin-dry the lettuce. Place in a large bowl, add 3 tablespoons of the vinaigrette, and toss lightly.

6. Place the lettuce on a platter. Arrange the string beans, potatoes, tuna, tomatoes, eggs, and bell pepper on top of the greens in a decorative fashion. Sprinkle olives, capers, and anchovies over the salad, drizzle with the remaining vinaigrette, and serve.

— *www.fooddownunder.com*

. . . .

PICKLED GREEN BEANS   MAKES 4 PINTS

2 pounds fresh green beans, rinsed and trimmed
4 cloves garlic, peeled
8 sprigs fresh dill weed
4 teaspoons salt
2½ cups white vinegar

"It's so beautifully arranged on the plate you know someone's fingers have been all over it."

— *Julia Child,
French chef and TV cooking personality*

2½ cups water

1. Cut the green beans to fit inside 1-pint canning jars.

2. Place the green beans in a steamer over 1 inch of boiling water, and cover. Cook until tender but still firm, about 3 minutes. Plunge the beans into ice water. Drain well.

3. Pack the beans into 4 hot, sterilized 1-pint jars. Place 1 garlic clove and 2 sprigs of dill weed inside each jar, against the glass. Add 1 teaspoon of salt to each jar.

4. In a large saucepan over high heat, bring the vinegar and water to a boil. Pour over the beans.

5. Fit the jars with lids and rings and process for 10 minutes in a boiling water bath.

— *Kimber, www.allrecipes.com*

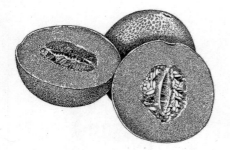

Cantaloupe

CUCUMIS MELO

Like sweet corn and tomatoes, melons herald the arrival of summer plenty, plump balls of juicy refreshment best savored on sweltering evenings or warm early mornings. Melons belong to the Cucurbitaceae family, a large group of vine-type plants that also include squashes, luffas, and cucumbers.

Although the terms "cantaloupe" and "muskmelon" are sometimes used interchangeably in the United States, they are different fruits in Europe. Cucumis melo var. reticulatus, commonly called canteloupe in the U.S., is called muskmelon in Europe. The American varieties have netted rinds and a round or oval shape, but they often have regional differences; some of the eastern types are larger and have skins that are divided into deep ridges by long sutures.

In Europe, the true cantaloupe (Cucumis melo var. cantaloupensis) looks completely different, with deep grooves, a hard, warty rind, and orange or greenish flesh. They are little known outside their home countries.

HISTORY

Although its exact origins are unclear, melons probably first grew in the Middle East, near Persia. Early Egyptians and Sumerians displayed melons in their art, around 2200 B.C.E., and the Greeks had melons by the third century B.C.E. At the peak of their power, the Romans imported melons from Asia to Europe, but after the Empire fell, melons disappeared from European tables until possibly the fourteenth century.

Throughout recorded humanity, melons seem to have aroused passionate feelings, including a French obsession with the fruit at the end of the fifteenth century. In the sixteenth century, melon seeds were brought from Armenia to the Papal domain of Cantalupo, near Tivoli, hence the cantaloupe. Melons did not arrive in the United States until the late 1800s.

NUTRITION

Cantaloupe is rich in vitamin A (a 1-cup serving contains an adult's complete daily allowance) and vitamin C, and provides some potassium, folate, vitamin B6, and dietary fiber. A single cup contains 56 calories.

SELECTION

Once picked, melons do not continue to ripen, even in the sun. For full flavor, choose melons that are perfectly ripe. One dead giveaway is that unmistakable, mouthwatering aroma wafting from the blossom end. Also, fully ripe melons easily separate from the vine with very light pressure, so a melon showing signs of damage in that area was plucked unripe. Melons should be firm and heavy, with no soft or depressed areas. Very ripe melons are yellowish around the "netting" on their skins; a very jaundiced melon with a strong smell is probably overripe.

STORAGE

You can store melons at room temperature, but they are susceptible to spoiling if kept too long. Store them in the refrigerator if you can; they keep a bit longer this way and are extremely appetizing chilled on a hot summer day.

TRIMMING & CLEANING

Bacteria sometimes grows on the outside of melons (the 2001 U.S. salmonella outbreak was traced to cantaloupe), so a thorough washing is a good idea before slicing into the fruit. Once the luscious orange flesh has yielded to the blade, scoop out the seeds and get ready for a taste treat.

STEAMING & BOILING

Cantaloupe is usually eaten fresh in the United States, but it can be cooked for jam, melon chutney, bread, or even pie. Low heat is best for cantaloupe, to preserve its delicate flavor and aroma.

BLANCHING & FREEZING

Cantaloupe and other types of melon can be frozen as-is, or prepared in a light sugar syrup to better preserve their flavor and color. Peel and cut melons into ½- or ¾-inch cubes or balls. To make the syrup, combine 9 cups of water or fruit juice with 2¼ cups of sugar. Combine the sugar and water in a saucepan, and bring to a boil until the sugar dissolves. Chill, then pour ½ cup of syrup into the freezer container, add the melon, and keep adding syrup until the fruit is covered. Leave ½ inch of headspace for pints, 1 inch for quarts.

You can also prepare your fruit unsweetened by arranging pieces on a single layer on a cookie sheet and freezing. Transfer the frozen pieces into zipper-lock freezer or vacuum food sealer-type bags, or freezer containers. Squeeze out excess air and leave ½ inch of headspace (unless you are using the vacuum sealing method). Frozen cantaloupe should keep for 8 months to 1 year.

EQUIVALENTS, MEASURES & SERVINGS

- 1 pound = ½ medium cantaloupe = 1½ cups cubed

COMPLEMENTARY HERBS, SEASONINGS & FOODS

Basil, Champagne, chiles, cognac, Cointreau, cucumber, ginger, Grand Marnier, grapefruit, honey, ice cream, kirsch, lemon, lime, mint, oranges, pear, prosciutto, raspberries, salt, sherry, strawberries, vanilla, wine.

SERVING SUGGESTIONS

- Combine different types of melons, along with mango, pineapple, and pomegranate seeds for an exotic fruit salad.
- Try using muskmelons in your favorite homemade sorbet or popsicle recipe.
- Wrap muskmelon with proscuitto and sprinkle lightly with a high-quality balsamic vinegar and coarsely ground black pepper for a taste explosion. Or try really ripe melon with a bit of sea salt.
- Chop cantaloupe with diced kiwi and strawberries for a fun fruit salsa.
- Combine cantaloupe with orange and lemon juice, candied ginger or ginger ale, and whole milk for a refreshing soup.
- Get kids to drink their fruit by combining cantaloupe, milk, and honey in a blender to make a tasty melon milkshake.

"There are three things which cannot support mediocrity: poetry, wine, and melons."

— *Unknown French poet*

"There are only two good things in the world— women and roses— and two choice tidbits— women and melons."

— *French poet Malherbe*

MINTY MELON SALAD

SERVES 2

Inspired by the chile- and salt-sprinkled pineapple found in the fresh fruit stalls of Mexico, this amazing melon salad is delightfully refreshing. Salt, tangy lime juice, and spicy chili powder enhance the sweetness of summer melon while fresh mint adds a cool finish.

1 medium-sized ripe cantaloupe, cut into bite-sized pieces
2 tablespoons chopped fresh mint
Juice from 1 medium lime
1 to 3 teaspoons chili powder
¼ teaspoon sea salt

Simply combine all of the ingredients and toss well.

— *Whole Foods Market*

BACON, LETTUCE, AND CANTALOUPE SANDWICH

MAKES 4 SANDWICHES

12 bacon slices (about ¾ pound)
6 tablespoons mayonnaise
2 tablespoons Dijon mustard
2 teaspoons fresh lemon juice
2 teaspoons honey
½ cantaloupe
8 soft lettuce leaves, such as Boston or bibb
8 slices crusty bread

1. Preheat the oven to 425°F.

2. In a shallow baking pan, cook the bacon in one layer in the middle of the oven, turning occasionally, until golden and crisp, 16 to 18 minutes. Transfer to paper towels to drain.

3. In a small bowl, whisk together the mayonnaise, mustard, lemon juice, and honey until smooth. Seed the cantaloupe. Cut the melon into 12 thin slices and discard the rind. Cut out and discard the lettuce ribs.

4. Spread the mayonnaise mixture on all 8 slices of bread. Stack the lettuce, melon, and bacon on 4 of the bread slices, and top with the remaining slices, gently pressing them together.

— Gourmet, *August 1999, as appeared on www.fooddownunder.com*

SPICY CANTALOUPE SALSA

MAKES ABOUT 8 CUPS

2 medium-sized cantaloupes, peeled, seeded, and finely chopped
1 habañero chile, finely chopped
1 red onion, chopped

¼ cup cilantro, chopped
1 red bell pepper, roasted and chopped
1 papaya, chopped
1 tablespoon pineapple juice
1 tablespoon lemon juice
1 tablespoon rice vinegar
½ teaspoon salt
1 tablespoon sugar

Mix all of the ingredients together. Chill and serve.

— *Davis Farmers Market*

. . . .

Cantaloupe Pie

MAKES 1 9-INCH PIE

1 very ripe cantaloupe
½ cup white sugar, plus 6 tablespoons
8 tablespoons all-purpose flour
¼ teaspoon salt
3 egg yolks
2 tablespoons water
1 tablespoon butter
¼ teaspoon butter-flavored extract
3 egg whites
¼ teaspoon cream of tartar
1 (9 inch) pie crust, baked

1. Cut the cantaloupe in half, remove the seeds, and scoop the pulp into a saucepan. Place the pulp in a pan over medium heat until it comes to a gentle boil. Mash the cantaloupe as it heats. This should make about 2 cups of pulp.

2. Combine the ½ cup sugar, flour, and salt. Add to the heated cantaloupe pulp and cook, stirring constantly, until thick. (The amount of flour seems large, but it takes considerable thickening to achieve the correct consistency.)

3. Preheat the oven to 400°F.

4. In a large bowl, beat the egg yolks; add water to the yolks. Add a little of the cantaloupe to the yolks in order to heat the yolks gradually, then stir the yolk mixture into the cantaloupe mixture. Continue cooking, stirring constantly, until the mixture becomes thick and creamy. Remove from heat. Add the butter or margarine and flavoring to the cantaloupe mixture. Pour into a baked pie shell.

5. Beat the egg whites and cream of tartar together until frothy. Continue beating, adding the 6 tablespoons of sugar gradually; beat until thick peaks form. Top the pie with this meringue.

6. Bake at 400°F until the meringue turns delicately brown on top.

— *Kathi Duerr, www.allrecipes.com*

"In my garden
I pick a muskmelon
feeling like a thief."

— *Yosa Buson,*
Japanese haiku poet

Cilantro

CORIANDRUM SATIVUM

Cilantro has a bright, assertive, sage-citrus flavor that people either love or hate. (Those of the latter persuasion say it tastes like soap or rubber.) Resembling flat-leaf parsley, it is an essential ingredient in many world cuisines, including Vietnamese, Middle Eastern, Indian, and Latin American. Cilantro is sometimes called Chinese parsley, Mexican parsley, or Vietnamese mint. It is one of the few herbs in the world that has different names for the herb and spice forms: the seeds of fresh cilantro are coriander.

HISTORY

Coriander is one of humanity's earliest spices, and it is probably safe to assume that cilantro was also used. The plant probably originated in the North Africa or the Middle East, but it grows wild in Mediterranean Europe.

Coriander seeds have been found in Bronze Age ruins and Egyptian tombs, mentioned in the Bible, and were brought to northern Europe by the Romans. Spanish conquistadors introduced it to Latin America, where, paired with chiles and tomatoes, it became a staple.

NUTRITION

Cilantro is a good source of vitamins A and K, as well as dietary fiber, potassium, calcium, phosphorus, magnesium, and trace amounts of B vitamins. Coriander and cilantro have been used as an aphrodisiac, diuretic, and appetite stimulant. Cilantro leaves contain an antibacterial agent in its essential oils.

SELECTION

Look for very fresh bunches, with no signs of bruising or sliminess.

STORAGE

Handle cilantro carefully, for its leaves wilt and bruise easily. Cilantro is often bunched, with the root ends conveniently close together. If the roots are still attached, you can place your cilantro bouquet in a small glass of water, cover it loosely with plastic, and store it in the refrigerator. If you change the water every few days, your cilantro should last for up to 2 weeks.

Or you can wrap it loosely in a damp paper towel and store it in a perforated plastic bag in the refrigerator vegetable crisper. Avoid washing it until you are ready to use it, because excess moisture causes rapid spoilage.

TRIMMING & CLEANING

Cilantro needs thorough rinsing to remove grit. Fill a sink or large bowl with water, submerge the cilantro bunch, and swish it vigorously. Repeat if necessary, then drain and pat it gently dry with paper towels or cloth. Strip the leaves from the stems, discarding the tough stems.

BLANCHING & FREEZING

Place a small amount of dry cilantro leaves in a single layer on a cookie sheet, and place in the freezer. When they are frozen, place them in zipper-lock freezer or vacuum food sealer-type bags and return them to the freezer immediately. Use within 6 months. Do not thaw before using.

DRYING

Because cilantro almost completely loses its fragrance and flavor when dried, this type of preparation is not recommended.

COMPLEMENTARY HERBS, SEASONINGS & FOODS

Avocado, beef, borage, chicken, chiles, fish, garlic, ginger, ice cream, lamb, lentils, lime, mayonnaise, onion, peppers, pork, rice, salads, salsas, shellfish, shrimp, tomatoes, turkey, yogurt.

SERVING SUGGESTIONS

- Use cilantro in fresh salsa.
- Add several tablespoons of chopped fresh cilantro to green salads.
- Try tossing it in your potato salad or adding it to soups for a fresh zing.
- Use cilantro instead of basil to make pesto.
- Add cilantro and lime juice to your favorite guacamole recipe.
- In Vietnamese and Thai cuisines, cilantro is one of the several raw green herbs that accompany savory dishes.
- Mix cilantro with lime juice, honey, and shredded cabbage to make an unusual coleslaw.

· ·

CILANTRO LIME VINAIGRETTE   MAKES ABOUT 1¼ CUPS

⅔ cup (6 ounces) lime juice
3 tablespoons minced garlic
¼ cup apple cider vinegar
Pinch of salt
⅔ cup packed cilantro leaves
2 to 4 dashes Tabasco sauce
1 tablespoon cumin
¼ cup canola oil

Place all of the ingredients except the oil in a blender. Turn on the blender and very slowly add the oil to the "hole" in the middle. Use a little water if you lose the hole, just enough to maintain it so the oil will get properly blended.

— *MACSAC*, From Asparagus to Zucchini

· ·

ARROZ VERDE (GREEN RICE)   SERVES 4

This Mexican holiday rice is adapted from Aída Gabilondo's Mexican

Family Cooking *(Ballantine Books, 1992)*.

1 small white onion, peeled and quartered
2 poblano chiles, deveined, seeded, and quartered
3 cloves garlic, peeled
1 cup fresh cilantro
2 cups chicken stock
Salt and freshly ground black pepper
1 cup long-grain white rice
2 tablespoons vegetable oil

1. Place the onions, chiles, garlic, cilantro, and 1 cup of the stock in a blender. Blend, strain, and season with salt and pepper.

2. Rinse and drain the uncooked rice. Heat the oil in a heavy-bottomed pot over medium-low heat. Add the rice and sauté, stirring constantly, for 2 minutes. Add the sauce and the remaining 1 cup stock. Cover and simmer for 20 minutes.

3. Remove the pot from the heat, but keep covered, allowing the rice to cook for another 10 minutes.

— Saveur, *April 1998*

. . . .

SPAGHETTI WITH CILANTRO, CORN, AND TOMATOES

SERVES 2

Fragrant cilantro, sweet corn, and summer tomatoes have so much color and flavor that you may be surprised to find that this is a low-calorie meal.

2 very ripe medium tomatoes, stem ends removed
1 medium ear fresh corn, husked
½ pound spaghettini
1 egg
1 tablespoon red wine vinegar
½ teaspoon sugar
Salt and pepper
1 to 2 tablespoons full-flavored oil
¼ cup cilantro, finely minced
⅛ cup red onion, chopped

1. Drop the tomatoes and corn into a large pot of salted, boiling water; return to a boil on the highest heat. Boil 15 seconds. Remove the tomatoes; let the corn boil 1 minute, then remove. Cover the pot and lower the heat.

2. Peel the tomatoes, halve, and squeeze out the seeds. Cut 1 of the tomatos into ½-inch dice. Cut off the corn kernels from the cob.

3. Boil the sphagettini until it becomes just barely tender. Meanwhile, whirl the eggs in a food processor until they turn pale and fluffy; cut up the remaining tomato and add with vinegar, sugar, and salt and

pepper to taste. Whirl to blend well.

4. Toss the drained pasta in a warm serving dish with the oil, to taste. Add the egg-tomato sauce and toss to coat. Add the corn, cilantro, onion, and remaining tomato; toss gently and serve at once.

— *Elizabeth Schneider,* Uncommon Fruits and Vegetables

MEXICAN BLACK BEAN AND TOMATO SALAD SERVES 4

You can vary the spices to your palate. This salad tastes best when refrigerated for an hour or two before serving.

DRESSING
2 tablespoons olive, safflower, or canola oil
2 tablespoons fresh lemon or lime juice
1 to 2 cloves garlic, crushed
1 to 2 teaspoons cumin powder
1 to 2 teaspoons chili powder
Pinch of salt

1 (16-ounce) can black beans
1 to 2 chopped fresh tomatoes (or a pint of halved cherry tomatoes)
1 green bell pepper, chopped
A little red onion or a couple of green onions, chopped
Several sprigs of fresh cilantro, chopped

In a medium-sized bowl, mix the dressing ingredients. Then add the remaining ingredients and toss thoroughly.

— *Robin Taylor, Featherstone Farm CSA member*

Corn

Corn has a long history as a staple food, especially for peoples of the New World. Also known as maize, corn has evolved into an astonishing number of forms, from plants growing two to twenty feet tall and ears measuring the length of a thumbnail to two feet long. One characteristic common to all is the placement of seeds in orderly rows along a central cob.

Maize's value to modern humanity is inestimable. Most of the corn grown in the United States and Canada is used for livestock feed, the making of that ubiquitous sweetener, corn syrup, and for grain alcohol (and its sister product, the fuel alternative ethanol).

Sweet corn is a relatively recent phenomenon. The Iroquois were raising it in central New York by the early 1600s, but it was not widely cultivated until after the Civil War. Selective breeding has elevated the sugar levels of this crop to new heights, with "supersweet" and "sugar-enhanced" varieties available with higher sucrose levels than standard sweet corn (at the expense of traditional corn flavor, according to some).

HISTORY

Maize is native to the Americas, where it has been cultivated for thousands of years. The earliest maize probably came from Mexico, and pollen has been found in Mexico City dating 60,000 to 80,000 years ago. American Indians have long cultivated maize, where it is one in the famous trio of vegetables (corn, beans, and squash), which contain complementary vegetable proteins. Wherever maize was cultivated, it became a staple food, and it is no exaggeration to say that the Incan empire was built on the prosperity that corn provided.

When Europeans encountered maize in the New World in the 1500s, they were not so impressed, for its gluten-free seeds lacked the rising and baking qualities of their more familiar grains such as wheat. In many areas, such as Russia, where maize was imported in 1921 to ward off starvation, people stubbornly viewed it as food for swine and consumed it only because they had no choice.

NUTRITION

One medium ear of sweet corn offers 80 calories, with lots of dietary fiber, a few grams of protein, and a fair amount of vitamin C, vitamin A (unless it is white), potassium, niacin, and folate.

SELECTION

Try to buy corn with the husk on, and pierce a kernel with a fingernail to see what sort of juice spurts out. If you can puncture the kernel easily and a translucent, milky juice emerges, the corn is likely to be fresh. If you have a hard time piercing the kernel, and little or no juice comes out, pass it up for a better, more youthful ear.

Both the husks and tassel should be light green and moist, not dried out, brown, or mushy.

STORAGE

Cook your corn promptly; its sugars start converting to starch as soon as the ears are picked, although the newer supersweet hybrids may retain their sweetness for several days. Always refrigerate your corn until you are ready to cook it; this chilling slows down the sugar conversion. Keep the husks on to retain freshness.

TRIMMING & CLEANING

If you are preparing the ears for boiling and it is still husked, peel back the husks like a banana, pulling off the silks as you go. Then break off the whole kit and caboodle along with its stalk as close to the end of the ear as possible. You can rinse the ear under running water or wipe with a damp paper towel to help clear off any remaining silks. Corn destined for the barbecue grill should stay protected in their husks.

STEAMING & BOILING

Steam or boil corn for as little time as possible to maintain that crisp sweetness characteristic of this brief summer treat. To steam, place shucked whole or half-ears in a steamer and cook, covered, for 6 to 10 minutes.

To boil, place the ears in a large pot of boiling water, add a spoonful of sugar if desired (but no salt, which toughens corn), and boil for about 3 to 7 minutes, depending on the size of the ears. Drain and serve immediately.

STIR-FRYING & SAUTÉING

Use either fresh or frozen corn kernels in stir-fries or sautéed dishes, adding them in the last 3 minutes of the cooking time to preserve their texture and flavor.

GRILLING

You can make delicious corn on the cob on the grill. Pull back the husks, but do not remove them. Remove and discard the silk, and then soak the whole cobs in a pot of cold water for 15 minutes. Preheat the grill to a medium temperature. Remove the corn from the water and brush the kernels with olive oil. Before you rewrap the corn in the husks, add whatever seasonings you desire. Then reposition the husks over the kernels and tie each ear with a piece of loose husk or twine. Place the prepared ears on the grill over medium heat, turning every 2 minutes. After a couple of turns, place the corn on indirect heat or on the top shelf of your grill and close the cover. Allow the corn to slowly roast for another 15 minutes. The corn is done when the pierced kernels squirt a sweet liquid.

MICROWAVING

Rinse the shucked ears and wrap each one in a damp paper towel. Microwave on High power for 3 to 4 minutes. Then turn the cobs over and microwave an additional 3 to 4 minutes, depending on how tender you want them.

- ☛ 1 ear = 2 to 3 minutes
- ☛ 2 ears = 3 to 4 minutes

July Days

by Rhys Williams,
Former Featherstone
Farm Partner

July 21, 2004

Recently Rebecca Claypool wrote a brief piece for the newsletter on the life of salad mix. Salad mix is a relatively small crop for us, but it is a good example of the uniqueness of vegetable farming.

In the six years that I have been with Featherstone, I have enjoyed the variety of our crops and the idiosyncrasies of each. You really need to keep a lot of balls in the air.

With the wet conditions this year we have had to hustle to prevent problems. Disease in tomatoes and winter squash can be devastating. Although it is present in both of our crops, we have been able to keep it at bay.

The timing of seeding and transplanting has to be pretty precise or you will have everything coming on at once. You need a handle on the present and a plan for the next three weeks. Each year that goes by, we get better at some things but still have time to mess up something else.

- 4 ears = 8 to 10 minutes
- 2 cups kernels = 3 minutes

BLANCHING & FREEZING

To prepare corn for freezing, it should be blanched first, preferably in a 12- to 15-quart pot. Blanching times will vary, depending on the thickness of the cob. If the ears measure 1¼ to 1½ inches wide, blanch in boiling water for 9 minutes, or if over 1½ inches, for 11 minutes. (Some supersweet varieties require only a 4-minute blanching.) Then submerge the ears immediately in an ice water bath for about 20 minutes to allow cobs to cool.

You can either freeze the corn while still on the cob or remove the kernels. Place the corn in zipper-lock freezer or vacuum food sealer-type bags, or freezer containers, and squeeze out excess air. For the best flavor, frozen corn should be used within 3 months, but it will keep up to a year at 0°F.

EQUIVALENTS, MEASURES & SERVINGS

- 2 medium ears, kernels scraped = 1 cup kernels

COMPLEMENTARY HERBS, SEASONINGS & FOODS

Butter, cayenne pepper, chile, cream, cumin, curry powder, garlic salt, lima beans, lime juice, Old Bay seasoning, paprika, parsley, peas, pepper, salt, sugar.

SERVING SUGGESTIONS

- It's awfully hard to beat simple, freshly boiled corn on the cob served with nothing but butter and salt and pepper. An interesting variation is corn on the cob with thick cream, ground chile powder, and lime juice (recipe below).
- If you actually get tired of fresh corn on the cob or find you have a lot of corn on your hands, try making creamed corn, corn pudding, corn au gratin, corn soup, or scalloped corn.
- Combine sweet corn kernels and lima beans with bits of onion and bacon for that traditional American dish, succotash.
- In a Boston baked beans recipe, substitute fresh sweet corn kernels for the beans.
- Barbecue corn on the grill, along with potatoes, onions, and meat.
- Strip off the kernels from older corn and use them in chowders, soups, stews, omelets, quiches, fried rice, and pancake batter.
- Add fresh, whole kernels to cornbread batter.
- If the corn is really fresh and just-picked, try enjoying a tender, sweet ear raw.

MEXICAN-STYLE CORN ON THE COB   SERVES 4

A lively alternative to butter and salt. This type of corn on the cob, slathered with thick cream and ground chile and sprinkled with lime juice is street food in Mexico. If you live near a Mexican market, you may be able to find thick Mexican crema. If not, substitute French crème fraîche; it's available in many cheese stores, or you can make your own.

CRÈME FRAÎCHE

1 cup heavy cream
1 tablespoon buttermilk

1. Put 1 cup of heavy cream (not ultra-pasteurized) in a saucepan and heat over low heat until it is just lukewarm (about 100°F). Pour the cream into a clean lidded glass jar.

2. Add 1 tablespoon buttermilk, cover, and shake for 1 minute. Let the jar stand at room temperature until the cream thickens, 12 to 24 hours. Refrigerate when thick. It will keep for at least 1 week.

4 ears fresh corn, shucked
6 to 8 tablespoons Mexican crema or crème fraîche, whisked
(recipe above)
Salt
Chile powder
Lime wedges (optional)

1. Bring a large pot of water to a boil over high heat. Add the corn, cover the pot, and remove it from the heat. Let stand 5 minutes.

2. Season the crème fraîche to taste with salt. When the corn is ready, remove the ears from the pot with tongs and let the excess water drip back into the pot. Using a rubber spatula, spread each ear generously with crème (the larger the ears, the more crème you will need), then sprinkle liberally with chili powder, and add a squeeze of lime if you like.

— *Janet Fletcher,* More Vegetables, Please

. . . .

CORN OYSTERS SERVES 4

A lovely use for fresh corn—and perhaps the only oysters that will ever pass your child's lips. Isn't it funny how giving a food a disgusting name makes children more willing to try it? Traditionally, these little pancakes are a side dish. By adding some chopped cooked bacon or ham, you can turn them into a light main course.

2 cups grated off-the-cob fresh corn
2 large eggs, beaten
½ cup flour
Salt and pepper
4 tablespoons (½ stick) unsalted butter, plus more as needed

1. Preheat the oven to 200°F so that you can keep the finished corn oysters warm.

2. Mix the corn, eggs, flour, salt, and pepper in a medium-sized bowl until they are well combined. Shape the mixture into little oyster-sized cakes.

Last year at a farm conference, I fell into a conversation with a business planner from the Minnesota Department of Agriculture. In the course of this discussion, this fellow asked me what it was that I wanted our farm to be, in some broader sense.

It was a very good question, one that I had never been asked to consider before. My response was a series of ideas—both abstract and concrete—that I now classify into the first two levels of the "Philosophy of Featherstone Farm" pyramid, outlined below.

"It sounds like you've achieved your vision," he began, and I felt a flash of satisfaction that indeed, ten years into our lives at Featherstone, we have created a farm that is essentially what I hoped it would become.

"But I didn't hear you say anything about making a profit doing it," he continued (as I began to squirm in my seat), "which explains why you say your balance sheet looks so bad!"

It was as though a light bulb had been turned on in my head. What this man had said was absolutely true, and I realized all at once that high ideals alone are not enough to constitute a workable statement of purpose. Not unless I intended to take a vow of poverty for myself and my family of five.

And what about other aspiring farmers, who might look to Featherstone as a model for a successful vegetable farm; what kind of message do we send them by struggling financially? In an instant, the third tier of the pyramid was born.

Then last spring I read The Omnivore's Dilemma *by Michael Pollan, an imaginative and lively critique of the modern food system of which our small farm is a part. Much of what this book relates*

3. Heat the butter in a large skillet until it begins to foam; then carefully set as many oysters into the skillet as will fit. Cook them for 4 minutes per side, or until they are medium-brown. Keep them warm on a cookie sheet in the oven until they are all done, adding more butter to the pan as needed.

— *Ann Hodgman,* One Bite Won't Kill You

BIG JIM CHILES STUFFED WITH CORN AND JACK CHEESE   SERVES 2 TO 4

Poblanos are a good substitute for the large, medium-hot Big Jim chiles.

1½ cups flour
1 teaspoon baking powder
Salt
1 (12-ounce) bottle of beer
2 tablespoons extra-virgin olive oil
1 small yellow onion, peeled and finely chopped
1 clove garlic, peeled and minced
1½ cups fresh corn kernels (about 4 ears)
Freshly ground black pepper
½ cup grated Monterey jack cheese
6 medium Big Jim or poblano chiles, charred and peeled
Corn oil

1. Combine 1 cup of the flour, the baking powder, and ½ teaspoon salt in a large bowl. Gradually add the beer, whisking until the batter is smooth. Cover with plastic wrap and refrigerate for 1 hour.

2. Heat the olive oil in a medium-sized skillet over medium heat. Add the onion and garlic and cook until soft, 4 to 5 minutes. Add the corn and cook for 2 to 3 minutes. Season to taste with salt and pepper, allow to cool, add the cheese, and set aside.

3. Make an incision the length of each chile and remove stems and seeds. Stuff the corn filling into the chiles, then close with toothpicks.

4. Pour oil to a depth of 1½ inch into a large deep skillet. Heat over medium heat until hot. Dredge the chiles in the remaining ½ cup flour; shake off the excess, dip the chiles into batter, and fry until golden, about 1 minute per side. Drain on paper towels and season with salt. Serve with sour cream and lime wedges, if you like.

— Saveur, *July–August 2001*

CORN PUDDING   SERVES 6

It is not dessert—it is a sumptuous side dish from a simpler era. The sim-

plicity of the ingredients allows the natural flavors to shine through. No flashy spices or herbs are needed.

2 tablespoons butter
2 eggs
1 teaspoon kosher salt
½ teaspoon freshly ground black pepper
1 cup organic milk
1 cup organic heavy cream
6 large ears of sweet organically grown corn

1. Preheat oven to 350°F and spread the 2 tablespoons butter liberally over the inside of a 13 × 9-inch baking dish.

2. Crack the eggs into a large mixing bowl and whisk in the salt and pepper. Then whisk in the milk and cream.

3. Trim the base of each ear of corn to make it stand flat on the cutting board. Working with one ear at a time, use a sharp knife to cut the kernels off of each ear. Add the kernels to the bowl with the egg mixture.

4. After the kernels are cut from the ears, use the dull side of the knife blade to scrape down the ear and press out any juices clinging to the ear and stir the juices into the mixture in the mixing bowl.

5. Transfer the pudding mixture to the buttered baking dish and bake 35 minutes, or until the corn pudding is browned on top and smells faintly of popcorn; the pudding should jiggle when the pan is moved briskly back and forth. Serve hot as a side dish with fish or pork, or as a simple main dish for lunch.

— *Greg Atkinson*

CORN SALSA

A great summer dish for all those family potlucks.

Quality olive oil
Red wine vinegar
Grilled corn, removed from the cob
Grilled serrano pepper, chopped fine
Tomato, diced
Basil, chopped roughly
Ground black pepper
Salt

Mix the olive oil slowly into the vinegar. Add everything else. Mix and refrigerate until well-chilled. Great on many things (with chips, pita, hummus, grilled veggies, and meat) or by itself.

— *Amy Chen, Featherstone Farm CSA member*

was nothing new to me, and yet it was said so eloquently as to refresh its urgency. Essentially, I concluded that Featherstone is a benign practitioner of what Pollan calls "industrial organic" agriculture, with all of its shortcomings—such as the dependence on fossil fuels—and that the farm can and must hold itself to a higher ecological standard.

Thus, the fourth and crowning piece of the Featherstone Philosophy pyramid took shape: the Featherstone Farm for the Future (FFF), described in greater detail on pages XVI–XVII.

As a student of anthropology and political economy years ago, I was intrigued with the philosophy of Karl Marx. Like Marx, I've organized my view of things into a pyramid.

The first level constitutes the material foundation that allows the other levels to exist. Higher levels are more abstract and idealistic, and they engage the material in a dialectic relationship that Marx would recognize.

So here, on this page and the next, is the Philosophy of Featherstone Farm pyramid as I now see it. It could be said that we took a decade to achieve some measure of success in Levels 1 and 2. With any luck we can make real progress in Level 3 (and dig ourselves out of debt!) in somewhat less time.

The biggest and ultimately most important idea for me—demonstrating a more environmentally sound way of farming—can't wait another decade if drastic climate changes are taking place.

LEVEL 1

Create the Featherstone Farm of the Future— a practical experiment in real sustainability.

CORN CHOWDER SERVES 6

2 pounds white potatoes, diced
1 bay leaf
Water
3 teaspoons margarine
3 medium onions, chopped
4 celery ribs, chopped
2 teaspoons cumin seeds
3 tablespoons all-purpose flour
½ teaspoon crushed dried sage
½ teaspoon crushed white pepper
2 cups skim milk
1⅓ cups cooked fresh or frozen whole kernel corn
Parsley, for garnish (optional)
Red bell pepper slices, for garnish (optional)

1. In a large saucepan, combine the potatoes, bay leaf, and 4 cups of water; bring to a boil. Cover, and cook 15 minutes, or until the potatoes are tender. Discard the bay leaf. Drain the potatoes, reserving the liquid. Set aside.

2. In the same saucepan, melt the margarine. Add the onions, celery, and cumin; cook until the onions are tender. Stir in the flour, sage, and white pepper. Stir in enough reserved potato liquid to make a paste. Stir in the remaining potato liquid and potatoes, and heat through. Stir in the milk and corn; heat through.

3. If desired, top with snipped parsley and bell pepper slices.

— *Fruits and Veggies—More Matters; Centers for Disease Control & Prevention*

SHEILA LUKINS'S SUMMER SUCCOTASH SALAD SERVES 8

This unusual succotash is Lukins's bright variation on an old theme. Fresh lima beans come to market in late summer. If you can't wait, frozen limas, quickly cooked, are a fine substitute.

3 cups cooked baby lima beans
3 cups fresh corn kernels, blanched
1 cup diced, peeled, seeded cucumber
2 ripe plum tomatoes, seeded and diced
¼ cup finely chopped red onion
1 scallion with 3 inches of green leaf, thinly sliced
2 tablespoons cider vinegar
½ teaspoon Dijon mustard
1 clove garlic, minced
½ teaspoon sugar
⅛ teaspoon curry powder

Salt and freshly ground black pepper
3 tablespoons olive oil
2 tablespoons chopped cilantro

1. Combine the lima beans, corn, cucumber, tomatoes, onions, and scallions in a bowl.

2. In a separate bowl, whisk the vinegar, mustard, garlic, sugar, and curry powder together. Season to taste with salt and pepper. Slowly drizzle in the oil, whisking constantly. Pour over the vegetables and mix well with a rubber spatula.

3. Refrigerate until ready to serve. Shortly before serving, toss with cilantro. Taste and adjust seasonings. Serve cold.

— Saveur, *May–June 1995*

. . . .

CORN SOUP WITH BASIL

SERVES 4

This soup, which can be made in advance, has a smooth, subtle taste.

4 ears of corn on the cob, cut in half crosswise
6 fresh bay leaves
Freshly ground black pepper and salt
1 ounce butter
1 small onion, finely chopped
1 clove garlic, finely chopped
3 small tomatoes, skinned and chopped
1½ pints chicken or vegetable stock
5 fluid ounces heavy cream
1 tablespoon cumin seeds, freshly ground
12 fresh basil leaves, chopped

1. Bring a large pan of water to a boil and add the corn and bay leaves. Cook for about 20 minutes, or until the kernels are soft. Drain the corn cobs and leave to cool.

2. Meanwhile, in a large saucepan, melt the butter. Add the onion and garlic and cook gently for about 5 minutes, until the onion is transparent. Add the tomatoes. Simmer gently for 10 minutes.

3. Cut the corn off the cobs with a sharp knife. Add the stock and sweet corn kernels to the tomato-onion mixture. Season to taste. Bring to a boil, then decrease the heat, and simmer for 10 minutes.

4. Pour the soup into a blender or food processor and process until smooth (you may need to do this in batches). Sieve the mixture into a saucepan. Stir in the cream and heat gently, making sure not to let the soup come to a boil. Add the cumin and stir well.

5. Serve in individual bowls and garnish with chopped basil. This soup is normally served hot, but it is also delicious cold on a hot summer day.

— *Robert Budwig,* The Vegetable Market Cookbook

"Sex is good, but not as good as fresh, sweet corn."

— *Garrison Keillor,
American humorist*

CORN-MAC CASSEROLE

SERVES 4 TO 6

2¾ cups fresh corn kernels, or 1 (16-ounce) can whole-kernel corn, juice and all
1 (16-ounce) can cream-style corn
1 full cup uncooked macaroni
1 full cup cubed Velveeta or American cheese
2 tablespoons margarine, cut into bits and stirred in as the above ingredients are combined

1. Combine all of the ingredients in a large, well-buttered casserole or 8 × 10-inch cake pan.

2. Let stand overnight in the refrigerator, covered, or combine at least 2 to 3 hours before baking.

3. Bake at 350°F for 1 hour.

Tips

☛ If you are using fresh corn, or your canned corn does not contain much liquid, add ⅔ cup water as the macaroni takes up the liquid.

☛ For a filling one-dish meal, add a can of sliced Vienna sausage or a cup of diced ham.

— *Donna Kaliff*, The Schoenleber Family Cookbook

Cucumber

CUCUMIS SATIVUS

The Cucurbits are a large, rambunctious family, which includes pumpkins, squashes, melons, gourds, and yes, cucumbers. The cucumber is beloved the world over for its cool, crisp, thirst-quenching flesh and clean flavor when raw and for its capacity to absorb salt, vinegar, water, and spices as a delectable pickle.

Cucumbers come in two varieties: pickling and slicing. Pickling types include the tiny gherkin and the French cornichon, as well as the American dill; all have skins with warts or spines. Slicing varieties are bigger, range about 8 to 15 inches in length, and have smooth, dark-green skins. Older varieties of slicing cucumbers used to have rather tough, thick skins full of spines; most modern varieties today lack the spines and are considered more digestible (or "burpless") than their cousins of yesteryear.

HISTORY

Cucumbers are believed to be native to India, although seeds have been found near Thailand that carbon-date to nearly 10,000 years ago. Cucumbers were brought from Asia to Europe, where the Romans became particularly fond of them, even soaking the seeds in honeyed wine in the hope of sweetening the resulting fruit. The Spaniards brought cucumbers to America, where they were received so enthusiastically by some of the indigenous peoples that the Pueblo Indians were falsely reported as using it as a native food.

NUTRITION

Cucumbers are lower in nutrients than many vegetables, but they do contain some vitamin C, dietary fiber, potassium, and magnesium. Cucumbers also contain significant silica, water, and caffeic acid, all of which benefit the skin—one reason why cucumber slices are often recommended for treating swollen eyes and topical burns.

SELECTION

Cucumbers should be uniformly firm with no soft spots or shriveled ends. Yellowing cucumbers (except lemon cucumbers) may be too old, and large cukes may not have the best flavor.

STORAGE

Supermarket cucumbers are usually coated with a food-grade wax, which allows them to be stored for about a week in the refrigerator vegetable crisper. Unwaxed cucumbers should be used within a few days.

TRIMMING & CLEANING

Whether to peel a cucumber depends on your personal preference and whether it is waxed or not. Supermarket cucumbers usually have a thin, edible wax coating, but if you don't enjoy ingesting unknown substances, they should be peeled first. An advantage to obtaining unwaxed or or-

Cooking Tip

You can revive most of the crispness of a wilted cuke by soaking it in salted ice water for 1 to 2 hours.

ganic cucumbers is that no peeling is necessary, so you also get the benefit of the nutrient-rich skin. You may want to peel unwaxed cucumbers anyway if the skin is tough or bitter, or if the skin's presence would detract from its texture (such as in thinly sliced cucumbers for tea sandwiches).

STEAMING & BOILING

Sliced cucumbers can be steamed for 5 to 8 minutes, or until just tender. Boiling cucumbers tends to make them soggy and is not recommended.

STIR-FRYING & SAUTÉING

Although we tend to think of cucumbers as exclusively a vegetable to be eaten raw or pickled, cucumbers do respond well to a light, quick sauté in butter or olive oil for a few minutes, and flavored with fresh herbs.

MICROWAVING

Cut cucumbers into slices or chunks and microwave on High power for 7 to 9 minutes, depending on the thickness of the pieces.

BLANCHING & FREEZING

Because of their high water content, cucumbers should not be frozen, or they will turn mushy.

MEASURES & EQUIVALENTS

- 1 medium cucumber = 1 cup chopped
- 2 medium cucumbers = 1 pound = 4 cups cubed = 3 cups sliced = 2 cups shredded
- 1 pound peeled, seeded, sliced, salted, drained, pressed cucumber = about 1⅓ cups

COMPLEMENTARY HERBS, SEASONINGS & FOODS

Butter, cayenne pepper, chile, cream, cream cheese, cumin, curry powder, dill, garlic salt, hummus, lemon, lima beans, lime juice, mint, Old Bay seasoning, paprika, parsley, peas, pepper, salt, sugar, yogurt.

SERVING SUGGESTIONS

- Cooked cucumbers go well with white-fleshed fish; cut them into strips or cubes and sauté in butter until tender.
- For an unusual alternative to zucchini, try thin-slicing cucumbers and deep frying.
- Make little "sandwiches" by cutting cucumbers into ¼-inch-thick slices and pressing deviled ham or chicken spread between them.
- Add bits of diced cucumber, tomato, and onion to a chilled gazpacho soup just before serving.
- Make fun cucumber boats by splitting a large cucumber lengthwise, then filling it with cheese, onions, or meat, and broiling until lightly browned.
- Place a few slices of cucumber in a glass of ice water for a refreshing drink.
- The traditional English cucumber tea sandwich is made with thinly sliced cucumber on white bread spread with the finest sweet butter you can afford, and with the crusts cut off.
- Liven up the usual carrots and celery on the relish tray by adding cucumber sticks.

✎ Combine diced cucumbers, sugar snap peas, and mint with Italian dressing or sour cream for a refreshing summer salad.

· ·

BARELY PICKLED CUCUMBERS

Kids love these crisp, salty, slightly acid, and yet sweet cucumber slices, which make excellent refreshers on hot summer days.

2 or 3 cucumbers
Water
White wine vinegar or apple cider vinegar
Salt
Sugar
Freshly ground black pepper
Fresh dill, slightly crushed

1. Fill a large container that has a cover about half full of water. Add the vinegar, salt, sugar, pepper, and dill in the proportions desired (taste constantly to check acidity, sweetness, and saltiness).

2. Wash and dry the cucumbers (peeling is optional). Slice the cucumbers as thinly as possible and add to the "brine."

3. Cover and refrigerate. Chill for at least 1 hour before serving. These cucumbers taste better on the second day, and will keep for about 3 days. As you use up the slices, you can add fresh cucumber to the brine.

Note

✎ For spicier cucumbers, add 2 or 3 slices of jalapeño pepper.

— *Mi Ae Lipe, Featherstone Farm CSA member*

· ·

SEEDLESS CUCUMBERS, YOGURT, MINT, AND GARLIC SALAD
SERVES 4 TO 6

2 European cucumbers or 3 medium regular (Persian) cucumbers
1 clove garlic, mashed and minced
2 to 3 tablespoons mint, fresh, chopped or 1 tablespoon dried mint
½ teaspoon salt
1 pint nonfat yogurt

Peel and slice or dice the cucumbers. Mash the garlic with salt and add to the yogurt. Add the cucumbers and mint to the yogurt, and gently stir until the cucumbers are well-dispersed throughout the salad.

— *From Produce for Better Health; Fruits and Veggies—More Matters; Centers for Disease Control & Prevention*

A Week's Cycle
by Rebecca Claypool
former Featherstone Farm
CSA Manager
July 14, 2004

It is cold and wet at Featherstone today. I actually enjoyed the rainy day although there was plenty to do out in the field.

Mondays are always busy filling orders for the stores and wholesalers. Every Tuesday and Friday we do deliveries to the Twin Cities, so we pick and pack all of the produce on Monday and Thursday.

During the height of the season, we send our own van to the Wedge Co-op early Tuesday and Friday mornings, as well as load produce on Avalanche Organics' truck that delivers to a variety of stores and wholesalers in the Twin Cities. As more and more crops go out of season, we won't need to do an exclusive delivery to our biggest buyer.

So… we pick and pack for stores Monday, pick and bag for CSA Tuesday, pack boxes and deliver CSA boxes Wednesday, pick and pack again for stores Thursday, and pick for the farmers market Friday. Saturday we go to the farmers market, and continue to pick the crops that are abundant.

Usually there is flexibility on Tuesdays, Wednesdays, and Fridays, so other projects such as planting, cultivating, fencing, and cleaning can get done. Then we start all over on Monday.

WHITE BEAN AND BASIL SALAD

SERVES 4

DRESSING

2 tablespoons olive or safflower oil
2 tablespoons lemon juice or salad vinegar
1 to 2 cloves garlic, crushed
2 teaspoons dry basil, or several leaves of chopped fresh basil
Pinch of salt
Freshly ground pepper

1 (16-ounce) can of Great Northern beans (or cannellini),
    drained and rinsed
1 cucumber, peeled, quartered, and sliced into little chunks
1 sweet red or green bell pepper, chopped
Several sprigs of fresh parsley, chopped
1 small red onion or 2 to 3 green onions, chopped

1. In a medium-sized bowl, mix the dressing ingredients, grinding the garlic and salt into the oil with the back of a spoon.

2. Then add the salad ingredients and stir. This salad tastes best when refrigerated for an hour or two before serving.

— *Robin Taylor, Featherstone Farm CSA member*

One Big Pickle

The world record for the largest cucumber is 59 pounds, grown in Queensland, Australia, in 1988.

VEGETABLE SUBS

MAKES 2 SANDWICHES

Depending on what part of the country you live in, this popular vegetarian sandwich could be called a sub, hero, or grinder. Whatever its name, it is made with a long sandwich roll and, in this case, stuffed with salad vegetables and sliced cheese.

This delicious sandwich has become a staple in my house because I can easily keep the rolls in the freezer to have on hand, and my vegetable bin always contains some lettuce and other salad ingredients. Don't hesitate to improvise here. You can include sliced olives, roasted red peppers, scallions, hot peppers, sprouts, mushrooms, and your favorite cheese.

2 submarine (grinder) rolls, sliced horizontally almost all of the way
    through
2 tablespoons mayonnaise (see Tips)
Freshly ground black pepper
4 lettuce leaves
4 thin slices tomato
2 thin slices red onion
4 thin rings green or red bell pepper
8 thin slices cucumber
6 thin slices smoked Gouda cheese (see Tips)

1. Spread the bread halves with the mayonnaise, then season generously

with pepper.

2. Divide the ingredients in half. Layer them in each sandwich and close tightly, pressing down on the bread gently to help it adhere. Slice each sandwich in half.

Tips

- Smoked cheese gives this sandwich a rich, dynamic flavor that is hauntingly good. Other cheeses will also work well, such as muenster, provolone, Monterey jack with jalapeño peppers, and Swiss.

- If you are going to pack these sandwiches for lunch or a picnic, wrap the tomato slices separately and then place them in the sandwiches just before eating.

- Vinaigrette dressing is a wonderful substitute for the mayonnaise.

— *Jeanne Lemlin,* Vegetarian Classics

AGUA DE PEPINO (CUCUMBER LIMEADE)

MAKES 2 LARGE GLASSES

This is a very refreshing drink. You can add a section of ripe pineapple as an alternative to using so much sugar.

4 cucumbers, cut into chunks
2 apples, cored
3 to 4 mint sprigs
Juice of 2 to 3 limes
Sugar to taste (about 2 ounces is enough unless you like it sweeter)
Ice
Mint sprigs, for garnish
Cucumber slices, for garnish

Put the cucumber, apples, and mint through a juicer, add the remaining ingredients, and blend well. Pour over ice and garnish with mint sprigs and cucumber slices.

— *Fire and Ice Café, Midleton, County Cork, Ireland*

Dill

Familiar to most of us as the seasoning of the ubiquitous pickle bearing its name, dill is a much-loved fixture of a number of world cuisines, particularly Polish, Russian, and Scandinavian. An annual member of the Apiaceae or Umbelliferae family, which includes such familiar plants as Queen Anne's Lace, carrot, celery, fennel, and parsnip, dill is grown for its feathery, caraway-tasting leaves in the spring and early summer, and harvested for its seeds in late summer. Its name comes from the old Norse word dylla, *meaning to soothe or lull, and the herb has long been used as a digestive tonic and for its calming effects.*

HISTORY

Dill hails from Asia and southern Europe, where the Romans reveled in its springy, ferny fronds, even making wreaths of it to wear at their feasts. In the Middle Ages, dill was thought to protect from the effects of witchcraft. Beverages made from dill seeds were drunk, and charms created from the leaves were worn as an antidote to spells.

Dill has been valued for its cleansing and digestive properties for centuries. In America during the 1700s and 1800s, both dill and fennel seeds were given to children to chew on during church services to keep them calm and quiet, hence the moniker "meetin' seeds."

NUTRITION

Dill has long been used as medicine; it contains carvone, which relieves intestinal gas. The seeds are high in calcium, with 1 tablespoon containing the equivalent of a third of a cup of milk, and fresh dill weed is a decent source of manganese and iron.

SELECTION

Dill weed should be bright green and fresh, not wilted or yellowish. Avoid slimy or tired-looking dill.

STORAGE

The leaves wilt quickly upon harvesting, but this will not affect flavor. To store, mist the whole stems lightly with a fine spray of water, wrap loosely in paper towels, place in a plastic bag, and store in your refrigerator crisper drawer. It should last up to a week or longer. You can also trim the stems, place them in a glass with an inch of cold water, loosely wrap the top with a damp paper towel, and place a plastic bag over the herbal bouquet; store it in the refrigerator.

TRIMMING & CLEANING

Dill benefits from a quick rinse under running water. To dry, gently roll up the stems in a paper towel. Then snip or trim sprigs with a pair of kitchen scissors.

BLANCHING AND FREEZING

Fresh dill sprigs can be frozen for up to two months, but their color will darken. To freeze, place the entire stalk with its leaves still attached in a zipper-lock freezer or vacuum food sealer-type bag or freezer container. Squeeze out the excess air. Or you can snip off the leaves, spread them out on a cookie sheet to dry overnight, then package them for the freezer the next day. They do not need to be thawed before using. To use, simply snip the leaves off as though it were fresh.

DRYING

Fresh dill weed can be dried in a dehydrator (about 6 to 8 hours at 110°F) or outdoors by hanging upside-down in an airy, shaded place for 3 to 4 days. Dried dill, however, contains only a fraction of the flavor of its fresh counterpart, and is vastly inferior for cooking.

MEASURES & EQUIVALENTS

- 1 tablespoon chopped fresh dill = 1 teaspoon dried dill weed = 3 heads fresh dill weed
- ½ ounce fresh dill = about ½ cup leaves

COMPLEMENTARY HERBS, SEASONINGS & FOODS

Beets, breads, cabbage, carrots, chicken, cucumbers, cream cheese, cream sauces, cucumbers, dips, dressings, eggs, fish, lamb, mild cheeses, pickles, potatoes, salads, salmon, scallops, seafood, soups, sour cream, tomatoes, veal.

SERVING SUGGESTIONS

- Snip dill sprigs and add to your favorite tossed green salad for extra flavor.
- Make dill butter by adding ¼ cup minced fresh dill weed to ½ cup softened butter. Mix well, cover, and refrigerate at least 2 hours before using to let the flavors blend.
- Dill is a vital ingredient in the beloved Swedish dish, gravlax. Fresh, raw salmon filets are layered with generous amounts of salt, sugar, and dill weed, and cured for several days.
- Snip bits of dill over summer potato, beet, and tomato soups for a zingy flavor.
- Add freshly minced dill weed to chilled tomato juice.
- Stir minced dill weed and other fresh herbs into cottage cheese.

The flavor of dill weed diminishes greatly the longer it is cooked, so add it at the last minute for full flavor and aroma.

SABZI (HERB SALAD)

SERVES 3 TO 4

Sabzi refers to greens or potherbs, usually a Middle Eastern combination of dill, parsley, and mint. Serve sabzi with a warm cheese-filled turnover or falafel, or add it to a pita sandwich along with tomatoes and feta cheese or ricotta salata.

3 cups small spinach leaves
1 cup arugula
¼ cup flat-leaf parsley leaves
¼ cup cilantro leaves

*Featherstone Fruits and Vegetables
manages over a hundred acres of
farmland for vegetable and fruit
crops, all in the varied topography of southeast Minnesota's bluff
country.*

*This topography contains very
diverse microclimates. Pockets of
land that are higher or lower on
hillsides have different degrees of
sun and wind exposure and a great
variety of soil types. These microclimates define the growing conditions in which certain crops will
mature.*

*Because we grow such a wide
range of fruits and vegetables, each
with its own specific needs, we have
been able to take full advantage of
these microclimates when we determine what to plant where.*

*Currently Featherstone rents
farmland in five separate locations
within a seven-mile radius of the
home farm:*

1. *Fifty-five acres of flat bottom-
land in two locations in the
narrow Wiscoy Valley, adja-
cent to a perennial waterway
and surrounded by steep
wooded hillsides. The soil here
is a very rich silt loam, very
high in organic matter.*

   *The depth of this valley
shelters it from high winds,
creating a cool, moist microclimate ideal for spring crops
such as leaf lettuce and peas,
which like to mature slowly
with lots of moisture. We
seldom notice any bitterness
in our salads from this farm
well into the summer because
these crops are grown in such
ideal conditions.*

2. *Eighteen acres of ridge land
on the surrounding bluffs,
again in two locations. These*

¼ cup dill sprigs
6 mint leaves, torn into small pieces
Several celery or lovage leaves, torn
2 scallions, including a few inches of the greens, thinly sliced
Salt
1 tablespoon extra-virgin olive oil or as needed
Fresh lemon juice

1. Carefully sort through the greens, then wash and dry them well. Tear
   or cut the spinach and arugula into bite-sized pieces and toss with the
   herbs, scallions, and a few pinches of salt.

2. Drizzle on enough oil to lightly coat the leaves, then squeeze on a little
   lemon juice and toss again.

— *Deborah Madison,* Vegetarian Cooking for Everyone

....

DILLED VEGETABLE-BARLEY SOUP   SERVES 6

*This soup tastes best the day after it is made. However, as it sits around, the
barley expands, so it usually needs a little additional water upon reheating.
Adjust the seasonings, if necessary.*

½ cup uncooked pearl barley
5½ cups water
2 to 3 tablespoons butter or canola oil
2 cups minced onion
1½ to 2 teaspoons salt
1 bay leaf
2 medium carrots, diced
1 medium stalk celery, minced
1 pound mushrooms, chopped
4 cups water
6 tablespoons dry white wine (optional)
1 tablespoon fresh lemon juice
3 tablespoons minced fresh dill or 1 tablespoon dried dill
½ cup minced fresh fennel (optional)
2 large cloves garlic, minced
Fresh black pepper

Optional toppings: Sour cream or yogurt, toasted sunflower seeds,
minced fresh parsley, and chives.

1. Place the barley and 1½ cups of the water in a small saucepan. Bring
   to a boil, cover, and lower the heat to a simmer. Cook about 30 to 40
   minutes—until tender.

2. Melt the butter or heat the oil in a soup pot or Dutch oven. Add the
   onion, salt, and bay leaf, and cook over medium heat until the onion
   begins to soften (5 to 8 minutes).

3. Add the carrots, celery, and mushrooms, and cook over medium heat,

stirring occasionally for about 10 minutes. Add the remaining 4 cups water, the optional wine, lemon juice, and cooked barley. Lower the heat to a quiet simmer. Cover, and let it bubble peacefully for about 30 minutes. The soup will thicken, and you might want to add more water.

4. Shortly before serving, stir in the dill, fennel, garlic, and black pepper. Taste to adjust the seasonings. Serve hot, with all, some, or none of the optional toppings.

— *Mollie Katzen,* The New Enchanted Broccoli Forest

. . . .

SALMON, CUCUMBER, AND DILL SALAD SERVES 4

This very summery dish is light and refreshing. The dill complements the rich taste of salmon beautifully. And it can be made in just 15 minutes from start to finish.

1 large cucumber, peeled, cut in half lengthwise, seeds scooped out, diced in ½-inch cubes (3 cups)
1 large ripe fresh tomato, seeds and excess pulp removed, diced
1 medium-sized ripe but firm avocado, diced into ½-inch cubes
2 tablespoons chopped chives
3 medium cloves garlic, pressed
1½ tablespoons chopped fresh dill
2 tablespoons plus 1 tablespoon fresh lemon juice
1 tablespoon extra-virgin olive oil
Salt and cracked black pepper
1½ pounds salmon fillet, cut into 4 pieces, skin and bones removed
½ tablespoon honey
1 tablespoon Dijon mustard

1. Mix together the cucumber, tomato, avocado, chives, garlic, and dill in a bowl and set aside.

2. Whisk together the 2 tablespoons lemon juice, olive oil, salt, and pepper in a separate bowl. Toss with the cucumber mix when you are ready to serve.

3. Preheat a stainless steel skillet over medium-high heat for 2 minutes. Rub salmon with the remaining 1 tablespoon of lemon juice and season with salt and pepper. Place in a hot pan bottom-side-up. Cook for 2 minutes.

4. While the salmon is cooking, mix together the honey and mustard. Turn the salmon and spread the honey mustard over the top of the fish. Continue to cook for another 2 minutes, depending on how thick the salmon is (it should still be pink on the inside). Season with pepper.

5. Divide the cucumber mixture between 4 plates and serve with the salmon.

— *www.whfoods.com*

fields are chosen to be as high as possible, perched at the edge of steep slopes into the valley below. Such sites have the warmest sun exposure and dry out quickly in the breeze after rains or morning dew.

They are ideal for crops like tomatoes and winter squash, which need heat to develop full flavor, and which would otherwise develop foliar diseases in the moist valley. Increasingly, we are growing late-fall crops such as broccoli and cauliflower on the ridge tops as well, because they are the very last fields to get killing freezes in early November.

Soils on the ridge fields tend to be heavy clays, which store moisture well and limit the need for irrigation.

3. Twenty-seven acres of prime floodplain land in the Root River basin, a broad valley just west of Rushford. Here we have found a black sandy loam soil and warm dry microclimate that (with irrigation) is ideal for a range of summer crops, including potatoes, zucchini, and most importantly, cantaloupes and watermelons.

One of the core principles of organic farming (and sound agriculture in general) is crop rotation. Groups of vegetable crops are moved year to year, season to season, from one field to the next, alternating with soil-building crops known as green manures. Another purpose of crop rotation is to prevent the buildup of soil-borne diseases and insect pests.

At Featherstone, having farmland in such geographically distinct sites (in some cases miles apart) allows us the luxury of a full rotation of vegetables in microclimates where they are most likely to thrive.

CREAMY DILL DRESSING

MAKES 1½ CUPS

This creamy dressing has no added oil; it is made with silken tofu.

1 (10½-ounce) package of firm silken tofu
1½ teaspoons garlic powder or granules
½ teaspoon dill weed
½ teaspoon salt
2 tablespoons water
1½ tablespoons lemon juice
1 tablespoon seasoned rice vinegar

Combine all of the ingredients in a food processor or blender, and blend until completely smooth. Store any extra dressing in an airtight container in the refrigerator.

— *Amanda Formaro,* The Chamomile Times and Herbal News

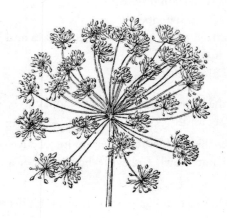

Eggplant

SOLANUM MELONGENA

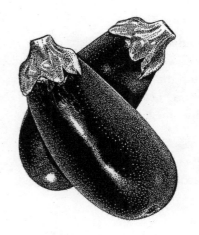

Eggplants are a curiosity, since they are neither much like a vegetable nor meat, but are blessed with the personality traits of both. They also have a popularity complex, since they are either much loved or frequently shunned. Part of this may have been because they are a member of the Solanaceae family, which includes such common vegetables as the potato, tomato, and pepper, but also the infamous deadly nightshade. This kinship has caused many to believe for centuries that eggplants and tomatoes were both poisonous.

Happily, eggplants are not, and they are much beloved in Asia and the Middle East, where they are a staple in those cuisines. Although their American name (they are called aubergines in Europe) comes from the fact that some varieties resemble the chicken's rounded ovum, Asian eggplants are slender and elongated, perfect for slicing into stir-fries. Modern hybrids come in different colors as well, with some beautiful green, pure white, and delightfully speckled varieties.

A versatile vegetable, eggplant can be baked, sautéed, grilled, broiled, steamed, or braised in a sauce. They also adapt beautifully to roasting. One rule of thumb about this vegetable is that it should never be undercooked; a tough eggplant is an unappetizing eggplant.

HISTORY

India is the eggplant's ancient homeland, where it is believed to have been cultivated over 4,000 years ago. Despite its modern-day association with Mediterranean cuisine, eggplants' trek to southern Europe was a slow journey, and the vegetable always seemed to be more popular in the Middle East. (The Turks claim they know a thousand ways to prepare it.) The French blamed eggplant for causing epileptic seizures, but southern Italians adored it. Eggplant found favor with Thomas Jefferson, who had it grown in his gardens at Monticello, Virginia.

NUTRITION

Eggplants contain modest nutrition, mostly in the form of dietary fiber, potassium, manganese, copper, and some B vitamins. Recent research has revealed that eggplant skins contain a potent antioxident, as well as phenolic compounds that possess anticancer and antiviral properties.

SELECTION

Choose eggplants that are uniformly firm and heavy for their size. Avoid lightweights that have soft spots, signs of shriveling, or brown patches on their skins. Smaller eggplants are generally much sweeter and less bitter than overly large ones.

STORAGE

Refrigerate eggplants in a perforated plastic bag in the refrigerator vegetable crisper. They do not keep well and should be used within a few days.

TRIMMING & CLEANING

Thoroughly wash the outside of eggplants before slicing, then trim off the stem end. The skins are edible but they may be tough on older, larger specimens or white eggplants. You may peel the skins before cutting, or, if you are baking the eggplant, scoop the flesh out of the shell after cooking.

Some people feel that salting and rinsing eggplant slices prior to cooking removes bitterness and makes them more tender. The effectiveness of this method is debatable in some circles, and it generally applies only to larger, older fruits. Slice eggplants into ½-inch-thick rounds, sprinkle with salt, and let the slices sit in a colander in the sink for 30 minutes to "sweat." Before cooking, rinse the slices briefly under running water to remove the salt.

STEAMING & BOILING

Whole eggplants can be steamed for 15 to 20 minutes; slices or cubes should be steamed only 4 to 8 minutes, or until meltingly tender. Boiling eggplant results in a more watery vegetable, so steaming is preferable. Nevertheless this method can yield tasty results if garlic, tea, or other herbs and seasonings are added to the cooking water, as the eggplant will absorb these flavors. Boil 1-inch cubes on medium heat for 8 to 10 minutes.

STIR-FRYING & SAUTÉING

Eggplants have an insatiable thirst for oil, which their porous flesh soaks up like a sponge. This should be taken into account when cooking. If you keep adding more oil, the eggplant will get more greasy. Sauté or stir-fry cubed eggplant in a well-oiled pan over high heat for 7 to 10 minutes, or until tender. Take care the eggplant doesn't burn, and stir often to keep the heat distributed, or the vegetable may come out unevenly cooked.

BAKING & ROASTING

Eggplants respond very well to baking in the oven. To bake whole, pierce an eggplant several times with a fork to allow steam to escape, then bake at 350°F for 15 to 25 minutes, depending on its size. Test for doneness by inserting a knife or fork, which should pass through easily.

BRAISING & STEWING

Because eggplants readily absorb the flavors of whatever food or sauces they come into contact with, they can be excellent braised in a highly flavored sauce, heated to boiling for a few minutes, then allowed to cook on decreased heat for 12 to 15 minutes, or until tender. Eggplants can also be stewed, either on their own with savory seasonings or in combination with other vegetables, in a little butter or oil on medium-low heat for about 30 minutes.

MICROWAVING

Placed cubed or whole eggplant (pierced with a folk) in a microwave-safe dish, add 2 tablespoons water, cover, and cook on High power, rotating every 2 minutes.

- 1 pound, cubed = 6 to 8 minutes
- Whole 1-pound eggplant = 4 to 7 minutes for scooping out flesh, 8 to 9 minutes for puréeing

BLANCHING & FREEZING

Eggplants can be frozen if blanched first. Peel them first if desired, then slice them into ⅓-inch-thick rounds or cubes. Bring a pot of water with to a rapid boil, add ½ cup of lemon juice to the water, add the eggplant, cover, and boil for 4 minutes. Then plunge the eggplant quickly into ice water to stop the cooking process, drain, and pack in zipper-lock freezer or vacuum food sealer-type bags, or freezer containers. Squeeze out excess air and leave ½ inch of headspace (unless you are using the vacuum sealing method).

If you are preparing slices for frying, pack with sheets of wax paper or freezer wrap between the drained slices. Frozen eggplant will keep up to 9 months or 1 year, depending on the coldness of the freezer.

MEASURES & EQUIVALENTS

- 1 medium eggplant = about 1 pound = 4 to 6 servings
- 1 pound eggplant = 3 to 4 cups diced = 1½ cups cooked
- 1 serving = ⅓ pound as a side dish
- 1 serving = ½ to ¾ pound as a main dish
- 6 cups raw cubed flesh = 3 cups cooked = 2 cups puréed
- 1½ pounds raw = 2 to 2¼ cups mashed or puréed

COMPLEMENTARY HERBS, SEASONINGS & FOODS

Aïoli, anchovies, bacon, balsamic vinegar, basil, béchamel sauce, breadcrumbs, capers, cream, cumin, garlic, goat cheese, Gruyére cheese, ham, lamb, lemon, mint, mozzarella cheese, mushrooms, olive oil, olives, onions, oregano, Parmesan cheese, parsley, peppers, pesto, pine nuts, rice, ricotta cheese, rosemary, shallots, thyme, tomatoes, walnuts, yogurt, zucchini.

SERVING SUGGESTIONS

- Here's a salty, savory, simple dish: Heat a preferred oil in a saucepan until hot (peanut or vegetable are good choices). Add eggplant that has been cut into 1-inch chunks and brown them on each side. Then add garlic, shallots, and tamari or soy sauce. Top with chopped scallions and serve hot or cold.
- Because of their substantial, rich texture, eggplants have been used as a meat substitute for centuries. Try using grilled, seasoned slices in sandwiches, lasagna, and casseroles.
- Grill or broil eggplant slices and use them in combination with mushrooms in sandwiches or other dishes.
- Top a pizza with strips of eggplant, sweet red peppers, and ripe tomatoes.
- Eggplants stuffed with shellfish (such as shrimp, crab, and lobster) and combined with a cream sauce make a delicious, filling meal, rounded out with a green or tomato salad and good crusty bread.
- For a twist on a traditional dish, mash and whip eggplants the same way you prepare mashed potatoes.
- Baba ghanoush, that traditional Middle Eastern preparation of puréed, roasted eggplant, makes a delicious dip or sandwich filling. Combine the

"The smell of manure, of sun on foliage, of evaporating water, rose to my head; two steps farther, and I could look down into the vegetable garden enclosed within its tall pale of reeds—rich chocolate earth studded emerald green, frothed with the white of cauliflowers, jeweled with the purple globes of eggplant and the scarlet wealth of tomatoes."

— *Doris Lessing,*
British writer

eggplant with garlic, tahini, lemon juice, sea salt, and olive oil.

- Add tender eggplant cubes to an Indian curry or Asian stir-fry.
- Hollow out eggplant "shells," stuff them with ground meat and spices, and bake them in the oven.
- Create a delicious, hearty, vegetarian spaghetti sauce by steaming eggplant slices until tender; sautéing garlic, onion, and Italian-style stewed tomatoes; combining the eggplant with the tomato mixture and adding chopped fresh basil; and simmering on low heat for 20 minutes.

....

RATATOUILLE NIÇOISE

SERVES 4

In this recipe, quantities depend on what you have, and varying the proportions doesn't matter—it is great no matter what!

1 onion, chopped
2 tablespoons olive oil
3 cloves garlic, chopped
1 eggplant, cut into thin slices, each slice quartered
1 medium zucchini, sliced
1 large tomato, chopped
1 green bell pepper, chopped
Salt and pepper
Handful of fresh basil, chopped

1. Sauté the onion in the olive oil until it turns translucent. Add the chopped garlic and sauté briefly. Add the eggplant, then the zucchini and tomato, and finally the green bell pepper, along with some salt, pepper, and basil. Simmer as long as you like.

2. Serve with crusty bread. You can also put some ratatouille in the bottom of a baking pan, make indentations in the vegetables, and then crack an egg into each indentation. This is then baked in a 350°F oven for about 15 minutes, or until the egg is cooked to your taste. Then you grate cheese over all of this—the benefits of the veggies far outweigh the fat in the cheese!

— *Margaret Houston, Featherstone Farm CSA member*

....

ROASTED EGGPLANT SALAD WITH BEANS AND CASHEWS

SERVES 6

2 eggplants, diced into 1-inch cubes
3 tablespoons olive oil
1 teaspoon coarse salt
½ pound green beans, cut into 1-inch pieces
3 tablespoons fresh lime juice
2 tablespoons vegetable oil
1 teaspoon curry powder

When I was fourteen, my aunt (a French professor at the University of Saskatchewan) took me to France for a month. We crossed the English Channel on a ferry and I was a bit queasy by the time we landed., and not very interested in food.

Until, that is, we sat down in a little café, and a perfect omelet, speckled brown on the outside and slightly runny with fresh herbs on the inside, was placed in front of me on a heavy white plate with a basket of the crispy-crusted, soft-centered slices of baguette.

That was a turning point in my life, and I fell in love with French food. My aunt had to attend a conference in Caen, in Normandy, and I was free to roam around all day until she was done. But one daily responsibility involved getting to the market and buying ripe, scarlet tomatoes, soft local cheeses, bread, and fruit for lunch. I loved the market. I had never before seen open-air stalls selling small amounts of such beautiful produce. And everyone was so friendly, helping me use my high school French to ask for what I wanted.

Two other food experiences stand out from that trip: jam and ratatouille. Our tiny hotel, which hung out over a very noisy and nar-

¼ teaspoon ground pepper
½ cup roasted cashews, chopped
½ cup fresh cilantro, chopped

1. Preheat the oven to 475°F.

2. Toss the eggplant in olive oil and ½ teaspoon of the coarse salt. Place the eggplant in a single layer on a cookie sheet in the oven for 25 to 30 minutes or until it becomes golden brown.

3. Cook the beans in a large saucepan of boiling salted water until they become crisp-tender, about 2 minutes. Drain. Transfer them to a bowl of ice water to stop the cooking process. Drain, and pat dry with paper towels.

4. In a large bowl, whisk together the lime juice, vegetable oil, curry powder, the remaining salt, and pepper. Toss the eggplant, beans, cashews, and cilantro with the dressing and serve immediately.

— *Featherstone Farm*

KHAJI NAMUL
(EGGPLANT SALAD WITH SESAME SEEDS)   SERVES 4 TO 6

Considered both a salad and an appetizer, this Korean dish is generally served at the start of a meal but stays on the table until the very end. It also goes well with cold lamb and chicken. The ideal eggplants for this recipe are the slim, long, Asian variety; if you cannot get them, use the smallest globe eggplants you can find.

1¼ pounds eggplants, preferably Asian
2 cloves garlic, peeled and crushed
1 scallion, cut into very thin rings all of the way up its green section
2 tablespoons roasted, lightly crushed sesame seeds
1 tablespoon sesame oil
3 tablespoons Japanese light soy sauce
2 tablespoons distilled white vinegar
¼ teaspoon salt
1 tablespoon sugar

1. If you are using Asian eggplants, quarter them lengthwise and then cut each piece crossways into half. If you are using regular globe eggplants, cut them into long sections that are about 1 inch thick and wide.

2. Steam covered for about 15 minutes or until tender. Let the pieces cool slightly, then pull them by hand into thin, long strips.

3. Add all of the other ingredients and mix well. Taste and make adjustments, if needed. Serve at room temperature or cold.

— *Madhur Jaffrey*, A Taste of the Far East

row street, served perfect apricot and plum jams for breakfast in our tiny little hotel, with more of that wonderful bread (nothing like the soft-crusted stuff we got at home) and fresh butter.

After the conference was over, we went to Provence, where we stayed with a college exchange student my aunt knew. Now that I think about it, this girl was probably a little apprehensive about a visit from a college professor and her teenage niece, but she was charming and hospitable, even if she did not know much about cooking.

She did know how to make ratatouille, though. We went out to the market and chose the perfect aubergines, as eggplants are called in France. (I had never even seen an eggplant. What were we going to do with this thing?!)

We also purchased peppers, courgettes (zucchini, which were also exotic to me at that time), luscious tomatoes, and onions. The onions were sliced and gently sautéed with chopped garlic, then the eggplant followed by the zucchini and tomatoes, and finally the peppers, along with some salt and pepper and herbs.

I did not like it. What was worse, it appeared again the next day. "We always make this on a ski trip, and it tastes better the next day," said Colette. I didn't buy it.

Since then, somehow, I learned to love ratatouille! I have tried a lot of different foods in different countries—but if there is a market where I am visiting, I am sure to attend.

Books

Mediterranean Vegetables:
A Cook's ABC of Vegetables and Their
Preparation in Spain, France, Italy,
Greece, Turkey, the Middle East, and
North Africa, with More than 200
Authentic Recipes for the Home Cook
Clifford A. Wright;
The Harvard Common Press, 2001.

The Eggplant Cookbook:
Classic and Contemporary Recipes
for Today's Healthy Diet
Rosemary Moon; Book Sales, 1998.

Essentially Eggplant
Nina Kehayan; Fisher Books, 1996.

Essentials of Classic Italian Cooking
Marcella Hazan; Knopf, 1992.

A Taste of the Far East
Madhur Jaffrey; BBC Books, 1993.

MIDI-POCHE (EGGPLANT BAKE) SERVES 4

This dish is a staple in Provence, served up at least once a week for dinner, supper, and sometimes next morning's breakfast as well. It is good both cold and hot.

2 small eggplants (about ¾ pound total), sliced
2 tablespoons lemon juice
1 tablespoon plus ½ teaspoon salt
4 tablespoons (½ stick) unsalted butter
2 tablespoons olive oil
1 shallot, minced
1 small onion, finely chopped
1 clove garlic, minced
3 cups chopped, seeded tomatoes (about 2 pounds)
Pinch of sugar
½ teaspoon chopped fresh thyme, or a pinch of dried thyme
1 tablespoon minced fresh basil, or 1½ teaspoons dried basil
1 teaspoon crushed allspice
¼ cup all-purpose flour
1 cup cooked rice
¼ cup freshly grated Parmesan cheese

1. Place the sliced eggplant in a colander. Sprinkle it with the lemon juice and 1 tablespoon salt; let stand 30 minutes to "sweat" and drain.

2. Meanwhile, heat 2 tablespoons of the butter with 1 tablespoon of the oil in a medium-sized saucepan over medium heat. Add the shallot and onion; cook 2 minutes. Stir in the garlic; cook 1 minute longer. Add the tomatoes; sprinkle with sugar. Add the thyme, basil, allspice, and ½ teaspoon salt. Cook, uncovered, over medium-low heat 20 minutes. Set aside.

3. Preheat the oven to 350°F.

4. Brush the eggplant with paper towels to remove the salt; pat dry. Dust the eggplant slices lightly with the flour. Heat the remaining butter and oil in a heavy-bottomed skillet and sauté the eggplant over medium heat until golden on both sides. Drain on paper towels.

5. Spoon ¼ of the tomato sauce over the bottom of an ovenproof baking dish or casserole. Layer half of the eggplant over the sauce. Sprinkle the eggplant with half of the rice and then spoon half of the remaining tomato sauce over the rice. Top with half of the grated cheese. Repeat the layers of eggplant, rice, tomato sauce, and cheese.

6. Bake until bubbly, about 15 to 20 minutes. Serve hot or at room temperature.

— *Bert Greene,* Greene on Greens

GRILLED EGGPLANT QUESADILLAS

SERVES 8

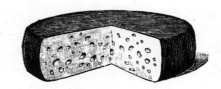

You can obtain the Dorothy Soils Gourmet Foods basil canola oil at www.dorothysoils.com.

2 large eggplants, grilled (recipe below)
1½ cups red wine vinaigrette
8 ounces low-fat shredded Monterey jack cheese
1 bunch fresh basil, chopped
2 to 3 tomatoes
2 cups sliced roasted peppers
4 (12-inch) tortillas
Dorothy Soils Gourmet Foods Basil Canola Oil

FOR THE GRILLED EGGPLANT

Slice the eggplant into ½-inch slices. Brush the slices with red wine vinaigrette. Grill the eggplant over hot coals, basting occasionally with more vinaigrette until the slices turn very soft. Cover the eggplant until ready to use.

FOR THE QUESADILLAS

1. If you plan to use an oven rather than a griddle to cook the tortillas, preheat the oven to 400°F.

2. Layer the cheese, basil, eggplant, tomatoes, and peppers inside the tortillas. Fold the tortillas in half. Brush the outside of the tortillas with basil canola oil.

3. Bake the tortillas or cook them on a hot griddle until their centers are hot and their exteriors are brown and crisp. While the tortillas are still hot, brush the quesadillas with a bit more basil canola oil.

— *Marc Casale of Dos Coyotes Border Cafe, Davis Farmers Market*

....

BABA GHANOUSH (EGGPLANT DIP)

SERVES 8

2 large eggplants (1¼ pounds)
2 level tablespoons tahini
4 cloves garlic, peeled and crushed with salt
½ cup onion, diced
1 cup tomato, chopped
3 tablespoons fresh lemon juice, or more to taste
3 to 4 tablespoons cold water
¼ teaspoon salt
Dash of freshly ground black pepper
1 teaspoon olive oil

1. Pierce the eggplants in several places with a toothpick. If you are cooking indoors, wrap the whole eggplant in aluminum foil and place it over a gas stove or indoor grill to cook on all sides until it collapses

and begins to release steam. If you are cooking outdoors over coals, grill the eggplant until it is blackened, collapsed, and cooked through.

2. Dump the grilled eggplant into a basin of cold water; peel it while it is still hot, and allow it to drain in a colander until cool. Squeeze the pulp to remove any bitter juices. Mash the eggplant to a purée.

3. In a food processor, mix the tahini with the garlic, onion, tomato, and lemon juice until the mixture contracts. Thin with water. With the machine still running, add the eggplant, salt, pepper, and oil.

4. Spread the mixture evenly throughout a shallow dish and garnish with pepper, parsley, and tomatoes.

— *Fruits and Veggies—More Matters; Centers for Disease Control & Prevention*

EGGPLANT, TOMATO, AND RED POTATO CASSEROLE

SERVES 8 TO 10

This is hearty for a vegetarian dish and even satisfies folks who usually prefer meat dishes.

1 large eggplant, cut into ½-inch cubes
4 to 5 medium-sized red potatoes, cut into 1-inch cubes
1 cup cooked garbanzo beans, or 1 (8-ounce) can, drained and
    well-rinsed
¼ cup olive oil
1 large onion, sliced into medium pieces
1 medium-sized garlic head, cloves quartered
1 red bell pepper, sliced into small pieces
10 to 15 cremini mushrooms, thickly sliced
5 medium-sized tomatoes, diced, or 1 (16-ounce) can diced tomatoes
Oregano, fresh or dried
Basil, fresh or dried

1. Preheat the oven to 350°F.

2. Slice all of the ingredients in advance, preparing the eggplant and mushrooms last to prevent discoloration.

3. Place the eggplant, potatoes, and garbanzo beans in a large casserole dish.

4. Heat the olive oil in a large skillet and sauté the onion, adding the garlic, bell pepper, and mushrooms when the onions have almost turned translucent. Do not brown. Add the tomatoes and sauté just until they are heated through. Add generous amounts of oregano and basil.

5. Pour the skillet ingredients over the casserole ingredients and mix them all together. Cover the casserole and bake for 45 minutes.

— *Nelda Danz*

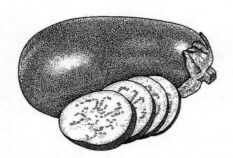

Honeydew Melon

CUCUMIS MELO,
INODORUS GROUP

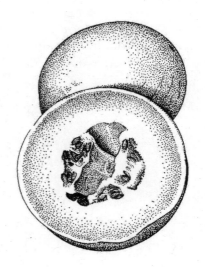

This alabaster, smooth-skinned beauty is a close cousin of the crenshaw, casaba, Persian, and winter melon, and is considered the sweetest of all melons. Honeydews can be round or oval and weigh up to 4 to 8 pounds, with sweet, juicy, pale green flesh that can be absolutely scrumptious when ripe. Determining ripeness can be tricky, because unlike muskmelons, the stem does not "slip" or separate cleanly from the fruit. Honeydew maturity is not based on size, but rather on the fruit's skin color (ripe melons are creamy yellow, not greenish white) and sometimes exterior texture (often an extremely subtle, almost undetectable wrinkling of the skin is perceptible).

HISTORY

Like its other melon cousins, honeydews or their forerunners probably originated in Persia (now modern-day Iran). Confusion reigns in melon history, and the name has frequently referred to multiple types of melons or sometimes even to gourds. It is known that the honeydew was imported to the United States by the French, who call it White Antibes winter melon, around 1900.

NUTRITION

Like many melons, honeydews are mostly water and mildly diuretic. They do contain significant vitamin C, potassium, and folate.

SELECTION

A choice honeydew should be uniformly firm and heavy for its size, and its skin more on the yellow than white side. A ripe honeydew may have a faint, characteristic odor, plus a slight wrinkling on its skin. Avoid melons with cracks, soft spots, or other surface blemishes. Honeydews are sometimes available year-round, but they are at their best from June through October.

STORAGE

Fresh honeydew can be stored for a week or two at room temperature, provided that they are not overripe and have no cracks or blemishes. Cut melons will keep in the refrigerator for up to a few days, but wrap the pieces well or store the melon in tightly sealed containers, as their odor tends to permeate other nearby foods, and vice versa.

TRIMMING & CLEANING

Bacteria sometimes grows on the outside of melons, so washing the skin thoroughly with warm, soapy water is a good idea before slicing into the fruit. Scoop out the seeds and you are ready to enjoy.

BLANCHING & FREEZING

Honeydew and other types of melon can be frozen as-is, but preparing them in a light sugar syrup can enhance their flavor and color. Peel and cut melons into ½- or ¾-inch cubes or balls. To make the syrup, combine 9 cups of water or fruit juice with 2¼ cups of sugar. Combine the sugar and water in a saucepan, and bring to a boil until the sugar dissolves. Chill, then pour ½ cup of syrup into the freezer container, add the melon, and keep adding syrup until the fruit is covered. Leave ½ inch of headspace for pints, 1 inch for quarts.

Or, if you prefer your fruit unsweetened, arrange pieces on a single layer on a cookie sheet and freeze. Either way, transfer the pieces into zipper-lock freezer or vacuum food sealer-type bags, or freezer containers. Squeeze out excess air and leave ½ inch of headspace (unless you are using the vacuum sealing method). Honeydew frozen this way should keep for 8 months to 1 year.

EQUIVALENTS, MEASURES & SERVINGS

- 1 pound = 1 cup cubed

COMPLEMENTARY HERBS, SEASONINGS & FOODS

Berries, Brie and Camembert cheeses, cantaloupes, cilantro, ginger, honey, ice cream, lemon, lime, mint, orange, other melons, pineapple, prosciutto, rum, salami, tequila, watermelon, yogurt.

SERVING SUGGESTIONS

- Wrap thin slices of honeydew with proscuitto, salami, or other high-quality charcuterie meats.
- Cut a honeydew in half, scoop out the seeds, and fill the cavity with berries or other cut fruit. Then drizzle honey, maple syrup, a little lemon or lime juice, or whipped cream over the top, and break out the spoons.
- Dice honeydew and add to your favorite salsa recipe; its sweetness helps balance out an especially fiery salsa.
- Honeydews and other melons make wonderfully refreshing sorbets and sherbets.
- For the ultimate in sophistication, serve thin slices of honeydew with the finest smoked salmon.
- Honeydew pairs well with rustic foods like artisan cheeses, crusty breads, and cured meats. Use it as a palate cleanser between tastings.
- Combine balls or chunks of honeydew with cantaloupe, crenshaw or casaba melons, watermelon, berries, mandarin oranges, pineapple, guava, and kiwi. This can be great fun for kids, especially with "dipping sauces" such as yogurt, honey, or maple syrup.
- Melon wedges can be grown-up, even sophisticated, when dressed up with vanilla ice cream, bits of candied ginger, orange-flavored liqueur, rosewater, or lavender syrup.

RASPBERRY-HONEYDEW PARFAITS   SERVES 4

Raspberries, honeydew melon, and pineapple sherbet are layered in parfait glasses for a refreshing and light meal ending.

1½ cups pineapple sherbet
1½ cups raspberries
¼ cup all-fruit raspberry spread, melted
1 cup honeydew melon, diced

1. Spoon about 2 tablespoons of the sherbet into each of 4 parfait glasses or dessert dishes.

2. In a small bowl, gently mix the raspberries and raspberry spread. Spoon about 3 tablespoons of the raspberry mixture over the sherbet in each glass.

3. Top each with ¼ cup melon, 2 tablespoons sherbet, 3 tablespoons raspberry mixture, and 2 tablespoons more sherbet. Garnish with a favorite cookie, if desired.

— Pillsburys Most Requested Recipes, as appeared on www.fooddownunder.com

HONEYDEW AND CUCUMBER SALAD WITH SESAME

SERVES 4 TO 6

DRESSING

1 tablespoon plus 2 teaspoons rice-wine vinegar
1 tablespoon fresh ginger, peeled and minced
2 teaspoons tamari or soy sauce
1½ teaspoons sugar
1 teaspoon Asian, (toasted) sesame oil, or to taste
¼ teaspoon dried hot red pepper flakes, or to taste
¼ cup vegetable oil

1 seedless cucumber, halved lengthwise and thinly sliced
      (about 2 cups)
2 cups 1-inch cubes of honeydew melon
2 scallions, minced
1 tablespoon sesame seeds, toasted lightly and cooled

1. In a bowl, whisk together the vinegar, ginger, tamari or soy sauce, sugar, sesame oil, red pepper flakes, and the vegetable oil until the dressing is well-combined.

2. Add the cucumber, melon, and scallions. Toss the salad until it is well-combined. Sprinkle with sesame seeds.

— Pillsbury Most Requested Recipes, as appeared at www.fooddownunder.com

ICED HONEYDEW AND
GEWÜRZTRAMINER SOUP

SERVES 6

The Honeydew Diet
Honeydew melon is supposedly one of the few foods that has a negative calorie value; that is, one expends more calories to eat and digest it than the melon actually contains.

1 honeydew melon
1 tablespoon chopped fresh mint
1 cup Gewürztraminer white wine
6 tablespoons low-fat peach yogurt

1. Cut the honeydew in half, then into quarters and cut away the rind. Cut the honeydew into cubes (you will need about 7 cups).

2. Purée the honeydew in a blender until smooth, working in batches if necessary. Pour the purée into a bowl. Stir in the mint and wine.

3. Divide the soup among 6 chilled bowls and top with a dollop of yogurt. Serve the soup by placing the bowls onto plates lined with crushed ice, setting the bowls into the ice.

— *www.fooddownunder.com*

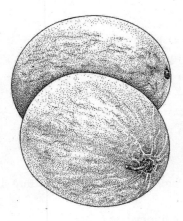

Lemongrass

CYMBOPOGON CITRATUS OR C. FLEXUOSUS

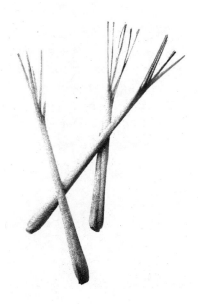

Until the U.S. interest in ethnic cuisines exploded about a decade ago, lemongrass was little known outside of its home countries in Southeast Asia, Africa, and the Caribbean. The plant is a type of perennial grass related to citronella, grown for its aromatic, citrusy flavor that adds a refreshing touch to teas, soups, marinades, curries, meats, vegetables, desserts, and beverages. Its essential oils (including citral, its main aromatic compound) are also widely used in perfumes, soaps, and cosmetics, often substituting for more expensive oils like lemon verbena or lemon balm. Lemongrass is extensively used in aromatherapy, and is also valued as an insect repellent.

The edible portion of the plant is its stalk, which is extremely tough and fibrous. To render its lemony pulp and fragrant oils, the stalk must be thoroughly crushed or bruised. Cooked pieces, unless very finely chopped or crushed to a pulp, are too fibrous to eat and should be removed before serving.

HISTORY

Cymbopogon citratus, or West-Indian lemongrass, is a tropical plant assumed to be native to Malaysia. East-Indian lemongrass, or *C. flexuosus,* is native to India and Sri Lanka. Both species are used interchangeably, but *C. citratus* is considered culinarily superior, valued as food, medicine, perfume, and antiseptic for centuries.

NUTRITION

Lemongrass is not usually consumed in enough quantity to be nutritionally significantly, but this versatile plant is nonetheless valued for many uses. Traditional Indian auryvedic medicine has long employed lemongrass in treating infection and fevers. Its essential oil contains antibacterial and antiviral qualities that rival many antibiotics. In aromatherapy, the stimulating yet soothing scent of lemongrass is used to treat depression.

SELECTION

Lemongrass should have plump bases and green, fresh-looking leaves. Avoid specimens that are brown, discolored, or dried-out. If you happen to find a stalk with roots attached, you can place it in water and grow it into a plant.

STORAGE

Lemongrass stalks will keep for up to 2 weeks individually wrapped in plastic wrap or aluminum foil in the refrigerator.

TRIMMING & CLEANING

Lemongrass requires some preparation to release its lemony scent and flavor. If you are using it fresh, remove the tough outer leaves until you reach the more tender inner core, and cut off the bottom root end. Diagonally slice the bulbous stalk into ¼-inch rings if you will serve it in well-cooked dishes; otherwise, you can slice long strips if you plan to just infuse your food with its oils—just be sure to remove these tough pieces before serving. If you plan to mince lemongrass, use only the bottom 4 inches of the stalk. To release its fragrant, flavorful oils, bruise the peeled stalks with the side of a cleaver or knife, mortar and pestle, or rolling pin.

BLANCHING AND FREEZING

Lemongrass does freeze well, with no need for blanching first. You can either freeze the stalks whole (freezing also softens the tough fibers a bit, making them easier to slice and chop), or just prepare them as you would normally for cooking, finely chopping the stalks first. Then pack them in zipper-lock freezer or vacuum food sealer-type bags, squeezing out excess air. Lemongrass will keep in the freezer for up to 5 months.

DRYING

Dried lemongrass lacks the full potency of the fresh herb, but it is acceptable when fresh or frozen alternatives are unavailable. You can air-dry it by hanging bunches in a well-ventilated, dark place for a few weeks. Or place the stalks on a screen and store them in a dark, airy area for several days, then finish them in a 120°F oven for a few minutes. The herb is dry when the stems crumble easily. It should then be stored in an airtight container away from light and heat.

When you are ready to use it, reconstitute dried lemongrass in a little warm water or simmered liquid first to release its oils. Be aware that the dried product usually cannot be softened enough to chew and should be strained out before serving in a finished dish.

COMPLEMENTARY HERBS, SEASONINGS & FOODS

Broccoli, butter, chiles, cilantro, coconut milk, cucumbers, fennel, garlic, geraniums, ginger, green tea, honey, kaffir lime leaves, lavender, limes, melon, orange juice, peaches, pears, pineapple, rosemary, seafood.

SERVING SUGGESTIONS

- If you are making ice cream, add a lemongrass simple syrup: Boil a cup of water with minced lemongrass, add the sugar required for the ice cream recipe, and cook to the desired strength. Then cool the mixture and add to the remaining ingredients. This syrup is especially good for poaching pears or peaches.
- Crush lemongrass into a glass of homemade lemonade.
- Add small pieces or pound stalks to a pulp for stir-fries.
- Use lemongrass to add flavor and life to marinades, clear soups, and sauces.
- Lemongrass-infused butter (using the most tender parts ground with a mortar and pestle and blended with butter) makes a perfect complement to lightly steamed broccoli or young, tender peas.
- Lemongrass tea is a relaxing, calming beverage: bruise a 2-inch section of the stalk and drop it into a pot of steeping tea.
- As an antidote to colds and flu, infuse clear chicken broth or a light chicken soup with plenty of garlic, ginger, hot peppers, and lemongrass.
- Lemongrass provides the delicate flavor of lemon without the sourness and bite of the citrus fruit; add finely chopped stalks or pulp to seafood dishes.
- For a surprising twist, add a tablespoon or two of finely mashed lemongrass to your favorite salsa recipe.

CHICKEN COCONUT SOUP WITH LEMONGRASS

SERVES 4 TO 6

Also known as Tom Kha Gai, this is one of the most requested dishes in Thai restaurants. This recipe uses two ingredients that are flavoring staples in Southeast Asian cuisine. Kaffir lime leaves are widely used in Thai cooking, imparting a haunting lime-lemony scent to soups, curries, and salads. And few Southeast Asian savory dishes lack fish sauce, a ubiquitous condiment derived from fermented fish that adds saltiness and piquancy.

Although they were considered exotic years ago, thanks to well-stocked supermarkets, gourmet shops, and a booming interest in ethnic cuisines, you can find these ingredients and more. A visit to an Asian neighborhood market in your city will yield an even grander selection of choices.

4 cups chicken stock
4 slices peeled fresh ginger
1 large lemongrass stalk, cut into 2-inch pieces and crushed
    (or 1 teaspoon fresh lemon zest)
16 fresh kaffir lime leaves or the grated zest of 1 large lime
2 (14-ounce) cans unsweetened coconut milk
¼ cup lime or lemon juice, freshly squeezed
2 to 3 tablespoons fish sauce
2 tablespoons light brown sugar
1 tablespoon red chili paste
1 pound boneless, skinless chicken breasts, cut into bite-sized pieces
½ pound fresh white mushrooms, thinly sliced
5 small fresh green or red chiles, sliced crosswise, paper-thin
Fresh cilantro leaves

1. In a large saucepan, combine the stock, ginger, lemongrass, and kaffir lime leaves or lime zest. Place over medium heat and slowly bring to a boil. Boil for 1 minute.

2. Decrease the heat to low, and add the coconut milk. Stir to combine, and bring to a simmer. Add the lime or lemon juice, fish sauce, brown sugar, and chili paste. Mix well and simmer for 5 minutes. Add the chicken pieces and simmer until tender, 4 to 5 minutes. Then add the mushrooms and simmer until tender, about 1 minute.

3. To serve, ladle the soup into warmed bowls. Float the chile slices and cilantro leaves on top.

— *www.fooddownunder.com*

RICE WITH LEMONGRASS AND GREEN ONION

SERVES 4

2 tablespoons vegetable oil
⅔ cup finely chopped onion
¼ teaspoon turmeric

Maybe Hospitals Should Use It

Lemongrass is more effective in treating staphylococcus infection than either penicillin or streptomycin antibiotics.

1 cup long-grain white rice, uncooked
1¾ cups water
2 (12-inch) lemongrass stalks, cut into 2-inch-long pieces
½ teaspoon salt
1 large green onion, chopped

1. Heat 1½ tablespoons of the oil in a medium-sized, heavy-bottomed saucepan over medium heat. Add the ⅔ cup onion and turmeric and sauté 5 minutes. Mix in the rice. Add the water, lemongrass, and salt, and bring to a simmer. Cover, decrease the heat to medium-low, and simmer until the rice is tender and the liquid is absorbed, about 18 minutes. Remove from the heat; let stand, covered, about 10 minutes. Discard the lemongrass.

2. Heat the remaining ½ tablespoon oil in a large, heavy-bottomed skillet over medium heat. Add the green onion and sauté 1 minute. Add the rice and stir until heated through. Season to taste with salt.

— Bon Appétit, *June 1992, as appeared at www.cooksrecipes.com*

MAINE LOBSTER CHOWDER WITH COCONUT, CORN, AND LEMONGRASS   SERVES 8

Galangal is a spicy root that resembles ginger and lends a pungent flavor to many Southeast Asian dishes. You can find it fresh or frozen in Asian markets or through online merchants.

2 tablespoons vegetable oil
4 ounces shallot, thinly sliced
6 cloves garlic, sliced
2 tablespoons lemongrass, minced
2 teaspoons red chile flakes, dried
½ teaspoon chili paste, ground
1-inch piece frozen or fresh galangal or ginger, thinly sliced
4 cups lobster stock
2 cups chicken stock
4 cups coconut milk, unsweetened
2 kaffir lime leaves, center rib removed, crushed (or zest of 1 lime)
4 tablespoons fish sauce
2 teaspoons granulated sugar
1 pound Maine lobster tail meat, cooked and cut into ¾-inch dice
2 cups sweet corn, blanched on the cob and kernels cut off
½ cup enoki mushrooms
1 cup cherry tomatoes, halved
2 tablespoons lime juice
Maine lobster claw meat, cooked whole and shelled, for garnish
12 cilantro sprigs, for garnish
12 Thai basil leaves, halved, for garnish
4 tablespoons fried shallots, for garnish

1. Heat the oil in a saucepan over medium heat until moderately hot. Add the shallot, garlic, lemongrass, chile flakes, and chili paste, and brown slightly, about 30 seconds.

2. Working quickly and without burning the spices, add the galangal, lobster stock, chicken stock, coconut milk, and kaffir lime leaves. Bring to a boil and let simmer for 5 minutes so the flavors can meld.

3. Adjust the seasoning with the fish sauce and sugar, and then add the lobster tail meat. Bring to a simmer and let the lobster heat through.

4. Add the corn and mushrooms. As soon as the mixture comes to a second boil, turn off the heat and add the tomatoes and lime juice.

5. Garnish with the lobster claws, cilantro, Thai basil leaves, and fried shallots. Serve immediately.

— Recipe provided courtesy of the Maine Lobster Promotion Council, as appeared on Cookrecipes.com

. . . .

Iced Green Tea with Lemongrass and Ginger

MAKES 4 CUPS

1 stalk fresh lemongrass
1 (1-inch) piece of peeled ginger, cut into 4 slices
2 green tea bags
¼ cup honey
4 cups boiling water
¼ cup fresh lemon juice
Ice cubes

1. Cut the dry ends off the lemongrass stalk, peel off the stalk's outer layer, and discard. Cut off the top half of the lemongrass stalk and save to use as swizzle sticks, wrapping them in a damp paper towel and refrigerating until needed. Split the remaining end of the lemongrass and cut into 4 pieces, bruising it a bit.

2. Place the ginger, split lemongrass, tea bags, and honey in a heatproof container or bowl. Pour boiling water over them. Let steep and cool to room temperature.

3. Remove the tea bags, and stir in the lemon juice. Chill until ready to serve. Separate the inner layers of the reserved lemongrass stalk into 4 stir sticks. Serve the tea in tall glasses over lots of ice with the lemongrass sticks.

— www.fooddownunder.com

. . . .

Summer Fruit in Wine Dessert

1 stalk lemongrass
1 to 2 tablespoons sugar, honey, or other sweetener

½ cup water

Mixed summer fruits: Melon balls or chunks, strawberries, blueberries, currants, cherries, plums, peaches, apricots, raspberries (plan on about 1 cup of fruit per person)

White wine (Riesling, Gewürztraminer, or Muscat canelli)

Mint or lemon balm sprigs

Edible flowers (nasturtium, pansy, violet, mint, lavender, calendula, borage, rosemary, etc.)

1. Chop the lemongrass and make a simple syrup by boiling the sweetener, lemongrass, and water until the sweetener is dissolved. Remove from heat and let cool and steep for a few hours or overnight.

2. In the meantime, wash and stem, pit, slice, and chop the fruit into bite-sized pieces, and place it in a nonreactive bowl.

3. Strain the lemongrass syrup and combine with enough wine to barely cover the fruit; pour over the fruit. Chill for several hours.

4. This can be served in large wine goblets or clear glass dessert bowls. Or for a fancy presentation, use a melon shell. Garnish with herb sprigs and flowers.

Variation

- Use other fresh herbs such as lemon balm, mint, lemon or regular thyme, sweet woodruff, or rosemary instead of the lemongrass.

— *Melinda McBride*

Mizuna

Mizuna is a relatively new green to American shores, brought by the Japanese, who use it extensively in their casseroles, soups, stir-fries, and as a pickled vegetable, but not as a raw green. Like all mustard greens, mizuna packs a peppery bite and a full-bodied flavor in its delicate-looking, heavily incised leaves, which resemble those of an elaborate dandelion. Young mizuna is zesty in salads and is often used as a beautiful garnish; larger specimens are best cooked. It is often found in mesclun, that European mix of baby salad greens, and it is sometimes known as Japanese mustard, mizu-na, kyona, or California pepper.

HISTORY

Mizuna is thoroughly associated with Japanese cooking, but the plant may have originated in China. Many mustard greens are thought to have grown wild in parts of Asia and India, where they have been eaten for thousands of years.

NUTRITION

As a cruciferous vegetable (a member of the cabbage family), this delicate green pulls its own weight nutritionally, containing folic acid, carotenes, vitamin C, and a number of antioxidants.

SELECTION

Like a dress uniform, mizuna should look fresh and crisp. Pass up slimy, wilted, or discolored leaves. The pepperiness of mizuna varies widely from plant to plant, depending on its growing conditions, so sample a few leaves before purchasing.

STORAGE

Refrigerate fresh mizuna unwashed in a plastic bag in the vegetable crisper for up to 5 days. If the greens are particularly wet, insert a paper towel in the bag to absorb excess moisture and prevent rotting.

TRIMMING & CLEANING

Mizuna should be thoroughly washed before using, preferably by submerging and swishing it in a sinkful of water to remove all impurities and stray insects. The stem ends are often woody and should be trimmed and discarded.

STEAMING & BOILING

Mizuna can be steamed briefly, about 2 to 3 minutes, or until it is just wilted. If you are steaming it in quantity, it may benefit from a slight squeezing and draining to remove excess water. To boil, mizuna should then be plunged into rapidly boiling water, stem-end first, for about 2 minutes, then removed and inserted leaf-end for 30 seconds or up to 1 minute.

STIR-FRYING & SAUTÉING

Mizuna responds to light stir-frying extremely well, maintaining its crisp texture and spicy flavor if added to the wok or sauté pan during the last 1 or 2 minutes of cooking.

MICROWAVING

Place mizuna in a microwave-safe bowl, add a few drops of water, and cover. Microwave on High power for 2 to 3 minutes, or until it is wilted; the greens will steam in their own moisture this way.

BLANCHING & FREEZING

Freezing is not recommended because of mizuna's high water content and delicate texture.

COMPLEMENTARY HERBS, SEASONINGS & FOODS

Almonds, apples, chestnuts, crab, fish, ginger, ham, hot chiles, lemon, lettuce, lobster, peanuts, rice, scallops, sesame, shrimp, soy sauce, spinach, tofu, vinegar, walnuts.

SERVING SUGGESTIONS

- Mizuna's assertive flavor makes it a good addition to mixed salads, combined with milder lettuces and spinach.
- Mizuna adds sophistication, elegance, and surprising flavor to seafood salads. Its zestiness provides a great contrast to milder shellfish, such as scallops and lobster.
- Combine mizuna in a salad with toasted almonds, slivered green apples, and a little grated pecorino or other hard cheese; lightly toss with walnut oil.
- Slice mizuna leaves and add to stir-fries during the final minutes of cooking.
- Add mizuna leaves to freshly made miso soup or dashi broth.
- Mizuna's highly decorative appearance and surprising durability makes it a great garnish. Use larger leaves as a bed for meats, seafood, and poultry.
- Substitute a few leaves of mizuna for the usual lettuce in tacos and sandwiches.

WILD MUSHROOM AND MIZUNA SALAD WITH WHITE TRUFFLE VINAIGRETTE AND SAGE   SERVES 4

If you don't have access to white truffles, you can omit the truffles and just use the rest of the vinaigrette recipe.

WHITE TRUFFLE VINAIGRETTE

2 tablespoons chopped shallots
¼ cup balsamic vinegar
1 teaspoon Dijon mustard
¾ cup extra-virgin olive oil
1 tablespoon white truffle oil
Salt and pepper

Place the shallots, vinegar, and mustard in a blender and blend until

 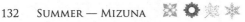

smooth. With the blender still running, add the olive oil and blend until the mixture is emulsified. Add the truffle oil, salt, and pepper and blend for 2 seconds more.

2 tablespoons olive oil
2 portobello mushrooms, stems removed, cleaned with a brush, and cut into ¼-inch slices
12 chanterelle mushrooms, cleaned with a soft brush
2 tablespoons minced garlic
Salt and freshly ground pepper
4 cups mizuna greens, rinsed well and dried
White Truffle Vinaigrette (recipe above)
¼ cup sage leaves, cut into chiffonade

1. Heat the oil in a large pan over high heat until it is almost smoking. Add the mushrooms and cook until they turn golden brown. Add the garlic and cook 1 minute. Add salt and pepper to taste.

2. Divide the mizuna and mushrooms among 4 plates.

3. Drizzle with the white truffle vinaigrette and sprinkle with sage leaves.

— *Teresa Johnson, www.epicurean.com*

. . . .

MIZUNA AND SUMMER SQUASH   SERVES 2 TO 4

3 tablespoons olive oil
1 to 2 cups summer squash, thinly sliced
3 to 4 cloves garlic, chopped
1 bunch mizuna, roughly chopped
Salt and pepper
Hard cheese for grating, such as Parmesan

1. In a large saucepan, heat the olive oil over high heat, then add the summer squash and cook for 3 to 4 minutes, stirring a bit.

2. When the squash is somewhat cooked, add the garlic, mizuna, salt, and pepper. Cook for 2 to 3 minutes longer. Sprinkle with cheese to finish off the dish.

— *Mariquita Farm*

. . . .

SPINACH, ROCKET, AND MIZUNA SALAD   SERVES 4

2 to 3 ounces smoked streaky bacon
¾ pound spinach leaves
¾ pound arugula leaves
¾ pound mizuna leaves

used insecticide is made from the roots of the chrysanthemum plant. It is highly effective against insects, but it breaks down in the sun and leaves no residue on the plant. To prevent worms on the broccoli, we use Bacillus thuringiensis, a bacteria that is found in the stomachs of most mammals (including humans) but is deadly to caterpillars. It also degrades very quickly with no residue.

The downside of an organic spray program is the number of times we must apply. Since all of the sprays we use remain only on the surface of the plant, they break down very quickly. To prevent tomato blight, a conventional farmer uses a fungicide that enters the plant through the leaves and fights the blight internally.

We, on the other hand, use a copper spray that is applied after the rain falls. It has a short life span but requires monitoring, or it can affect copper levels in the soil; too much copper harms our soil by killing off beneficial organisms.

When I began farming organically, I was surprised at the amount of spraying it involves. But the majority of organic customers don't want the holes caused by beetles and worms in their arugula or cabbage. If people see worms on our crops at the farmers market, they won't buy our produce.

So we try very hard to grow healthy plants that are able to repel pests in the first place, to reduce the amount of spraying needed. But knowing we do have the ability and resources to spray allows us to maintain a balance between the beneficial insects and the more harmful ones.

Books

Vegetables from Amaranth to Zucchini: The Essential Reference
Elizabeth Schneider;
William Morrow, 2001.

Ani's Raw Food Kitchen: Easy, Delectable Living Foods Recipes
Ani Phyo; Marlowe & Company, 2007.

Cider vinegar
Walnut or extra-virgin olive oil (optional)
Edible flowers

1. Cut the bacon into matchsticks. First render it slowly in a frying pan, then cook it more quickly to allow it to crisp.

2. Quickly wash the greens and shake or towel them dry. Tear the spinach into manageable pieces. Place it with the rest of the leaves in a salad bowl.

3. Pour the hot bacon and its fat over the greens and toss quickly.

4. Sprinkle a little cider vinegar, drizzle oil if desired, and scatter the flowers over the greens. Serve immediately.

   Note

   ☞ For a vegetarian salad, omit the bacon and simply dress the salad. Edible flowers in season will provide a decorative extra.

   — *www.fooddownunder.com*

· ·

MARINATED TOFU WITH MIZUNA OR SWISS CHARD   SERVES 2

This savory vegan dish may be served over white or brown rice or noodles.

½ pound firm tofu
Mizuna or Swiss chard, washed, stems removed and torn into pieces
Sesame seeds

MARINADE
Balsamic vinegar
Sesame seed oil
Olive oil
Garlic chives, minced
Fresh ginger, minced or grated
Pinch of red pepper
Tamari sauce or Braggs Amino Acids

1. Drain the tofu and cut into cubes.

2. Mix together all of the marinade ingredients in a separate bowl.

3. Set the tofu cubes in the marinade, and marinate for at least 2 hours at room temperature, turning the cubes over occasionally.

4. Pour off the marinade into a skillet on medium heat, and simmer 1 to 2 minutes.

5. Add the mizuna or Swiss chard, and cover the pan. Stir occasionally, and continue simmering until the greens wilt.

6. Add the tofu and sesame seeds and heat through. Serve immediately.

   — *Seabreeze Organic Farm*

Oregano

ORIGANUM VULGARE

This perennial member of the mint family is sometimes almost indistinguishable in taste from majoram, another staple herb in Italian and Greek cooking, and whose name is often incorrectly used in conjunction with oregano. Mexican oregano is actually not an oregano at all, but a plant closely related to lemon verbena, with a sweeter, more subtle flavor.

Treasured for its aromatic, warm, spicy taste with a touch of bitterness, oregano is one of the very few herbs whose flavor is actually stronger in dried form than when fresh. Its name comes from a Greek word meaning "joy of the mountains," and it grows abundantly in that country's hillsides. Surprisingly, this heat-loving plant also grows wild in cool climates, such as in England.

HISTORY

Oregano was born in the Mediterranean region, whose arid climate concentrates the hardy herb's oils. Certainly the ancient Greeks and Romans knew this showy, purple-flowered herb and used it in not only their cuisines but also their wedding ceremonies, as it was believed it would banish sadness.

Oregano has also been widely cultivated for its essential oil, which is used to flavor food and as a fragrance for soaps, detergents, and perfumes. Interestingly, oregano was virtually unknown in America until World War II, when returning soldiers craved the pizza they had eaten in Italy. In fact, this demand for pizza caused oregano sales to skyrocket 5,200 percent in the late 1940s and early 1950s.

NUTRITION

Normally, oregano is not consumed in large enough quantities to make it nutritionally significant, but 2 teaspoons of the dried herb do contain nearly one quarter of the adult daily requirement for vitamin K, as well as significant manganese, iron, and dietary fiber. Oregano has also been found to have incredibly high levels of antioxidants—42 times more than apples and 12 times more than blueberries.

SELECTION

Fresh oregano should be uniformly bright green, with no signs of wilting or yellowing.

STORAGE

You can treat fresh oregano sprigs like any living flower or plant cutting; just snip off the stem ends, place them in a glass of water, and cover loosely with a plastic bag. Or you can extend the life of oregano by wrapping it in damp paper towels and storing it in a plastic bag in the refrigerator vegetable crisper, where it will keep for 3 to 4 days.

TRIMMING & CLEANING

Wash the sprigs under running water, and strip the leaves off the stems.

Cooking Tip

Oregano's dominant flavor can quickly overpower other foods, so be careful when using it in cooking, especially with mild foods.

Books

Recipes from an
American Herb Garden
Maggie Oster; Macmillan, 1993.

The Herbfarm Cookbook
Jerry Traunfeld; Scribner, 2000.

The Complete Medicinal Herbal
Penelope Ody; Dorling Kindersley, 1993.

Rodale's Illustrated Encyclopedia of Herbs
Rodale Press, 2000.

BLANCHING & FREEZING

To prepare oregano for freezing, thoroughly wash and dry the oregano sprigs. Strip the leaves from the stems, place them loosely in a zipper-lock freezer or vacuum food sealer-type bag, and gently squeeze out the air.

You can also mix chopped leaves with a small amount of water, olive oil, or butter, and freeze in ice cube trays. Once frozen, pop out the cubes into a plastic bag and seal tightly. These cubes can be added as needed to soups, stews, casseroles, and other cooked dishes. Use frozen oregano within 1 year.

DRYING

Tie fresh sprigs into a bunch and hang in a cool, dark place with good ventilation. Once they are dried, seal them tightly in a container with a lid or a zipper-lock plastic bag and store away from light and heat.

Or you can oven-dry oregano by spreading a layer of leaves on a cookie sheet and placing it in a warm (up to 180°F) oven for 3 to 4 hours, stirring the herbs periodically until they are thoroughly dry. Or remove the best leaves from the stems and arrange them on a paper towel without letting them touch. This layer is covered with another paper towel and another layer of leaves is added. Five layers may be dried at one time using this method.

A microwave oven can also be used to dry small quantities of herbs. Place 4 or 5 herb branches in the microwave between paper towels. Heat for 2 to 3 minutes over High power. If the herbs are not brittle and dry when removed, repeat the microwave drying for 30 seconds more. (Be aware that the heat generated during microwaving not only removes moisture but also some of the oils, so these herbs may not have as intense a flavor as herbs dried by other methods.) Keep dried oregano in a cool, dark place away from light and heat, and use within 6 to 9 months.

EQUIVALENTS, MEASURES & SERVINGS

- 1 tablespoon fresh oregano = 1 teaspoon dried
- 1 ounce fresh oregano = ½ cup chopped
- 1 teaspoon dried oregano = 1 teaspoon liquid oregano

COMPLEMENTARY HERBS, SEASONINGS & FOODS

Basil, beans, breads, broccoli, capers, cauliflower, chili, eggs, eggplant, garlic, green beans, lemon, majoram, mushrooms, olives, olive oil, onions, parsley, pasta, pizza, pork, poultry, spaghetti sauce, thyme, tomatoes, veal, zucchini.

SUBSTITUTIONS

If your recipe calls for Italian oregano and you do not have any on hand, substitute thyme, basil, or majoram.

SERVING SUGGESTIONS

- Few self-respecting Italian pizzas reach their full flavor potential until they've been baptized with a couple generous shakes of the oregano jar.
- For a delicious twist to homemade garlic bread, add chopped fresh oregano and basil to the bread just after seasoning it with garlic and prior to toasting.
- Add oregano or oregano-infused oil to salad dressings.

- Oregano is the quintessential ingredient in Italian dishes—sprinkle it in pastas, pizza, sauces, meat dishes, and lasagna.
- Add a touch of oregano to egg dishes such as omelets, frittatas, or just plain old scrambled eggs.
- Toss in fresh or dried oregano with roast chicken, lamb, or meatloaf.
- For tasty oven-fried potatoes, season them with a mixture of finely chopped oregano and rosemary.

S. NARDECCHIA'S SPAGHETTI SAUCE   SERVES 4

SAUCE

1 large yellow onion, sliced
5 tablespoons olive oil
2 tablespoons salt
Freshly ground pepper
2 large cloves garlic, minced
1 (12-ounce) can tomato paste
1 medium green bell pepper, minced
1 (28-ounce) can tomatoes
1 (28-ounce) can of water
1 cup red wine (optional)
3 whole bay leaves
¼ cup parsley flakes
1 teaspoon ground fennel
1 tablespoon chopped fresh basil or 1 teaspoon dried basil
1 tablespoon chopped fresh oregano or 1 teaspoon dried oregano
1 tablespoon chopped fresh rosemary or 1 teaspoon dried rosemary
2 pounds ground chuck

2 pounds thin spaghetti
Parmesan cheese

1. In a large saucepan, sauté the onion in 3 tablespoons of the olive oil until it turns limp.

2. Add 1 tablespoon of the salt, pepper to taste, garlic, tomato paste, and green bell pepper. Stir and cook for 15 minutes.

3. Add the tomatoes, water, wine (if desired), bay leaves, parsley, fennel, basil, oregano, and rosemary. Simmer 3 hours or longer, stirring occasionally.

4. Meanwhile, in a large skillet, cook the ground chuck in the remaining 2 tablespoons olive oil. Add the remaining 1 tablespoon salt, as well as pepper to taste. Brown the meat until all of the liquid in the pan evaporates, then add the meat to the sauce 1 hour prior to the end of the sauce's simmering period.

5. Prepare the sphagetti according to the package instructions. Serve with the sauce and Parmesan cheese.

— *Maureen Cooney,* The Bluff Country Co-op Cookbook

"No man is lonely eating spaghetti; it requires so much attention."

— *Christopher Morley,*
American journalist and novelist

VEGETABLE LASAGNA

SERVES 4

1 medium zucchini, sliced
1 cup mushrooms, sliced
1 medium onion, chopped
1 clove garlic, cut into small pieces
2 (8-ounce) cans tomato sauce
1 tablespoon fresh oregano or 1 teaspoon dried oregano
1 tablespoon fresh basil or 1 teaspoon dried basil
¼ teaspoon freshly ground pepper
1 cup low-fat cottage cheese
1 cup mozzarella cheese, shredded
1 large tomato, chopped
6 lasagna noodles, uncooked

1. Preheat the oven to 400°F.

2. Mix the zucchini, mushrooms, onion, and garlic with the tomato sauce, oregano, basil, and pepper in a saucepan. Cover, and cook 15 minutes, stirring occasionally. Set aside. In a separate bowl, mix the cheeses and chopped tomato.

3. Spread a third of the sauce over the bottom of an 8 × 8-inch baking dish. Add half of the uncooked noodles and half of the cheese mixture. Repeat these layers and end with a third layer of sauce.

4. Cover tightly with aluminum foil; bake 45 minutes. Remove from the oven and let stand 5 minutes before serving.

— *Massachusetts Department of Agricultural Resources, Farmers Market Vegetable Recipes*

Cooking Tip

Soak sprigs of fresh herbs like oregano, thyme, majoram, sage, or rosemary in water for an hour, shake them partially dry, and lay them on the hot coals of your grill just before cooking meat.

MARINATED BEAN SALAD

SERVES 4

This is a healthy, fresh-tasting bean salad that will give you an easy way to enjoy the many nutritional benefits of beans with little effort. The fresh herbs make it very flavorful, and it will keep in your refrigerator for up to 3 to 4 days. In fact, it actually gets better as it marinates. The lima beans and fresh herbs add a nice twist to the more traditional version.

2 cups fresh green beans, cut into 1-inch lengths
1 (15-ounce) can lima beans
1 (15-ounce) can kidney beans
2 tablespoons minced onion
3 medium cloves garlic, pressed
1 large ripe fresh tomato, seeds and excess pulp removed, diced
2 tablespoons chopped fresh basil
1 tablespoon chopped fresh oregano
1 tablespoon chopped fresh parsley
3 tablespoons fresh lemon juice

2 to 3 tablespoons extra-virgin olive oil
Salt and cracked black pepper

1. In a pan, bring lightly salted water to a boil. Trim the green beans by cutting off the ends a handful at once (this saves time). Boil them for about 3 to 5 minutes, or until they are tender. Then drain them in a colander and pat dry with paper towels so that the excess water does not dilute their flavor.

2. Rinse the canned beans under running water in a colander, letting them sit for a couple of minutes to drain the excess water.

3. Mix all of the ingredients together. If you have the time, let this salad marinate for at least 15 minutes. It can keep in the refrigerator for a few days.

— www.whfoods.com

CONGRI (CUBAN BEANS AND RICE)   SERVES 6

1 pound dry red kidney or black beans
Water
3 teaspoons vegetable oil
1 pound long-grain rice, uncooked
4 cloves garlic, minced
1 large onion, chopped
1 medium bell pepper, chopped
¼ teaspoon cumin
1 bay leaf
¾ teaspoon fresh oregano, chopped
¼ teaspoon freshly ground black pepper
1 teaspoon salt
3 teaspoons olive oil

1. Soak the dry beans overnight before cooking.

2. Cook the beans in 6 cups of water by bringing them to a boil. Remove from the heat and let stand for about 60 minutes. Do not discard the liquid.

3. In a cast-iron or aluminum pot, combine the vegetable oil and rice and stir until the rice grains are evenly covered with oil. (This prevents them from sticking to one another.) Add 3 cloves of the garlic, onion, bell pepper, cumin, bay leaf, oregano, black pepper, and salt.

4. Add 2 cups of the liquid from the beans, bring to a boil, and cook on low heat for about 15 to 20 minutes, or until the liquid is almost absorbed by the rice. Lower the heat to a simmer, and cover the pot with aluminum foil or a lid to seal in the steam. (If the rice is still hard, add more bean liquid, a little at a time. Cook for an additional 4 to 5 minutes or until the rice is tender.)

5. Once the rice is ready, add the drained beans and stir.

6. Sauté the remaining chopped garlic clove with olive oil in a small pan for 1 to 2 minutes, then pour over the rice to add additional flavor and shine.

— *Havana Journal*

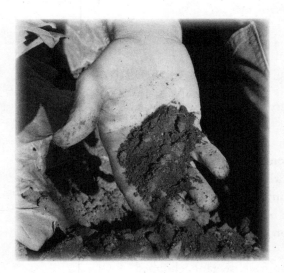

Our soil, our black gold.

Pepper (Sweet)

CAPSICUM
ANNUUM

Even if they weren't edible, humans might cultivate peppers just for their beautiful colors and shapes. But happily this is not the case, and peppers of all kinds—sweet and hot—add taste, texture, color, and a little (or a lot) of zip to our gustatory lives.

All peppers are members of the genus Solanaceae, the same family as tomatoes, potatoes, eggplants, tobacco, and deadly nightshade. The pepper family is a vast one, with literally thousands of varieties, many of them hot ones. Bell peppers simply refer to a subset of capsicums whose fruits are typically bell-shaped and taste sweet, with none of the sharp bite that characterizes their spicy cousins. (The latter warrant such different culinary treatment that they appear in a separate section in this book, on pages 148–153).

Peppers are heat-loving plants, and although they are available year-round in supermarkets, their best season is mid- to late summer. All bell peppers start out green and slowly change to red, yellow, or orange as they mature, depending on the variety, so do not be surprised if the peppers in your CSA basket are "blushing." As their color changes, they become milder and sweeter.

Featherstone grows a mix of red, yellow, and green bell peppers. Another variety may be lurking in your box as well—the apple pepper, which is a small, heart-shaped, sweet red pepper with fleshy walls.

HISTORY

Peppers originated in South and Central America, where they have been a part of the human diet for over 7,500 years and domesticated nearly as long. Dried peppers have been found in Incan tombs, and it is thought that chile peppers were one of the first cultivated crops on that continent. Christopher Columbus brought peppers back to Europe, and Spanish and Portuguese trade routes quickly spread both sweet peppers and hot chiles to the Philippines, India, and the rest of Asia.

NUTRITION

Bell peppers are outstanding sources of vitamin C (a 1-cup serving contains 300 percent of the adult daily requirement) and vitamin A. They also contain significant vitamin B6, folate, vitamin K, and dietary fiber. Red, yellow, and orange bell peppers are higher in vitamins A and C than green ones, since their color comes from beta-carotenes, antioxidant compounds that help eye health. Red peppers are one of the few vegetable sources of lycopene, which may help prevent prostate and bladder cancers.

SELECTION

Choose bell peppers that are heavy for their size, and firm all over, with no soft spots, bruises, or signs of shriveling or decay. Red bell peppers are just green bells that are fully ripened; the redder the pepper, the sweeter it is.

Cooking Tip

To transport and serve stuffed peppers, use a bundt cake pan.

It's rare that a single day at Feath-erstone Farm encapsulates a bit of everything we do in the course of producing and distributing a veg-etable crop. This past Wednesday was one of those remarkable days; I am writing now to recount the events of the day, and to reflect a bit on what I think they mean in the broader context of our mission as organic farmers.

The day started with half of our crew transplanting bok choy and broccoli—the last of the season—at the Lacher farm on the ridge, while the rest of us finished packing a substantial order of heirloom to-matoes for a wholesaler in Chicago. By mid-morning our CSA manager Sarah Stone and a few assistants were assembling CSA boxes. I went back up to the Lacher farm to fin-ish cultivating and fertilizing the mid-sized broccoli and cabbage there; My partner Rhys organized one crew of pickers in the cherry tomatoes and another group in the heirlooms.

In the afternoon, Sarah and our shop manager Trina delivered CSA boxes, while the tomato pick-ing continued under a bright sunny sky. This is when the day became particularly interesting for me. The forecast of rain showers for the end of the week had me thinking about planting—not just fall CSA crops like turnips, radishes, and salad mix, but also cover crops like rye and vetch, which help replenish the soil..

So Rhys and I fired up a pair of tractors, finished the necessary groundwork, and hooked up the seeders. As the clouds collected on the horizon, we charged the hop-pers and went at it. By the time I finally switched off the John Deere, it was 9 P.M. and drizzling, but the

STORAGE

Store peppers unwashed in the refrigerator in a perforated plastic bag in the vegetable crisper, where they will keep for a few days.

TRIMMING & CLEANING

Wash peppers well before cutting. Supermarket peppers may be covered with a fine coating of food-grade wax; be sure to scrub these well. To prepare, cut around the stem and gently lift this "cap" out; most of the pepper's seeds are attached to this inside stem end and will be removed this way. Then reach inside and clean out any stray seeds and white inner ribs.

STEAMING & BOILING

Bell peppers can be steamed whole or in strips. Place whole peppers in a steamer basket or pan and steam for 10 minutes; strips will be done in about 5 minutes. Boiling is generally not recommended for bell peppers, since this makes them watery.

STIR-FRYING & SAUTÉING

Bell peppers love the wok or sauté pan: Slice them into rings or strips, and stir-fry or sauté them in a little butter or oil, either by themselves or with other vegetables, for 2 to 4 minutes. Great accompaniments for bell peppers include onions, leeks, snow peas, tomatoes, green beans, cabbage, mustard greens, or tiny broccoli or cauliflower florets.

BAKING & ROASTING

Peppers respond well to oven baking, although for stuffed pepper prepa-rations, bells benefit from a parboiling in salted water for 5 minutes before baking. Bake at 400°F for about 20 minutes, or until the peppers are soft but not collapsing. For nonstuffed-pepper recipes, cut the peppers into 1½- to 2-inch chunks, combine them with other vegetables and ingredients if desired (like onions and potatoes), and bake for 20 to 30 minutes at 425°F, or 45 minutes at 375°F.

Roasting peppers caramelizes their natural sugars, making them sweeter. To roast on the grill, halve or quarter them, depending on their size, remove their seeds and ribs, and brush the pieces with olive oil. Place the peppers directly on the grill on medium heat, and cook for 6 to 10 minutes, turning them over at least once during the cooking time. When done, the peppers should be browned but still somewhat crisp. Or you can roast whole peppers on medium-high heat for 10 to 12 minutes, turning often, until the skins are well-charred.

Once they have finished grilling, place the peppers in a large bowl, seal the bowl tightly with plastic wrap, and let them stand for about 20 minutes. The trapped steam within the bowl will loosen the skins from the peppers. Then cut the peppers open and remove the ribs, seeds, stems, and skins. Now they are ready for use in dishes calling for roasted pep-pers.

BLANCHING & FREEZING

Blanch peppers if you want to use them in heated dishes, and for un-cooked preparations, don't blanch if you want a more crispy texture. To blanch peppers, wash them and remove their seeds. Cut peppers into halves, or slice or dice them. Blanch halved peppers in boiling water for 3 minutes; sliced or diced ones for 2 minutes. Then chill them in ice water to halt the cooking process. Drain and pack in zipper-lock freezer or vacuum food sealer-type bags, or freezer containers. Squeeze out excess air and leave ½ inch of headspace (unless you are using the vacuum sealing method). Chopped peppers do not need to be blanched. Peppers will keep for up to 10 to 12 months at 0°F.

MICROWAVING

Microwave stuffed bell peppers (fillings should be precooked) over High power for about 10 to 15 minutes, depending on the size of the pepper. Pepper chunks can be microwaved in a little liquid on High power for 6 to 8 minutes, or until tender-crisp.

COMPLEMENTARY HERBS, SEASONINGS & FOODS

Anchovies, basil, cheese, chiles, coriander, corn, crab, eggplant, fish, garlic, lemon, lobster, meat, olive oil, onions, peppers, potatoes, rice, tomatoes, vinegar.

EQUIVALENTS, MEASURES & SERVINGS

- 1 large pepper = 1 cup chopped
- 3 medium peppers = about 1 pound = 2 cups chopped
- 1 pound peeled, seeded peppers = ½ pound flesh = 1 to 1¼ cups
- 1 pound raw, cleaned, trimmed, thinly sliced peppers = about 4 cups

SERVING SUGGESTIONS

- Thinly slice fresh bell peppers into rings or strips and serve with a favorite dressing as a dip. Kids love bell peppers like this, especially the sweeter orange and red ones.
- Grill bell peppers that have been marinated in olive oil, garlic, and herbs.
- Add chunks of bell pepper, onion, and tomatoes to shish kebobs.
- Combine bell peppers with other vegetables for tasty, colorful stir-fries: broccoli, onions, greens, mushrooms, cabbage, tomatoes, carrots.
- Bell peppers are wonderful stewed or cooked in sauces, paired with veal or savory pork sausage.
- That old classic, stuffed peppers, can be livened up from its traditional ground beef and rice filling with different ingredients, like cooked cracked wheat berries, sliced jalapeños, barbecued chicken, honey-laced ahi (raw tuna), sushi rice, sweet onions, eggplant, breadcrumbs, deep-fried parsley sprigs, miniature meatballs....
- Thinly slice bell peppers and add them to sandwiches as a substitute for lettuce. (Great with onions and cucumbers!)
- For a crunchy texture and distinctive flavor, add finely chopped bell peppers to tuna, ham, chicken, or egg salad.

VEGETARIAN STUFFED PEPPERS   SERVES 8

4 red or green bell peppers
1 pint or 2 cups cherry tomatoes

work was done: satisfaction of the highest order.

Circling a tractor around a 26-acre, soon-to-be rye and vetch field in the gathering twilight provides a unique opportunity for reflection. This particular evening, my head was filled with an odd but potentially related collection of ideas: thoughts of the wonderful newsletter article contributed by CSA member Becky Bodonyi subtitled "The Revolution Will Come in a Box." Thoughts of an article last year in Harper's, assessing the utter dependence of modern agribusiness on petroleum (for fuel, fertilizer, etc.).

And finally, thoughts of a commencement address delivered this spring by writer Barbara Kingsolver in which she proposes (brilliantly, I may add) a paradigm shift for thinking and acting in the future from a global ecological perspective, creating the "first American generation that behaves as if there's going to be a tomorrow."

Essentially, it boiled down to this in my somewhat weary and tractor-shaken mind: The first ninety percent of my day had been spent at the zenith of the current paradigm: petrol-sucking machines producing vegetables in big fields for shipment between 50 and 250 miles away on refrigerated trucks.

It is what we have set out to accomplish here, and we've grown good at it. I am proud of our farm and all it is able to produce. But what about sustainability? The organic codes are strict and we follow them in both letter and spirit. But what about all these fossil fuels and internal combustion engines? I am clearly ambivalent about this paradigm, and look forward to its ultimate demise (when the petrol or our current atmosphere expires, whichever comes first) with a mixture of dread and relief.

I concluded my tractor-seat philosophizing with this more hopeful realization: The last ten percent of

1 medium onion
1 cup fresh basil leaves
3 cloves garlic
2 teaspoons olive oil
¼ teaspoon salt
¼ teaspoon pepper

1. Preheat the oven to 425°F.

2. Lightly oil a large shallow baking pan. Cut the peppers in half lengthwise and remove their seeds. Arrange the peppers, cut sides up, in a baking pan, and lightly oil the cut edges of the stems.

3. Halve the cherry tomatoes, and chop the onion and basil. Finely chop the garlic.

4. In a bowl, toss the tomatoes, onion, basil, garlic, oil, salt, and pepper. Divide the mixture among the peppers and roast in the upper rack of the oven until the peppers are tender, about 20 minutes.

— *Fruits and Veggies—More Matters; Centers for Disease Control & Prevention*

SPICY ROASTED VEGETABLE SOUP　　　　SERVES 8 TO 10

1 medium eggplant, cut into 1-inch dice
2 red or green bell peppers, cut into 1-inch dice
2 large sweet onions, cut into 1-inch dice
3 large carrots, peeled and cut into ½-inch slices
1 medium zucchini, cut into ½-inch slices
1 garlic head, peeled and minced
1 large sweet potato, peeled and cut into ½-inch dice (or substitute winter squash)
¼ cup olive oil
1 tablespoon ground cumin seed
1 tablespoon ground coriander seed
1 tablespoon fennel seed
1 teaspoon red pepper flakes
½ pint of cherry tomatoes or 1 cup diced tomato
3 tablespoons balsamic vinegar
¼ cup tamari sauce
1 tablespoon brown sugar or honey
3 tablespoons tomato paste
3 tablespoons dried currants
12 cups vegetable stock
Salt and black pepper

1. Preheat the oven to 400°F.

2. Toss all of the vegetables (except the tomatoes) and spices with the olive oil. Bake for 30 minutes, stirring a few times, until the vegetables start to brown.

3. Remove the vegetables from the oven and place all of the ingredients in a large stockpot. Mix the vinegar, tamari, sugar or honey, tomato paste, and currants into the stockpot along with the vegetable stock. Simmer 10 to 15 minutes. Correct the seasonings, and add salt and pepper to taste.

— Blue Heron Coffeehouse, Winona, Minnesota, The Bluff Country Co-op Cookbook

. . . .

VEGETARIAN STIR-FRY   SERVES 4

This recipe gives you a delicious and easy way of receiving the many health benefits of vegetables in your meal in just 20 minutes. This cooking method makes it even healthier by not using heated oils. Feel free to add other vegetables you may have on hand to this dish.

1 tablespoon vegetable broth
1 medium onion, cut in half and sliced medium-thick
1 red bell pepper, cut into ½-inch pieces
1 cup thinly sliced fresh shiitake mushrooms, stems removed
4 medium cloves garlic, pressed
1 tablespoon minced fresh ginger
2 cups thinly sliced green cabbage
1 red bell pepper, cut into ½-inch pieces
1 cup sliced fresh shiitake mushrooms, stems removed
2 cups sliced green cabbage
5 ounces extra-firm tofu, cut into ½-inch cubes
2 tablespoons soy sauce
1 tablespoon rice vinegar
2 tablespoons chopped fresh cilantro
1 tablespoon sesame seeds
Salt and white pepper

1. Heat the broth in a stainless-steel wok or a 12-inch skillet. Stir-fry the onion for about 2 minutes in the broth over medium-high heat, stirring constantly.

2. Add the red bell pepper and mushrooms. Continue to stir-fry for another 2 minutes. Add the garlic and ginger and continue to cook, stirring for another 2 to 3 minutes.

3. Add the rest of the ingredients and cook for another 2 minutes. Sprinkle with sesame seeds.

— www.whfoods.com

. . . .

LAYERED VEGETABLE CASSEROLE   SERVES 6

1 tablespoon vegetable oil

Books

The Peppers Cookbook: 200 Recipes from the Pepper Lady's Kitchen
Jean Andrews; University of North Texas Press, 2005.

The Chile Pepper Encyclopedia: Everything You'll Ever Need to Know About Hot Peppers, With More Than 100 Recipes
Dave DeWitt;
Diane Publishing, 2003.

The Great Chile Book
Mark Miller;
Ten Speed Press, 1991.

1 large onion, coarsely chopped
1 large green bell pepper, seeded and cut into 1-inch pieces
1 small eggplant or zucchini, peeled and diced
½ pound fresh mushrooms, sliced
1 large tomato, peeled and chopped
¾ teaspoon dried leaf thyme or 1 tablespoon fresh thyme
⅛ teaspoon pepper
1 cup herb-seasoned stuffing mix
2 cups shredded Swiss cheese, divided

1. Preheat the oven to 350°F.

2. In a skillet, heat the oil. Add the onion and green bell pepper, and sauté on medium heat for about 3 minutes. Add the eggplant or zucchini and mushrooms. Sauté for 3 more minutes. Add the tomato and seasonings and simmer for 1 more minute.

3. Spread the stuffing mix on the bottom of greased 2-quart casserole. Make a layer of about half of the vegetable mixture. Spread 1 cup of the cheese over the top. Top with the remaining vegetable mixture.

4. Bake for about 30 minutes.

5. Sprinkle the remaining cup of cheese on top and return to the oven for about 10 minutes, or until the cheese is melted.

— *Aria Boydston,* The Schoenleber Family Cookbook

VEGETARIAN PAELLA   SERVES 6

1½ tablespoons olive oil
1 large onion, chopped
3 cloves garlic, chopped
½ teaspoon paprika
1½ cups long-grain brown rice, uncooked
3¾ cups low-sodium vegetable broth
¾ cup dry white wine
1 (14-ounce) can tomatoes, chopped with juice
1 tablespoon tomato paste
½ tablespoon fresh tarragon or ½ teaspoon dried tarragon
1 tablespoon fresh basil or ½ teaspoon dried basil
1 tablespoon fresh oregano or ½ teaspoon dried oregano
1 red bell pepper, roughly chopped
1 green bell pepper, roughly chopped
3 stalks celery, finely chopped
3 cups mushrooms, washed and sliced
½ cup snow pea pods
⅔ cup frozen peas
⅓ cup cashew nut pieces
Salt and pepper

1. Heat the oil in a large, deep skillet, and sauté the onions and garlic until they become soft.

2. Add the paprika and rice and continue to cook for 4 to 5 minutes, or until the rice becomes transparent. Stir occasionally.

3. Add the broth, wine, tomatoes, tomato paste, and herbs. Simmer for 10 to 15 minutes.

4. Add the peppers, celery, mushrooms, and pea pods. Continue to cook for another 30 minutes, or until the rice is cooked through.

5. Add the peas, cashews, salt, and pepper to taste. Heat through and place on a large heated serving dish.

Nonvegetarian Variation

> Add chopped country ham, clams, mussels, cooked shrimp, chunks of crab, lobster, andouille or chorizo sausage, or rabbit.

— *Fruits and Veggies—More Matters; Centers for Disease Control & Prevention*

Transplanting garlic.

Pepper (Hot)

CAPSICUM FRUTESCENS

How much more boring and bland our gastronomic universe would be were it not for the fiery heat and distinctive flavors of hot peppers, those brazen denizens of the vegetable world. Nearly 4,000 varieties of hot peppers exist around in the world, in all shapes, colors, flavors, and sizes, from the diminutive Thai bird peppers to the mild, fleshy poblanos. In such a large family, confusion runs rampant, for all peppers cross-pollinate easily to form new varieties, and common names may refer to completely different peppers in various cultures.

What is common to all hot peppers (often called chiles) is the presence of capsaicin, a fat-soluble compound that reacts with pain receptors in the mouth and throat to produce that characteristic burning sensation. If we eat a lot of hot-pepper-seasoned foods over time, these receptors often desensitize, which is why we may need to consume more to get the same capsaicin "kick."

Capsaicin has a long history as medicine, valued for its antibacterial and anti-inflammatory properties. It is also used as a circulatory stimulant and pain reliever in dermatological ointments. And despite popular belief, hot peppers do not cause ulcers or hemorrhoids; in fact, they may actually help relieve the conditions.

Featherstone grows three varieties of hot peppers: long cayenne (long and skinny), jalapeño (fat, short, and green), and serrano (a little skinnier than the jalapeños, but shorter than the long cayenne).

HISTORY

Peppers originated in South and Central America, where they have been a part of the human diet for over 7,500 years and domesticated nearly as long. Dried peppers have been found in Incan tombs, and chiles may have been one of the first cultivated crops on that continent.

Christopher Columbus brought peppers back to Europe, and Spanish and Portuguese trade routes quickly spread both chile and sweet peppers to the Philippines, India, and the rest of Asia. Since those times, hot peppers have become an indispensable part of the cuisines of China, Korea, southeast Asia, Africa, and the Middle East, making it one of the world's more universal seasonings.

NUTRITION

Hot peppers are usually not consumed in large enough quantity to be nutritionally significant, but they do contain vitamin A. Capsaicin, the substance that gives chiles their heat, has its own health benefits, helping lower cholesterol, reduce pain (especially arthritis), possibly prevent stomach ulcers, and stimulate circulation.

SELECTION

Choose peppers that are heavy for their size (signaling a greater proportion of flesh) and firm all over, with no soft spots, bruises, or signs of shriveling or decay.

Hot Peppers By Any Other Name

Hot peppers are called many names throughout the world, depending on where you are.

In Mexico, they are "chiles." In parts of South America, they are known as *aji.*

In the United States, they are "chile/chiles," "chili/chilies," or "chili/chile pepper" (with a single "l").

In the United Kingdom and Canada, they are "chilli/chillies" or "chilli peppers" (with a double "l").

STORAGE

Do not wash peppers until you are just about to use them. Store them in the refrigerator vegetable crisper in a perforated plastic bag, where they will keep for up to 1 to 2 weeks.

TRIMMING & CLEANING

Wash and dry the peppers. The trickiest part of handling hot peppers is to avoid direct contact with its innards; its fiery capsaicin can severely irritate the skin and mucous membranes. Some cooks protect their hands, eyes, noses, and mouths by wearing thin gloves and face masks while preparing chiles.

To deseed hot peppers (and if you are not planning to peel them), slice off the stem end and then slice them in half lengthwise. With the halves exposed, carefully scrape off the seeds and cut out the whitish inner ribs (which contain the highest capsaicin concentration) and discard.

After cutting peppers, always thoroughly wash your hands, utensils, and cutting surfaces with plenty of soap and water to prevent the capsaicin from inadvertently burning your skin or coming into contact with your face. For more tips, please see the "Chile Handling Safety" sidebar on this page.

STEAMING & BOILING

For a bit of zip, add a few slices of jalepeño or other hot pepper to the steam basket or pan while other vegetables are steaming or boiling. The longer the pepper cooks, the milder it will become (although you may not notice much difference with the hottest chiles!).

STIR-FRYING & SAUTÉING

Thinly sliced or slivered fresh hot peppers add a lovely bite to stir-fries or sautéed mixtures. Stir-fry or sauté in a little butter or oil, either by themselves or with other ingredients, for 2 to 4 minutes.

ROASTING & BROILING

Roasting peppers in the oven or over a grill gives them a luscious, smoky flavor. It also loosens the tough skins, making them easier to remove and discard so that the pepper flesh can be used in recipes and for canning.

To grill-roast, place whole or cut-up peppers directly atop a charcoal or gas grill about 5 to 6 inches above the coals. Use tongs to constantly turn the peppers on all sides until their skins start to blacken and blister, about 2 to 3 minutes.

To roast in the oven or broiler, preheat to 425°F, and use tongs to turn the peppers constantly until their skins blister on all sides. To roast over the stove, place the peppers on a wire mesh directly atop the electric or gas burner, and roast and turn until the skins are evenly blistered.

Once the peppers are blistered, allow them to cool for 20 to 30 minutes. Then peel by gently pulling at the skin and occasionally rinsing with water. Remaining skins that did not blister can be persuaded to come off with a vegetable peeler. Be sure to handle these peppers carefully, avoiding direct contact with the skin if possible (see Trimming and Cleaning, above).

Cooking Tip

When you cook with hot peppers, taste-test the pepper (and the dish if feasible) during preparation, and adjust the seasoning accordingly.

The heat of individual peppers (even ones of the same species and from the same plant) varies tremendously. Better for you and your diners to not be unpleasantly surprised at the table!

Chile Handling Safety

There is a reason why capsaicin is an ingredient in self-defense sprays; the stuff can be a mighty irritant if not respected. When handling fresh chiles, consider wearing gloves. After cutting or chopping hot peppers, always thoroughly wash your hands, cutting utensils, and cooking surfaces with soap and water (not just a rinsing with water, as capsaicin is not water-soluble).

If you have touched hot peppers, avoid rubbing your eyes or bringing your fingers anywhere near your nose, mouth, or eyes until you have thoroughly washed your hands with soap and water. Avoid inhaling the fine dust created when you grind dried chiles. When cooking with some of the hottest chile varieties in the world, some chefs even use inhalers to avoid breathing the fumes.

If you do burn your skin with chiles, dress the affected area with a baking powder paste or a burn ointment. Skin burns can also be soaked in cold milk.

If your eyes get burned, immediately flush them with cold water. If a juicy pepper squirts you in the eyes, cry for a while—the tears and the passage of time will eventually do the trick.

How To Beat the Heat

- *Don't drink water. Consuming water does little to quench a capsaicin burn, because this compound is fat- (but not water) soluble.*

- *Got milk? Capsaicin does bind with the fat and protein in dairy products, so drinking milk or eating yogurt or ice cream is one of the more effective ways to soothe a flaming tongue.*

- *Serve starchy foods like rice, potatoes, pasta, bread, or plantains. For the very hottest burns, some swear by sucking on a slice of bread soaked in olive oil, ingesting a mouthful of sugar, or chewing on a large piece of cheese.*

- *Have a beer. Capsaicin is also alcohol-soluble, so consuming spicy, chile-laced foods with beer, margaritas, or wine can help calm the burn.*

- *Eat acid foods and drinks. Tomato juice, lemonade, lime juice, mangos, and oranges can help counteract the akalinity of hot peppers.*

- *Keep it moving. If you love eating hot pepper pods or fiery chunks of chiles, but don't want to subject yourself to the full capsaicin punch (or if you really want to impress your friends), here is a trick: Try to wrap or surround the hot pepper with other food, take a bite, and then move the pepper toward the back of your mouth as quickly as possible, and swallow. (The most sensitive receptors of the tongue that capsaicin affects lie on the tip and sides.)*

- *Eat more hot peppers. Over time, humans often become desensitized to the effects of*

MICROWAVING

To soften their skins, place the peppers in a microwave-safe container, then cover with a tight-fitting lid to allow steam to build up inside. Microwave on High power for 7 to 8 minutes, then allow the steam to accumulate inside the dish for another 1 to 2 minutes. Be careful when you open the dish, as the steam will be extremely hot and may burn on contact. The skins will not appear blistered, but they will be tougher and more brittle, making them easier to peel.

BLANCHING & FREEZING

Blanch peppers if you want to use them in heated dishes; for uncooked preparations, do not blanch if you want a more crispy texture. Whole peppers that will not be blanched do not need any preparation; simply insert them into zipper-lock freezer bags and freeze.

To blanch peppers, wash them and remove their seeds. Cut peppers into halves or slice into rings. Blanch halved peppers in boiling water for 3 minutes, sliced ones for 2 minutes. (Chopped or diced peppers do not require blanching.) Then promptly chill them in ice water to halt their cooking. Drain and pack them in zipper-lock freezer or vacuum food sealer-type bags, or freezer containers. Squeeze out excess air and leave ½ inch of headspace (unless you are using the vacuum sealing method). They will keep for up to 10 to 12 months at 0°F.

DRYING

Drying is a very popular method to preserve hot peppers. Using string and wire, tie quantities of whole, fresh, unblemished peppers into a layered bunch called a *ristra*, and hang it up to dry in a cool, well-ventilated spot away from heat, humidity, and sunlight.

Peppers also dry well in a food dehydrator. Simply wash them, slice them into desired lengths, and dry them on the dehydrator shelves until they turn brittle. Then package the dried chiles into plastic bags or glass jars for later use, or crumble or grind them into a powder (but beware of the dust produced in the process, which can irritate eyes and throats).

EQUIVALENTS, MEASURES & SERVINGS

1-inch segment = 2 teaspoons finely chopped
20 peppers 3 to 6 inches long and ½ to ¾ inch in diameter = ½ pound

COMPLEMENTARY HERBS, SEASONINGS & FOODS

Bananas, beans, cheese, chutney, cilantro, corn, crab, cream, eggplant, fish, fruit, garlic, ginger, ketchup, lime, lobster, onions, peppers, pineapple, potatoes, rice, tomatoes, yogurt.

SERVING SUGGESTIONS

- Make salsa!
- Preserve hot peppers in vinegar or oil for a spicy seasoning that is handy for sprinkling over cooked dishes or in dresssings. To make pepper vinegar, put enough fresh, sliced hot peppers in a sterilized Mason-type jar to fill it about a quarter- to half-full. Then add enough white vinegar to fill the jar, add a little salt and powdered cayenne if desired, and seal. Let the vinegar stand for several weeks; it will keep for up to 6 months. For a recipe to create the oil, see Chili Oil on page 151.

- For an eye-opening tossed salad, add a few very thinly sliced hot pepper rings and finely shredded or slivered fresh ginger.
- Add a teaspoon of finely chopped chiles to your favorite cornbread recipe.
- Add jalapeños or serranos to soups, stews, casseroles, omelets, and stir-fries.
- Combine hot peppers with garlic, olive oil, coriander, cumin, peppermint, and other herbs and spices to make *harissa,* a Tunisian hot pepper paste that is commonly used in North African cuisines.
- Add a little chopped hot pepper to yogurt- and sour cream-based dips.
- Use hot peppers in Southeast Asian, Szechuan and Hunan Chinese, Korean, and Latin American dishes.

capsaicin if they repeatedly consume quantities of hot peppers, gradually needing to eat more to feel the same burn (and that peculiar high that accompanies it). So go ahead and indulge!

. . . .

CHILI OIL
MAKES ABOUT 1 CUP

1 medium jalapeño with half of the seeds and veins removed, minced
1 shallot, minced
⅓ cup peanut, corn, or blended vegetable oil
3 tablespoons water
½ teaspoon sugar
1 teaspoon salt
¼ teaspoon white pepper

1. Heat the jalapeño, shallot, and oil in a small saucepan over medium heat for several minutes. Let stand for 5 to 10 minutes for flavors to meld.

2. While the oil is still warm, stir in the water, sugar, salt, and pepper.

3. When ready to serve, spoon the flavored oil over steamed vegetables and toss gently.

— *Shirley O. Corriher,* Cookwise

. . . .

SALSA MARINADE
MAKES ABOUT 8 CUPS

2½ cups fresh starfruit, finely diced
1 cup fresh mango, finely diced
1 cup fresh pineapple, finely diced
½ cup red bell pepper, finely diced
½ cup yellow bell pepper, finely diced
1 cup green bell pepper, finely diced
1 cup yellow onion, finely diced
½ teaspoon salt
3 tablespoons jalapeño pepper, minced, or to taste
1 teaspoon dried hot pepper flakes, or to taste
2 fresh tomatoes, peeled, seeded, and finely diced
3 tablespoons fresh cilantro, minced
Juice of 1 lemon

Books

Hot Spots
David DeWitt; Prima Publishing, 1992.

Peppers: A Story of Hot Pursuits
Amal Naj; Knopf, 1992.

The Chile Pepper Encyclopedia: Everything You'll Ever Need to Know About Hot Peppers, With More Than 100 Recipes
Dave DeWitt; Diane Publishing, 2003.

The Great Chile Book
Mark Miller; Ten Speed Press, 1991.

The Tabasco Cookbook
McIlhenny Company with Barbara Hunter; Clarkson Potter, 1993.

Salsa, Sambals, Chutneys and Chow-Chows
Christopher Schlesinger; Morrow Cookbooks, 1995.

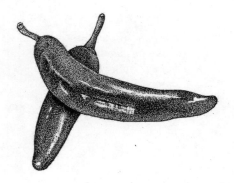

Combine all of the ingredients and let marinate for at least 1 hour before serving.

— *Maureen Cooney,* The Bluff Country Co-op Cookbook

ROASTED CHILES IN SAUCE WITH PINE NUTS AND CREAM

SERVES 2

½ green bell pepper
½ red bell pepper
2 hot yellow banana peppers
¼ cup pine nuts
2 tablespoons olive oil
2 tablespoons chopped fresh cilantro
3 tablespoons pesto, or chopped fresh basil with 4 or 5 cloves of garlic, minced
1 tablespoon white flour
½ pint (or more) half-and-half

1. Clean the peppers and remove the seeds. Slice them into slivers 1½ to 2 inches long. Spray a nonstick skillet with a squirt of nonstick cooking spray, and roast the peppers over high heat. They will not be soft, but should have some dark brown spots.

2. Remove the peppers and then roast the pine nuts in the same pan for 1 or 2 minutes.

3. Mix the peppers back in the skillet with the pine nuts and the olive oil. Add the cilantro, pesto, and flour. Stir for a minute; the mixture will start to thicken. Lower the heat.

4. Stir in enough half-and-half until it thins the sauce to the desired consistency.

— *Greg Smith,* The Bluff Country Co-op Cookbook

ENCHILADAS VERDES

SERVES 3 TO 4

1 pound fresh tomatillos
2 jalapeño peppers
1 clove garlic
4 large red tomatoes
Olive oil
1 red onion, thinly sliced
Salt and pepper
2 chicken breasts, cooked and pulled
1 cup Parmesan cheese, shredded
1 head iceberg lettuce, washed and shredded
12 ounces sour cream

Sources

Peppers in Rehoboth Beach, Delaware, is the world's largest hot sauce museum, with 6,500 different kinds on exhibit.

Its retail store offers 1,500 to 2,000 brands for sale, with 100 to 150 available for tasting at any given time.

Visit their entertaining website to find out more about hot peppers and order from their vast selection of chile-related products:

www.peppers.com

10 flour tortillas, warmed

1. Boil the tomatillos with the jalapeño peppers until they become soft; remove from the liquid and drain. Blend in a food processor, adding the garlic.

2. Blanch and peel the tomatoes; cut into cubes.

3. In a small frying pan, heat 1 to 2 tablespoons of olive oil over medium heat; add the red onion. Add the tomato cubes, and cook until the onions become translucent. Add the blended tomatillo, pepper, and garlic mixture. Simmer 10 minutes. Add salt and pepper to taste.

4. Heat more olive oil in a pan over high heat. Lightly fry the tortillas in the hot oil on both sides (or they may also be served without frying). Drain on paper towels to absorb the excess oil.

5. Assemble the ingredients on each tortilla shell (chicken, cheese, tomatillo sauce, lettuce, and sour cream). Serve topped with salsa or guacamole.

— *Terhune Orchards*

Cayenne pepper seedlings in the greenhouse awaiting transplanting.

It's Getting Warm in Here

The heat of hot peppers is measured on the Scoville scale, developed by chemist Wilbur Scoville in 1912.

Sweet bell peppers rate a zero on the Scoville scale, while the most intense is the Naga Jolokia pepper, a Bangladeshi variety that has measured a whopping 1,041,427 Scoville units.

By contrast, the previous records for the hottest peppers in the world were the Red Savina, a cultivar of the habañero chile, at 580,000 Scoville units, and the habañero itself, which measures about 260,000 units, about 65 times hotter than a jalapeño!

Pure capsaicin measures between 15 and 16 million Scoville units.

Turning Up the Heat

If you are looking to add more fire to a recipe, use more of the seeds and white inner ribs, where the fiery capsaicin is concentrated.

Conversely, if you prefer a milder dish, use just the flesh instead.

Potato

SOLANUM TUBEROSUM

One of the planet's most versatile, staple foods, the value of potatoes to humanity is inestimable. It is the number-one vegetable crop internationally, grown in 130 of the world's 167 countries, and the fourth most-grown food plant, after rice, wheat, and maize. It is also one of the most genetically diverse plants—at least 5,000 varieties were once known to the Andean peoples. Today, only a fraction of these still survive, and scientists at Peru's International Potato Center are desperately trying to save the remaining rarer species.

The potato is a member of the Solanaceae family, which includes tomatoes, eggplants, and the deadly nightshade. Because of this association, potatoes were not widely trusted as food plants outside their native Peru and Andes regions until the seventeenth and eighteenth centuries. Eventually recognizing their value as a high-starch, high-yielding crop that would thrive in soils too poor to grow other food plants, different countries employed fascinating tactics to entice their populations to consume this unfamiliar tuber. Today, the average American eats about 140 pounds of potatoes annually.

All of Featherstone's spuds are dug by hand as new potatoes in July and early August. These potatoes are so delicate that, to protect their skins, the sand is not washed off. Unlike cured potatoes, they need to be refrigerated. Featherstone grows its potatoes in sandy soil to minimize the incidence of potato scab (a black, hard growth). The sand also makes it easier for the potato to grow downward with less resistance. Later in the season, Featherstone's spuds are machine-dug and cured as finished potatoes, to be used from September to New Year's.

Featherstone grows several potato varieties:

All Blue
A curious-looking variety that is sure to attract attention in salads and french fries, All Blue has a deep bluish-purple hue that extends from its skin all the way through the center of its flesh. This potato has an excellent flavor, wonderful for baking, frying, and mashing. When boiled the flesh turns light blue.

Bintje
This is an extremely popular yellow-fleshed variety from the Netherlands. Its versatile, waxy flesh is excellent for making french fries.

Desiree Pink
This variety has pastel pink skins and pale-yellow, almost white flesh that has a creamy texture and a mild flavor, excellent for baking and roasting.

Langlade White
This is a white-fleshed variety that is a good, all-purpose spud.

Red Norland
Featherstone's cured, mature Norlands are much bigger, starchier, and sturdier than the spring "new" ones. They tend to be more soggy and wet when baked than Russets, but they make good boiling potatoes.

Russet Burbank

This large, brown-skinned beauty is the classic baking potato, with a dry, mealy texture that also makes it excellent for boiling and mashing.

Russian Fingerling

Russian Fingerlings are skinny (like a finger) and creamy, with tender skins. Try leaving these unpeeled; doing so will add texture, color, and nutrition. These are terrific for roasting.

Yukon Gold

Yukons are an all-purpose potato with golden, waxy, buttery flesh that is ideal for boiling, baking, and roasting. Their creamy texture makes outstanding mashed potatoes.

Romance

Romance is a beautiful, red-skinned potato with gold flesh, similar in appearance to the Red Gold variety but much larger, like a Russet.

HISTORY

Potatoes are native to the mountainous Andes regions of Bolivia and Peru in South America, where they have been domesticated for over 7,000 years. The earliest wild potatoes were small, wrinkled, and extremely bitter, which challenged the native peoples to find ways to make these tubers edible. In the sixteenth century, Spanish explorers introduced the potato to Europe and throughout other countries that they colonized.

Despite their obvious value as a potentially nutritious, easily cultivated sustenance crop, potatoes were not welcomed with open arms by most of Europe. In part this was due to a predictable resistance to strange, new foods and also because of the potato's kinship to the deadly nightshade. Indeed, contact with the plant's leaves can produce skin rashes, and before advanced medical science proved otherwise, it was believed that potatoes could spread leprosy.

Much of Europe regarded the tuber with disdain, calling it suitable only for lowly riffraffe. However, many governments, wanting to take advantage of this economical food source, practically ordered their citizenry to eat these unfamilar roots, or devised ingenous psychological means to overcome public resistance to them.

By the 1800s, potatoes were widely consumed across Europe. The degree to which humans can be dependent on a single food source was dramatically and tragically demonstrated during the Irish Potato Famine of 1845–49. A blight triggered by severe plant inbreeding caused a total crop failure, leading to the starvation of nearly a million people and a massive immigration of Irish to American shores.

Ironically, despite the potato's origins in the New World, it was the Scotch-Irish who brought potatoes to America. Today, Idaho is the top potato-growing state in the U.S., which annually produces 45.6 billion pounds valued at over $2.6 billion.

NUTRITION

Potatoes tend to be unfairly maligned nutritionally, usually because of how they are prepared—deep fried into french fries, made into potato

---

One Potato, Two Potato

Celebrity chef Wolfgang Puck prefers Yukon Golds for making his signature mashed potatoes.

The Russet Burbank variety was developed by famed horticulturist and plant breeder Luther Burbank in the early 1870s. The primary potato used in American french-fries, it is the number-one crop in Idaho and the most widely cultivated commercial potato variety.

Cooking Tip

Steaming instead of boiling the potatoes makes a less watery mashed product.

Cooking Tip

When making oven fries,
chill the potatoes, unpeeled,
in the refrigerator for a day
or two to make them browner.

Cooking Tip

Potato varieties that are high in
starch make good baked and
mashed spuds, because they are
drier and lower in moisture.

Low-starch varieties are firmer
in texture and are best-suited
for boiling, sautéing, and
using in potato salads.

chips, or mashed and adorned with plenty of high-fat toppings such as butter, cheese, bacon, and sour cream. Actually, potatoes are extremely healthy for you, being high in fiber, low in calories, rich in vitamins C and B6, as well as copper, potassium (more than bananas), manganese, and tryptophan, all for just 132 calories per cup. In addition, researchers have recently identified compounds called kukoamines, which may help lower blood pressure.

For maximum nutrients, leave the skins on your potatoes, where most of the tuber's vitamins, minerals, and fiber reside.

SELECTION

Potatoes of any type should be smooth and firm, with no signs of shriveling or soft or green spots.

STORAGE

New potatoes should be stored in a perforated plastic bag in the refrigerator vegetable crisper and used within 1 to 2 weeks. Mature, cured potatoes do best kept quite cool (around 45°F) in a well-ventilated, dark place, out of direct sunlight, which will trigger the formation of sprouts. Do not store potatoes next to onions; they produce gases that will hasten the spoilage of both. Mature potatoes may keep for up to 2 months, depending on temperature and humidity levels.

If the potatoes start to sprout or develop isolated green patches on their skins as a result of being exposed to light and warm temperatures, they may still be edible. Just cut off the sprouted "eyes" and peel any green skins. If, however, the green portion (actually caused by the presence of chlorophyll) is widespread throughout the surface of the potato or within its flesh, discard such specimens.

Potatoes can also keep quite well in a basement, root cellar, or other place with the proper cool temperature and lack of humidity (for more information, see "Preserving the Bounty" on page 331).

TRIMMING & CLEANING

The most preparation that properly stored potatoes usually require is a thorough scrubbing with a vegetable brush and peeling, if desired. If a potato has begun to sprout, simply cut away the sprouted areas and their surrounding "eyes," and peel away any green areas on or just under the surface of the skin.

STEAMING & BOILING

Potatoes can be steamed for 10 to 20 minutes, or until they are tender throughout. Steaming is a good alternative to boiling, which tends to make potatoes soggy and leach out their flavor. Average-sized potatoes usually require about 20 to 30 minutes of boiling time, but accurate cooking times are impossible to generalize because they depend on the variety and size of the potato. Always test cooked potatoes with an inserted fork or knife to be sure of their doneness. Also, if potatoes will be used in a chilled salad, take care to halt cooking while they are still firm.

STIR-FRYING AND SAUTÉING

Stir-frying and sautéing are usually not the first cooking methods that come to mind when preparing spuds, but potatoes can be quite delicious prepared this way, either by themselves or in combination with other vegetables. Waxy or new potatoes work better than baking types.

For these cooking methods, potatoes cook faster and more evenly if they are sliced quite thinly (julienned, shredded, or cut into small dice). Soaking potatoes beforehand in cold water helps to leach out their starch and make them cook up more crisply. Some recipes recommend parboiling potatoes first.

Stir-fry or sauté on medium-high heat in oil or butter (use 4 to 6 tablespoons for every 2 pounds of spuds) for 5 to 7 minutes, or until they reach the desired tenderness and are golden brown. Potatoes cut into rounds or small chunks will take about 10 to 15 minutes to cook.

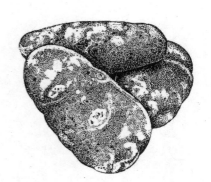

BAKING & ROASTING

Baked potatoes are an old, trusty standby that are also wonderfully simple to prepare. Resist the urge to wrap potatoes in aluminum foil; this only results in steamed potatoes with soggy, wet skins and flesh.

Place washed potatoes in a baking pan or directly on the oven rack, and pierce their skins several times to allow steam to escape. Baking times will vary immensely, depending on the potato variety and size, but a large baking-type potato will usually take about 40 to 50 minutes in a 425°F oven. Test by inserting the point of a large, sharp knife into the center of the spud; if the blade meets no resistance, the potato is done.

Roasting the potatoes concentrates their flavor, which can be accentuated with seasonings. (I personally love roasting potatoes with onions, shallots, or even garlic cloves along with olive oil and chopped fresh rosemary.) Some cooks recommend parboiling potatoes for 5 minutes first to soften them, then rubbing them with oil and seasoning, and placing them in a 400°F oven for 30 to 40 minutes, or a 350°F oven for 45 to 55 minutes. Turn them occasionally to prevent scorching.

For a real treat, make potato skins. Scoop out the inner flesh from baked potato skins, cut them into strips, spread butter and sprinkle salt over them, and bake them in a 450°F oven until they turn crisp.

MICROWAVING

To prepare potatoes for microwaving, puncture them a few times with a fork to prevent explosions; then place them on a paper towel or directly on the oven plate. Microwave on High power.

At the end of the cooking time, insert a knife into the center of the potato. If the knife sticks or meets resistance, then cook another 1 or 2 minutes, then let them stand for 5 minutes. They will finish cooking during the standing time.

- 1 to 2 medium potatoes (6 to 8 ounces) = 4 to 6 minutes
- 4 large baking potatoes = 16 to 18 minutes
- 2 pounds boiling potatoes in a covered dish with ¼ cup water = 10 to 12 minutes
- 6 small new potatoes in a covered dish with ¼ cup water = 8 to 10 minutes

New Potatoes
- 6 to 8 (about 1 pound), plus 3 tablespoons water = 8 to 12 minutes

Books

A Passion for Potatoes
Lydie Marshall;
HarperPerennial, 1992.

Potatoes: A Country Garden Cookbook
Maggie Waldron;
Collins Publishers, 1993.

The Potato: How the Humble Spud
Rescued the Western World
·Larry Zuckerman;
North Point Press, 1999.

The Ultimate Potato Book: Hundreds
of Ways To Turn America's
Favorite Side Dish into a Meal
Bruce Weinstein and Mark
Scarbrough; William Morrow
Cookbooks, 2003.

BLANCHING & FREEZING

Raw potatoes do not respond well to freezing; they will discolor and their texture will deteriorate. Boiled potatoes do not fare much better, unless they are frozen along with other ingredients.

Potatoes to be frozen must be blanched first by boiling in salted water for 4 to 5 minutes, then plunging into ice water for 5 minutes. Drain well, pack in zipper-lock freezer or vacuum food sealer-type bags, or freezer containers. Squeeze out excess air and leave ½ inch of headspace (unless you are using the vacuum sealing method). Sliced, lightly fried potatoes can also be frozen.

EQUIVALENTS, MEASURES & SERVINGS

- 3 medium to large potatoes = 1¾ cups mashed
- 1 pound = 2 to 3 medium russet or 6 to 8 new = 3 to 3½ cups chopped, sliced, or cubed = 1¾ to 2 cups cooked and mashed

COMPLEMENTARY HERBS, SEASONINGS & FOODS

Bacon, basil, butter, caviar, cayenne, celery root, chard, cheese, chervil, chives, cream, crème fraîche, dill, fennel, garlic, ham, horseradish, kale, leeks, lovage, mint, mushrooms, mustard, nutmeg, olive oil, olives, onions, paprika, parsley, pepper, pork, sage, salt, savory, smoked salmon, sour cream, squash, sweet potatoes, thyme, turnips.

SERVING SUGGESTIONS

- Combine diced potatoes with green and red peppers, onions, olives, slices of chorizo or other sausage, and diced ham to add to your favorite omelet, scrambled eggs, or frittata for an easy, nutrious, one-dish meal.
- Leftover mashed potatoes can be reincarnated in breads, doughnuts, and cakes.
- Make hash browns by finely shredding potatoes and frying them, covered, in butter or oil over low heat for 10 minutes. Then remove the cover, turn them over, and continue to fry until they become crispy.
- Enjoy new potatoes boiled simply and topped with butter, salt, cheese, garlic, and dill or other fresh herbs.
- Make oven fries by cutting potatoes into wedges, drizzling them with oil and seasonings of your choice, and baking in a 375°F oven for 30 minutes.
- Use puréed potatoes to thicken soups, or to make that cold leek-potato soup, vichyssoise (see recipe on page 232 and Yukon Gold Potato Soup on page 159).
- Finely shred potatoes to make potato latkes or pancakes.
- For new potatoes like Russian Fingerlings, toss the washed potatoes in oil, salt, pepper, and a spice of your choice (rosemary, tarragon, and sage are nice complements). Then roast them at 375°F until they are fork-tender, about 45 minutes to 1 hour.
- Prepare garlic mashed potatoes by puréeing roasted garlic, potatoes, and olive oil together. (This is also fantastic with bacon bits!)

BARBECUED POTATOES   SERVES 4

2 pounds russet or Yukon Gold potatoes, unpeeled

1 teaspoon salt
1 teaspoon pepper
1 pound thick-sliced bacon, cut into 2-inch pieces
10 ounces extra-sharp Cheddar cheese, grated (about 2½ cups)
2 tablespoons (¼ stick) unsalted butter
1 large clove garlic, minced (optional)
1 (8-ounce) container sour cream

1. Prepare a fire in your grill.

2. Slice the potatoes as thinly as possible. (You should end up with about 6 cups.) Toss them with salt and pepper.

3. Spread about one-third of the bacon across the bottom of an 8 × 11-inch foil pan. Cover the bacon with a layer of sliced potatoes and cover them with one-third of the cheese. Cover the cheese with another layer of potatoes and dot that layer with one-third of the butter. Stir the optional garlic into the sour cream and spread one-third of that on top of the butter-dotted potatoes. Repeat the entire process twice more, making layers of the bacon, potatoes, cheese, more potatoes, butter, and the sour-cream mixture.

4. Wrap the foil pan tightly with a sheet of aluminum foil. Place the wrapped pan over the hot coals and cover the grill. Cook for 45 minutes. If you are really worried about whether the potatoes have cooked enough, you can try to unwrap a little corner of the foil—but that can be messy, and you would have to watch out for the hot steam.

5. With a sharp knife, slash the bottom of the foil in several places to let the fat drain out. Serve the potatoes right away.

— *Ann Hodgman*, One Bite Won't Kill You

Yukon Gold Potato Soup

SERVES 6

Served cold, this would be vichyssoise; served hot, it is sometimes called soup bonne femme, *or "good housewife" soup. Whatever it is called, it is inexpensive, satisfying, and very, very good. Thin-skinned Yukon Gold potatoes need not be peeled. In fact, the skins almost disappear when the soup is puréed, but their memory lends the soup more character.*

2 pounds (about 4 medium) Yukon Gold potatoes
2 large leeks (whiter ends only)
¼ cup butter
4 cups chicken or vegetable broth
2 teaspoons kosher salt, or to taste
1 teaspoon ground white pepper
1 cup organic whipping cream
Chives, for garnish

1. Cut the potatoes into 1-inch chunks. Split the leek ends in half

My hope is not some kind of wishful thinking. Rather, it is a gracious and honest hope rooted in the good work being done in communities.

Take, for example, our humble little CSA. By joining this cooperative, we are giving and receiving much more than money and veggies. We are saying to the farmers that we will be there to share the risk of a failed crop. We are telling our neighbors that there are alternatives to Wal*Mart and Cub Foods [a supermarket chain]. And we are telling ourselves that the food we eat is meant to nourish not only our bodies but the soil as well.

Every time someone asks you about a CSA is one more ripple of hope, as it is one more person who will begin to ask where his or her food came from. It is one more person who will likely see the benefits of local foods, sustainable agriculture, and small farms because it just makes sense.

No democracy will ever be perfect, nor will it ever be straightforward. It is actually really quite messy and it certainly is a lot of hard work (kind of like farming). It involves taking risks, asking questions, and trying new things.

Joining a CSA involves much of the same—and it certainly hasn't been easy. Adjusting to eating so many new foods is a lifestyle change, as my friend and fellow CSAer so candidly pointed out. But it is something that I know I must do. It's a kind of embodied democracy, as I've come to call it: a local foods revolution that changes the world one box at a time.

"Potatoes are to food what sensible shoes are to fashion."

— *Linda Wells*

lengthwise and rinse out any soil trapped between the layers; slice them crosswise into ¼-inch half-rounds.

2. In a large soup pot with a thick base, melt the butter over medium heat and cook the sliced leeks, stirring often until they are very tender but not brown, about 10 minutes. Add the cubed potatoes, broth, salt, and pepper and bring the soup to a boil. Cover and decrease the heat to low. Simmer gently for 15 minutes, or until the potatoes are very tender. (The soup may be served as a rustic country soup at this point, but it is even better when it is puréed.)

3. In a blender, purée the soup in small batches. Cover the top of the machine with a kitchen towel and process, using short pulses at first so that the hot mixture does not overflow when the machine is turned on. Bring the cream to a gentle simmer in the soup pot and stir in the puréed soup. Serve the soup hot with snipped chives on top.

— *Greg Atkinson*

PEPPERY POTATO AND ZUCCHINI PACKETS ON THE GRILL

SERVES 4

1½ pounds potatoes (6 medium), scrubbed and thinly sliced
1 zucchini, rinsed and thinly sliced
1 medium onion, thinly sliced
1 tablespoon olive oil
1 teaspoon fresh thyme or ½ teaspoon dried thyme
½ teaspoon salt

1. Heat the grill.

2. Mix all of the ingredients in a bowl. Divide the mixture among 4 pieces of aluminum foil, placing the mixture near one end. Fold in half to form a packet; then fold the edges to seal completely.

3. Grill the packets 25 to 30 minutes, turning over once, until the potatoes are tender when pierced.

— *Featherstone Farm*

VEGETABLE CORNMEAL CRÊPES

SERVES 6
(2 CRÊPES PER SERVING)

CRÊPES

1 cup all-purpose flour
⅓ cup yellow cornmeal
1 tablespoon sugar
2½ teaspoons baking powder
3 tablespoons grated Parmesan cheese
1¾ cup skim milk
2 tablespoons melted margarine

1 egg
2 egg whites
Vegetable cooking spray

FILLING

1 pound cooked new potatoes, cut into ½-inch pieces
1 cup mushrooms, sliced
½ medium red bell pepper, chopped
2 teaspoons olive or vegetable oil
2 small zucchini, coarsely shredded
2 cups broccoli florets, steamed until crisp-tender
3 tablespoons grated Parmesan cheese
2 teaspoons finely chopped fresh thyme or ½ teaspoon dried thyme
⅛ teaspoon salt
¼ teaspoon pepper
6 tablespoons reduced-fat sour cream
Parsley sprigs

FOR THE CRÊPES

1. In a medium-sized bowl, mix the flour, cornmeal, sugar, baking powder, and cheese. Then stir in the milk, margarine, egg, and egg whites until smooth.

2. Spray a crêpe pan or small skillet with cooking spray; heat over medium heat. Spoon 3 tablespoons of the crêpe batter into the skillet, rotating the pan quickly so that the batter covers the bottom of the pan in a thin layer. Cook over medium heat until the crêpe turns light brown on the bottom. With a spatula, loosen the edges of the crêpe; turn and cook until other side is light brown.

3. Stack the crêpes between sheets of waxed paper, and cover loosely with a clean kitchen towel.

FOR THE FILLING

1. In a large skillet, sauté the potatoes, mushrooms, and bell pepper in the oil until the potatoes begin to brown, about 5 minutes.

2. Stir in the zucchini and broccoli; sauté until the zucchini turns tender, about 3 minutes.

3. Stir in the cheese, thyme, salt, and pepper. Spoon the vegetable mixture into the center of the crêpes (about ⅓ cup per crêpe). Roll the crêpes and place, seam sides down, on the plates.

4. Garnish with dollops of sour cream and parsley.

— *Fruits and Veggies—More Matters; Centers for Disease Control & Prevention*

For More Information

Washington State Potato Commission
www.potatoes.com

Idaho Potato Commission
www.idahopotato.com

The United States Potato Board
www.healthypotato.com

PETER RABBIT'S BIRTHDAY SOUP   SERVES 8 TO 10

2 pounds carrots, peeled and chopped
4 cups chicken stock or water

1½ teaspoons salt
1 medium potato, chopped
1 cup onion, chopped
1 to 2 small cloves garlic, crushed
⅓ cup chopped cashews
3 to 4 tablespoons butter
¾ cup sour cream
½ to 1 teaspoon thyme
Toasted nuts and extra sour cream (optional)

1. Bring the carrots, chicken stock or water, salt, and potato to a boil. Cover and simmer for 12 to 15 minutes. Let cool.

2. Meanwhile, sauté the onion, garlic, and cashews in the butter until the onions turn translucent.

3. Purée everything together in a blender until the soup is smooth. Return the purée to a pan or double boiler and whisk in the sour cream. Heat very slowly and season with the thyme. Garnish with toasted nuts and sour cream, if desired.

— *Maureen Cooney,* The Bluff Country Co-op Cookbook

SOUR CREAM POTATO SALAD   SERVES 10

This is a real favorite. It is even better when refrigerated a day ahead to blend the flavors.

7 medium red or white potatoes, cooked in their jackets,
    peeled and sliced (6 cups)
⅓ cup Italian dressing
¾ cup celery, sliced
⅓ cup chopped scallions, white sections and green tops, plus extra
    for garnish, if desired
4 hard-cooked eggs
1 cup Miracle Whip salad dressing
½ cup sour cream
1½ teaspoons prepared horseradish mustard
    (or 1 teaspoon prepared mustard and ½ teaspoon horseradish)
Salt
Celery seed
⅓ cup cucumber, diced

1. While the potatoes are still warm, pour the Italian dressing over them. Chill them for 2 hours.

2. Add the celery and scallion.

3. Chop the egg whites and sieve the egg yolks, reserving some yolk for garnish if desired. Combine the remaining sieved yolk with Miracle Whip, sour cream, and horseradish mustard. Fold into the salad. Add salt and celery seed to taste.

"For me, a plain baked potato is the most delicious one … It is soothing and enough."

— *M. F. K. Fisher,*
American food writer

4. Chill the salad for at least 2 hours.

5. Add the diced cucumber just before serving. Garnish with the reserved sieved yolk and sliced onion tops, if desired.

— Matthew George Looper, The Schoenleber Family Cookbook

. . . .

LaVerne's Potato Candy   SERVES 8

As a child this was one of our favorite treats. My mother made potato candy for me and my siblings while we were growing up in the small company railroad and coal town of Delano, Pennsylvania. Potato candy still is often served as a special treat, because everyone likes it. Often it is made for social affairs at the local firehouse and church because it sells well and serves as a good fundraiser. Although it is hard work to make it, it's worth the effort because kids and adults like its taste.

1 medium, cooked mashed potato (instead of mashed potatoes, 4 ounces of cream cheese may be used)
1 tablespoon of butter
Dash of vanilla
1 pound powdered sugar
Peanut butter

1. Make the mashed potato, keeping it to a dough-like consistency, similar to pie dough. (Or instead of mashed potatoes, soften 4 ounces of cream cheese and combine with 1 tablespoon of butter).

2. Add a dash of vanilla and 1 pound of powdered sugar to the potatoes.

3. Roll out the dough on wax paper using some flour so the dough will not stick. (Dough is also a little easier to work with if chilled before rolling out.)

4. After you have rolled out the dough until it is somewhat smooth and to the desired thickness, spread peanut butter over the top.

5. Then roll up the dough and slice into pieces of candy. You can also roll it into small individual rolls. Refrigerate until chilled, and slice.

6. Enjoy eating this Pennsylvania Dutch treat!

— Library of Congress, American Memory Project, Immigration … The Great American Potluck

> "A diet that consists predominantly of rice leads to the use of opium, just as a diet that consists predominantly of potatoes leads to the use of liquor."
>
> *— Friedrich Nietzsche, German philosopher*

Rosemary

In the Mediterranean climates where this perennial herb grows rampantly, it can be hard to walk past it and resist plucking a sprig or crushing a few of its evergreen, needle-like leaves and inhaling its distinctive, pungent, piney-sweet scent. Rosemary seems equally happy growing wild in sprawling bushes, or contained in considerably more restrictive environments in the home garden, where it can be shaped into topiaries or grown as a pot plant. It definitely prefers a hot, arid climate where paradoxically, it is watered only by the moisture from daily morning fog or dew; constant wet feet quickly kills rosemary.

Humans have treasured rosemary throughout history as a culinary herb, a decorative ornamental, and a valuable medicine. Along the way, the herb became associated with memory and remembrance, for which it still remains a symbol. Christianity favored it, where it was once believed that rosemary never grows taller than the height of Jesus Christ, nor after 33 years (the age of Christ when he was crucified).

HISTORY

Rosemary's native shores lie in the Mediterranean region, where its hot, dry climate richly concentrates the herb's aromatic oils. Ancient Greeks used to wear rosemary wreaths while studying to enhance their memory. In ancient Rome, sprigs of the herb were placed in the hands of the dead for remembrance. In fact, rosemary symbolized both love and death in ancient Europe, where it was carried in wedding bouquets and laid on coffins. Rosemary was imported to England in the mid-1500s.

NUTRITION

Rosemary contains fiber, iron, calcium, and vitamins A and C. It is also rich in certain antioxidants, especially carnosol and ursolic acid.

SELECTION

Choose sprigs that look fresh and green, with no limp or discolored branches. Fresh rosemary has a far superior flavor than the dried form.

STORAGE

Store fresh rosemary in the refrigerator vegetable crisper, either in its original packaging or wrapped in a damp paper towel, where it will keep for up to 1 week. You can also trim the bottoms of rosemary stems, strip off the leaves from the first several inches of the stems, and place the sprigs in a glass of water. Dried rosemary will keep in a tightly sealed container in a cool, dark, dry place for about 6 months.

TRIMMING & CLEANING

Rinse fresh rosemary branches under running water briefly before patting dry. For recipes calling for just the leaves, grasp the stem between your forefinger and thumb and pull down, stripping the leaves off. Or you can use entire sprigs for grilling and roasting.

FREEZING

An easy way to freeze rosemary is to place whole sprigs in a zipper-lock freezer bag, freeze for a couple of weeks, then remove the bag, and run a rolling pin over the unopened bag. This removes many of the leaves from the stems. You can either continue to store the leaves in the freezer in the zipper-lock bag, package them in a vacuum food sealer-type bag, or place them in a tightly lidded canning jar. Rosemary should keep well this way for up to 1 year.

Another terrific way to freeze rosemary and other herbs is to chop them finely, mix them into a paste using ⅓ cup of olive oil to every 2 cups of herbs, and then freeze the resulting mixture in ice cube trays. To thaw, simply pop out a few cubes into a strainer and let the ice melt away, or just drop them frozen into sauces or soups.

DRYING

Rosemary can be dried, although freezing fresh rosemary does preserve more flavor. Hang fresh sprigs in a warm, dry, dark place with good ventilation, and store the dried leaves in an airtight container.

COMPLEMENTARY HERBS, SEASONINGS & FOODS

Bay, beans, beef, cheese, chervil, chives, eggs, fruit, garlic, lamb, lentils, mint, mushrooms, onions, parsley, pork, potatoes, poultry, sage, spinach, thyme, tomatoes, veal.

SERVING SUGGESTIONS

- Rosemary has a surprising affinity with fruit. Try sprinkling finely chopped fresh leaves over fruit salad, or simmering fruit juice with rosemary, straining and cooling it, and pouring it over fresh fruit such as melon, oranges, peaches, and pears.
- Infuse soups and stews by adding a sprig during the last half hour of cooking.
- Flavor butter by adding 2 teaspoons of finely chopped fresh rosemary to ½ cup softened butter.
- Place rosemary sprigs in vinegar for sprinkling over salads or meats.
- Insert whole sprigs under the skin of chicken or turkey, or into lamb or beef roasts, along with slivers of fresh garlic and whole baby onions, prior to cooking.
- Besides culinary uses, the scent of rosemary is both stimulating and yet soothing, useful for relieving headaches and tension. Place a few sprigs in a muslim bag when drawing a hot bath, or make tea from the fresh herb.

SUBSTITUTIONS

If you happen to be out of rosemary, substitute thyme, tarragon, or savory instead.

> ### Cooking Tip
> Rosemary is a powerful herb with a strong personality. It goes best with other robust foods and seasonings that can stand up to its distinctive scent and flavor, and it should not be used in dishes that are very delicate or where it may overpower.

. . . .

MYLAR'S ROSEMARY POTATO WEDGES   SERVES 4 (IF YOU'RE LUCKY)

3 to 5 large baking potatoes (depending on appetites)
2 to 4 cloves garlic
2 to 3 large rosemary sprigs
Olive or sesame oil

Sea salt
Freshly ground black pepper

1. Preheat the oven to 450°F.

2. Cut the potatoes into bite-sized wedges.

3. Strip the rosemary off their stems, and coarsely chop the leaves. Finely chop the garlic. (If you have one of those little miniature food processors, you can throw the garlic cloves and rosemary together into the machine.)

4. Place the potatoes in a big bowl and toss lightly with oil (sesame adds a deliciously nutty, smoky flavor), garlic, rosemary, salt, and pepper.

5. Line a large shallow baking dish or sheet with aluminum foil, then place the potatoes in a single layer on top. Bake for about 30 to 45 minutes, or until the potatoes are nicely golden brown on the outside but still moist inside. Serve immediately.

— *Mi Ae Lipe, Featherstone Farm CSA member*

ROSEMARY CROCKPOT CHICKEN   SERVES 4

1 roasting chicken
2 sprigs fresh rosemary
2 stalks celery with leaves, cut into pieces
2 small onions, quartered
16 cloves garlic
1 tablespoon lemon juice
½ teaspoon salt
½ teaspoon pepper
½ teaspoon paprika

1. Remove and discard the chicken giblets and neck, or freeze for making broth another time. Trim the excess fat. Rinse the chicken and pat dry.

2. Place the rosemary, celery, 4 of the onion wedges, and 4 of the garlic cloves in the cavity of the chicken. Tie the legs together with string. Place the chicken, breast side up, in a crockpot. Add the remaining onion and garlic.

3. Drizzle lemon juice over the chicken; sprinkle with the salt, pepper, and paprika. Cover, and cook on low heat for 8 hours.

— *Harmony, www.cdkitchen.com*

ROSEMARY- OR BASIL-INFUSED OIL   MAKES 1 CUP

1 cup mild olive or vegetable oil
¼ cup packed chopped fresh rosemary leaves or ½ cup packed roughly chopped fresh basil leaves

"How sweet I roam'd from field to field And tasted all the summer's pride."

— *William Blake,*
"Song (How Sweet I Roam'd),"
Poetical Sketches

1. Place the oil and rosemary (or basil) in a 3½- to 4-quart slow cooker. Cook uncovered over high heat for 1½ to 2 hours, then turn the cooker off.

2. Allow the oil to cool for about 20 minutes, and then pour it through a sieve lined with a clean paper towel or paper coffee filter into a metal bowl.

3. When the oil is completely cool, transfer it to a clean glass jar. Cover the jar and refrigerate for up to 1 month. (After that, the flavor may fade.) The oil may cloud under refrigeration, but it will become clear again at room temperature.

— *Kylan, www.cdkitchen.com*

. . . .

BRAISED LAMB WITH OLIVES AND MUSHROOMS

SERVES 2

1 tablespoon butter
1 tablespoon olive oil
6 sage leaves
2 tablespoons fresh rosemary leaves, chopped
1 bay leaf
1½ pounds lamb chops, bone removed and cubed
3 tablespoons white wine
6 shiitake mushroom caps, or 3 whole ones, or 4 with stems trimmed in half
¾ cup Sicilian green olives
2 tablespoons capers
¼ cup red or yellow bell pepper strips
Salt and pepper

1. Melt the butter and oil in a large skillet over medium heat. Add the sage, rosemary, and bay leaf.

2. Add the lamb cubes and lower the heat. Cook it, stirring continuously, until the meat is well-browned.

3. When the lamb is browned, pour the wine into the pan. Add the mushrooms, olives, and capers, and simmer for 5 minutes. Then add the bell peppers.

4. Season with salt and pepper to taste. Simmer for 5 more minutes, then serve immediately.

— *Jacob Wittenberg*

Savory

SATUREJA HORTENSIS OR
S. MONTANA

Savory is a spicy, distinctive herb reminiscent of a combination of sage and thyme—somewhat minty, green, and medicinal-tasting. The name can refer to two different species: summer savory (Satureja hortensis), which is an annual herb with a sweet, delicate flavor preferred for sausages and cabbage rolls, or winter savory (Satureja montana), a perennial, semiwoody shrub whose robust, tough leaves are more suitable for long cooking with meats such as chicken and turkey. The small leaves of both herbs share a similar aroma and flavor, and are often a part of herb mixtures such as herbes de Provençale *and* bouquet garni.

Although savory is used primarily as a culinary herb, it contains oils and tannins with mild astringent and antiseptic properties that can be useful in medicines. Rubbing a sprig of crushed savory on wasp or bee stings provides quick relief.

HISTORY

Savory originated in the Mediterranean, where the ancient Romans, including Pliny, regarded the herb as an effective aphrodisiac. While this use is somewhat questionable, the herb is well-known for its warming qualities and was used as an expectorant. It was also used to cure flatulence and colic, to soothe earaches, and even to restore vision. Shakespeare mentioned it, along with mint, majoram, and lavender in his play *The Winter's Tale*. Early English colonists brought savory to America to remind them of their home country.

NUTRITION

Savory is not usually consumed in large enough quantities to be of nutritive value, but the plant does contain essential oils with warming properties. The plant is reputed to be good for digestive upsets and a remedy for flatulence, and early California settlers made a tea from the herb.

SELECTION

Savory should be vibrantly green and fresh-looking, not wilted or discolored. Avoid specimens with dark spots, mold, or slime.

STORAGE

Store the fresh herb unwashed and wrapped in a plastic bag in the refrigerator vegetable crisper along with a damp paper towel for up to a few days. Or you can treat fresh savory sprigs like any living flower or plant cutting; just snip off the stem ends, place them in a glass of water, and cover loosely with a plastic bag.

TRIMMING & CLEANING

Rinse fresh savory thoroughly under running water, and strip the leaves from the tough, woody stems before using.

BLANCHING & FREEZING

You can freeze fresh savory in leaf form by washing and thoroughly drying the sprigs, stripping them of leaves, and placing them in zipper-lock freezer bags. Or package them using vacuum food sealer-type bags.

A terrific way to freeze savory and other herbs is to chop them finely, mix them into a paste using ⅓ cup of olive oil to every 2 cups of herbs, and then freeze the resulting mixture in ice cube trays. To thaw, simply pop out a few cubes into a strainer and let the ice melt away, or just drop them frozen into sauces or soups.

DRYING

Spread a layer of leaves on a cookie sheet and place the herbs in a warm (up to 180°F) oven for 3 to 4 hours, stirring the herbs periodically until they are thoroughly dry. Or remove the best leaves from the stems and arrange them on a paper towel without letting them touch. This layer is covered with another paper towel and a second layer of leaves is added. Five layers may be dried at one time using this method.

A microwave oven can also be used for small quantities of herbs. Place 4 or 5 herb branches in the microwave between paper towels. Heat for 2 to 3 minutes over High power. If the herbs are not brittle and dry when removed, repeat the microwave drying for 30 seconds more. (Be aware that the heat generated during microwaving not only removes moisture but some of its oils, so these herbs may not have as intense a flavor as herbs dried by other methods.)

COMPLEMENTARY HERBS, SEASONINGS, AND FOODS

Basil, beans, beef, cabbage, cheese, chervil, chives, eggs, fish, game, lamb, lemon, majoram, oregano, parsley, peas, pork, poultry, rabbit, sage, sausage, soups, thyme, tarragon.

SERVING SUGGESTIONS

- Add chopped fresh savory to your favorite stuffing, marinade, or gravy.
- Fry pork sausage in a bit of savory and sage, or add the herb to hamburgers.
- Fresh savory is delectable mixed with goat cheese and served with crackers.
- Add savory near the end of the cooking time to soups and stews.
- Use savory in making a bouquet garni, that little bundle of fresh or dried herbs added to dishes as they cook and removed just before serving.
- Try using strong-flavored savory as a salt substitute.
- Slow-cook winter savory with dried beans and peas.
- Sprinkle a mixture of chopped fresh savory, basil, oregano, and majoram over pizza.
- Combine fresh savory and tarragon with a little lemon or lime juice and sprinkle over sole, halibut, or other delicate white fish.
- A little chopped fresh savory livens up steamed green beans, peas, broccoli, and summer squash.
- Combine savory, chives, lemon juice, and mayonnaise and top poached chicken or fish.

SUBSTITUTIONS

Use thyme, majoram, or sage instead.

The Big Three

In Bulgaria, three seasonings regularly appear on the table: salt, paprika, and savory.

How Sweet It Is

In the first century B.C.E., Virgil grew savory for his bees, believing that it made their honey taste better.

SUMMER SAVORY SOUP — SERVES 4

1 tablespoon olive oil
2 small cloves garlic, minced
½ sweet onion, chopped
2 cups mixed vegetables (such as cabbage, cauliflower, green beans, spinach, etc.)
3 cups vegetable or chicken broth
¾ cup orzo or other small pasta
½ teaspoon fresh basil, minced
½ teaspoon fresh oregano, minced
1 tablespoon flour
¼ cup milk or half-and-half
½ teaspoon fresh summer savory, minced
Salt and pepper

1. Heat the oil in a medium-sized saucepan. Add the garlic and onion and cook until the onions are softened. Add any of the chunkier vegetables that will need extra time, and cook for 5 to 7 minutes on low heat, stirring occasionally.

2. Add the broth and the remaining vegetables. Bring to a boil. Add the orzo, basil, and oregano. Simmer for about 15 minutes.

3. In a separate bowl, whisk the flour into the milk or half-and-half until well-combined. Decrease the heat and stir in the flour mixture. Add the savory. Stir frequently while the soup thickens. Add salt and pepper to taste.

— *Brenda Hyde, www.oldfashionedliving.com*

BLACK BEAN SOUP
WITH GARLIC AND SUMMER SAVORY — SERVES 6

2 tablespoons olive oil
1 cup onion, finely chopped
1 jalapeño pepper, finely chopped
3 cloves garlic, minced
½ cup summer savory leaves
6 cups cooked black beans (if canned, drain well)
2 cups water
4 cups chicken or vegetable stock
Salt and paprika

1. In a very large saucepan, heat the olive oil and sauté the onion and jalapeño pepper for 3 minutes. Add the garlic and ¼ cup of the summer savory; sauté for another 3 minutes.

2. Add 2 cups of the black beans and 2 cups water. Sauté, mixing

constantly, until all of the water is absorbed by the beans, and the mixture is thick. Add the chicken or vegetable stock and boil for 5 minutes.

3. Strain the mixture through a sieve, pressing all of the ingredients so that they pass through the sieve. Return the liquid to the pot and add the remaining 4 cups of beans, salt, and paprika. Boil for another 5 minutes.

4. Sprinkle the remaining fresh summer savory leaves over the soup. Serve with tortilla chips.

— *Brenda Hyde, www.oldfashionedliving.com*

. . . .

SUNFLOWER MEATLOAF

SERVES 8

This meatloaf is a super-tasty and healthy vegetarian substitute for the real thing! Marmite is a savory, salty spread made from yeast extract that is popular in Great Britain; in the U.S. it can be ordered through online food retailers or found in stores specializing in British items.

1 cup raw sunflower seeds, ground
1 cup breadcrumbs
1 cup walnuts, ground
1 cup raw potatoes, grated
1 tablespoon Marmite
1 cup rice milk or soy milk
1 large onion, grated
2 tablespoons instant coffee or coffee substitute
1 tablespoon oil
1 tablespoon fresh savory or 1 teaspoon dried savory
1 clove garlic (optional)

1. Thoroughly mix the sunflower seeds, breadcrumbs, walnuts, and potato.

2. Preheat the oven to 350°F.

3. In a blender, blend the remaining ingredients. Add to the dry ingredients and mix well. Let stand for 15 minutes.

4. Bake for 1 hour. Serve with mushroom gravy.

— *www.recipezaar.com*

622 Selby Avenue
St. Paul, Minnesota
651-310-9469

➤ **Seward Co-op**
2111 East Franklin Avenue
Minneapolis, Minnesota
612-338-2465
www.seward.coop

➤ **Valley Natural Foods**
13750 CR 11
Burnsville, Minnesota
952-891-1212
www.valleynaturalfoods.com

➤ **The Wedge Co-op**
2105 Lyndale Avenue South
Minneapolis, Minnesota
612-871-3993
www.wedge.coop

➤ **Whole Foods Market**
3060 Excelsior Boulevard
Minneapolis, Minnesota
612-927-8141
www.wholefoodsmarket.com

30 Fairview Avenue South
St. Paul, Minnesota
651-690-0197

Squash (Summer)

CUCURBITA PEPO

Over 600 types of heirloom squash exist, each with distinguishing characteristics in appearance, flesh, and flavor. Some are round and elongated, while others are scalloped and pear-shaped, with flesh that ranges from ivory to brilliant orange. The terms "summer" and "winter" for squash can be confusing, as the "summer" types (zucchini, patty pan, and yellow) are frequently in the market all winter; and "winter" types can be found in late summer and fall.

These types were named based on their storage longevity. Summer varieties have thin skins and are highly perishable, whereas the thick-skinned winter squashes can be stored unrefrigerated for several months.

Featherstone grows three Cucurbita species for a total of ten different squashes: Cucurbita pepo *(to which the summer squashes belong), and the winter squash varieties* Cucurbita moschata *and* Cucurbita maxima.

For more information on zucchini, please see pages 202–210. For information on winter squashes, see pages 279–288.

HISTORY

The history of squash is sordid and confusing, as references to this New World vine have intertwined it since antiquity with the closely related gourds and pumpkins, some of which may have originated in the Old World. It is thought that most modern-day summer squashes came from a wild variety that grows between Guatemala and Mexico.

Squashes are possibly one of humanity's earliest cultivated foods, with seeds found in Mexican caves dated around 9000 B.C.E. Christopher Columbus brought squash back from the New World to Europe in the 1400s; subsequently Portuguese and Spanish explorers introduced squash to many other parts of the world.

NUTRITION

A 1-cup serving of summer squash contains nearly one-fifth of the adult daily requirement for manganese, as well as significant vitamins A, C, and K, magnesium, potassium, copper, folate, phosphorus, and dietary fiber, all for only 36 calories.

SELECTION

Summer squashes are best when they are still young, tender, and small. Avoid overly large squashes, for they may be bitter, tough, and tasteless. Choose firm, plump, heavy specimens with unblemished skins and no soft, bruised, shriveled, or watery spots.

STORAGE

Summer squashes are surprisingly perishable; avoid washing them until just before using, and keep them wrapped in a plastic bag in the refrigerator vegetable crisper for up to 4 days. Try to avoid bruising or puncturing the delicate skin, which will lead to decay.

TRIMMING & CLEANING

Summer squash requires little preparation; just wash thoroughly and slice into the desired-size pieces; peeling their thin skins is usually unnecessary.

STEAMING & BOILING

Summer squashes often become watery when cooked, so either choose cooking methods that dry them out a bit, or avoid those that may exacerbate this characteristic. For this reason, steaming summer squash is preferable to boiling it, which yields a more waterlogged product. Steam 1-inch chunks over rapidly boiling water for 10 to 15 minutes, or until the squash is tender.

STIR-FRYING & SAUTÉING

Cut squash into thin strips, coins, or slices. Sprinkle with oil, butter, broth, or soy sauce, and stir-fry or sauté it over high heat for about 3 to 6 minutes, or until the squash is tender and its edges lightly browned.

BAKING & ROASTING

Baking and roasting summer squash are better alternatives to boiling, as the oven or broiler heat helps dry out their copious moisture. Squashes do well fixed as casseroles with other ingredients, or you can cut them in half, drizzle them with olive oil, butter, or a marinade and bake at 350°F for 25 to 30 minutes.

MICROWAVING

Trim off the ends; cut into ¼-inch slices and place in a microwave-safe dish with ¼ cup water; cover and cook on High power.

- 1½ cups = 3 to 4 minutes
- 1 pound = 6 to 7 minutes

BLANCHING & FREEZING

Summer squash can be frozen, but its high water content causes it to turn mushy when thawed. To freeze raw squash, it must be blanched first. Wash it, trim off the stem ends, and cut it into slices or strips. Blanch in rapidly boiling water for 3 minutes, then pack it in zipper-lock freezer or vacuum food sealer-type bags, or freezer containers. Squeeze out the excess air and leave ½ inch of headspace (unless you are using the vacuum sealing method). Also, puréed or sautéed squash tends to freeze somewhat better. Frozen summer squash will keep up to 3 months.

MEASURES & EQUIVALENTS

- 1 pound squash = about 3½ cups sliced = 4 cups grated = 2 cups salted and squeezed = 2 to 3 servings

COMPLEMENTARY HERBS, SEASONINGS & FOODS

Basil, beans, butter, cheese, chives, cinnamon, cloves, corn, cream, curry

July Days

**by Rhys Williams,
Former Featherstone
Farm Partner**

August 25, 2004

Last Saturday morning, we thought we had dodged a bullet. At 4:00 A.M. the temperature at the shop was 37 degrees Fahrenheit. The shop is in a low spot so it is a good indication of the temperature of our valley. As we drove to market and listened to the lows across the state, we thought we had avoided the frost that blanketed many of the fields that we passed.

Unfortunately, the fields where our melons and cantaloupe were growing did get frosted, and many of the plants were damaged. It will be a few days until we can fully assess the crop.

So one of the strangest years continues. To have frost on August 20 is devastating to any agricultural enterprise. If it had happened in Florida, the papers would be full of pictures of ice-covered oranges. In the apple industry, the fruit would begin ripening at an increased rate and cause panic throughout the orchards.

powder, dill, garlic, marjoram, mint, nutmeg, onions, pepper, rosemary, sage, sausage, tomatoes.

SERVING SUGGESTIONS

- Add peeled summer squash cubes to soups, stews, beans, gratins, and vegetable ragouts.
- Serve chunks or slices of summer squash with other raw vegetables and your favorite dips and dressings.
- Finely grate or shred summer squash, sauté with onion in butter, and combine with milk, eggs, and seasonings. Top with butter and cracker crumbs, and bake in a 450°F oven for 15 minutes, or until the casserole is golden brown.
- Make a hearty one-dish meal of squash lasagne, combining summer squash, layers of meat, cheese, and noodles. Serve with salad and fruit.
- Shred summer squash with carrots, cucumbers, and cabbage for an unusual coleslaw.
- Thinly slice summer squash to substitute for cucumbers in sandwiches.
- Slice summer squashes in half and grill for 3 to 4 minutes on either side on the hottest part of the grill. Chunks of squash are terrific in shish kebobs.
- Make a batch of ratatouille by combining summer squash, eggplant, tomatoes, onions, garlic, herbs, and olive oil, and cooking slowly to reduce the liquid.
- Add diced summer squash to salads and pasta dishes.
- Bake sliced summer squash that has been brushed with melted butter and sprinkled with lemon pepper at 400°F for 20 to 25 minutes, or until tender.
- Sauté coins of summer squash with zucchini and other squashes of contrasting colors—yellow and light green, for instance—and dress with fresh herbs and garlic for a lovely summer dish.
- Of course, if all else fails, make that old standby—squash bread or muffins. Be sure to decrease the amount of liquid in the recipe by about a third to compensate for the vegetable's moisture.

STUFFED SQUASH WITH BASIL AND HONEY   SERVES 4 TO 6

This recipe comes from one of our regulars at the farmers market. She got it from New Zealand.

2 pounds summer squash (about 4 to 6 squashes)
Olive oil
1 small Walla Walla onion, finely chopped
1 clove garlic, crushed
1 tablespoon honey
1 teaspoon light soy sauce
1 tablespoon tahini
⅓ cup fresh basil
1 tablespoon toasted sesame seeds

1. Boil, steam, or microwave the squash whole until it is tender. Drain and cool. Trim the slices so that the squash can sit flat (either like a

canoe for the zucchini and yellow squash, or like a chair for the patty pan). Scoop a shallow hole from the top of each squash. Set the shells aside, and finely chop the scooped pieces.

2. Preheat the oven to 375°F.

3. Heat the oil in a small saucepan and add the onion and garlic. Sauté over medium heat until they become soft, about 2 minutes. Add the chopped squash, honey, soy sauce, tahini, and basil, and cook for 1 more minute. Place the squash shells onto an oven tray, spoon the basil mixture into the hollows, and sprinkle with sesame seeds.

4. Bake for 10 minutes. Serve the individual squashes on their own plates.

— *Featherstone Farm*

SUMMER SQUASH MUFFINS

MAKES 12 MUFFINS

These muffins are great for breakfast or as an addition to summer meals. Also, by using the microwave oven to cook the muffins, you won't heat up your kitchen!

1 cup all-bran cereal
¾ cup skim milk
2 cups grated zucchini or other summer squash
½ cup whole-wheat flour
½ cup all-purpose enriched flour
2 tablespoons frozen orange juice concentrate
2 tablespoons canola oil
1 tablespoon fresh lemon juice
1 teaspoon baking powder
1 teaspoon baking soda
1 teaspoon ground cinnamon
½ teaspoon ground ginger
⅛ teaspoon salt
1 medium egg, beaten

1. In a large bowl, combine the bran with the milk and grated squash. Let stand 5 minutes.

2. Meanwhile, in a medium-sized bowl, mix the remaining ingredients. Add this mixture to the bran mixture and stir until just combined. Do not overstir.

3. Line a microwave-safe muffin tin with 2 paper liners per cup, and fill each cup half full. Microwave on High power for 5 to 5½ minutes, or until the muffins are springy when touched. It is best to microwave only 6 muffins at a time.

— *Fruits and Veggies—More Matters; Centers for Disease Control & Prevention*

But in Minnesota it is just one more thing to deal with and one more adjustment to make. Many corn and soybean growers in northern Minnesota have been forced to write off the year. It was probably a merciful ending to a very wet, cold year.

But what are you going to do? You accept the notion in agriculture that your biggest variable is not one you can control. It puts you at the mercy of the weather, and you begin to understand why so many early farming communities were spiritually based.

Our farm will lose a couple of weeks of cantaloupe, and the growth of many of our crops will be slowed. Fortunately for our CSA, we still have a wide variety that will fill in any gaps that we may experience. Rebecca's planning and crop selection will help us to get through some of the problems that the weather has thrown at us.

Now, we at Featherstone await the arrival of the locust. We will be one of the few farms in the Midwest that expect their arrival and are already looking up recipes for all of you.

Books

Summer Squash & Squash Blossoms: From Seed to Supper
Jack W. Hazelton; Seed to Supper, 2000.

The Classic Zucchini Cookbook: 225 Recipes for All Kinds of Squash
Nancy C. Ralston, Marynor Jordan, Andrea Chesman; Storey Publishing, 2002.

Squash Lovers Cook Book
Golden West Publishers and Lee Fischer; Golden West Publishers, 2003.

SUMMER SQUASH CASSEROLE

SERVES 4 TO 6

For summer squash lovers, here is a tasty do-ahead casserole that can be a rustic supper when accompanied by crusty bread and a salad.

1 cup water
½ cup white rice, uncooked, preferably converted or basmati
2 tablespoons olive oil, plus extra for greasing
2 onions, finely diced
3 medium summer squash, quartered lengthwise and thinly sliced
1 red bell pepper, thinly cut into 2-inch-long strips
2 large eggs
½ cup milk
1½ cups grated extra-sharp Cheddar cheese
½ teaspoon salt
Freshly ground black pepper

TOPPING
2 slices white bread
1 tablespoon olive oil

1. Bring the water to a boil in a small saucepan and add the rice. Lower the heat to a simmer, and cook until all of the water is absorbed, about 17 minutes. Set aside.

2. Meanwhile, heat the oil in a large skillet over medium-high heat. Add the onions and sauté until lightly browned. Stir in the squash and red bell pepper, and continue to cook on medium-high heat, stirring often, until the vegetables are tender and the juices have evaporated, about 10 minutes. Set aside to cool.

3. Preheat the oven to 375°F. Lightly oil a 2½- to 3-quart baking dish.

4. Beat the eggs in a large bowl. Beat in the milk, cheese, salt, pepper, cooked rice, and vegetables. Spread the mixture evenly in the prepared baking dish.

5. To make the topping, tear up the bread and place it in a food processor or blender to make crumbs. Pour the crumbs into a small bowl and drizzle with oil. Rub the oil into the crumbs with your fingertips. Sprinkle the crumbs on top of the casserole. (The casserole may be prepared to this point up to 8 hours in advance. If it is chilled, warm it to room temperature before baking.)

6. Bake 40 to 45 minutes, or until it turns a deep golden brown. The casserole must sit at least 15 minutes before serving, to allow the juices to set and thicken.

— *Jeanne Lemlin,* Vegetarian Classics

VEGETABLE FRITTATA

SERVES 6 TO 8

3 ounces sautéed mushrooms, chopped

4 ounces sautéed squash, chopped
5 tablespoons butter or olive oil
Salt and pepper to taste
12 eggs, beaten and seasoned with salt and pepper
3 ounces grated Parmesan cheese
4 ounces shredded cheese (mozzarella, Cheddar, or jack)
4 ounces spinach, chopped

1. Preheat the oven to 325°F.

2. Sauté the mushrooms and squash in 2 tablespoons of the butter or olive oil, salt, and pepper in a nonstick pan over medium heat until they are just softened.

3. Spray an 8 × 10-inch cast-iron skillet with nonstick spray. Melt the remaining butter over medium heat and coat the entire inside of the pan. Add the egg mixture, Parmesan cheese, other shredded cheese, spinach, and squash-mushroom mixture. Stir lightly to make sure all of the ingredients are evenly distributed. Cook for 3 to 4 minutes until the egg mixture starts to adhere to the pan.

4. Bake in the oven for 25 to 30 minutes. (To check for doneness, make sure the eggs are firm in the middle. Insert a toothpick and pull it out; if no runny egg sticks to it, the frittata is done.) Remove from the oven and cool for 10 minutes.

5. Using a paring knife, separate the edges of the frittata from the pan. Cover the pan with a dinner plate and flip the frittata onto the plate. (If it sticks, turn the pan back over and use a paring knife or rubber spatula to separate the edges.) This frittata can be served warm but tastes best at room temperature.

— *Davis Farmers Market*

SUMMER VEGETABLE MEDLEY

SERVES 3

This recipe has no cholesterol, is very low in sodium, is high in vitamins A and C, and is a good source of iron and calcium.

1 tablespoon vegetable oil
¼ teaspoon powdered ginger or 1 teaspoon ginger, finely chopped
1 clove garlic, minced, or ⅛ teaspoon garlic powder
3 cups sliced cut vegetables (such as broccoli, cauliflower, greens, squash, beans, peas, or carrots)
½ green or red bell pepper, sliced
2 teaspoons water

Heat a 10-inch frying pan or wok over high heat. Add the oil. When the oil is hot, add the ginger and garlic, and cook about 30 seconds. Add the vegetables and water. Stir-fry until tender.

— *Massachusetts Department of Agricultural Resources*

Tarragon

ARTEMISIA DRACUNCULUS OR A. DRACUNCULOIDES

Few herbs are so uniquely linked to a specific culture as tarragon, which the French revere and feature prominently in their cuisine. Along with chervil, chives, and parsley, tarragon is one of the four components of fines herbs, that combination that graces so many French chicken, egg, and fish dishes, as well as salad dressings. Tarragon is also a prominent component of the egg-based béarnaise and hollandaise sauces and a favored flavoring for vinegar.

Fresh tarragon has a strong, robust flavor, a mélange of pungency, an anise-like sweetness, and a pepperish bite that slightly numbs the tongue. It should be used rather sparingly, as a little goes a long way. The tarragon that is most frequently available in the United States is Russian tarragon (Artemesia dracunculoides)*, which is harsher and more bitter than the French version* (Artemisia dracunculus)*, the one usually called for in cooking. Unfortunately, the latter tends to not produce fertile seeds, so seed companies prefer to distribute the easily propagatible Russian variety.*

HISTORY

Tarragon is likely a native of the Asian steppes. Despite its close association with European cooking, the herb was probably not widely cultivated or used there until the Tudor family introduced it from Siberia to its royal gardens in England. The Mongols brought the plant to the Near East, where its young shoots were eaten as a cooked vegetable. In fact, honored guests in Syria were often served tarragon. The plant traveled to America with the colonists, along with burnet, horehound, and chamomile.

NUTRITION

Although tarragon is usually not consumed in enough quantity to be a significant source of nutrients, the fresh herb does contain surprising amounts of potassium, iron, calcium, vitamins A, C, B6 and folate. Once thought to cure the effects of snakebite in ancient times, tarragon has been used medicinally as a sleep aid, digestive, and a breath sweetener.

SELECTION

When purchasing the raw herb, look for bunches that are uniformly green and fresh-looking. Avoid wilted or slimy specimens.

STORAGE

An easy way to store fresh tarragon (and many other cut herbs) is to treat them like flowers; simply trim the stem ends, strip off the leaves from the bottom several inches of the stems, and place them in a glass of water. Or wrap the herb in damp paper towels and place in a plastic bag in the refrigerator vegetable crisper, where it will keep for up to a week.

TRIMMING & CLEANING

Tarragon benefits from a quick rinse under running water to remove all traces of dust and dirt. Gently pat it dry between paper towels, and strip the leaves from the stems, discarding the tough stems.

FREEZING

Tarragon leaves, stripped from their stems, and chopped or left whole, can be frozen dry in a zipper-lock freezer bag. Or package them using vacuum food sealer-type bags.

An effective way to freeze tarragon and other herbs is to chop them finely, mix them into a paste using ⅓ cup of olive oil or butter to every 2 cups of herbs, and then freeze the resulting mixture in ice cube trays. To thaw, simply pop out a few cubes into a strainer and let the ice melt away, or just drop them frozen into sauces or soups. This is a good way to freeze conveniently sized portions for cooking.

DRYING

Tarragon can be dried, but its flavor deteriorates tremendously. Freezing the freshly chopped raw herb in olive oil or butter in ice cube trays yields a far better, full-flavored product (see above), as does preserving it in vinegar.

If you still want to dry the herb, spread a layer of leaves on a cookie sheet and place the herbs in a warm (up to 180°F) oven for 3 to 4 hours, stirring the herbs periodically until they are thoroughly dry. Or remove the best leaves from the stems and arrange on a paper towel without them touching. This layer is covered with another paper towel, and another layer of leaves is added. Five layers may be dried at one time using this method.

A microwave oven can also be used for small quantities of herbs. Place 4 or 5 herb branches in the microwave between paper towels. Heat for 2 to 3 minutes over High power. If the herbs are not brittle and dry when removed, repeat the microwave drying for 30 seconds more. (The heat generated during microwaving not only removes moisture, but some of the oils, so these herbs may not have as intense a flavor as herbs dried by other methods.)

COMPLEMENTARY HERBS, SEASONINGS & FOODS

Artichokes, béarnaise sauce, carrots, chervil, chicken, chives, eggs, fish, lobster, mushrooms, onions, parsley, potatoes, rabbit, salads, seafood, shellfish, sole, spinach, stuffings, tomatoes, veal.

SERVING SUGGESTIONS

- Tarragon is delicious on fruits like cantaloupe, honeydew melon, and peaches. It is wonderful even on citrus desserts like lime tarts or sorbets.
- Mix 1 tablespoon of chopped fresh tarragon leaves into ½ cup of softened butter, to use on grilled or roasted foods.
- Tarragon flavors eggs most wonderfully; use sparing amounts in quiches, frittatas, omelets, and scrambled eggs.
- Tarragon vinegar can be added to salad dressings, soups, sauces, stews, or wherever a hint of tarragon flavor is desired.
- Make a calming tea from tarragon leaves by pouring 1 cup of boiling water over 1 tablespoon of fresh tarragon, and steeping for 10 minutes.
- Tarragon combines well with parsley, chives, or chervil. When using tarragon on cooked food, always add it toward the end of the cooking process.

Books

Herbs & Spices: The Cook's Reference
Jill Norman;
DK Adult, 2002.

Rodale's Illustrated
Encyclopedia of Herbs
Rodale Press, 2000.

The Herbfarm Cookbook
Jerry Traunfeld; Scribner, 2000.

Sources

Tarragon Central
www.tarragoncentral.com

If you are out of tarragon, try substituting chervil or a dash of either fennel seed or aniseed.

. . . .

TARRAGON CHICKEN MARINADE

¼ cup fresh tarragon leaves
¼ cup chives, shallots, or green onions
1 cup dry white wine
½ cup olive oil

Combine all of the ingredients in a container large enough to hold the chicken pieces. Marinate the chicken thighs and drumsticks at least 1 hour or overnight, then broil, bake, or barbeque the chicken.

— *Jan Taylor, Zephyr Co-op member*

. . . .

SPICY VEAL ROAST

SERVES 12

¼ teaspoon salt
½ teaspoon black pepper
½ teaspoon cinnamon
1½ teaspoons cumin
3 pounds boned lean veal shoulder, trimmed, rolled, and tied
4 teaspoons olive oil
½ pound onions, peeled
½ clove garlic, peeled
2 tablespoons fresh tarragon or 2 teaspoons dried tarragon
4 sprigs fresh parsley
1 tablespoon fresh thyme or 1 teaspoon dried thyme
1 bay leaf

1. Mix together the salt, pepper, cinnamon, and cumin. Rub over the veal roast.

2. Heat 2 teaspoons of the oil in a large skillet. Add the onions, garlic, and tarragon. Cover and cook over low heat for 10 minutes. Set aside.

3. Preheat the oven to 325°F.

4. Heat the remaining 2 teaspoons of oil in an ovenproof pan large enough to hold all of the ingredients. Brown the meat on all sides. Add the onion-garlic mixture, then the parsley, thyme, and bay leaf. Cover and bake for 1½ hours, or until the meat is tender.

5. Remove the meat to a serving platter. Skim the fat from the cooking juices, and remove the bay leaf and parsley. Carve the roast into ¼- to ½-inch slices. Pour a little cooking juice over the roast and serve.

— Keep the Beat: Heart Healthy Recipes, *National Institutes of Health*

LOW-FAT RANCH DIP

MAKES ABOUT 2 CUPS

1 (15-ounce) can Great Northern beans, rinsed and drained
½ teaspoon garlic powder
¼ cup water
½ cup plain low-fat yogurt
⅛ teaspoon cayenne pepper
¼ teaspoon black pepper
1 tablespoon fresh chives, chopped
1 tablespoon fresh parsley, chopped
¼ tablespoon fresh tarragon, or ¼ teaspoon dried tarragon
¼ teaspoon salt
1 tablespoon lemon juice

1. Blend the beans and garlic powder in a blender, adding enough water to make it the desired consistency. Then blend for 2 minutes to make the mixure silky-smooth.

2. Use a spatula to scrape the mixture into a medium-sized bowl.

3. Stir in the yogurt, cayenne and black peppers, chives, parsley, tarragon, salt, and lemon juice until thoroughly blended. Serve in a bowl.

— *5aday.gov, National Cancer Institute*

TARRAGON VINEGAR

MAKES ABOUT 4 CUPS

2 cloves garlic, peeled
10 black peppercorns
10 mustard seeds
1 cup fresh tarragon leaves
4 cups white wine vinegar
Several branches of tarragon for decoration

1. In a large sterilized jar, combine the garlic, peppercorns, mustard seed, and tarragon leaves. Bring the vinegar to a boil in a saucepan, and pour it over the aromatics. Tightly close the jar and store it in a cool place for 15 days, shaking it occasionally.

2. After the 15 days, open the jar and filter the vinegar through paper coffee filters or a clean cheesecloth into a new, sterilized bottle. Slide a branch or two of the tarragon into the strained vinegar, and close tightly.

— *www.about.com*

Thyme

Thyme is a hardy Mediterranean herb that is related to mint. It loves arid climates and plenty of sun, which concentrates its aromatic oils. Its elliptical, gray-green leaves are tiny (only about an eighth of an inch long) and arranged along slender, woody stems that are often tipped with pale pink flowers in the summer. Many varieties of thyme exist, each with subtle differences in fragrance (orange, lemon, camphor, caraway). Wild thyme has a character all its own, so different from its cultivated cousins that some European herb references classify it under a separate name altogether. Wild thyme honey is sought after the world over for its uniquely herbal sweetness.

Assertive thyme is an incredibly versatile player in the herb world. Its distinctive, pungent odor and flavor (sometimes described as greenish with an undertone of cloves) melds beautifully with so many herbs and foods that the French consider it an essential ingredient in their famous bouquet garni, that bundle of herbs tied with string that flavors soups, stocks, and stews. Thyme also has a long medicinal history, used as an aphrodisiac, to dispel melancholy, and to treat animal bites and digestive disorders.

HISTORY

The homeland of the common or garden thyme is the western Mediterranean, although other members of the thyme family are native to North Africa and Asia. In its native countries, thyme has been treasured as medicine and a culinary herb since ancient times—Virgil, Hippocrates, and Pliny wrote of its merits in their texts, and the Egyptians used thyme oil to embalm their dead. Thyme grows wild in the Catskill Mountains in New York State, introduced when its seeds were carried in the fleece of sheep imported from England by colonial settlers.

NUTRITION

Although thyme is not usually consumed in large enough quantities to be nutritionally significant, two teaspoons of the herb contain over 50 percent of an adult's daily requirement for vitamin K and 20 percent of the iron, as well as manganese, calcium, and dietary fiber. Thymol, its primary volatile oil, possesses antioxidant, antibacterial, and antifungal properties. It is sometimes used to treat athlete's foot or is added to commercial mouthwashes and toothpastes.

SELECTION

Thyme should be fresh-looking and uniformly gray-green, free from dark spots or yellowish leaves.

STORAGE

Wrap fresh thyme in a damp paper towel and store in the refrigerator vegetable crisper; use within 1 week.

TRIMMING & CLEANING

Briefly rinse fresh thyme under running water to wash off the dust, then strip off the leaves from the stems and finely chop.

FREEZING

Thyme can be frozen while still on the branch. Just freeze whole sprigs on cookie sheets, strip off the leaves, and pack them in zipper-lock freezer or vacuum food sealer-type bags. Another easy way to freeze thyme is to place whole sprigs in a zipper-lock freezer bag, freeze for a couple of weeks, then remove the bag and run a rolling pin over the unopened bag. This removes many of the leaves from the stems. You can then either continue to store the leaves in the freezer in a bag, or you can place them in a tightly lidded canning jar. Thyme frozen this way does not need to be thawed before using.

Another way to freeze thyme is to chop the fresh herb, combine it with olive oil or butter, and pour the mixture into ice cube trays. This is a great way to freeze conveniently sized portions for cooking; just pop out the number of ice cubes you need and let them melt in soups or sauces.

Frozen thyme has a flavor that is superior to the dried herb, but its brownish appearance is rather unattractive, so you may want to reserve it for stews, casseroles, or other dishes where aesthetics are not critical.

DRYING

Thyme takes to drying better than most herbs, retaining more of its flavor. Tie fresh sprigs into bunches and hang them in a cool, dark place with good ventilation. Dried thyme should be stored in an airtight glass container away from light and heat, where it will keep for about 6 months.

MEASURES & EQUIVALENTS

- 1 tablespoon fresh = ¾ teaspoon dried
- 1 fresh sprig = 1 teaspoon dried

COMPLEMENTARY HERBS, SEASONINGS & FOODS

Basil, beans, beef, carrots, cheese, chervil, chicken, chives, eggs, figs, fish, fruit, garlic, ginger, goat cheese, lamb, lemon, lentils, marjoram, onions, oregano, parsley, peas, pork, potatoes, rosemary, sage, salads, savory, seafood, soups, stews, tomatoes, veal, venison.

SERVING SUGGESTIONS

- Thyme goes beautifully with eggs—sprinkle a little of the fresh herb on omelets, scrambled eggs, and frittatas.
- Thyme is a traditional seasoning, along with sage, in poultry stuffing.
- Thyme and oregano are a winning combination, wonderful in pasta sauces, pizza, and other tomato-based dishes.
- Certain types of fruit and thyme pair beautifully; try thyme with orange, lemon, pineapple, peaches, and mangoes.
- Thyme is excellent in herb butters, either by itself or in combination with majoram, basil, rosemary, or sage.
- Bruise fresh thyme and tarragon, and combine with red-wine vinegar and olive oil for a simple, yet delicious salad dressing.

Cooking Tip

Thyme should be added to dishes at the beginning of the cooking time, to allow its flavor to fully permeate the food.

"I know a bank where on the wild thyme blows, Where oxlips and the nodding violet grows, Quite over-canopied with luscious woodbine, With sweet musk-roses and with eglantine: There sleeps Titania some time of the night, Lull'd in these flowers with dances and delight. ..."

— *William Shakespeare, A Midsummer Night's Dream, Act II, Scene 1,*

Throughout history, thyme has been associated with courage, and medieval knights setting out for battle wore scarves with embroidered sprigs of thyme.

- Thyme goes well with many hearty root vegetables: carrots, onions, turnips, parsnips, and rutabagas.
- The woody stems of thyme can be tossed directly onto the grill to impart an aromatic, smoky flavor to meats and poultry.
- Thyme tea makes an effective cough remedy. To prepare, simply place 2 teaspoons of the dried herb in boiling water and steep for 10 minutes. Add sage if your cough is particularly potent.
- Sprinkle a teaspoon of fresh thyme over cottage cheese to add a vibrant, herbal flavor.
- Add freshly chopped thyme, basil, and parsley to cream cheese or sour cream for a delicious dip or baked potato dressing.
- Make freezer bouquet garni: Tie 3 to 4 sprigs of parsley, 2 sprigs of thyme, and 1 bay leaf together with kitchen twine and pack bouquets into zipper-lock freezer bags, and freeze. Place them in sauces, stocks, soups, or stews toward the end of cooking.
- Cook kidney, pinto, and black beans with thyme.

SUBSTITUTIONS

Basil, majoram, oregano, and savory are acceptable substitutes for thyme.

. . . .

JESSE'S CHICKEN STEW
SERVES 4

2 boneless chicken breasts, sliced
2 carrots, chopped
¾ cup fresh or frozen corn kernels
4 new potatoes, chopped
¾ cup fresh or frozen peas
1 stalk celery, chopped
3 cloves garlic, minced
1 cup fresh okra, sliced (frozen or canned is also acceptable)
1 cup fresh mushrooms, sliced
Green beans (about 20 young, tender specimens)
Tarragon, thyme, parsley, basil, oregano, or other chopped herbs
Water
2 chicken bouillon cubes
½ cup rotini pasta
Cornstarch (optional)
Tamari sauce

1. Combine all of the ingredients except the bouillon cubes, rotini, and cornstarch. Sauté them lightly in olive oil over medium heat in a large pan.

2. Cover with water, and add the bouillon cubes and rotini. Simmer until everything is tender and well-blended, about 1 hour or more. Thicken with cornstarch, if needed.

3. Add tamari sauce at the table, and garnish with oyster crackers and fresh parsley, if desired.

— *Jesse Smith*, The Bluff Country Co-op Cookbook

TERHUNE ORCHARDS VEGETABLE SOUP

SERVES 4

1 large onion, chopped
1 bunch celery, plus leaves
4 tomatoes, peeled and quartered, or 1 can stewed whole tomatoes
1 pound carrots
2 zucchinis, sliced
1 green bell pepper, cleaned and chopped
1 fennel bulb, including enough leaves to make 2 tablespoons, chopped
4 chicken bouillon cubes (or salt to taste)
4 cups chicken broth (or replace 2 cups of broth with V8 juice)
¼ cup barley, uncooked
1 bunch fresh thyme

Put all of the ingredients in a stockpot and bring to a boil. Turn the heat down to medium and simmer 1 hour, or until the barley is tender and the vegetables are cooked but not too soft.

— *Terhune Orchards*

THYME AND MUSHROOM GRAVY

SERVES 4

Serve with vegetarian or meat sausages, or pour onto a bed of mashed potatoes. Chase with beer.

2 tablespoons olive oil
1 onion, sliced
2 teaspoons fresh thyme leaves
1 bay leaf
1 cup mushrooms, coarsely chopped
2 tablespoons all-purpose flour
½ cup port wine
1 cup vegetable stock
2 tablespoons dark soy sauce or Braggs Liquid Aminos

1. Heat the oil in a saucepan and add the onion. Sauté until the onions turn golden.

2. Add the thyme, bay leaf, and mushrooms, and cook until they are softened, about 5 minutes. Stir in the flour, wine, vegetable stock, and soy sauce or Braggs, and simmer, stirring until the gravy has thickened slightly, about 3 to 5 minutes.

3. Remove the bay leaf. Pour into a gravy boat and serve.

— *www.recipezaar.com*

"An old-fashioned vegetable soup, without any enhancement, is a more powerful anticarcinogen than any known medicine."

— *James Duke, M.D., USDA medicinal phytochemicals expert*

Tomato

LYCOPERSICON ESCULENTUM

Tomatoes are so popular in European and American cuisines that it is easy to forget that at one time (not so long ago in some places) they were considered lethally poisonous. A member of the Solanaceae family, which includes peppers, potatoes, and eggplants, tomatoes were thought to be toxic because of their kinship to the deadly nightshade. Their leaves and stems are indeed poisonous, and apparently few thought to sample the fruit. Thus, for centuries tomatoes were grown strictly for their ornamental value.

Happily, today paints a far different picture, and tomatoes are a staple in many parts of the world. They rank as the number-one vegetable grown in home gardens in the United States, and are surpassed in commercial cultivation only by the potato, with over three billion pounds harvested annually.

Unfortunately, tomatoes are also a prime example of the follies of commercial production; modern breeding techniques have created tomatoes that are gorgeously appetizing and durable in every way except flavor—we are all familiar with those plastic supermarket beauties that have no taste. Luckily, this is where farmers markets, CSAs, and home growers fulfill our craving for that ubiquitous summer treat—a deeply colored, richly fragrant tomato ready to explode with juice and redolent flavor.

Technically a fruit rather than a vegetable, tomatoes come in literally thousands of varieties, but they tend to fall into one of several categories. There are our familiar slicers, the diminutive but sweet cherry, the paste or Roma (a drier variety used for pasta sauce), the lusciously flavorful heirlooms, and yellow and orange varieties, which contain less acid. Each has its own characteristics and uses in the kitchen.

Featherstone grows hybrid varieties, heirlooms, and cherry tomatoes, each with its own distinctive personalities.

Hybrids, or "Red Slicers"
These are familiar to us as the common supermarket tomato, with uniformly red skins and flesh. Featherstone grows its hybrids directly in the soil, but in greenhouses rather than the field. The greenhouses offer additional protection and an earlier start to the growing season. The skins on these tomatoes are a bit thick, but their flavor is wonderful.

Heirlooms
The wild children of the tomato world, heirlooms come in fantastic shapes and colors but have a true tomato flavor that rivals any hybrid. Featherstone grows several heirloom varieties:

- *Aunt Ruby's Green:* A large green slicing tomato with a rich flavor.
- *Brandywine:* This large, pinkish-red variety started the heirloom craze. Its very rich tomato taste is only slightly sweet but has a nice acidic burst.
- *Cherokee Purple:* This is a large, roundish tomato with a red-brown-

purple color; a rich, sharp, acidic flavor; and unbelievable body.

- *German Stripe:* This variety has green, yellow, and orange stripes! It is a large, very sweet tomato.
- *Green Zebra:* A small, green-striped tomato, zebras have a unique flavor that some claim are the best in the hybrid world.
- *Red Zebra:* This is the red version of the Green Zebra, with beautiful orange-red-green stripes and a very sweet, true tomato flavor.
- *Roma:* The Romas are long, cylindrical, drier-fleshed tomatoes that are typically used to make sauces and tomato paste. Featherstone grows three different Roma varieties: San Marzanos, Amish Paste, and Yellow. The San Marzanos have more flavor than the Amish Paste, but the latter has a better texture for cooking down into paste. The Amish Paste is skinnier than the San Marzanos. The Yellows are, well, yellow with a very mild flavor.

Cherry Tomatoes

These are sweet, succulent, bite-sized red and orange fruits of summer. The modern Sungold variety was developed in Japan, and Jack and Jenni "discovered" them in California's Sacramento Valley a decade ago. Its distinctive golden yellow-orange fruit bursts in the mouth with startling sweetness and subtle tropical undertones. Featherstone raises its Sungolds outdoors in well-composted soil, trellised in a "basket-weave" system with fence posts and twine. Hot, dry summers produce the most flavorful, disease-free fruit.

Our red grape cherry tomatoes are less sweet than the orange Sungolds, but they are very resilient and tasty nonetheless, great for grilling on kebobs, tossing with pasta, or simply eating straight from the box.

HISTORY

Tomatoes originated most likely in South America and Mexico, and were possibly cultivated in both areas. When the Spaniards conquered much of the Americas, they found this New World fruit quite palatable and later distributed it to their colonies in the Philippines and the Caribbean. They also introduced it to Europe, where the heat-loving plants particularly thrived in the Mediterranean climate.

Although the English were growing tomatoes for decoration by the beginning of the 1600s, they refused to eat them for many decades, thanks to an herbal text written by an influential physician who knew that tomatoes were eaten in Italy and Spain but still believed they were poisonous. This English belief still persisted when the British colonies brought tomatoes to North America in the early 1700s. With the exception of a few European-cultured people like Thomas Jefferson, tomatoes were grown primarily for ornamental value rather than as food.

NUTRITION

The nutritional value of tomatoes has been well-publicized in recent years because of studies on their lycopene content. This carotenoid has extensive antioxidant properties, possibly reducing the incidence and severity of many organ cancers, especially prostate. Lycopene is also important to eye health, particularly in warding off macular degeneration. Tomato juice consumption has also been shown to reduce blood clot-

---

Heirlooms versus Hybrids
by Jack Hedin, Featherstone Farm Owner

If you spend any time at all at either farmers markets or sifting through seed catalogs, you will soon encounter the terms "heirlooms" and "hybrids." Heirlooms are older cultivars of crops—anything from broccoli to zucchini—that are typically open-pollinated, meaning that they produce viable seed that can be saved and replanted to produce offspring with similar characteristics. Heirloom varieties have been selected naturally by gardeners looking for particular characteristics—like grandma saving seed from the tomato plant that produces the tastiest fruit, or the butternut squash that ripens earliest in the fall.

Hybrids, on other hand, are created by cross-pollinating two parent crops that otherwise might not be sexually compatible to force certain characteristics. When hybridizing is performed by plant breeders who use naturally occurring parent stock, this is a relatively benign process that has produced most of the cultivars we grow on our farm.

Unfortunately, this sort of breeding has been going on so long that the genetic base of hybrids nowadays is coming from an increasingly smaller pool. This results in less innate strength and resilience, such as in the case of corn in the United States (drawn from only five of the hundreds of distinct natural antecedents to modern hybrids). Also, modern hybrids are only as good as the criteria on which they are selected, which nowadays usually prizes cosmetic appearance and shelf life over eating quality.

With the exception of tomatoes, we grow mostly hybrids at Featherstone. Hybrids provide several big advantages to us as growers. For example, because less natural variability exists in hybrid seed genet-

---

ics, our crops tend to mature more evenly in the field. This is important with, say, broccoli, where we have many succession plantings in the fall and need to be able to predict how much will be ready to pick in each successive patch every week.

Another example is traditional sweet corn, which is not naturally very sweet and tends to lose its sugars extremely quickly after harvesting. Our modern hybrids not only contain far more sugar, but they retain it for days after picking—something we all enjoy!

Also, do not underestimate cosmetic appeal—whether we like it or not, we depend on aesthetics for 80 percent of our sales at stores and even farmers markets.

Hybrid development can have very positive consequences as well. Consider the Sungold cherry tomato. It was originally bred in Italy for one trait only—its sublime sweet flavor with slight citrus undertones. This plant has no disease resistance, and its thin-skinned fruit routinely cracks and splits. For this reason, Sungolds never became commercially viable in California, because it could not be shipped for long distances—they split and leak even when they are in their boxes. So we started growing them for local markets and the CSAs with great success. Now a new hybrid—Sunsugar—has been developed, which is indistinguishable from the Sungold except that it sports a thicker skin that makes the fruit ship better. We are trying both—let's see if anyone notices the difference!

Heirloom tomatoes are all the rage now—we usually grow six to eight varieties in a given year, and they are extremely popular with our CSA subscribers and at the farmers markets. Again, the big advantage is flavor, which is often very distinct from variety to variety. Striped Germans and Brandywines are rich and sweet, while Cherokee Purples are more sharp and acid.

No doubt that the potential ex-

ting and inflammation. Cooked tomato products, such as sauce or juice, contain up to five times more lycopene than the raw fruit, because the intense heat involved breaks down the cell walls and releases this compound. Interestingly, organic red and purple ketchups also contain much more lycopene than nonorganic counterparts.

Tomatoes are also rich in vitamins A, C, and K, as well as potassium, magnesium, dietary fiber, chromium, folate, thiamine, iron, and copper, all for just 37 calories a cup.

SELECTION

For maximum nutritional value, choose tomatoes with the richest, darkest color, which indicate high levels of lycopene. Tomatoes should be uniformly firm with no soft or bruised spots (although ripe specimens will yield slightly to fingertip pressure), no wrinkles, and no signs of decay. Although most books recommend avoiding tomatoes with cracks or splits, many heirloom and beefsteak varieties are naturally prone to cracking, especially if they received inconsistent watering during their development. Cracked tomatoes are still perfectly edible as long as they are not rotting or decaying; they simply will not keep as long.

STORAGE

Store tomatoes at room temperature, if possible, for best flavor and ripeness. Refrigeration tends to make them mealy. If they are not overripe, they will keep for up to 1 week. Tomatoes continue to ripen if stored away from sunlight at temperatures of 60 to 75°F. Tucking an apple or banana among them and storing them in a paper bag hastens ripening, because these fruits release ethylene gas. If you must store overripe tomatoes in the refrigerator, keep them in a warmer section, like the butter compartment.

TRIMMING & CLEANING

Most tomatoes need little more than a good washing before cutting and a bit of trimming to cut out the green stem end. If you want to peel tomatoes easily, blanch them in boiling water for 30 to 45 seconds, then immediately rinse them in cold running water. Insert a paring knife under the skins, which will slip off easily.

STIR-FRYING & SAUTÉING

Tomatoes make a delicious, healthy addition to your favorite stir-fry. Simply slice and toss in with other vegetables, some olive oil, and fresh herbs; sauté or stir-fry for 5 to 7 minutes over high heat.

BAKING & ROASTING

Baked tomatoes provide a pleasant change of pace as an easy-to-make side dish. Simply preheat the oven to 375°F, halve the tomatoes, and place them, cut sides up, in a baking dish lined with either a cooking parchment or a silicone baking mat. Sprinkle them with olive oil, herbs, salt, pepper, and grated Parmesan cheese, and bake uncovered for about 30 minutes. Other variations include butter, cinnamon, sugar, breadcrumbs, and butter.

To roast tomatoes quickly, preheat the oven to 425°F, halve them and place them, cut sides down, in a glass pan or parchment-lined metal pan

 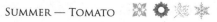

(do not let the tomatoes directly touch the metal). Brush them with olive oil, and roast for 30 minutes. Let cool, then peel.

Slow-roasting is a luscious way of cooking tomatoes, since it caramelizes their natural sugars and makes them even more sweet and piquant. To slow-roast, preheat the oven to 225°F; slice the tomatoes and place them on a cooking parchment-lined baking sheet. Sprinkle them with olive oil, salt, pepper, sugar, cayenne pepper, and fresh herbs, and bake for 2 to 4 hours. These roasted beauties will keep for up to 1 week in the refrigerator, or 6 months in the freezer.

BRAISING & STEWING

Slowly braising tomatoes concentrates their flavors, making a rich-tasting side dish or a great foundation for a vegetable sauce. To braise, place tomatoes (plum or Roma types work best) in a baking pan with enough olive oil to reach half way up the tomatoes. Cover them with sautéed garlic and onion if desired, and braise them in a 250°F oven for 2½ to 3 hours.

Stew tomatoes by cutting them into pieces, combining them with salt, pepper, sugar, butter, onion, and bell pepper, if desired, and simmering in a medium-sized saucepan for 15 to 20 minutes, stirring occasionally.

BLANCHING & FREEZING

Tomatoes can be frozen, although the resulting mushy product is good only for sauces or well-cooked tomato dishes, as their taste and texture suffer. Raw tomatoes can be frozen whole without blanching; just wash them, cut away the stem ends, place them on a cookie sheet, freeze, and place them in zipper-lock freezer or vacuum food sealer-type bags, or freezer containers. Squeeze out excess air and leave 1 inch of headspace (unless you are using the vacuum sealing method). If you prefer to freeze peeled tomatoes, you can dip the raw fruit in boiling water for 30 to 45 seconds first; their skins will slip off like a glove.

To peel frozen tomatoes, simply run warm water over the frozen fruit until their skins slip off easily.

DRYING

Dried tomatoes are concentrated summer, with an intense flavor and a versatility that is hard to beat. To get around the priciness of commercial sun-dried tomatoes, or if you have an overabundance from your garden, you can dry your own using the sun, a food dehydrator, or your oven. Plum-type or Roma tomatoes work best for drying because of their thicker, meatier walls and fewer seeds. Sungold cherry tomatoes produce wonderful, candylike fruits. A pound of fresh fruit will yield about 1 ounce dried.

Drying in the sun is easy, but it requires a climate that will kindly oblige with a number of contiguous days of temperatures in the 90s and less than 20 percent humidity. Wash and dry the tomatoes well, and slice them ½- to ¼-inch thick, and as uniformly as possible. Plum-type tomatoes should be halved or quartered lengthwise, and cherry tomatoes can be halved or left whole. Arrange the tomato slices in a single layer about 1 inch apart on plastic mesh screens (do not use metal wire ones, as the acid in the tomatoes may react with the metal and produce an off-taste).

ists for heirlooms to be much better eating than the more typical hybrid reds, but growing conditions matter a lot too. During cool, wet summers, for example, heirlooms might not be as tasty. And there is the ever-constant problem with cosmetic appearance and shipping—heirlooms ripen much faster than hybrids—so careful, more time-consuming handling is even more important.

We continue to be open to trying more heirlooms in other crops—if our customers want them. Growing more would add more management effort for us—and hybrids work well for us on a mass scale. In many ways, from a strictly commercial cultivation standpoint, heirlooms seem basically better suited for the home gardener, where their special qualities and charms can be better appreciated.

Cooking Tip

Do not cook tomatoes in aluminum cookware, as their acidity may leach the metal into the food, causing both an unpleasant taste and unwanted health effects.

Lay cheesecloth over the fruits to protect them, and place the trays in an area that receives reflective full sun, like a stone patio. Elevate the trays so air circulates underneath them, and bring them indoors every evening or if rain is forecast. The tomatoes should dry to a leathery but soft texture in 3 days to 1 week, depending on their water content, thickness, and the weather. Less moisture present in the final product means less of a possibility of spoilage and bacteria.

Oven-drying in a regular or convection home oven is a convenient method if you live where the weather is uncooperative. Preheat the oven to 140 to 145°F, and place the fruits on a plastic-mesh screen or on a cooking parchment-lined baking sheet. Prop open the oven door slightly, check the fruit regularly, and rotate the tray if necessary. Oven-drying can take between 6 to 12 hours, depending on the tomatoes' moisture content. They are done when they are dry, leathery, and pliable, but not sticky.

If you have a food dehydrator, follow the manufacturer's instructions. Good-quality dehydrators usually produce the best, most evenly dried fruits.

Once dried, keep the tomatoes in airtight bags in a cool, dry place for up to 6 months, or refrigerated for up to 8 months. They can be rehydrated in water, bouillon, vegetable stock, or wine for 1 to 2 hours, or tossed into soups and stews during the last 30 minutes of cooking. Or add them to pastas, sandwiches, sauces, and salads.

MICROWAVING

Core and halve the tomatoes, and dot them with butter or sprinkle with olive oil. Place in a microwave-safe dish and microwave on High power for 3 to 4 minutes for 4 halves, or 5 to 8 minutes for 6 to 8 halves.

MEASURES & EQUIVALENTS

- 3 to 4 medium globe tomatoes = 1 pound = 2 cups chopped
- 8 small plum tomatoes = 1 pound
- 25 to 30 cherry tomatoes = 1 pound = 2½ cups chopped tomatoes
- 2 cups chopped tomatoes = 1 pound
- ⅜ cup of tomato paste plus ½ cup water = 1 cup tomato sauce
- 1 cup canned tomatoes = 1½ cups fresh, chopped, cooked tomatoes
- ½ pound or 1 tomato = 1 serving
- 1 large tomato = 1 cup chopped
- 1 cup firmly packed fresh tomato = ½ cup tomato sauce plus ½ cup water
- 1 pound fresh = 1½ cups chopped
- 1 16-ounce can = 2 cups undrained or 1 cup drained
- 1 35-ounce can = 4 cups undrained = 2½ to 3 cups drained
- 1 28-ounce can = 3 cups undrained = 2 to 2½ cups drained
- 1 6-ounce can tomato paste = ¾ cup
- 2½ to 3 pounds fresh tomatoes = 1 large mason jar
- 1 bushel = 53 pounds fresh tomatoes

COMPLEMENTARY HERBS, SEASONINGS & FOODS

Anchovies, arugula, bacon, basil, bay leaf, beans, beef, breadcrumbs, cheese, chiles, chives, cilantro, cucumbers, dill, eggplant, eggs, garlic, honey, lemon, marjoram, mint, mushrooms, nutmeg, olive oil, olives, onions, oregano, parsley, pasta, peppers, rosemary, saffron, salt, seafood,

shallots, sugar, tarragon, thyme, vinegar, zucchini.

SERVING SUGGESTIONS

- Try serving a traditional English breakfast: Fry up some bacon in a pan and reserve the fat to fry thick slices of sourdough or French bread until crisp. Serve with poached eggs and grilled tomato slices on the side.
- Add whole cherry tomatoes to shish kebobs.
- Top sliced tomatoes with thin slices of Cheddar, American, or mozzarella cheese and broil until the tomatoes become soft and cheese is melted and bubbly.
- Who says BLTs are just for sandwiches? Try a bacon, lettuce, and tomato salad, along with hard-boiled eggs and a little bacon dripping added to the dressing.
- Stuffed tomatoes are a classic: Fill them with ground beef, bacon, rice, spinach, or for a vegetarian version, cracked wheat.
- For that quintessential Italian snack, bruschetta, top grilled or toasted slices of garlic-and-oil-rubbed baguette with a mixture of finely chopped or diced fresh, ripe, peeled tomatoes that have been combined with olive oil, salt, pepper, and fresh herbs.
- Combine tomato, mint, sugar, champagne, and lemon juice for a refreshing sorbet.
- For a stunning salad that will delight guests, slice and combine different-colored heirlooms on a platter for a "tomato tasting." Try pairing with different types of flavorful olive oils poured into separate dipping bowls, with balsamic vinegar on the side.
- One little-known use for tomatoes (and condensed tomato soup) is to add moisture (but not necessarily tomato flavor) to baked goods, like cakes and breads, even puddings.
- Green tomatoes, with their low acidity and fresh tomato taste, make great toppers for eggs and enchiladas.
- Add zip to tuna salad by adding chopped fresh tomatoes, scallions, and a touch of chopped fresh basil.
- Make salsa!

BAKED HONEY TOMATOES   SERVES 8

A lot of people don't realize how well the flavors of tomato and honey go together. These are easy, and once cooked may even wait if your timing of some other part of the meal is slightly off.

8 ripe medium tomatoes
½ cup fresh coarse breadcrumbs
2 teaspoons salt
2 teaspoons freshly ground black pepper
2 tablespoons fresh tarragon or 1 tablespoon dried tarragon
4 teaspoons honey
4 teaspoons unsalted butter

1. Preheat the oven to 350°F. Slice off the stem ends of the tomatoes and carefully scoop out the seeds. Place, open sides up, in a buttered baking dish.

The State of the Tomato

The South Arkansas Vine Ripe Pink Tomato was adopted as the Arkansas state fruit and vegetable in 1987. The Pink Tomato Festival is held each year in Bradley County.

V8, Anyone?

Tomato juice is the official state beverage of Ohio.

A Note about Tomato Shoulders

At certain times of the year, the majority of Featherstone's tomatoes may have "yellow shoulders"— patches of yellow coloring near the stem ends. These "shoulders" are usually caused by heat stress and are perfectly edible. They just don't have much taste (akin to a green tomato). If you prefer, cut away the shoulders, and the rest of the flesh is fine.

"The crooked little tomato branches, pulpy and pale as if made of cheap green paper, broke under the weight of so much fruit; there was something frantic in such fertility, a crying-out like that of children frantic to please."

— *John Updike,*
American novelist

2. Mix the breadcrumbs with the salt, pepper, and tarragon. Drizzle the honey over the tomatoes, rubbing it down into the cavities. Sprinkle tomatoes with the crumb mixture and dot with butter.

3. Bake, uncovered, for 30 minutes, until the tomato skins begin to wrinkle. Place under the broiler for another 5 minutes, or until the crumbs begin to brown. Serve hot or at room temperature.

— *Lee Bailey,* Lee Bailey's Southern Food

TOMATO, ONION, AND CUCUMBER SALAD

This salad is eaten throughout the Mediterranean in slightly different variations. It is easy to make and does not need any particularly exotic ingredients. The only requirements are that its components are the best quality possible, and that the diner appreciates flavors as fresh as the morning sun.

Fresh ripe tomatoes
Fresh cucumbers
White, red, or sweet onion
Extra-virgin olive oil (use the very best quality you can afford)
Sea salt or seasoned salt
Freshly ground black pepper
Fresh basil, torn or chopped

Slice up the vegetables in the proportions and shapes desired. Drizzle with olive oil, not too much but not too little, either. Season with salt, pepper, and basil to taste. (When I am just about to sneeze is how I know I have put enough pepper on my salad.)

— *Mi Ae Lipe, Featherstone Farm CSA member*

GOLDEN GAZPACHO

SERVES 4 TO 6

2 pints Sungold cherry tomatoes
1 cup peeled cucumber chunks
½ cup red or green bell pepper chunks
1 whole scallion
1 tablespoon red wine vinegar
2 teaspoons olive oil
1 clove garlic, minced
¼ teaspoon salt

Place all of the ingredients in a blender or a food processor fitted with a steel blade. Cover and process until the mixture is almost smooth, but still retains some texture. Chill to let the flavors blend.

Variation

For a spicier version, add ½ jalapeño pepper, or ⅛ to ¼ teaspoon

ground red pepper and a small bunch of fresh, chopped cilantro.

— Colleen Wolner, Blue Heron Coffeehouse, Winona, Minnesota

SPINACH AND WARM SUNGOLD TOMATO SALAD

SERVES 4

2 large bunches spinach
1 pint Sungold cherry tomatoes
3 tablespoons olive oil
1 clove garlic, minced
Salt and freshly ground pepper

1. Wash the spinach, removing and discarding the thick stems. Dry the spinach thoroughly, and divide it among 4 large plates.

2. Wash the tomatoes and cut them in half through their stem ends.

3. In a saucepan, heat the olive oil over medium-high heat and add the garlic and halved tomatoes. Cook for 5 minutes, until the tomatoes soften and release some of their juices (but do not overcook, as the tomatoes should hold their shape).

4. Season with salt and freshly ground pepper. Spoon the warm tomatoes, garlic, and pan juices evenly over the spinach. Serve immediately.

— Colleen Wolner, Blue Heron Coffeehouse, Winona, Minnesota

SUNGOLD SALAD WITH FETA AND CUMIN-YOGURT DRESSING

SERVES 6

2 pints Sungold cherry tomatoes
½ teaspoon salt
¼ cup plain yogurt, drained about 30 minutes, liquid discarded
1 tablespoon olive oil
1 tablespoon fresh lemon juice
1 clove garlic, minced
1 teaspoon ground cumin
3 scallions, white and green parts, thinly sliced
1 tablespoon chopped fresh oregano leaves
Freshly ground pepper
1 small chunk (about 3 ounces) feta cheese

1. Stem and halve the tomatoes and toss them with salt in a large bowl. Let them rest until a small pool of liquid accumulates—about 15 to 20 minutes.

2. Meanwhile, whisk the drained yogurt, oil, lemon juice, garlic, cumin, scallions, oregano, and pepper together in a small bowl. Pour the

Books

Lee Bailey's Tomatoes
Lee Bailey;
Clarkson Potter, 1992.

The Heirloom Tomato Cookbook
Mimi Luebbermann;
Chronicle Books, 2006.

The Tomato Festival Cookbook: 150 Recipes that Make the Most of Your Crop of Lush, Vine-Ripened, Sun-Warmed, Fat, Juicy, Ready-to-Burst Heirloom Tomatoes
Lawrence Davis-Hollander;
Storey Publishing, 2004.

In Praise of Tomatoes: Tasty Recipes, Garden Secrets, Legends & Lore
Ronni Lundy; Lark Books, 2006.

yogurt mixture over the tomatoes and accumulated liquid. Toss everything to coat. Set aside to blend the flavors, about 5 minutes.

3. Crumble the feta over the tomatoes and toss to combine. Adjust the seasonings and serve immediately.

— *Colleen Wolner, Blue Heron Coffeehouse, Winona, Minnesota*

HOMEMADE SALSA SERVES 8

1 cup finely chopped, peeled tomato
½ cup tomato sauce
¼ cup yellow or red onion
¼ cup finely chopped green bell pepper
2 tablespoons vinegar
2 cloves garlic, minced
1 to 3 jalapeño peppers, seeded and chopped
½ cup fresh cilantro, chopped (optional)

Mix all of the ingredients in a glass bowl. Refrigerate until serving.

— *Fruits and Veggies—More Matters; Centers for Disease Control & Prevention*

CHERRY TOMATO SHISH KEBOBS MAKES 4 TO 6 SHISH KEBOBS

My daughter, Miska, is always delighted when we find a little basket of cherry tomatoes in our produce box. This is our favorite recipe for these.

1 basket cherry tomatoes, rinsed
1 pound tofu, baked and cut into 1-inch chunks
1 cucumber, sliced
½ pound Cheddar cheese, cut into 1-inch chunks
2 cups green beans, steamed until just tender

Arrange all of the ingredients on toothpicks and serve on a platter. This is pretty and delicious as an appetizer, good with a vinaigrette dipping sauce. We sometimes make a whole meal of them!

— *Margaret Trott, Featherstone Farm CSA member*

QUICK TOMATO SAUCE FOR THE FREEZER

This sauce may be more watery than that yielded by the traditional canning method, but it is uncooked and so can be reduced later. When you defrost it months later, you will still have that great fresh tomato taste of summer, without the extensive labor of canning.

Mince 2 garlic cloves in a food processor. Add 1 minced onion, the number of tomatoes you desire, any herbs you prefer, and salt and pepper to taste, and process. (This can also be chopped by hand and the tomatoes puréed in a blender). Pour the sauce into zipper-lock freezer bags and lay the bags flat on a baking sheet in the freezer. (The sauce will then freeze in a thin, easy-to-handle shape.)

— *Featherstone Farm*

BAKED TOMATOES WITH FETA

SERVES 4

This is an extremely simple recipe and one you can make all summer long without tiring of it. Vary it by replacing the feta cheese topping with a swipe of pesto or store-bought tepenade (olive paste). Serve these soft, juicy tomatoes with grilled lamb chops, a leg of lamb, grilled fish, or shrimp. The leftover tomatoes are delicious as a sandwich the next day, between two slices of good toasted bread.

4 large ripe tomatoes
2 tablespoons olive oil
Salt and freshly ground black pepper
1 teaspoon minced fresh oregano
⅓ pound imported feta cheese, in one piece
1 tablespoon minced parsley

1. Preheat the oven to 325°F.

2. Core the tomatoes and slice off about ⅓ inch from the stem end of each to make a flat surface. Pour the olive oil in a baking dish just large enough to hold the tomatoes. Set the tomatoes in the dish, cut sides down. Bake for 45 minutes.

3. Using a spatula, turn the tomatoes, cut sides up. Spoon the pan juices over them and season them with salt, pepper, and oregano. Continue baking until the tomatoes turn soft but not mushy, about 30 to 45 minutes.

4. Transfer the tomatoes to a warm serving platter or individual dinner plates. Pour the pan juices over them. Grate the feta cheese thickly over the top, and garnish with minced parsley.

— *Janet Fletcher,* More Vegetables Please

TOMATOES STUFFED
WITH BLUE CHEESE AND WALNUTS

SERVES 4

2 large tomatoes (1 pound)
Salt and pepper
¼ pound blue cheese
¼ cup chopped walnuts

"It's not hard to breed a tomato that looks great and tastes like hell."

— *Charles M. Rick,*
Preeminent U.S. tomato breeder

¼ **cup dry breadcrumbs**
1 tablespoon chopped fresh parsley
Olive oil

1. Preheat the oven to 400°F.

2. Cut the tomatoes in half horizontally. Remove the seeds but leave the flesh intact. Sprinkle them with salt and let them drain upside-down for 30 minutes.

3. Crumble the cheese and stir in the walnuts, breadcrumbs, parsley, and ¼ teaspoon pepper. Pat the tomatoes dry and mound the cheese mixture on top, pushing some into the cavities. Brush the tomatoes with oil, and place them on a lightly oiled baking sheet.

4. Bake until the tomatoes are tender and soft, and their tops are golden brown, about 10 to 12 minutes.

— *Arlayne Fleming*

OVEN-ROASTED TOMATO SAUCE   MAKES ABOUT 3 CUPS

8 large tomatoes or 15 romas (about 3½ pounds)
Salt and pepper
Olive oil
Onions, quartered
Garlic cloves
Green bell pepper, cut into wedges
Fresh herbs (such as basil, oregano, and parsley)

1. Preheat the oven to 450°F.

2. Cut the tomatoes in half (in quarters if they are very large) and core them. Place them in a 9 × 13-inch baking pan in a single layer. Sprinkle with salt, pepper, and olive oil. Roast them in the oven for 30 minutes.

3. Add the quartered onion, several garlic cloves, and, if you like, green bell pepper wedges to the tomatoes. Drizzle again with oil and roast for another 30 minutes.

4. When the tomatoes are done, chop the fresh herbs in a food processor or blender. Add the tomato mixture and blend to a chunky consistency. This sauce is now ready to eat or freeze.

— *Maria Runde*

Watermelon CITRULLUS LANATUS

Along with sweet corn and tomatoes, watermelon is a quintessential sign of summer. Watermelon belongs to the Cucurbitaceae family, which also includes squash, cucumbers, gourds, and pumpkins. All of its members grow as rambling, sprawling annual vines with enormous appetites for space, heat, water, and fertilizer.

Featherstone grows three different types of watermelon: Yellow Doll, Sugar Baby, and Mickey Lee. The Yellow Doll is a beautiful, yellow-fleshed melon, with light green skin accented with dark green stripes and flesh that is sweet, light, and refreshing. The Mickey Lee and Sugar Baby fruits are both red-fleshed, with the former sporting light green stripes and the Sugar Baby having a solid dark-green exterior. The flesh of the Sugar Baby is rich and very sweet (hence its name), whereas the Mickey Lee has a lighter texture but great body. All three are icebox melons, which means that they are smaller melons that you can easily store in your refrigerator.

HISTORY

Watermelon is believed to have originated from Africa's Kalahari Desert, where it grows wild and serves as a convenient source of food and water for indigenous peoples in that area. Ancient Egyptians and Chinese cultivated watermelons, and watermelon seeds were found in Pharaoh Tutankhamen's tomb. The Moors probably introduced watermelon to Europe by the thirteenth century, and African slaves likely brought the seeds of their beloved native fruit to the United States.

Because of the fruit's surprising fragility, however, watermelons were not a commercially viable, large-scale crop in America until breeding efforts in South Carolina in the 1940s to create a disease-resistant strain produced a melon with an easy-to-stack shape and harder rind.

NUTRITION

A watermelon consists of … well, mostly water—about 92 percent, which is why these fruits weigh so much when they are ripe. A 2-cup serving of watermelon contains about 30 percent of an adult's daily requirement for vitamin A, 25 percent of vitamin C, and significant amounts of potassium and vitamin B6, all for about 80 calories. Watermelon also contains abundant lycopene, a carotenoid antioxidant that may help prevent certain cancers.

SELECTION

A good watermelon is a heavy, shiny one, with no soft or bruised areas. A ripe melon should sound hollow when thumped, and the underside that sat on the ground as it ripened should have a creamy yellow skin.

STORAGE

Whole, uncut melons will keep for 7 to 10 days at room temperature.

Don't Drop It on Your Foot

The largest watermelon, listed in the Guinness Book of World Records, tipped the scales at 262 pounds, grown by Bill Carson of Arrington, Tennessee, in 1990.

For More Information

National Watermelon
Promotion Board

www.watermelon.org

Made in China

Over 1,200 varieties of
watermelon are grown
in 96 countries. China
is the world's largest
producer of watermelons.

Waste Not

All parts of the watermelon are
edible, including the thick outer
rind, which can be pickled or
cooked into pies or preserves.

But store them too long, and they will lose flavor and texture. Once watermelons are cut, it should be tightly wrapped, stored in the coldest part of the refrigerator, and eaten within a day or two.

TRIMMING & CLEANING

Before cutting, thoroughly wash the melon (to avoid introducing contamination from the skin into the flesh). To remove the seeds, wash and quarter a whole melon, then cut each quarter into three or four wedges. Cut lengthwise along the seed line with a paring knife and lift off the piece. Using a fork, scrape the seeds from both the removed piece and the remaining flesh on the rind. Save the seeds for spitting and target practice.

To easily cube a watermelon, cut into the flesh in a grid pattern, and tilt—the cubes will practically tumble off.

BLANCHING & FREEZING

Freezing is a good way to preserve watermelon for those long winters when no decent melons are available, or when you have an overabundance of fruit. Cut the flesh out of the rind, cube, and place in zipper-lock freezer or vacuum food sealer-type bags, or freezer containers. Squeeze out excess air and leave ½ inch of headspace (unless you are using the vacuum sealing method). These frozen cubes work well for smoothies during non-watermelon seasons.

You can also prepare watermelon in a sugar syrup that will help preserve its flavor and color. Peel and cut melons into ½- or ¾-inch cubes or balls. To make the syrup, combine 9 cups of water or fruit juice with 2¼ cups of sugar. Combine the sugar and water in a saucepan, and bring to a boil until the sugar dissolves. Chill, then pour ½ cup of syrup into the freezer container, add the melon, and keep adding syrup until the fruit is covered. Leave ½ inch of headspace for pints, 1 inch for quarts.

EQUIVALENTS, MEASURES & SERVINGS

- 1 pound = 1 cup cubed

COMPLEMENTARY HERBS, SEASONINGS & FOODS

Apples, blueberries, coconut, ginger, grapefruit, ham, ice cream, lemon, lime, mango, mint, other melons, pepper, proscuitto, raspberries, salt, seafood, smoked meats, strawberries, sugar, yogurt.

SERVING SUGGESTIONS

- Watermelons are a wonderful, thirst-quenching snack anytime and are surprisingly filling, either by themselves or in conjunction with other fruit.
- Kids and adults alike love foods in fun shapes: Cut watermelon, cheese, and sausage into cubes or flat squares, and arrange to create checkerboards or a Rubik's cube. Serve with toothpicks and a variety of tasty dips and sauces.
- Hollow out a big watermelon shell and fill it with assorted fruits and melon balls tossed in a spicy-sweet ginger-lemon-mint dressing.
- Mince watermelon and toss with maple syrup to use as a topping on pancakes, waffles, ice cream, and sherbet.
- Use watermelon purée to add a subtle, sweet, fruity flavor to sauces, glazes, and marinades.
- Grill whole shrimp and watermelon cubes on skewers.

- Watermelon is delicious added to summer salads or made into a cold soup.
- A simple, refreshing summer meal is a fruit plate with cut-up watermelon, cantaloupe, pineapple, grapes, and raspberries, accompanied by a selection of fine cheeses like smoked Gouda, Brie, and Stilton, served with sangrias or mimosas.

WATERMELON PINEAPPLE PRESERVES MAKES ABOUT 2 CUPS

Do not double the recipe, or the mixture may not set.

1 cup finely chopped, peeled watermelon rind, red flesh removed
1 cup sugar
1 (8-ounce) can crushed pineapple, drained and juice reserved
¼ cup water
1 tablespoon grated orange peel
⅛ teaspoon pumpkin pie spice or cinnamon
1 (3-ounce) pouch liquid fruit pectin

1. In a saucepan, stir together the rind, sugar, pineapple, reserved pineapple juice, and water. Bring to a boil over high heat, stirring constantly. Decrease the heat, and simmer for 15 to 20 minutes, until the rind is tender and translucent.

2. Stir in the remaining ingredients. Increase the heat, bringing the mixture to a full rolling boil, stirring constantly. Boil 1 minute, stirring constantly.

3. Ladle into jars; cover. Let stand at room temperature 24 hours to set. These preserves will keep in the refrigerator for up to 3 weeks.

— *National Watermelon Promotion Board*

WATERMELON AND CHICKEN SALAD　　　　SERVES 4

1 (3-pound) red watermelon
12 ounces oriental noodles, uncooked
1 pound grilled boneless chicken breasts
10 ounces seedless cucumbers, thinly sliced with peel
2 ounces green onions, thinly sliced
Bamboo shoots, thinly sliced, for garnish
Parsley springs, for garnish
Sweet-and-Sour Ginger Dressing (recipe below)

SWEET-AND-SOUR GINGER DRESSING

2½ tablespoons rice vinegar
1 tablespoon soy sauce
1 teaspoon sugar
½ teaspoon minced fresh ginger
4 ounces soy oil

1 ounce sesame oil

1. To prepare the dressing, mix the vinegar, soy sauce, sugar, and ginger until thoroughly mixed; set aside. Combine the soy and sesame oils in a salad dressing shaker; gradually add the vinegar mixture until blended. Shake well before serving.

2. Remove the rind from the watermelon and cut the flesh into 1- to 1½-inch cubes. Cover and refrigerate.

3. Cook and drain the noodles; set aside.

4. To make an individual serving, arrange 1 sliced chicken breast in a spiral on top of 3 ounces of cooked noodles. Place ¾ cup cubed watermelon and ⅓ cup sliced cucumbers beside the chicken. Sprinkle with green onions. Garnish with bamboo shoots and parsley sprigs, and serve with the Sweet-and-Sour Ginger Dressing.

— *National Watermelon Promotion Board*

WATERMELON STRAWBERRY MINT SALSA   SERVES 4

For a dynamite combination, serve this salsa with grilled chicken breasts that have been marinaded in jerk seasoning before cooking.

1 cup diced watermelon, seeds removed
¾ cup diced strawberries
¼ cup diced red onion
2 tablespoons diced, seeded jalapeño
2 tablespoons finely chopped fresh mint leaves
2 tablespoons olive oil
1 tablespoon lime juice
1 teaspoon sugar

Gently stir together all of the ingredients in a bowl. Let stand to blend flavors, about 1 hour.

— *Chef Marty Blitz, Mise En Place, Tampa, Florida; National Watermelon Promotion Board*

WATERMELON BITS   SERVES 6

1 cup fresh lime juice
½ teaspoon salt
¼ teaspoon hot pepper sauce
6 cups watermelon, seeded

1. In a small bowl suitable for dipping, stir together the lime juice, salt, and hot pepper sauce; adjust the seasoning to taste.

2. Place the bowl in the center of a large platter, arrange the watermelon

around the bowl, and serve with toothpicks.

— *Produce for Better Health; Fruits and Veggies—More Matters; Centers for Disease Control & Prevention*

. . . .

WATERMELON SMOOTHIE   SERVES 2

2 cups watermelon, cut into seeded chunks
1 cup cracked ice
½ cup plain yogurt
1 tablespoon sugar
½ teaspoon ground ginger
⅛ teaspoon almond extract

Combine all of the ingredients in a blender, then blend until smooth.

— *Produce for Better Health; Fruits and Veggies—More Matters; Centers for Disease Control & Prevention*

. . . .

WATERMELON GAZPACHO   SERVES 4

Surprise your family or guests with this spicy (not sweet) soup! A garnish of thin apple slices adds a special touch.

6 cups cubed, seeded watermelon
1½ cups chopped Golden Delicious apples
½ cup finely chopped onion
½ cup finely chopped green bell pepper
1 tablespoon fresh basil or 1 teaspoon dried basil
½ teaspoon salt
¼ teaspoon coarsely ground pepper
¼ teaspoon chili powder
1 tablespoon cider vinegar
1 Granny Smith or other tart apple, thinly sliced, for garnish

1. In a blender, purée the watermelon; pour into a large mixing bowl.

2. Stir in the remaining ingredients, except the apple slices. Refrigerate, covered, at least 1 hour to blend the flavors. Garnish with thinly sliced apple.

— *National Watermelon Promotion Board*

Zucchini

To the home gardener, prolific zucchini are the rabbits of the cucurbit world, thus earning this summer squash a reputation for being given away to people already weary of too much of a good thing. Zucchinis do not keep, however, and just as quickly as the floodgates of summer open to overflowing armfuls of this succulent green vegetable, they are gone as soon as cold weather nips the vines.

Like many vegetables, zucchini is best as a small package. Zucchinis that are 4 inches long or under are the most succulent. Anything over 8 and certainly over 12 inches long tend to be tasteless and are more fit for the compost heap than the dinner table.

These vines are astoundingly productive, but if you happen to have one or more in your garden, you can help stem the flow of fruits by indulging in another of life's culinary pleasures—squash blossoms, a delectable treat when stuffed and delicately fried, or made into a quesadilla.

HISTORY

Zucchini was relatively unknown in America until surprisingly recently. Although both summer and winter squashes are one of humankind's oldest foods, zucchini was mostly confined to Europe in general and Italy in particular, where it was developed.

In the mid-1900s, Italian immigrants brought this green summer squash to America. From then on, its popularity in the U.S. grew nearly as quickly as the plant in July.

Like many summer squashes, zucchini was often not well-liked in Europe outside of its home country. In particular, the French shunned it until they learned to use just the smallest, most succulent fruits; they call them *courgettes,* which also refers to yellow summer squash.

NUTRITION

Zucchinis are mostly water (over 95 percent) and thus are extremely low in calories (one cup contains only 36 calories). Like other summer squashes, zucchini contains significant vitamins A, C, and K, as well as manganese, magnesium, potassium, copper, folate, and dietary fiber.

SELECTION

Zucchinis taste best when they are still quite young, tender, and small—about 2 to 8 inches long. Avoid zucchinis that are any bigger, for they may be bitter, tough, and tasteless. Choose firm, plump specimens with unblemished skins and no bruised, shriveled, or watery areas.

STORAGE

Zucchini is a rather perishable vegetable; avoid washing until just before using, and keep wrapped in a plastic bag in the refrigerator vegetable crisper for up to 4 days.

Trimming & Cleaning

Like most summer squash, zucchini needs little preparation. Just wash them thoroughly and slice into the desired-size pieces. Peeling their thin skins is usually not necessary.

Steaming & Boiling

Zucchini and other summer squashes tend to be watery when cooked, so either choose cooking methods that dry them out a bit, or avoid those that may exacerbate this characteristic. For this reason, steaming zucchini is preferable to boiling it, which yields a more waterlogged product. Steam 1-inch chunks for 10 to 15 minutes, or until they become tender.

To boil zucchini, cook in rapidly boiling water for 8 to 10 minutes, or until tender. Drain thoroughly.

Stir-Frying & Sautéing

Cut zucchini into thin strips or slices; coat with oil, butter, or soy sauce; and stir-fry or sauté over high heat for about 3 to 6 minutes, or until it becomes tender and is lightly browned on the edges.

Baking & Roasting

Baking is a good way to prepare zucchini, especially with other vegetables such as onions, peppers, and tomatoes. Layer these in a casserole dish with herbs and seasonings of your choice, drizzle with olive oil, cover, and bake in a 350°F oven for 45 minutes.

Grilling

Zucchini responds well to grilling, especially the larger fruits. Use about twice what you think you will want, as they will soften and shrink considerably. Trim the ends from about 2 pounds of zucchini; cut them into ¼-inch slabs and slather them with ½ cup bottled Italian salad dressing or other vinaigrette. Grill over a medium-hot fire until they are soft and somewhat charred, about 2 to 3 minutes per side.

Blanching & Freezing

Zucchini can be frozen, but like most vegetables, it must be blanched first. Wash, trim off the stem ends, and cut into slices or strips. Blanch in rapidly boiling water for 3 minutes and pack in in zipper-lock freezer or vacuum food sealer-type bags, or freezer containers. Squeeze out excess air and leave ½ inch of headspace (unless you are using the vacuum sealing method).

Or you can freeze preshredded zucchini for future batches of zucchini bread. Simply shred the zucchini manually or in a food processor and package in recipe-sized amounts in zipper-lock freezer or vacuum food sealer-type bags. Squeeze out excess air.

You can also prepare preseasoned and breaded zucchini for freezing by cutting the desired number of squash into wedges or sticks. Then moisten them with water and dredge them in a mixture of cornmeal or breadcrumbs, salt, and pepper. Arrange the sticks on a baking sheet lined with wax paper and place in the freezer. Once the sticks are frozen, package them in a freezer bag. When you are ready to use them, simply take out what you need and deep-fry—no need to thaw them first.

Books

The Classic Zucchini Cookbook: 225 Recipes for All Kinds of Squash
Nancy C. Ralston, Marynor Jordan, and Andrea Chesman; Storey Publishing, 2002.

The New Zucchini Cookbook
Nancy C. Ralston and Jordan Marynor; Storey Publishing, 1990.

Zucchini: You Can Never Have Enough
John Butler; The University of Alberta Press, 2001.

> "The trouble is, you cannot grow just one zucchini. Minutes after you plant a single seed, hundreds of zucchini will barge out of the ground and sprawl around the garden, menacing the other vegetables. At night, you will be able to hear the ground quake as more and more zucchinis erupt."
>
> — *Dave Barry, comic writer*

MICROWAVING

Trim off the stem ends; cut the zucchini into ¼-inch slices and put in a microwave-safe dish with ¼ cup water; cover and cook on High power.

- 1½ cups = 3 to 4 minutes
- 1 pounds = 6 to 7 minutes

MEASURES & EQUIVALENTS

- 3 medium-sized zucchini = 1 pound or about 3 cups sliced or chopped

COMPLEMENTARY HERBS, SEASONINGS & FOODS

Basil, breadcrumbs, butter, cayenne, cheese, cilantro, cream, cumin, dill, eggplant, garlic, lemon, marjoram, mushrooms, olive oil, onions, oregano, parsley, pesto, pine nuts, rosemary, sage, salmon, savory, tarragon, thyme, tomatoes, vinegar, walnuts.

SERVING SUGGESTIONS

- Combine with eggs, tomatoes, and basil to make a summer frittata.
- Roast zucchini with sliced onions, olive oil, salt, pepper, and other herbs and seasonings.
- Shred zucchini along with carrots, cucumbers, and cabbage for an unusual coleslaw.
- Sauté coins of zucchini with other summer squashes of contrasting colors—yellow and light green, for instance—and dress with fresh herbs and garlic for a lovely summer dish.
- Add diced zucchini to salads and pasta dishes.
- Thinly slice zucchini and use it like cucumbers in sandwiches and hoagies.
- Cut zucchini into thin strips and serve them with other fresh vegetables for dipping.
- Bake sliced zucchini that has been brushed with melted butter and sprinkled with lemon pepper at 400°F for 20 to 25 minutes, or until tender.
- Stuff zucchini by coring out the centers of the bigger squash; stuffing with a mixture of vegetables, ground meat, tofu, cooked garbanzo beans, herbs, and seasonings; and baking, covered, with or without tomato sauce at 350°F for 45 to 60 minutes.
- Of course, if all else fails, make that old standby—zucchini bread or muffins. Be sure to decrease the amount of liquid in the recipe by about a third to compensate for the vegetable's moisture.

BAKED CHICKEN AND ZUCCHINI   SERVES 4

1 egg
1 tablespoon water
¾ teaspoon salt, divided
⅛ teaspoon pepper
1 cup dry breadcrumbs
4 boneless, skinless chicken breast halves
4 tablespoons olive or vegetable oil
5 medium zucchinis, sliced

4 medium tomatoes, sliced
1 cup shredded mozzarella cheese, divided
2 teaspoons minced fresh basil

1. In a shallow bowl, beat the egg, water, ½ teaspoon of the salt, and pepper.

2. Set aside 2 tablespoons of the breadcrumbs. Place the remaining crumbs in a large zipper-lock bag. Dip the chicken in the egg mixture, then place it in the bag and shake to coat.

3. Preheat the oven to 400°F.

4. In a skillet, cook the chicken in 2 tablespoons of the oil for 2 to 3 minutes on each side, or until it turns golden brown. Remove and set aside.

5. In the same skillet, sauté the zucchinis in the remaining oil until they are crisp-tender; drain. Transfer to a greased 9 × 13-inch baking dish. Sprinkle the reserved breadcrumbs over the zucchini. Top with tomato slices; sprinkle with ⅔ cup of the mozzarella, basil, and remaining salt. Top with the chicken.

6. Cover and bake for 25 minutes. Uncover; sprinkle with the remaining mozzarella. Bake 10 minutes longer, or until the cheese is melted.

— *Mariquita Farm*

SOUPE AU PISTOU (FRENCH VEGETABLE SOUP WITH PESTO)
SERVES 12 (MAKES 6 CUPS)

This Provençale "Soup with Pesto" is a casual, family-style soup that is frequently featured in cafés and even fine-dining restaurants in the south of France. With vegetables, beans, and pasta drifting around in a pesto-laced broth, the soup reflects the cultural connection between the Côte d'Azure (or French Riviera) and Liguria, the region of Italy that lies just around the bend. Italians call Nice "La Bella Nizza" and seem barely cognizant of the fact that this part of the Mediterranean coast slipped out of their grasp a few hundred years ago to become a part of France. Serve the soup hot with a spoonful of pesto on top of each bowlful.

FOR THE BEANS

4 cups water, plus additional water if needed
1 cup dried white beans
1 bay leaf
1 teaspoon salt

TO COMPLETE THE SOUP

¼ cup olive oil
1 medium onion, peeled and thinly sliced
1 large leek, white and pale green end only, split, rinsed, and sliced
2 celery stalks, sliced
3 cloves garlic, peeled and thinly sliced

"Vegetables are a must on a diet. I suggest carrot cake, zucchini bread, and pumpkin pie."

— *Jim Davis*

A Zucchini Flower Primer

**by Nickolas Vassili,
Vegetable Lover and Former
Restaurant Owner**

Featherstone does not usually offer CSAers squash blossoms, but those who grow summer squash or zucchini in their home gardens may be missing out on a wonderful treat right under their noses. Besides, preparing squash blossoms may help curb your plants' prolific yield!

Squash blossoms are one of my favorite treats when delicately battered and fried. Although they are not well-known in American cuisine, both Italians and Mexicans know what a delicacy they can be, stocking them in produce markets and serving them in their restaurants when they are in season.

Not knowing about these delicious flowers is a shame, for this could make use of the prolific blooms that every home grower of zucchini and summer squash witnesses. To the best of my knowledge, a book has never been written on "The Skill of Picking and Preserving Zucchini Flowers." So here goes:

First, you must pick only the male flowers, which contain one stamen, as opposed to female flowers, which contain a cluster.

Second, you must not pick all of the male flowers because then the plant will not continue to bear fruit. (That makes sense—doesn't it?)

Third, the flowers should only be picked between approximately 8 and 10 in the morning, as that is the only time when the flowers are wide-open and bell-shaped. Once they close, they should not be picked because then they shrivel and lose shape, making them smaller and less appetizing. (Additionally, you're liable to cook them up with ants or bees inside.)

Fourth, if you don't get along with bees, picking zucchini flowers might not be the right activity for you simply because bees pollinate

1 medium-sized zucchini
2 medium-sized Yukon Gold or other thin-skinned, waxy potatoes, scrubbed
1 (14½-ounce) can diced tomatoes in their own juice
8 cups water, plus more if needed
Salt
1 teaspoon freshly ground black pepper
2 cups (about ¼ pound) haricots verts (tiny French-style green beans)
¼ pound spaghetti noodles, broken into 2-inch lengths
Prepared pesto (homemade or Cibo Naturals brand), for garnish

1. Presoak and cook the beans. In a large kettle over high heat, bring the water to a boil. Add the beans, bay leaves, and salt, and as soon as the water returns to a boil, turn off the heat. Cover the pan and leave undisturbed for 1 hour.

2. When the hour has passed, turn the burner on high heat and bring the beans to a boil again, then decrease the heat to medium-low. Cook, adding more water if necessary to keep the beans barely covered, until the beans are tender, about 90 minutes.

3. While the beans are cooking, prepare the other elements of the soup. In a very large, heavy-bottomed Dutch oven or soup pot, heat the olive oil over medium heat, and sauté the onion, leek, celery, and garlic until the vegetables are tender and just beginning to color, about 10 minutes.

4. While the onion mixture is sautéing, prepare the zucchini. Cut the sides of the vegetable away from the seedy center and discard the center. Cut the sides into matchsticks about 2 inches long and ¼ inch wide. Add the cut zucchini to the pot. Cut the potatoes into matchsticks the same size as the zucchini and stir them in.

5. Stir the tomatoes and water in with the sautéed vegetables and increase the heat to high. Bring the soup to a full rolling boil and add a little salt; taste to make sure the salt is correct, then stir in the green beans and spaghetti noodles. Cook until the spaghetti is tender, then stir in the cooked beans with their cooking liquid. Decrease the heat to low, and allow the soup to simmer until the flavors merge and the broth surrounding the vegetables thickens slightly, about 10 minutes.

— *Greg Atkinson*

TEN-MINUTE ZUCCHINI PIZZA   SERVES 6

6 medium zucchinis
Olive oil
¾ cup pizza sauce
½ cup finely chopped basil
1¾ cups freshly grated mozzarella cheese
⅓ to ½ cup freshly grated Parmesan cheese

1. Preheat the oven to 425°F.

2. Cut the zucchinis lengthwise into ¼-inch-thick slices. Pat them dry and brush both sides with olive oil. Arrange them side-by-side on a baking sheet or pizza pan lined with aluminum foil. Bake 7 minutes, or until they are just tender when pierced with a fork.

3. Top the zucchinis generously with pizza sauce. Sprinkle with basil and the mozzarella and Parmesan cheeses. Return the pan to the oven and bake until the sauce is hot and bubbly and the cheese is melted, 2 to 3 minutes.

— *MACSAC*, From Asparagus to Zucchini

ZUCCHINI PICKLES

MAKES 3 PINTS

4 medium zucchinis (about 1½ pounds), trimmed and thinly sliced
2 small yellow onions, thinly sliced
3 tablespoons salt
Cold water
2 cups distilled vinegar
1 cup sugar
1 teaspoon celery seeds
1 teaspoon anise seeds
2 teaspoons dry mustard

1. Place the zucchinis and onions in a medium-sized bowl. Sprinkle with the salt. Cover with cold water; let stand for 1 hour.

2. Meanwhile, combine the vinegar, sugar, celery seeds, anise seeds, and mustard in a medium-sized saucepan. Heat to boiling, then remove from the heat.

3. Drain the zucchini and onions. Place them in a large pot and pour the hot vinegar liquid over them. Let stand for 1 hour.

4. After an hour, heat the mixture to boiling; simmer 3 minutes. Remove from the heat and pour into sterilized jars.

— *Bert Greene*, Greene on Greens

MARINATED ZUCCHINI

Garlic whistles (also called "scapes") are the garlic plant's immature flower buds, borne on whimsically curving stems in early summer. Chopped, these whistles taste delightfully of garlic without the harsh pungency of the mature bulb.

About 1 pound zucchini
2 tablespoons olive oil
Garlic whistles, minced

flowers and are often found at work between 8 and 10 A.M. They can get quite nasty when someone decides to chase them off or out. I personally have a way with them and have never been stung, but I know lots of people who have.

Fifth, immediately after picking the flowers, you must lightly spray the inside of the flower with cool water to remove any soil or creatures that may still be inside.

Sixth, hold the flower firmly by the stem and gently shake off all of the excess water, then place the flowers in separate rows of paper toweling. After covering each row with toweling and securely wrapping them with aluminum foil, store the packaged flowers in plastic containers and refrigerate until ready to use. The flowers will maintain their peak condition for up to a couple of weeks.

Fried Squash Blossoms

6 to 8 flowers per person for an entrée, 3 to 4 as an appetizer.

20 squash blossoms, trimmed and
    washed
½ cup milk
⅔ cup flour
⅔ cup beer (not dark) or club soda
Salt and pepper to taste
Oregano or other seasonings
1 teaspoon olive oil (optional)
1 teaspoon lemon juice (optional)
Deep-fat fryer thermometer

Whisk together the milk, flour, beer or club soda, salt, pepper, seasoning, olive oil, and lemon juice in a bowl until smooth. Heat 1 inch of oil in a large, heavy saucepan over moderate heat until it registers 375°F. Working in batches of 3 or 4, dip the blossoms in the batter to coat and fry until golden, about 30 seconds on each side, or 1 to 2 minutes per batch. Transfer to paper towels to drain and sprinkle lightly with salt. (Return oil to 375°F between batches.)

Serve at once, while still warm.

Basil, chopped
1 tablespoon red wine vinegar
Salt

1. Wash and dry the zucchini and cut diagonally into long, oval-shaped ⅓-inch-thick slices.

2. In a large skillet, heat just enough oil to coat the bottom of the skillet. Quickly fry the zucchini in a couple of batches (adding more oil if necessary) until it is golden-speckled on both sides and tender in the center. Drain on paper towels.

3. Lower the heat and sauté the garlic whistles until tender.

4. Arrange the zucchini in a bowl and sprinkle with basil, vinegar, salt, and garlic. Cover and serve at room temperature.

— *Featherstone Farm*

ZUCCHINI SALAD   SERVES 6

2 medium zucchinis, thinly sliced
3 or 4 radishes, sliced
½ medium white onion, chopped
⅓ cup green peppers, coarsely diced
1 cup sliced cauliflower
1 medium tomato, cut into bite-sized pieces
3 to 4 sprigs parsley, diced
1 clove garlic, finely diced and crushed
Several leaves fresh basil, chopped
6 tablespoons salad oil
1 to 2 tablespoons lemon juice
⅔ cup sugar
⅔ cup vinegar
Salt and pepper
Onion or garlic powder
Seasoned salt
Parmesan cheese, grated

1. Toss the zucchini, radishes, onion, green peppers, cauliflower, tomato, parsley, garlic, and basil together in a bowl. Sprinkle with the salad oil and lemon juice.

2. Dissolve the sugar and vinegar in a saucepan over medium heat. Pour over the salad. Season to taste with salt, pepper, onion or garlic powders, seasoned salt, and grated Parmesan cheese.

3. Chill several hours before serving.

— *Betty Culp,* Daisies Do Tell … A Recipe Book

ZUCCHINI CASSEROLE

SERVES 6

1 pound hamburger meat or ground venison
6 cups sliced zucchini or yellow squash
¼ cup chopped onion
1 can cream of chicken soup
1 cup sour cream
1 cup shredded carrots
1 (8-ounce) package herb bread stuffing mix
½ cup melted butter

1. Cook and brown the meat and drain. Set aside.

2. Boil the zucchini or squash in salted water for 5 minutes, and drain.

3. Preheat the oven to 350°F.

4. Add the onion, chicken soup, sour cream, and carrots to the squash, and mix well.

5. Cook the stuffing as directed on the package, and combine it with the melted butter.

6. Place half of the stuffing mixture on the bottom of a 12 × 7½ × 2-inch pan. Top with ground beef and then the vegetable mixture. Top with the rest of the stuffing mixture. Bake for 30 minutes.

— *Arlayne Fleming*

OREGANO AND ZUCCHINI PASTA

SERVES 4

Campanelle pasta are small and fluted, resembling little tubular flowers, whereas orecchiette look like tiny ears or bowls. Both pastas are excellent with chunky, heartier sauces.

Pecorino is a type of hard cheese made from sheep's milk. Like Parmesan, it has a strong, salty flavor that pairs well with pasta dishes dressed with robust sauces. If you cannot find genuine pecorino, substitute a quality Parmesan instead.

1 pound campanelle or orecchiette pasta
6 tablespoons extra-virgin olive oil, divided
2 pounds zucchini, trimmed and cut into ⅓-inch-thick slices
6 cloves garlic, chopped
2 tablespoons chopped fresh basil
2 tablespoons chopped fresh oregano
Dash red pepper flakes or hot pepper sauce (optional)
Salt and freshly ground black pepper
½ cup grated pecorino cheese, plus additional for sprinkling

1. Cook the pasta in a large pot of boiling salted water until its texture becomes al dente, stirring occasionally. Drain, reserving ½ cup of the cooking liquid. Return the pasta to the pot.

2. Heat 2 tablespoons of the olive oil in a large skillet over high heat.

Add the zucchini and sauté until tender, about 3 to 4 minutes. Add the garlic, basil, oregano, and red pepper, if desired; remove from heat.

3. Combine the zucchini mixture with the pasta, adding the reserved pasta cooking liquid as needed to moisten. Season to taste with salt and pepper. Add the pecorino cheese, stirring until melted and ready to serve. Sprinkle on additional cheese for garnish.

— *Mi Ae Lipe, Featherstone Farm CSA member*

Brandywine heirloom tomatoes, ready for eating.

Fall

FALL CROPS AT FEATHERSTONE FARM FALL INTO TWO CATEGORIES. FIRST, THERE ARE CROPS THAT ARE PLANTED IN THE SPRING AND TAKE THE FULL LENGTH OF THE SUMMER TO PRODUCE A CROP (WINTER SQUASH, FOR EXAMPLE). THEN THERE ARE OTHERS, SUCH AS BROCCOLI AND SALAD CROPS, THAT MAY HAVE BEEN PLANTED AND HARVESTED IN EARLY SUMMER, AND ARE THEN REPLANTED FOR A SECOND CROP TO BE PICKED IN THE MONTHS OF SEPTEMBER AND OCTOBER.

THE FIRST GROUP LARGELY CONSISTS OF FRUITS, BULBS, AND TUBERS THAT ARE PICKED EN MASSE WHEN THEY MATURE IN THE FIELD, THEN ARE CURED AND STORED INDOORS FOR LATER DISTRIBUTION. OUR ENTIRE GARLIC CROP, FOR EXAMPLE, IS HARVESTED OVER TWO DAYS AT THE END OF JULY.

We distribute new heads in August that must be refrigerated like any fresh vegetable. It is not until the garlic has been hung to cure, or dry down, in the barn for four to five weeks that it takes on that familiar dry, papery form, and that makes it a real fall (or even winter) crop.

This first group of fall crops—the garlic and onions and leeks, the potatoes and sweet potatoes, the winter squashes and the root crops—can also be considered long-storage crops. Their eating quality is determined as much by how they are cured and stored as how they are grown and harvested. In fact, they improve with age.

The months of September and October produce some of the very best crops of certain vegetables that are available all year. Many of the crops we associate with spring—radishes, spinach, arugula, and beets, among others—are significantly higher quality in the fall. In June, under strong sun and warmer soil, they grow too fast, resulting in lighter foliage that turns bitter fast. In the moist soil and long nights of autumn, however, they thrive, producing snappy sweet radishes, nutty arugula with no sharpness … and the list goes on.

Then there are the cole crops—broccoli, cauliflower, bok choy, napa cabbage, kohlrabis, collards, and kales. This group also makes an adequate early summer crop, but a truly wonderful fall harvest. Cole crops remarkably tolerate the cold, not only surviving temperatures in the mid- to low 20s, but thriving in them. Broccoli, for example, responds to the first nip of frost by generating more natural antifreeze … sugar!

So we always greet the first cold snap of September as a mixed blessing here in Minnesota. The tomatoes and basil are done for good, but the cole crops make huge leaps forward in terms of eating quality.

The month of September offers the fullest cornucopia of farm-fresh produce of the year. The summer crops are still around, even if their rich glow is finally subsiding. The new lettuces and spinach and radishes are just maturing as the heat of August recedes into memory. The big plantings of broccoli and cabbage are nearing their peak form. And the promise of the winter squash and carrots and leeks of October awaits, just around the corner.

Farmer's Table Menu — Fall
— up to December 15 —

by Jack Hedin

Salad
Coleslaw with Grated Daikon Radish,
Kohlrabi, and Vinaigrette Dressing

Soup
Kabocha Squash with White Beans and Ginger

On the Side
Brown Rice
Steamed Carrots, Leeks, Broccoli, and Cauliflower
Fresh Bread

Dessert
Apple Crisp

This time of year finds me working to take advantage of the very last fresh produce of the season, before embarking on the long winter of storage crops. In early November I pack our cooler with boxes of broccoli, cauliflower, kale, and, when I think of visiting the orchard, apples. You can do the same on a smaller scale in the vegetable crisper drawers of your refrigerator. Wrapped in plastic, these crops will keep remarkably well into December.

This is also the time of year when long, slow cooking overtakes the harried stir-fries around our house, and the squash soup is a prime example. Heat the oven to 350°F in the morning and pop in a kabocha and a butternut (or some other combination—two varieties make a fuller flavor, but kabocha or buttercup should be included as at least one).

When the squash is 80 percent cooked (beginning to soften but still firm enough to handle), peel it and chop it into chunks. Then simmer it with grated ginger in a full-bodied vegetable stock all afternoon. At some point, mash it all together and add some well-cooked white beans. This is a full-bodied, incredibly satisfying soup that constitutes a whole meal around our house, along with fresh bread, some steamed veggies, and apple crisp for dessert.

Fall Crops Available

Arugula (October)
Basil (Italian)
Beans (String)
    Green Snap, Haricots Verts,
    Royal Burgundy, Yellow Wax
Beets
    Chioggia, Detroit Red
Bok Choy
Braising Mix
Broccoli
    Green, Purple
Cabbage
    Green and Red Head, Napa,
    Savoy
Cauliflower
Collards
Garlic (Mature)
Kale
    Winterbor, Redbor, Lacinato
Kohlrabi
    White Vienna
Leeks
Mizuna
Mustard greens
    Green and Red
Onions (Cooking and storage;
    August through New Year's)
Potatoes (All mature; September
    and later)
    All Blue, Bintje, Desiree Pink,
    Langlade White, Red Norland,
    Romance, Russian Fingerling,
    Yukon Gold
Pumpkin
    Pie pumpkins
Radishes (September to October)
Raspberries (September)
Squash (Winter) (November)
    Acorn, Butternut, Carnival,
    Heart of Gold, Kabocha/
    Buttercup, Red Kuri, Spaghetti,
    Sweet Dumpling
Spinach (Salad)
Tatsoi
Turnips (October)

Beet

Beets are a bargain vegetable, because they are actually two in one: the delicious roots that everyone knows, and also the beet tops, or greens, which are extremely nutritious and a wonderful spring treat. Unfortunately, too many adults dislike beets, having eaten (or been forced to eat) poorly prepared specimens as children.

Beets are biennials, meaning that they take two years to grow to maturity. In their first year they develop their familiar swollen roots, and during the second year they flower and seed.

Featherstone grows two types of beets: Detroit Red and Chioggia (pronounced kee-oh-ja). Detroit Reds are deep red, while Chioggia roots have striking, concentric red and white rings. Both are extremely sweet and flavorful. Sometimes the CSA boxes offer just the greens, which are usually cut from the Detroit Red variety when they are young and tender.

HISTORY

It is thought that beets originated in the Mediterranean area, possibly Italy, although they have been cultivated since prehistoric times and thus their true origins are unknown. The original beets were closer to chard (a cultivar of the beet family) than the root vegetable we know today, and the early Romans ate only the leaves. Humans and livestock alike have enjoyed beets and their cultivars, which include chard, mangel-wurzel, and sugar beets.

Throughout recorded history, beets have been thought to have medicinal powers, combating digestive disorders, lack of sexual interest, and even AIDs.

NUTRITION

Beets have one of the highest sugar contents of all vegetables but are fairly low in calories, at 74 per cup. They are extremely high in folate and manganese and are a decent source of dietary fiber, vitamin C, and potassium. Betacyanin, which gives beets their distinctive rich pigment, is a powerful cancer-fighting agent and antioxidant.

The roots also contain betaine, supplements of which are sometimes prescribed to lower toxic levels of homocysteine, which can contribute to heart disease and stroke.

SELECTION

Avoid beets that are overly large; they may be old and woody. The smaller beets are, the sweeter they tend to be. They should be firm and their tops unwilted, with no soft or flabby areas.

STORAGE

If you are lucky enough to acquire beets with their greens still attached, cut all but 2 inches of the greens and stems from the roots, so they do not pull moisture away from the roots. Store the unwashed greens in a separate perforated plastic bag in the refrigerator vegetable crisper, where they will keep for about 4 days.

The roots should be placed in the coldest place possible. Beets that are unwashed in the refrigerator vegetable crisper will keep for about 3 weeks. Beets will also keep quite well in a basement, root cellar, or other place with the proper cool temperature and lack of humidity (for more information, see "Preserving the Bounty" on page 331).

TRIMMING & CLEANING

Like spinach, beet greens must be very thoroughly washed and rinsed several times, as they usually harbor sand and debris.

Once you are ready to use the roots, scrub their necks gently with a soft vegetable brush to work off any clinging dirt, but be careful not to break the skin, which will cause them to "bleed."

STEAMING & BOILING

Boiling cooks beets quickly but tends to leach out nutrients and some color (although red beets usually have plenty of pigment to spare).

To prevent bleeding when boiling, leave them whole with their root ends and 1 inch of stem attached. Boil for 25 to 30 minutes for small beets; 45 to 50 minutes for medium beets, or until they are tender. Test by piercing them with a knife. Once the beets are cool enough to touch, peel them by slipping the skins, which should slide off like a glove.

The Chioggia beets (the ones with concentric red and white circles) do not bleed. When cooked their rings will turn orange or rose.

STIR-FRYING & SAUTÉING

Beet greens adapt well to stir-fries, but add them only during the last 1 to 2 minutes of cooking. The dense, sometimes fibrous quality of the roots means that they should be parboiled before being tossed into the wok. Or else they should be julienned (but cooked separately and added at the very end so they don't bleed all over the rest of the ingredients). If thinly sliced, stir-fry beets for only 2 to 4 minutes.

Sautéed beets should also be thinly sliced (about ⅛ to ¼-inch rounds) and cooked on medium heat for 5 to 7 minutes.

BAKING & ROASTING

Beets respond very well to slow roasting in the oven. To prepare, preheat the oven to 375°F. Slice the beets into wedges (similar to potatoes), or if they are very small, leave them whole and place them as a single layer on a roasting pan or baking dish. Drizzle with oil, garlic, and seasonings if desired, and roast them for about 30 to 40 minutes, or until they are tender when pierced with a fork. If necessary, peel them (the skins should slip off easily after they are cooked).

MICROWAVING

Cut unpeeled beets into evenly sized pieces. Place in a microwave-safe dish and cover with 1 inch of water. Microwave on High power for 8 to 15 minutes, depending on their size and age, or until they are just tender. If you prefer them peeled, rub off their skins right after cooking, while they are still warm.

"The beet is the most intense of vegetables. The radish, admittedly, is more feverish, but the fire of the radish is a cold fire, the fire of discontent, not of passion. Tomatoes are lusty enough, yet there runs through tomatoes an undercurrent of frivolity. Beets are deadly serious."

— *Tom Robbins*

BLANCHING & FREEZING

Beets should be fully cooked before freezing, as frozen raw beets will soften undesirably upon thawing. Frozen cooked beets, however, will retain their flavor and texture. To freeze, follow the boiling instructions above. Then chill them and remove their skins. Slice or cube them if necessary, and pack in zipper-lock freezer or vacuum food sealer-type bags, or freezer containers. Squeeze out excess air and leave ½ inch of headspace (unless you are using the vacuum sealing method). Beets will keep in the freezer for about 8 months, but their texture may diminish considerably.

EQUIVALENTS, MEASURES & SERVINGS

- 1 pound = 1¾ cups shredded = 2 cups chopped or sliced

COMPLEMENTARY HERBS, SEASONINGS & FOODS

Allspice, apples, bacon, beef, brown sugar, butter, cheese, chestnuts, cinnamon, citrus, cloves, cream, cucumber, curry, dill, eggs, fennel, honey, horseradish, lamb, lemon, mustard, nutmeg, onions, oranges, parsley, pork, potatoes, smoked fish, sour cream, tarragon, vinaigrette, vinegar.

SERVING SUGGESTIONS

- Because of their dense texture and sweet flavor, beets go best with rich meats like pork, beef brisket, duck, and ham, as well as oilier fish like salmon and swordfish.
- Baking and oven-roasting are wonderful ways to accentuate the natural sweetness of beets because these cooking methods caramelize their sugars.
- Shred beets and carrots for an airy, colorful salad. Toss with raisins and a sweet dressing.
- Beets can be juiced, but be sure to use this juice sparingly and mix with apple juice (or you will have a sugar high unlike any other).
- Beet soup, or borscht, is a perennial Eastern European favorite. Top it with sour cream and serve with pork tenderloin, a green salad, and a dark bread like rye or pumpernickel.
- Shred beets and red cabbage, and cook them together with a little balsamic vinegar, sea salt, and butter.
- Don't forget the beet greens—they are incredibly healthy and tasty when sautéed with garlic and a nice olive oil. Try them in stir-fries and soups, or eat them raw in salads. Older beet greens are more flavorful and slightly bitter, which make them a perfect foil to goat cheese, rich soups, stews, and meats.
- Sprinkle cooked beets with the grated zest or juice of either lemons or oranges.
- Bake whole beets along with new potatoes in the oven until tender. They are delicious with salt and pepper, and served with steak or corned beef.

ICED BEET AND ORANGE SOUP   SERVES 8

This soup freezes well if you have any left over.

3 pounds beets, peeled and cut into thin slices
1 cup chopped onions
1 tablespoon fresh basil, or 1 teaspoon dried basil

4 cups chicken stock
2 cups freshly squeezed orange juice

Place all of the ingredients except the orange juice in a saucepan, and simmer over medium heat until the beets are tender, about 15 to 20 minutes. Cool and purée. Add the orange juice and chill.

— *Lee Bailey,* Lee Bailey's Southern Food

. . . .

TRINA'S GREEN SALMON

SERVES 2

This recipe was given to us by Trina, our shop manager. This is a perfect fusion of her many lives: her time cooking at her family's restaurant, her work on a CSA in Alaska, and her love of good food. This dish can be found as a first course at many Japanese restaurants, and it is very simple to make.

8 ounces salmon
8 ounces spinach
Handful of beet greens
¼ cup wasabi paste
Juice from ½ lemon (about 2 tablespoons)
Salt and pepper

1. Preheat the oven to 300°F.

2. Blanch the spinach.

3. Coat the salmon thickly with the wasabi paste. Wrap the salmon up in the spinach and beet greens and top with 1 tablespoon lemon juice.

4. Bake slowly for 1 hour. Remove from the oven and top with the remaining lemon juice. Add salt and pepper to taste.

— *Trina, Featherstone Farm shop manager*

. . . .

BEETS AND THEIR GREENS WITH AÏOLI

SERVES 4

16 to 20 small (not baby) beets with greens attached
Coarse salt
1 tablespoon extra-virgin olive oil
Freshly ground black pepper

AÏOLI

3 cloves garlic, peeled and minced
1 teaspoon Dijon mustard
1 teaspoon salt
1 egg yolk, at room temperature
3 tablespoons fresh lemon juice

Seasonality: A True Definition

by Jack Hedin, Featherstone Farm Owner

As consumers of supermarket produce, we have grown accustomed to eating pretty much any vegetable or fruit all year round, rather than waiting for certain crops to come into season. This concept of eating something in season and what this means to me as a farmer—pulling leaves off broccoli, eating green beans at different times of the year, harvesting the perfect radish—grows increasingly important as the years pass.

To me, seasonality is not just when something is available, but when it is good, and dependably so. Weather, climate, and soil conditions enormously impact the quality of both fruits and vegetables.

We humans tend to perceive the seasons as how we experience weather when we are out and about (always during the day). Plants, on the other hand, experience seasons as night and day: dew sets that occur because of humidity, moisture, wind, (or the lack of them), and temperatures.

In particular, here in southeast Minnesota, temperature differences during the day and night can range in June from 45 degrees Fahrenheit at night to 86 degrees during the day. In August, that nighttime temperature might not get below 70 degrees.

Moisture in the field and how soil and its organic matter retains moisture in the root zone are also extremely important factors. Dewfalls play critical roles too. Every single morning in August, the fields will be completely soaked. When the sun rises, even if it is brightly shining, its solar energy goes first into drying things out, not into the leaves to make energy.

Such fluctuations really affect how a melon ripens in the field, for

½ cup vegetable oil
½ cup mild olive oil

FOR THE AÏOLI

1. Put the garlic, mustard, and salt into a medium-sized bowl. Use the back of a wooden spoon to crush them into a paste.

2. Add the egg yolk to the garlic and mustard and whisk in until the mixture turns pale. Add the lemon juice and whisk until the mixture becomes frothy. Gradually add the vegetable oil, then the olive oil, in slow, steady streams, whisking constantly until the oils are fully incorporated and the mixture is emulsified.

3. Adjust the seasonings.

FOR THE SALAD

1. Preheat the oven to 350°F.

2. Cut the greens off the beets, leaving 2 inches of the stalks attached. Wash the greens and beets and set them aside separately.

3. Line a large pan with aluminum foil, and place the beets in a single layer in the pan. Roast the beets in the oven until they turn soft, about 1 hour. Unwrap the beets and set aside to cool, then peel.

4. Meanwhile, cook the beet greens in a medium-sized pot of boiling salted water over high heat until tender, about 5 minutes. Drain, squeezing out excess water, and put into a bowl. Toss with extra-virgin olive oil and salt and pepper to taste. Set aside to cool.

5. To serve, spoon some of the aïoli onto 4 small plates. Then divide the greens and beets between the plates, putting the greens on top of the aïoli and the beets on top of the greens. Season to taste with salt and pepper.

— Saveur, *September–October 2002*

. . . .

MOEN CREEK PICKLED BEETS   MAKES 4 PINTS

These will keep in the refrigerator several weeks but may disappear long before. Use as a condiment or a salad topping (chopped or sliced). Delicious as an appetizer with cottage or hard cheeses.

4 pounds beets
3 cups thinly sliced onions
1½ cups cider vinegar
1½ cups sugar
1 tablespoon mustard seed
1 teaspoon whole allspice
1 teaspoon whole cloves
3 sticks cinnamon, broken
1 teaspoon salt

1. Scrub the beets with a vegetable brush and trim off the tops, leaving 2 inches of the stems attached to the roots. (Young tops can be added as greens to salads or steamed as a vegetable.) Cover the beetroots with boiling water and cook until they become tender. Lift out the beets and drain. Peel and remove the stems (quarter any roots that are larger than golf-ball size); set aside.

2. Combine the remaining ingredients with 1½ cups water in a large pot. Bring to a boil, decrease the heat, and simmer 5 minutes.

3. Add the beets and heat through. Remove the cinnamon sticks, and chill in the juice.

— *MACSAC, From Asparagus to Zucchini*

....

BEET-CHOCOLATE CAKE   SERVES 10

  2 cups sugar
  2 cups flour
  ½ teaspoon salt
  2 teaspoons baking powder
  1 teaspoon baking soda
  3 to 4 ounces unsweetened chocolate
  4 eggs
  ¼ cup oil
  3 cups shredded beets

1. Preheat the oven to 325°F.

2. Combine the sugar, flour, salt, baking powder, and baking soda. Sift or mix well together.

3. Melt the chocolate very slowly over low heat or in a double boiler.

instance. Squash and melons need accumulated heat to ripen. That means that they do not start to ripen until all of their leaves are dry, so those dewfalls in the valley hugely impact how these crops develop.

Having worked on farms in California, I often think in terms of the conditions of where a crop is grown in that agricultural state, where so many different microenvironments exist.

Here in our valley in southeastern Minnesota, the nightly dewsets mimic the coastal fogs of California's heavily cultivated Salinas Valley, which is why we grow so much leaf lettuce and broccoli. Both prefer cool soils and plenty of moisture.

One of the most striking examples of the divide between the consumer perception of seasonality and actual seasonality occurs with radishes. When we come to the farmers market in June, everyone lines up to get radishes because they are psyched up for it.

What is happening in the field, however, is that the lengthening days are causing the radishes to grow so fast in May and June that they get pithy and hollow inside. When the soil reaches above 65 degrees, the roots lose crunch, juiciness, and sweetness, and turn very spicy. What people perceive as peak radish time in early June is, in my mind, a pretty risky season.

Although radishes can be good at this time, what I believe people are really responding to is the lack of fresh fruits and vegetables during the previous six or eight months. They are not necessarily looking for radishes; they are seeking something good, and even though these radishes might be fresher than those from California, they are nothing like the fall radishes we harvest.

In September and October, the radishes are growing so much more slowly. The nights are cooler, and

Allow the chocolate to cool, then blend thoroughly with the eggs and oil.

4. Combine the flour mixture with the chocolate mixture, alternating with the beets. Pour into 2 greased 9-inch cake pans.

5. Bake for 40 to 50 minutes, or until an inserted fork can be removed cleanly from the center.

— *MACSAC*, From Asparagus to Zucchini

BORSCHT

SERVES 6

Although there are many versions of borscht—the famous Eastern European soup—most are made with beet stock and bacon, with a huge dollop of sour cream on top. If you want a tart topping, you can try a spoonful of soy yogurt, or blend silken tofu with a bit of lemon, a small amount of oil, and some sugar using a hand blender. In this vegetarian version of borscht, I have created a creamy base with the addition of a baked potato for a hearty dinner soup.

½ tablespoon canola or olive oil
1 large onion, chopped
4 to 5 cloves garlic, minced or pressed
2 stalks celery, chopped
1 or 2 carrots, sliced
2 tablespoons tomato paste
6 cups water or vegetable stock (or use a combination of the two)
½ tablespoon fresh dill or ½ teaspoon dried dill
4 cups sliced beets
Salt and pepper
1 potato, baked
Juice and zest of 1 lemon
1 to 2 tablespoons granulated sweetener

1. Heat a large, heavy-bottomed soup pot over medium heat. Add the oil and onion. Stir, decrease the heat, cover, and "sweat" the onions until they are translucent. Add the garlic, celery, and carrots. Stir and cook for about 5 more minutes. Stir in the tomato paste. Mix well and continue to cook for another minute or two. Add the water or stock, dill, and beets. Bring to a boil. Decrease the heat to a simmer. Cover and cook for 15 minutes or until the beets are tender. Add salt and pepper to taste.

2. In a medium-sized bowl, use a hand blender or electric blender to purée the potato, lemon juice, zest, granulated sweetener, and approximately ½ cup of the soup liquid until it turns smooth and creamy. Stir into the rest of the soup, and adjust the salt and pepper seasoning. Serve topped with a dollop of plain soy yogurt or tofu-lemon mixture.

— *Debra Daniels-Zeller,* Vegetarian Journal, *September 2000*

ROASTED BABY BEET SALAD   SERVES 4

1 pound mixed red and candy-striped baby beets, stems trimmed
    to 1-inch pieces
1 tablespoon minced shallot
1 tablespoon fresh lemon juice
3 tablespoons fresh orange juice
1 teaspoon freshly grated orange zest
½ teaspoon Dijon mustard
1 tablespoon extra-virgin olive oil
Salt and pepper
1 head Bibb or butterhead lettuce, leaves separated

1. Preheat the oven to 400°F.

2. Rinse the beets. Wrap the colors separately in aluminum foil and roast in the middle of the oven until they become tender, 45 minutes to 1 hour. Cool.

3. Peel the beets and halve them lengthwise. Whisk together the shallot, lemon and orange juices, zest, and mustard. Whisk in the oil until emulsified and season with salt and pepper.

4. Drizzle the lettuce with three-quarters of the dressing. Sprinkle with the beets and drizzle with the remaining dressing.

— Gourmet, *as appeared on www.foodnetwork.com*

"Everything I do, I do on the principle of Russian borscht. You can throw everything into it—beets, carrots, cabbage, onions—everything you want. What's important is the result, the taste of the borscht."

— *Yevgeny Yevtushenko, Russian poet*

Broccoli

Broccoli is a member of the large and venerable Brassica family, which includes many of the world's familiar vegetables—cabbage, cauliflower, kale, Brussels sprouts, and collards, to name just a few. As with many of its cousins, the mere mention of its name often evokes passionate feelings, either of fond gustatory pleasure or pure fear and loathing.

Broccoli is one of the few plants we savor for its floral abundance, since its distinctive green heads are actually huge clusters of flower buds that are consumed before they open. But the plant's stems make a perfectly respectable vegetable on their own, a tasty, healthy alternative to carrot and celery sticks on the crudité tray or cooked as a sturdy addition to stir-fries.

Broccoli grows best in cool weather, responding to frost by actually becoming sweeter. Heat drives the plants to bolt, or flower, prematurely, so the best season for broccoli is in the fall, from mid-September to late October. Featherstone grows sprouting broccoli, which is the most familiar type of broccoli. (For more information on the different types of broccoli, see the sidebar "A Broccoli Primer" on pages 224–225.)

HISTORY

Broccoli's name suggests that it came from the Mediterranean, particularly Italy, where the ancient Romans knew of it. But since the plant does not grow well in hot climates, it was probably eaten and cultivated long before its mention in the famous Roman cookbook *Apicius,* compiled around the fifth century C.E. Possibly the plant originated in Asia. The Italian noblewoman Catherine de' Medici introduced a type of broccoli to France in the mid-1500s, but it remained unfamiliar to English tables until the 1700s. Later, Thomas Jefferson had broccoli planted in his extensive gardens at Monticello, Virginia, where it joined the ranks of other vegetables rare and exotic at that time, like tomatoes and cauliflower.

Broccoli was not commercially cultivated in America until brothers Stephano and Andrea D'Arrigo planted some experimental plots in San Jose, California, in 1922. They shipped a few crates to Boston, where broccoli became a hit in that city's Italian community. In part because of the D'Arrigos' aggressive marketing under their Andy Boy label, broccoli finally became a mainstream vegetable in the United States—and a food of distaste to many American children.

NUTRITION

Broccoli is one of nature's most nutritious foods, packing formidable amounts of vitamins A, C, and K, as well as folate, fiber, vitamins B6 and B2, phosphorus, potassium, and manganese. Like other cruciferous vegetables, broccoli contains abundant phytonutrients such as sulforaphane and indoles, which in studies have proven to fight cancer, especially prostate, colorectal, and lung. Broccoli also is a good source of lutein, an antioxidant crucial for eye health.

SELECTION

Choose broccoli that is young and very firm. Supermarket broccoli is susceptible to being dried out; limp florets will lack flavor. The entire head should be a consistent gray-green color. Avoid heads with yellowing buds or opening flowers, which indicate overmaturity.

STORAGE

Store broccoli unwashed in a perforated bag in the coldest part of the refrigerator. It will keep for up to 2 weeks, depending on its original condition.

TRIMMING & CLEANING

Broccoli florets and stems should be cooked separately to retain their nutrients and optimum texture. Trim the florets from the thicker stems. Unless the stems are very thin, you will probably have to trim their skins with a vegetable peeler and slice them in half or in pieces about 2½ to 3 inches long, so they cook faster.

STEAMING & BOILING

Steaming is the best way to cook broccoli to preserve its nutrients, much of which are leached out or destroyed by boiling and even microwaving. Steam florets for about 5 to 10 minutes; boil for about 4 to 7 minutes, depending on your preference for doneness. Remember that the vegetable will continue to cook as it cools down, so it is better to slightly undercook than overdo it.

STIR-FRYING & SAUTÉING

Divide broccoli florets into smaller, bite-sized chunks, with a minimum of the stem attached (since these will be tougher). With the stems, peel them first, then cut them diagonally into thin slices, so they will cook faster. Stir-fry in oil, butter, or water for about 3 to 5 minutes on high heat in a wok or large frying pan, or until the pieces are crisp-tender.

For sautéing, it may be better to parboil or steam the broccoli lightly first, so that they are not too tough by the time they hit the pan. In a large skillet, melt a couple of tablespoons of butter until it begins to foam, then add the cooked broccoli along with any herbs, seasonings, or salt desired, and sauté for 2 to 3 minutes.

BAKING & ROASTING

Broccoli can be baked in a 350°F oven for 45 minutes to 1 hour as a casserole or by itself, wrapped in aluminum foil with herbs, oil, and chicken broth. Roasted broccoli calls for shorter cooking times and a hotter oven, about 17 to 20 minutes at 425°F.

BLANCHING & FREEZING

For best results, blanch no more than one pound at a time. Blanch in boiling water for 4 minutes, then plunge into ice water for 5 minutes or until cooled. Remove and drain. Then package the broccoli in zipper-lock freezer or vacuum food sealer-type bags, or freezer containers. Squeeze out excess air and leave 1 inch of headspace (unless you are using the vacuum sealing method). It will keep to up to a year at 0°F.

Cooking Tip

As with all members of the Brassica (cabbage) family, some of the very compounds that make broccoli so healthful also produce a distinctive sulfurous odor.

To minimize the scent, do not overcook. As with some people, broccoli that's old and tough will smell more. You can also try adding a few chunks of bread into the cooking water to absorb the smell.

A Broccoli Primer

All of the varieties of broccoli available in the markets these days are bound to trigger some confusion for the consumer.

Sprouting broccoli or Calabrese broccoli: *This is the type of broccoli most familiar to us, with a thick central stalk bearing a large head of florets, with some smaller branching stems and florets.*

Purple broccoli: *This variety looks almost identical to the familiar green sprouting broccoli, except that its florets have a purplish cast to them and they are often a bit smaller. The chemical compounds responsible for the purple color also have additional antioxidant properties. Unfortunately, its attractive purple color tends to fade during cooking.*

Broccolini or baby broccoli: *A cross between broccoli and Chinese kale, these cute stalks look like rather leggy, unkempt versions of our familiar broccoli, with looser florets, narrow but succulent stems, and broad leaves.*

Although it is sometimes called baby broccoli, it is a separate vegetable in and of itself, and not a youthful version of our familiar sprouting type.

Broccoli raab or rapini: *This plant is actually not related to broccoli, but more to the turnip. Still, it bears close-knit tufts of flower buds atop its stalks that closely resemble broccoli.*

(One way to tell it apart from broccolini is the presence of its

MICROWAVING

Peel the largest stalks, or cut into spears. Arrange the pieces in a microwave-safe dish, with florets pointed toward the center. Add 2 tablespoons water, cover, and cook on High power.

- 1 cup = 2 to 3 minutes
- 2 cups = 3 to 4 minutes
- 1 pound = 8 to 10 minutes

MEASURES & EQUIVALENTS

- ½ pound broccoli = 1 serving
- 1 medium bunch = 3 to 4 servings
- 1 bunch = 1½ to 2 pounds
- 1 pound fresh broccoli = 2 heads
- 1 pound fresh broccoli = 9 ounces trimmed
- 1 pound fresh broccoli = 2 cups chopped
- 10 ounces frozen broccoli = 2½ cups chopped

COMPLEMENTARY HERBS, SEASONINGS & FOODS

Anchovies, bacon, basil, beef, breadcrumbs, butter, carrots, cheese, chiles, cream, cumin, dill, fish, garlic, hollandaise sauce, lemon balm, lemon juice, marjoram, nuts, olive oil, orange, oregano, peppers, potatoes, shallots, tarragon, thyme, vinaigrette.

SERVING SUGGESTIONS

- To make broccoli and other vegetables more appealing to kids (and adults too!), serve bite-sized pieces with a variety of dressings and dipping sauces.

- Chop broccoli into small pieces and sprinkle them over pizzas, salads, casseroles, and just about anything that could use color and vegetable crunch.

- Few vegetable dishes beat the simple preparation of steamed broccoli with a little lemon juice, melted butter, and freshly ground pepper.

- A quick soup: First blanch cut-up broccoli (tops and stems). Then place broccoli, cut-up cooked potatoes, and a couple of garlic cloves and onions (both sautéed in olive oil or butter) into a food processor or blender and blend. Reheat the mixture, and add salt and pepper to taste.

- Broccoli is also great blanched until bright green and sautéed with garlic, onion, and olive oil.

- Toss steamed broccoli with butter and herbs. Cool and use in a salad.

- Peeled broccoli stems make a great raw vegetable on their own. Slice them long and serve with carrot and celery sticks on the crudité tray.

BROCCOLI STEM SALAD

Broccoli stems
Onion, chopped
Green olives, chopped
Mayonnaise

1. Peel and trim the tough outer layer of the broccoli stems. In a pan, simmer them in a little water until they turn just tender but not mushy.

2. Cool, add the onion and olives, and toss with mayonnaise.

3. Chill and serve.

— Susan Roehl, Featherstone Farm CSA member

. . . .

BROCCOLI SOUP   SERVES 4

1½ cups chopped broccoli or 1 (10-ounce) package frozen broccoli
¼ cup diced celery
¼ cup chopped onion
1 cup low-sodium chicken broth
2 cups nonfat milk
2 tablespoons cornstarch
¼ teaspoon salt
Dash pepper
Dash ground thyme
¼ cup grated Swiss cheese

1. Place the broccoli, celery, onion, and broth in a large saucepan. Bring to a boil, decrease the heat, cover, and cook until the vegetables are tender, about 8 minutes.

2. In a separate bowl, mix the milk, cornstarch, salt, pepper, and thyme; add to the cooked vegetables. Cook, stirring constantly, until the soup is lightly thickened and the mixture just begins to boil. Remove from the heat.

3. Add the cheese and stir it in until it is melted.

— Fruits and Veggies—More Matters; Centers for Disease Control & Prevention

. . . .

THE ENCHANTED BROCCOLI FOREST   SERVES 4 TO 6

1 pound broccoli
1 tablespoon butter or canola oil (plus a little for the pan)
1 cup chopped onion
¾ teaspoon salt
1 large clove garlic, minced
2 tablespoons fresh lemon juice
About 6 cups cooked brown or white rice
Freshly ground black pepper
Cayenne to taste
2 tablespoons minced fresh dill or 2 teaspoons dried dill
3 tablespoons minced fresh mint or 3 teaspoons dried mint
¼ cup minced fresh parsley
½ cup toasted sunflower seeds (optional)
1 packed cup grated Cheddar or Swiss (about ¼ pound) (optional)
A little melted butter for the top (optional)

distinctive, lacy-edged foliage.) But unlike its sweeter namesake, broccoli raab is a strongly flavored vegetable, pleasantly bitter and aggressive.

Broccoflower: This vegetable looks like a green cauliflower, which along with sprouting broccoli is what makes up its heritage. Raw, it tastes somewhat sweeter than regular white cauliflower but much like broccoli when cooked.

Chinese broccoli or Chinese kale: This is not a broccoli or kale as we know it, but a whole different subspecies of the vast Brassica family. They look distinctively different, with broad, smooth, flat leaves, waxy-looking stems, and very small clusters of floral buds atop their juicy, crunchy stems. They taste milder and sweeter than sprouting broccoli, and they certainly lack the bitter pungency of broccoli raab.

Romanesco broccoli: An exotic-looking plant that appears to be from an alien vegetable world, this is actually another type of green cauliflower, like broccoflower. It is hard to mistake this for any other member of the Brassica family, with its conical, chartreuse heads tightly arranged on a central stalk.

(Incidentally, this beautifully geometrical pattern of Romanesco's florets are one of nature's more perfect examples of mathematically accurate fractal design.)

Broccoli sprouts: Last but not least are these little alfalfa-sprout-like veggies, which are simply sprouting broccoli seeds that have germinated.

1. Trim the tough bottoms from the broccoli stalks, and cut the tops into smallish spears of whatever size suits you. Cook them in a steamer over boiling water until bright green and just barely tender. Rinse under cold running water, drain well, and set aside.

2. Preheat the oven to 325°F. Lightly grease a 9 × 13-inch baking pan.

3. Melt the butter or heat the oil in a large, deep skillet or a Dutch oven. Add the onion and salt, and sauté over medium heat for about 5 minutes, or until the onion begins to soften. Add the garlic and lemon juice, and sauté for about 2 minutes longer. Stir in the rice, some black pepper and cayenne to taste, the herbs, and the optional sunflower seeds and cheese. Taste to correct the salt, if necessary, and spread into the prepared pan.

4. Now for the fun part. Arrange the broccoli upright in the rice, and, if desired, drizzle with melted butter. Cover loosely with aluminum foil, and bake until just heated through (15 to 20 minutes). Serve right away.

— *Mollie Katzen,* The New Enchanted Broccoli Forest

BASMATI RICE WITH MUSHROOMS, BROCCOLI, AND ONION
SERVES 4

2 tablespoons extra-virgin olive oil
40 pearl onions, peeled and ends removed
    (or substitute 3 cups white or yellow onions, cut into chunks)
1 clove garlic, peeled and minced
2 cups basmati rice, uncooked
1 tablespoon paprika
½ cup dry white wine
6 cups hot vegetable stock
Salt and freshly ground black pepper
2 cups mushrooms, wild or domestic, sliced
2 cups broccoli florets, blanched
¼ cup chives (or scallions), diced, plus ¼ cup for garnish
¼ cup Parmesan cheese, grated, for garnish

1. In a very large nonstick saucepan, heat 1 tablespoon of the olive oil over medium-high heat. Add the onions; cook until they are tender and browned on both sides, about 7 minutes.

2. Add the garlic; cook until it begins to brown, about 2 minutes. Add the rice; heat until it is lightly toasted. Add the paprika and mix well. Add the white wine and cook until all of the liquid is gone, about 3 minutes. Add the hot vegetable stock. Season well with salt and pepper.

3. Cover with a tight-fitting lid and lower the heat to a simmer. Cook until the rice is just about tender, about 15 to 25 minutes, depending upon your choice of rice.

Books

Broccoli and Company
Audra Hendrickson and Jack Hendrickson; Storey Communications, 1989.

The Big Broccoli Book
Georgia Downard; Random House, 1992.

Cooking Tip

Cut a criss-cross incision about an inch deep in the stem of each floret before steaming or boiling. The cooking heat can then penetrate the tougher stem faster.

4. Meanwhile, in a large nonstick skillet over high heat, add the remaining 1 tablespoon of oil. Add the mushrooms; cook until they become golden, about 5 minutes. Add the broccoli, cooking until al dente, about 3 minutes.

5. Transfer the mushrooms and broccoli to the saucepan with the rice. Season with salt and pepper. Add ¼ cup of the chives. Cover the pan; remove from the heat and allow to sit for 5 minutes before serving. Spoon onto warm serving plates and sprinkle with the remaining chives and Parmesan cheese, if desired.

— *www.fooddownunder.com*

BLASTED BROCCOLI   SERVES 4

A few years ago, Food & Wine *editor Tina Ujlaki offered this recipe to a reader who wrote requesting a healthy vegetable side dish. "Blasting" vegetables was in the wind that year. Chefs and home cooks alike were popping asparagus and green beans into hot ovens all over the country, but this recipe captured the mini-trend and codified it. The intense heat assures that the vegetable is irresistibly crisp, and the trace of bitterness from the browning is trumped by the sweet tang of balsamic vinegar.*

4 cups broccoli florets
2 tablespoons olive oil
1 teaspoon sea salt, or to taste
1 tablespoon balsamic vinegar

1. Preheat the oven to 500°F. Rinse the broccoli florets and let them drain in a large strainer or colander.

2. Put the florets in a bowl with the olive oil and toss to coat. Sprinkle with the sea salt and toss again. Spread the seasoned broccoli in a single layer on a baking sheet and pop it in the preheated oven. Bake until the edges of the florets are browned and crisp, about 4 minutes.

3. Put the cooked florets back into the bowl and toss with balsamic vinegar to coat. Taste and add more salt if desired. Serve hot.

— *Greg Atkinson (Adapted from* Food & Wine *Magazine)*

Cauliflower

Cauliflower is one of the many members of the Brassica family, which includes cabbage, broccoli, bok choy, kale, and collards. Broccoli and cauliflower are kissing cousins; at one point they were actually identical plants until humans began breeding them for their most desired traits.

Cauliflower is grown for its distinctive heads of modified, undeveloped flowers, called curds, which can be white, green, purple, and even orange. Technically, all parts of the cauliflower plant are edible, although the leaves and stalks are (sadly!) usually ignored.

Like most Brassicas, cauliflower thrives in cooler weather, and Featherstone's crop starts coming into its own in the fall and remains one of the last vegetables to appear in its CSA baskets. It is a slower-growing crop than broccoli and cabbage, but its sweet mellowness, heightened by the season's first frosts, make it well worth the wait.

HISTORY

Cauliflower probably originated in Asia Minor, and there is some evidence that the ancient Romans cultivated it. It was slow to enter the rest of Europe, appearing on French tables only in the 1600s and on American shores about a hundred years later. Cauliflower remains a popular vegetable in China, India, and Europe.

NUTRITION

A cup of boiled cauliflower contains about 29 calories and is an extremely good source of vitamins C and K. It also provides folate, dietary fiber, vitamin B6, manganese, and potassium. Along with its other Brassica relatives, cauliflower is a cruciferous vegetable, containing phytonutrients that may help prevent cancer.

SELECTION

Look for clean, tightly compact heads of uniform color, with no soft or discolored areas, which indicate rot, extreme age, or sliminess. The size of the heads is not related to quality, but a head that is enveloped in green leaves is likely to be fresher.

STORAGE

Cauliflower should be stored in the refrigerator vegetable crisper, tightly wrapped in a plastic bag, stem-side down so as not to trap moisture in the florets. It is not the best keeper, especially cut florets, and should be used within 1 week.

TRIMMING & CLEANING

To prepare, snap off the green leaves surrounding the curd, and cut the entire head in half. Then slice the florets away from the central stem and core. (If desired, you can save this stem and core and prepare them like broccoli stems, or use them in soup stocks.) Or you can keep the entire head intact to steam or roast whole.

STEAMING & BOILING

Cauliflower should be cooked at a bare minimum, as its unpleasant sulfurous odor becomes stronger with overcooking. Steaming is far preferable to boiling, which makes the curds watery. Place the florets in a steamer and cook for about 5 to 7 minutes, depending on their size. An entire head may take 10 to 12 minutes, depending on its size.

If you must boil cauliflower, cook it, covered, as briefly as possible in about 2 inches of boiling, salted water for about 7 to 10 minutes for florets, or 10 to 15 minutes for a whole head.

STIR-FRYING & SAUTÉING

Break up the florets into small, uniform pieces, with a minimum of stem attached, since they will cook unevenly. Stir-fry in oil, butter, ghee, or water for about 5 to 7 minutes, or until it becomes tender.

As with broccoli, cauliflower benefits from parboiling or a brief steaming for a few minutes prior to sautéing. Then sauté in butter, oil, and seasonings for about 2 to 3 minutes.

BAKING & ROASTING

Cauliflower is terrific baked and roasted, for this cooking method caramelizes the vegetable's natural sugars. Before baking, cauliflower should be steamed or boiled first until it turns tender. Then combine it with breadcrumbs, cheese, herbs, and seasonings, and bake for 10 to 15 minutes in a 375°F oven, or until the top is golden brown.

To roast, separate cauliflower into florets, place in a lightly greased roasting pan, drizzle with oil and seasonings, and put in a 500°F oven for 15 minutes. An entire head may take 1 to 1¼ hours in a 450°F oven.

MICROWAVING

Arrange florets in a microwave-safe dish, with them pointed toward the center. Add 2 tablespoons water, cover, and cook on High power. (Depending on your microwave wattage and the size of your cauliflower, you might need to increase cooking times, as cauliflower often cooks unevenly in the microwave.)

- 1 cup = 2 to 3 minutes
- 2 cups = 3 to 4 minutes
- 1 pound = 8 to 10 minutes
- Whole cauliflower = 11 to 15 minutes

BLANCHING & FREEZING

Freezing cauliflower affects its texture significantly, causing it to break down. Still, frozen cauliflower is fine for recipes calling it to be puréed.

For best results, blanch no more than 1 pound at a time. Cut the heads into individual pieces about 1 inch in diameter. Soak for about ½ hour in a salt or vinegar brine (using ½ cup salt or 1 teaspoon of vinegar per quart of water) to drive out any insects or worms lurking inside. Rinse and drain. Bring a large pot of water to a boil, add the cauliflower,

"Cauliflower is nothing but cabbage with a college education."

— *Mark Twain,*
American satirist and writer

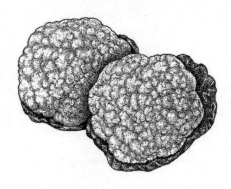

Food Choices

**by Rebecca Claypool,
former CSA Manager**

October 13, 2004

For the last few weeks I have been mulling over this topic of food choices, and I never quite get anywhere with my thoughts, so this seems like the perfect avenue for reflection. I come from a family of six (I am the youngest of four children), and when I was growing up most nights we shared a family meal. We sat around our kitchen table and ate the same meal together that more often than not was cooked in collaboration. In recent conversations with various people it appears that my experience eating dinner with my family is greatly different than how some families operate today. I ate what was given to me or I went to bed hungry, and as a result I love vegetables and all sorts of food. Honestly I absolutely love food, and truly believe that we are what we eat.

Every time I begin thinking about this topic, an article from The Nation *by Barbara Kingsolver comes to mind. "A Good Farmer" was an article in the November issue of last year, and I had to dig it up when I thought of it again. She writes "Recall that whatever lofty things you might accomplish today, you will do them only because you first ate something that grew out of dirt." Kingsolver reminds us of how dependent we are to the land for our most basic needs, so why not feed ourselves and families*

cover, and blanch for 3 minutes. Then drain and plunge the cauliflower into ice water to halt the cooking. Pack in zipper-lock freezer or vacuum food sealer-type bags, or freezer containers. Squeeze out excess air (unless you are using the vacuum sealing method), but no headspace is necessary. Frozen cauliflower will keep for up to a year at 0°F or below. It does not need to be thawed before adding to cooking dishes.

EQUIVALENTS, MEASURES & SERVINGS

- 1 head = 1½ pounds = 6 cups florets = 1½ cups chopped

COMPLEMENTARY HERBS, SEASONINGS & FOODS

Almonds, bacon, basil, béchamel sauce, breadcrumbs, broccoli, butter, cayenne pepper, cheese, chervil, chives, citrus, cream, créme fraîche, curry, dill, garlic, ham, hollandaise sauce, leeks, lemon, mushrooms, mussels, mustard, nutmeg, nuts, olive oil, onion, paprika, parsley, pepper, potatoes, saffron, tomato sauce, turmeric, walnuts.

SERVING SUGGESTIONS

- Cauliflower's neutral flavor and color makes it an excellent backdrop for spicy seasonings such as curry. In India, cauliflower is often cooked with turmeric, cumin, and saffron.
- A classic cauliflower dish calls for steamed or boiled florets topped with a cheese or cream sauce.
- Cooked cauliflower can be puréed and used as a soup base, along with cream, seasonings, broth, potatoes, etc.
- Add tiny bits of raw cauliflower to chopped vegetable salads for crunch.
- Use it in casseroles by itself or with broccoli.
- Serve raw cauliflower florets with a variety of taste-tempting dipping sauces.
- Boil cauliflower just until done, dredge in flour and seasonings, and fry until brown.
- Try tossing cauliflower florets with a mixture of butter, sugar, salt, cinnamon, cumin, and pepper, and baking until they are caramelized.
- Marinate steamed cauliflower pieces with other vegetables such as peppers, broccoli, cucumbers, and carrots; season to taste. Serve chilled.

GREEN CURRY CHICKEN WITH BROCCOLI AND CAULIFLOWER SERVES 2

½ head broccoli
½ head cauliflower
1 to 2 cloves garlic, chopped
2 chicken breasts, sliced
1 tablespoon olive oil
2 tablespoons butter
3 tablespoons heavy cream
2 to 3 tablespoons green curry paste

1. Cut the broccoli and cauliflower into bite-sized pieces and steam until they are tender-crisp. Set aside.

2. In a large skillet, sauté the garlic and chicken breasts in the olive oil. When the chicken is cooked through, push it to the outer edges of the pan.

3. Then melt the butter in the center of the pan over low heat. Add the cream and curry paste; blend and stir in the chicken; then turn off the heat. Add the broccoli and cauliflower, cover, and let the flavors meld about 5 minutes.

— *Nadine Bayer, The Bluff Country Co-op Cookbook*

. . . .

PASTA WITH VEGGIES AND CHEESE   SERVES 3 TO 4

I have convinced my 2-year-old daughter, Miska, that this is the best macaroni and cheese around.

8 ounces bowtie, penne, elbow, or other short, chunky pasta
2 large plum tomatoes, sliced, or ¼ cup diced, canned organic
    tomatoes, drained
1 clove garlic, crushed
1½ cups or 1 can white beans, drained
¼ cup broth, homemade or canned organic
5 cups fresh spinach, or 1 bunch broccoli, or ½ head cauliflower,
    coarsely chopped
¾ cup (3 ounces) shredded or cubed part-skim mozzarella cheese
½ cup (1 ounce) grated Parmesan cheese

1. Cook the pasta according to the package directions.

2. While the pasta cooks, lightly oil a large nonstick skillet. Heat it over medium-high heat until hot. Add the tomatoes and garlic. Cook and stir 2 minutes. Then stir in the beans, broth, and spinach, and stir constantly until the spinach wilts.

3. Drain the pasta and add to the skillet. Then stir in the cheeses, toss, and serve.

— *Margaret Trott, Featherstone Farm CSA member*

. . . .

ROASTED CAULIFLOWER   SERVES 4

Unopened nut oils will keep for up to 1 year; after opening, store them in the refrigerator and use within a couple months. Pecan oil can also be used in this recipe, but the delicate taste of peanut oil goes exceptionally well with cauliflower.

1 large head cauliflower
½ cup peanut oil
Salt and freshly ground pepper

1. Preheat the oven to 375°F.

wholesome food from clean dirt, so when we rise out of bed and know that nutritious food will supply us with mental and physical health throughout the day. I feel that Kingsolver makes some terrific points about how food is regarded and she puts it into words better than I ever could so here is an excerpt from the same article.

"In my professional life I've learned that as long as I write novels and nonfiction books about strictly human conventions and constructions, I'm taken seriously. But when my writing strays into the muddy territory where humans are forced to own up to our dependency on the land, I'm apt to be declared quaintly irrelevant by the small, acutely urban clique that decides in this country what will be called worthy literature ... I understand their purview, I think. I realize I'm beholden to people working in urban centers for many things I love: They publish books, invent theater, produce films and music. But if I had not been raised such a polite Southern girl, I'd offer these critics a blunt proposition: I'll go a week without attending a movie or concert, you go a week without eating food, and at the end of it we'll sit down together and renegotiate 'quaintly irrelevant.'"

I love this part of her article and it only reinforces to me that what Featherstone is trying to do is incredibly worthy. I am grateful for our CSA and it is the highlight of my week to deliver healthy food to all of you.

2. Remove the green leaves from the underside of the cauliflower, cut the head in half, and rinse it briefly under running water. Drain for a few minutes, then pat dry. Slice vertically into ½-inch-thick slices.

3. Brush both sides of the slices lightly with peanut oil and season with salt and pepper. Lay the slices in a single layer on a clean baking sheet and roast in the oven for 30 to 35 minutes, or until the top of the cauliflower is lightly browned and tender (the bottoms will be a deeper golden brown). Serve warm or at room temperature.

Variations

- Slice a large yam crosswise into ½-inch-thick slices and toss with 2 to 4 tablespoons regular or toasted sesame oil mixed with a little salt, pepper, powdered ginger, cumin, and cardamom. Using a jelly-roll pan, lay the slices in a single layer, then bake in a 375°F oven for 10 to 15 minutes. Remove the pan from the oven, add the cauliflower slices, and continue baking as directed.

- This dish becomes a one-dish meal by adding raw, peeled, marinated shrimp or chicken breast. The medium-sized shrimp usually take about 6 minutes to bake. Serve with cooked basmati rice.

— *Pam Garetto, Featherstone Farm CSA member*

VICHYSSOISE (WITH CAULIFLOWER)　　SERVES 4

This soup is traditionally made with leeks and potatoes, but in this version, the addition of cauliflower is really good too.

3 tablespoons unsalted butter
8 ounces peeled, sliced potato
8 ounces leeks, white part only, halved, cleaned, and sliced into
**　　½-inch pieces**
8 ounces onion, quartered and sliced (about 1 medium onion)
8 ounces cauliflower, chopped
Salt and white pepper
4 cups chicken stock
1 cup cream
Chives or finely chopped green onion, for garnish

1. Melt 2 tablespoons of the butter in a hot pan. Add the potato, leek, onion, and cauliflower. Season with salt and pepper and sauté lightly for 3 to 4 minutes.

2. Add the chicken stock, bring to a boil, decrease the heat, and simmer until the vegetables are cooked soft. Purée in a blender or food mill. Return the soup to the pan, reheat, and mix in the cream. Chill thoroughly, season to taste, and serve chilled, garnished with finely chopped chives or green onion.

— *Richard Wright, www.epicurean.com*

Collard

BRASSICA OLERACEA, ACEPHALA GROUP

The collard is a vigorous member of the rather crowded Brassica family. It is a actually a type of kale, and although both are low-growing plants with robust leaves growing on sturdy stalks, collards are flat and paddle-shaped in contrast with kale's often intricately curled or wrinkled foliage.

Collards are forever associated in American cuisine with Southern soul food. It is thought that African slaves brought with them from their homeland seeds of the vegetables they knew and loved, including collards, black-eyed peas, and okra. Collards are a staple ingredient in the famous "mess o' greens," that nutritious mass of dark green leaves slow-cooked for hours with that other Southern staple, the pig. Collard's rich, meaty leaves hold up well even to hours of boiling, and make a wonderful foil to robust meats, or as a fulfilling vegetable side dish with rice and beans.

HISTORY

The exact origins of wild cabbage are lost to history, but collards are thought to be possibly native to the eastern Mediterranean region and Asia Minor. The ancient Greeks were rather unimpressed with them, but the Romans doted on them and their other cabbage brethen, unlike much of the rest of Europe. By the mid-1500s, collards were flourishing in the West Indies, and collards were growing in Virginia by the early 1600s.

NUTRITION

Dark-green leafy vegetables are among nature's most healthful foods, with abundant vitamins A and C, folic acid, iron, fiber, and calcium. Per calorie, collards have more calcium than milk, are an excellent source of organic and highly absorbable iron, contain phenomenal amounts of vitamin K, and are also twice as high in vitamin A as carrots. Additionally, like other cruciferous vegetables, collards contain abundant phytonutrients, which have proven in studies to fight cancer.

SELECTION

Collards should be fresh-looking, not wilted or yellowing. Younger leaves will be more tender and have a milder flavor.

STORAGE

Collards should not be stored for too long, as their moisture content makes them susceptible to rot or wilting. Wrap collards in a damp paper towel and store in a perforated plastic bag in the refrigerator vegetable crisper. They will keep for up to 1 week. Avoid washing them until just before preparation.

TRIMMING & CLEANING

Greens often host dirt and insects, so they require a thorough washing.

Southerners believed that a fresh collard leaf hung over the door assured that evil spirits would not enter. (And we always thought garlic was the magic deterrent.)

Some believed that placing a fresh collard leaf on the forehead could chase a headache away.

One of the best ways to wash them is to fill the kitchen sink with water, completely submerge the greens, and swish them around several times to dislodge any impurities. Drain the greens in a colander, or if they are small, use a salad spinner. If the water that drains still looks dirty, repeat the washing.

Sturdy greens like collards, kale, and turnip greens have tough central stems or ribs that should be trimmed from the leaves before cooking, either by hand or knife.

STEAMING & BOILING

Steaming is not the best way to cook collards because it gives them a somewhat tough texture. If you want to try it nevertheless, steam using just the greens' own moisture in a covered pan. Greens can be boiled in water or broth for 15 to 30 minutes, but even this cooking method yields a slightly firmer texture. Long, slow simmering over a couple of hours is the best way to soften these meaty greens and mellow their flavor.

STIR-FRYING & SAUTÉING

Simmer collards first in a small amount of water for 10 minutes. Then drain them and sauté in olive oil with herbs or spices until tender, about 10 minutes.

MICROWAVING

Thoroughly wash the collards, then place the leaves, with water still clinging to them, in a microwave-safe dish. Cover, and cook on High power for 7 to 10 minutes, stirring half way through.

- 2 cups leaves = ½ cup cooked greens
- 2 cups = 2 minutes
- 1¼ pounds = 7 to 10 minutes

BLANCHING & FREEZING

Collards do freeze well. After washing, trimming, and cutting them into 1-inch pieces, blanch the leaves in rapidly boiling water for 3 minutes. Then drain and plunge them into ice water to stop the cooking process. Squeeze out the excess water and place them in zipper-lock freezer or vacuum food sealer-type bags. Squeeze out excess air and leave 1 inch of headspace (unless you are using the vacuum sealing method). Collards will keep for up to 1 year this way.

EQUIVALENTS, MEASURES & SERVINGS

- 1 pound = 10 cups pieces = 2 cups cooked

COMPLEMENTARY HERBS, SEASONINGS & FOODS

Bacon, basil, beans, brown sugar, butter, cayenne peppers, chiles, cinnamon, cream, curry, dill, fresh ginger, garlic, ham, hot pepper sauce, lemon, liquid smoke seasoning, mint, molasses, mustard, onion, oregano, parsley, pork, salt pork, sausage, soy, vinegar, walnuts.

SERVING SUGGESTIONS

- Boiled or pan-steamed greens are tasty seasoned with onion, garlic, and chopped fresh herbs such as mint, dill, and basil.

- Sauté collards with tofu, garlic, and red pepper flecks for a quick, nutritious, vegetarian meal.

- Serve collards with beans—especially black-eyed peas. An avant-garde approach to spring rolls and sushi: cooked collard greens with black-eyed peas and brown rice.

- Add chopped collards to soups and stews.

- Greens go especially well with ham, bacon, and pork fatback. Sauté chopped greens with a little bacon fat or a hunk of salt pork, sugar, and pepper. Splash liberally with hot pepper vinegar just before serving.

- The liquid left after slow-cooking collards with pork is extremely nutritious and delicious, the famed "pot liquor." Drink this broth on its own as a savory soup, or use it as you would vegetable stock.

- Try a vegetarian stew of collard greens, cabbage, sweet bell peppers, garlic, onions, mushrooms, tomatoes, and hot red peppers, seasoned with molasses, vinegar, and seasoned salt.

· ·

SOUTHERN-STYLE GREENS WITH SLAB BACON   SERVES 4

These irresistible greens are absolutely better the second day. They seem to absorb more of the smoky bacon flavor, and the braising liquid ("pot likker") tastes better, too. In contrast to what you are served in some restaurants, greens prepared this way are neither salty nor greasy. You can almost taste the nutrition in them. Don't throw away the pot liquor. Use it for making vegetable soup or enjoy a steaming-hot cup of it for lunch the next day.

½ pound slab bacon (not salt pork), in one piece
2 pounds collards or turnip greens
2 cloves garlic, peeled and thinly sliced
Salt and freshly ground black pepper
Hot pepper vinegar

1. Put the bacon in a large pot. Add 3 quarts of cold water and bring it to a simmer over moderately high heat. Decrease the heat and continue simmering until the liquid is reduced to about 5 cups. This will take about 1½ hours, depending on the size and shape of your pot.

2. Meanwhile, wash the greens well and let them drain (no need to dry them). Remove and discard the stems. Stack the leaves and slice them crosswise at 1-inch intervals. When the stock is ready, add the garlic, then add the greens a few at a time, poking them down into the liquid with a wooden spoon until they wilt. When all of the greens have been added, simmer them until they become tender, about 30 to 40 minutes. Stir occasionally to keep the greens below the surface of the liquid. Turn off the heat, and let them cool in the liquid.

3. To serve, reheat the greens in their liquid; season if necessary with salt and black pepper. Serve in warm bowls, with a smidgen of the bacon and some of the braising liquid. Offer hot pepper vinegar on the side.

— *Janet Fletcher,* More Vegetables Please

Books

The Collard Patch
Mary Lou Cheatham
and Paul Elliott;
Blue Moon Books Louisiana, 2006.

For More Information

Collard Greens Festival
www.epa.net/collardgreens

MILLET GARDEN MEDLEY

SERVES 6

In-season vegetables, including carrots, parsnips, greens, and sweet potatoes, combine with kidney beans, chickpeas, and millet for this hearty winter meal. Feel free to vary the vegetables, selecting your seasonal favorites for this flavorful garden medley. Millet, a tiny, round, golden grain, turns light and fluffy when cooked and is simple to prepare.

1 cup dried kidney beans
1 cup dried chickpeas
2 tablespoons olive oil
1 large onion, chopped
2 cloves garlic, diced
1 carrot, diced
1 stalk celery, diced
2 parsnips, chopped
1 teaspoon chili powder
6 cups vegetable stock or water
1 stalk broccoli, cut into bite-sized pieces
5 plum tomatoes, diced
3 medium sweet potatoes, scrubbed and cut into bite-sized pieces
6 fingerling potatoes, cut in half
2 cups chopped greens (such as kale or collards)
1 cup corn kernels (fresh or frozen)
2 teaspoons sea salt
Cooked millet (see recipe below)
2 scallions, sliced (for garnish if desired)

1. Rinse the kidney beans and chickpeas, then soak them in water overnight. Drain and rinse before proceeding.

2. Heat the olive oil in a Dutch oven over medium-high heat. Add the onion, garlic, carrot, and celery.

3. Sauté for 5 minutes, or until the onions are translucent. Add the parsnips and sauté another 2 minutes. Add the chili powder and cook 1 more minute.

4. Add the vegetable stock and drained beans, and bring to a boil over high heat. Lower the heat, cover, and simmer for 1 hour. (Check the beans half way through the cooking time, and, if necessary, add water just to cover.)

5. Add the broccoli, tomatoes, sweet potatoes, fingerling potatoes, greens, corn, and salt. Bring to a boil, then cover and simmer for 1 hour, or until the beans and vegetables are tender.

6. Serve over the cooked millet. Garnish with sliced scallions, if desired.

FOR THE MILLET

1 cup millet, rinsed and drained
3 cups spring water or vegetable stock

Pinch of sea salt

1. Place the millet in a fine mesh strainer. Briefly rinse it under cool water and drain for a few minutes.

2. Heat a heavy-bottomed skillet with a lid over medium heat. Add the drained millet to the hot pan and, stirring frequently, roast the millet for a few minutes until it becomes dry and fragrant, but not brown. Remove the millet from the heat and set aside in a separate container.

3. In the skillet, bring the water or stock to a boil, add salt, and toss in the roasted millet. Return to a boil, decrease the heat to a simmer, and cover. Cook for 20 to 30 minutes until all of the liquid is absorbed. Remove from the heat and leave covered for a few minutes.

— *Whole Foods Market*

. . . .

AYIB BE GOMEN (COLLARDS WITH COTTAGE CHEESE) SERVES 3 TO 4

This is one of the national dishes of Ethiopia, where collards and spinach are often paired with dairy products.

1 pound collards
3 tablespoons butter
1 teaspoon black pepper
1 pound cottage cheese (dry-curd is fine)
Salt to taste

Wash, shred, and steam or boil the collards. Mix the butter, black pepper, and cottage cheese. Add the drained collards and salt to taste.

— *www.egforums.com*

"I ran out of Tupperware one day, so I took my cottage cheese to work tied up in a condom. I'm not allowed to use the employee refrigerator anymore."

— *Rolf Lundgren*

Kale

BRASSICA OLERACEA,
ACEPHALA GROUP

Kale will probably never become a favorite vegetable on American shores, which is a shame, and not just because it is one of the most nutritionally packed vegetables in existence. It is amazingly versatile in cooking, with the curious trait of keeping its texture and earthy, nutty flavor even when cooked for long periods. Hardy kale loves cold weather, becoming sweeter after a frost.

Kale has long been a favorite of Scots, who likely eat more of it than any other ethnic group, but other northern Europeans, like the Danish and Germans, favor it too.

Your CSA boxes may contain one of three different kales Featherstone grows: Winterbor (a green, curly kale), Lacinato (a flat, bluish leafy green, also called "Dinosaur kale," an heirloom variety), and Redbor, which has beautiful red greens. All three varieties can be prepared the same way and share similar nutritional values.

HISTORY

Some people believe that kale is actually wild cabbage and that it may be the ancestor to all of our modern cabbage varieties. Kale is a hardy and hearty green that humans have cultivated for over 2,000 years. It is particularly popular in Scotland, whose cold, damp climate provides kale's ideal growing conditions. In the United States, kale is mostly eaten in the South, where, along with collards and turnip leaves, it forms those famous, savory, long-cooked "mess o' greens."

NUTRITION

Few vegetables are as nutrient-rich as kale. A 1-cup serving contains staggering amounts of vitamins A, C, and K, as well as manganese, dietary fiber, copper, B vitamins, potassium, iron, calcium, phosphorus, and vitamin E, all for only 36 calories. Like other members of the Brassica family, kale packs huge amounts of phytonutrients that are believed to have anticancer properties. It is also a rich source of the carotenoids lutein and zeaxanthin, which are known to promote eye health.

SELECTION

Choose kale that is fresh-looking, crisp, and evenly colored; yellowing or spotted leaves indicate advanced age or poor storage. Smaller leaves will be sweeter and more tender than larger ones.

STORAGE

Kale should not be stored for too long, as their moisture content makes them susceptible to rot or wilting. Kale also tends to become bitter the longer it is stored. Wrap the leaves in a damp paper towel and store them in a perforated plastic bag in the refrigerator vegetable crisper, where they will keep for up to 1 week. Avoid washing until ready to prepare.

TRIMMING & CLEANING

Kale's finely curled, crimped leaves provide perfect hiding places for insects. The easiest way to flush unwanted critters out is to fill a sinkful of water and submerge the leaves completely, swishing them back and forth vigorously, before draining them in a colander. To prepare kale for cooking, trim the leaves away from the tough stems and discard the stems. If you want the leaves to cook faster, shred or coarsely cut the leaves into strips.

STEAMING & BOILING

To prepare kale for steaming, trim the leaves away from their stems with a knife. Place the leaves in a steamer basket, and steam them for about 5 to 10 minutes, depending on the size of the leaves, or until they become tender and bright green in color. Kale can be boiled for 5 to 15 minutes, or until tender and still bright green.

STIR-FRYING & SAUTÉING

Kale leaves, stripped from their stems and coarsely shredded, can be stir-fried. For best results, parboil them for 5 minutes, then add to a well-oiled stir-fry pan or wok and cook for an additional 5 minutes.

MICROWAVING

Thoroughly wash kale, then place the leaves, with water still clinging to them, in a microwave-safe dish. Cover, and cook on High power for 7 to 10 minutes, stirring half way through.

- 2 cups leaves = ½ cup cooked greens
- 2 cups = 2 minutes
- 1¼ pounds = 7 to 10 minutes

BLANCHING & FREEZING

Unlike many greens, kale freezes well. Blanch the leaves first in rapidly boiling water for 3 minutes, drain, and plunge into ice water to stop the cooking. Squeeze out the excess water and place in zipper-lock freezer or vacuum food sealer-type bags, or freezer containers. Squeeze out excess air and leave 1 inch of headspace (unless you are using the vacuum sealing method).

EQUIVALENTS, MEASURES & SERVINGS

- 1 pound = 2 cups cooked

COMPLEMENTARY HERBS, SEASONINGS & FOODS

Almonds, bacon, beans, caraway seeds, cheese, cinnamon, cream, garlic, ginger, goat cheese, ham, lemon, miso, olive oil, onions, pine nuts, pork, potatoes, red pepper, sausage, sesame, tomatoes, walnuts, yams.

SERVING SUGGESTIONS

- Kale's ability to maintain its texture and flavor make it ideal for stews, casseroles, and slow-cooking soups.
- For a quick, nutritious meal, stir-fry kale with chunks of tofu and season with garlic, ginger, and red chiles.

Cooking Tip

Boiling kale in vegetable or chicken broth adds a hearty flavor to this already substantial vegetable.

How Green Was My Soup

Portugal's national dish is *caldo verde*, or green soup, made from thinly sliced kale strips, light broth, a little olive oil, and topped with slices of garlicky pork sausage.

- Add kale to your favorite pasta recipe, as a substitute for spinach. Especially good with pine nuts!
- Serve boiled or steamed kale with vinaigrette or sesame dressing.
- Slow-cook kale just as you would collards (see page 235).
- Kale and pork sausage or ham are natural soul mates.
- Scramble eggs with a bit of cooked kale stirred in instead of spinach.
- Chop up plenty of garlic, fry it crisp in olive oil and salt, and sprinkle it over a bunch of steamed kale.
- For another quick and hearty soup, add cooked kale to canned tomatoes, canned white beans, chicken or vegetable broth, parsley, rosemary, and plenty of onion and garlic to taste.

SIMPLE KALE   SERVES 2

1 bunch kale, leaves chopped into thin strips and stems discarded
1 tablespoon olive oil
2 thinly sliced green garlic scapes
1 tablespoon tamari or soy sauce

1. Rinse the kale and toss it, still wet, into a large heated pan. After the kale begins to wilt (about 5 minutes), add the olive oil and green garlic to the pan. Cook until the kale reaches the desired doneness.

2. If you are cooking the kale for a longer time, you will need to add a liquid to ensure that the kale does not burn. Sherry, broth, vermouth, green tea, or water all work well. (I like kale lightly cooked, while others prefer it well-done. The beauty of kale is that it will not become bitter, even if it is cooked for a long time).

3. Right before serving, cook off or drain any remaining liquid and add the tamari or soy sauce to the hot greens. Toss, serve, and enjoy.

— *Sarah Libertus, former Featherstone Farm CSA manager*

KALE MASHED POTATOES   SERVES 4 TO 6

Everyone asks what to do with kale. This is my favorite way to prepare it. If this is your first time with kale, or you are trying to introduce others to this wondrous green, start them off slowly with these Kale Mashed Potatoes.

4 to 5 medium Russet or Yukon potatoes, peeled and sliced
    into 1/3-inch-thick pieces
1/2 teaspoon cider vinegar
3 tablespoons butter
1 cup heavy whipping cream
1/2 cup half-and-half
1/4 teaspoon white pepper
Salt and pepper
Kale from Simple Kale recipe (above)

1. In a large pot, add the potatoes, vinegar, and salt to 6 cups of hot water. Simmer on very low heat for 20 minutes. Drain the potato water, and run cold water over the potatoes to halt their cooking.

2. Heat the butter in a heavy-bottomed saucepan; add the cream, half-and-half, white pepper, and salt. Add water back to the cooled potatoes, bring to a boil, and simmer until fork-tender, about 5 minutes.

3. Mash the potatoes by putting them through a ricer or using a masher, gradually adding the hot cream mixture. Once the potatoes become creamy, add the kale.

— *Sarah Libertus, former Featherstone Farm CSA manager*

. . . .

GINGER KALE   SERVES 2 TO 4

1 large bunch kale, stems removed and leaves cut into strips
2 tablespoons olive oil
1 tablespoon butter
2 large cloves garlic, minced
1 medium onion, chopped
1 tablespoon minced fresh ginger or 1 teaspoon dried ginger
Juice of 1 fresh lime
Freshly ground black pepper

1. Steam the kale until it wilts slightly.

2. In a large skillet or wok, heat the oil and butter. Then add the garlic, onion, and ginger; sauté until onion turns soft. Toss in the kale. Cover and cook on low heat until the kale is tender.

3. Sprinkle lime juice and pepper to taste.

— *MACSAC,* From Asparagus to Zucchini

. . . .

MOTHER AFRICA'S SPICY KALE AND YAM   SERVES 3 TO 4

The term "yam" is something of a misnomer; in America it actually refers to the orange-fleshed, moist sweet potato, whereas the rest of the world knows yams as enormous tubers that measure several feet long, can weigh over a hundred pounds, and have a firmer, drier, white flesh. The garnet yams in this recipe are sweet potatoes with distinctive purplish-red exterior skins.

Nama shoyu is a type of unpasteurized soy sauce that is naturally aged for several years in cedar kegs, giving it a much more full-bodied flavor and complex bouquet than regular soy sauce. It can be found in natural foods stores and through online retailers.

1 large bunch kale (about 4 cups chopped, firmly pressed)
4 cups garnet yams, well-rinsed and chopped

This effort to simplify and mechanize the growing process by reducing the variables of the farming system suits the modern scientific mind, but it also results in unanticipated results. Nature abhors a vacuum, and this leads to resorting to chemical responses to problems that inevitably result.

The organic system encourages the broad diversity of all species in and around the field in an effort to mirror nature as much as possible. Organic farming encourages insect diversity with the planting of perennial flowers around the fields and leaving insect habitat such as tall grasses and legumes unmowed nearby. It creates and promotes balance in the entire farm ecosystem, with the premise that pests and diseases and their enemies will balance themselves out, thus preventing any one factor from getting out of control.

Farming organically does not necessarily mean "no spray." In fact, we spray quite a bit on our farm (see page 132). This is primarily in the form of Bacillus thuringiensis, a naturally occurring bacteria that is toxic only to certain worms (primarily cabbage worms in broccoli). We also spray copper, a fungicide that controls disease in tomatoes, and because our soils are naturally low in copper.

But anything we spray meets organic standards, which means that it is 100 percent naturally occurring (not synthesized or altered in a laboratory), is nonresidual in the crop or field, and used only as a last resort after following the organic farming system approaches outlined above.

1½ tablespoons olive oil
1½ cups onion, chopped
1 tablespoon garlic, minced
1 tablespoon fresh ginger, peeled and minced
1 teaspoon serrano chile, seeded and diced
2 cups purple cabbage, sliced
3 tablespoons nama shoyu soy sauce
2 tablespoons sea salt, or to taste
Abba's African Hot Sauce (recipe below) to taste

1. Rinse and drain the kale well. Steam the kale and yams; when done, the kale should still be colorful and the yams should retain some firmness.

2. While the kale and yams are steaming, place the olive oil in a large saucepan and heat over medium-high heat. Add the onion, garlic, ginger, and chile pepper and cook for 5 minutes, stirring frequently.

3. Add the cabbage and cook for 5 minutes, stirring frequently. (Add small amounts of water if necessary to prevent sticking.)

4. Place the cabbage in a large bowl with the remaining ingredients, add the kale, and mix well. Add the yams and gently mix well.

ABBA'S AFRICAN HOT SAUCE   MAKES ABOUT 2 CUPS

1 cup filtered water or stock
8 to 10 assorted hot peppers, chopped (such as habañero, serrano, and jalapeño, about ½ cup total)
1 medium diced green bell pepper (about ¾ cup)
1½ teaspoons minced garlic
½ cup shallots or diced green onions
¼ cup tomato paste
2 tablespoons raw apple cider vinegar
1 teaspoon freshly ground black pepper
1 teaspoon sea salt
¼ teaspoon cardamom powder
¼ teaspoon cayenne powder

Place all of the ingredients in a blender and blend until smooth. Place in a small saucepan on low heat and cook for 20 minutes, stirring frequently.

— *Gladys, www.recipelink.com*

RAW KALE SALAD   SERVES 4

A less fattening alternative to the typical creamy coleslaw.

1 pound kale, very finely chopped, stems removed
1 medium-sized red onion, diced

3 carrots, grated
1 cup green beans, chopped
¼ cup olive oil
¼ cup balsamic vinegar
2 tablespoons brown sugar
2 cloves garlic, crushed
1 teaspoon salt
Ground pepper
1 teaspoon curry powder
2 teaspoons Dijon mustard
Several fresh purple basil leaves, chopped

Thoroughly mix all of the ingredients together, and toss to evenly coat with the dressing.

Optional toppings: Crumbled bacon, vegetarian bacon bits, gorgonzola cheese, toasted slivered almonds.

— *Robin Taylor, Featherstone Farm CSA member*

Kohlrabi

BRASSICA OLERACEA,
GONGYLODES GROUP

A curious member of the cabbage family, kohlrabi is sometimes called "cabbage turnip," because its name consists of the German words "kohl" (cabbage) and "rabi" (turnip). Some botanists believe that kohlrabi is a hybrid of the two, whereas others maintain that it is actually a variant of mustard; its exact origins are rather mysterious.

The vegetable's most distinguishing feature is its large, light green (or sometimes purple), globe-shaped swollen stem which grows above ground and is not a root, topped with turnip-like leaves. The plant is grown for this stem, which is crunchy, juicy, sweet, and quite delicately flavored, with a distinct cabbage flavor, similar to broccoli stems or turnips.

Most people eat kohlrabi raw, peeling and slicing the vegetable into rounds and sprinkling it with a little salt. But kohlrabi is just as good cooked, braised, steamed, or shredded.

HISTORY

The history of kohlrabi is an elusive one. By some accounts, the vegetable appeared rather suddenly and without explanation in Europe in the middle of the 1500s, but this may be due more to linguistic confusion than the kohlrabi's actual existence. Charlemagne ordered kohlrabi grown in his gardens during the Middle Ages, the ancient Romans likely knew of it, and northern and eastern Europeans have consumed it for centuries. In the U.S., kohlrabi is sometimes eaten as part of southern-style mixed greens, and it is popular throughout Africa and Madagascar. Until recently, kohlrabi was not commercially cultivated or available in U.S. supermarkets, and most Americans who wanted to enjoy this unusual vegetable had to grow it in their home gardens. Kohlrabi has also long been cultivated in Europe for livestock food.

NUTRITION

Like other cruciferous vegetables, kohlrabi is very nutritious, containing vitamin C, potassium, iron, thiamin, magnesium, folate, copper, and dietary fiber, all for just 36 calories a cup. Kohlrabi also contains abundant phytonutrients such as sulforaphane and indoles, which have proven in studies to fight cancer, especially prostate, colorectal, and lung. Its green tops are similar to turnip greens in nutrient value, extremely rich in vitamins A, C, and K.

SELECTION

Choose kohlrabi that is firm, evenly colored, and with fresh green tops. Avoid specimens that are shriveled, cracked, blemished, or have wilted or yellowing leaves. Overly large specimens may be woody.

STORAGE

If their tops are intact, kohlrabi will keep refrigerated in a perforated plastic bag in the refrigerator vegetable crisper for up to 5 days. Detopped bulbs will last longer, keeping for up to 2 to 3 weeks.

TRIMMING & CLEANING

Kohlrabi must be peeled before eating. Trim off the tops (save them if desired for cooking), then use a paring knife or sharp vegetable peeler to cut off the thick outer skin. Wash its leaves thoroughly to remove traces of grit, sand, and insects by submerging them in a sinkful of water and swishing well, then draining.

STEAMING & BOILING

Steam whole, peeled or unpeeled kohlrabis for 15 to 20 minutes, depending on their size, and sliced kohlrabi for 5 to 10 minutes, or until tender when pierced with a fork. Boil cubed, peeled kohlrabi for 15 to 30 minutes, then drain.

STIR-FRYING & SAUTÉING

Stir-fry or sauté kohlrabi bulbs, cut into ½-inch dice or cubes, in a well-oiled pan or wok over high heat for about 8 minutes, or until crisp-tender. Leeks, jalapeños, and sweet peppers make delicious stir-fry accompaniments. Kohlrabi greens can be sautéed after a quick parboiling for 2 to 7 minutes, depending on their size and thickness.

BAKING & BRAISING

Bake whole kohlrabis in a 350°F oven for about 20 to 30 minutes, depending on their size. Or prepare kohlrabi like oven-roasted potatoes (see recipe on page 157). To braise, trim and peel kohlrabi, and cook in butter or pan juices for 10 to 15 minutes over medium heat, or until kohlrabi is lightly colored and tender.

MICROWAVING

Trim and peel 2 cups of kohlrabi, cutting into ¼-inch-thick slices. Place in a covered dish with ¼ cup water and microwave on High power until tender, about 10 to 15 minutes, while stirring every 5 minutes. Let stand 5 minutes before serving.

BLANCHING & FREEZING

Cube or slice kohlrabi into ½-inch-thick pieces, boil for 2 to 3 minutes, and then plunge into ice water to stop the cooking. Let cool, drain, and pack in zipper-lock freezer or vacuum food sealer-type bags, or freezer containers. Squeeze out excess air and leave ½ inch of headspace (unless you are using the vacuum sealing method).

MEASURES & EQUIVALENTS

- 4 to 5 medium kohlrabi = 2 pounds = 5 cups chopped

COMPLEMENTARY HERBS, SEASONINGS & FOODS

Bacon, béchamel sauce, butter, caraway seed, cinnamon, cream, dill, garlic, ginger, hollandaise sauce, lemon, majoram, mustard, nutmeg, onion, parsley, pork, sausage, thyme, vinaigrette dressing.

Kohlrabi Kapital
Hamburg Township in Michigan proclaims itself as the Kohlrabi capital of the world. In 1985, the township's Kohlrabi Festival attracted 600 visitors.

- Boil and mash kohlrabis like potatoes, and serve with butter, salt and pepper, and other seasonings.
- Combine cubes of kohlrabi with Granny Smith or Yellow Delicious apples and your favorite creamy, sweet or mustard dressing for an unusual, refreshing summer salad.
- Make a cheesy casserole or gratin with kohlrabi instead of potatoes.
- Try substituting kohlrabi for cabbage in a kohl-slaw.
- Add sliced rounds of kohlrabi to the vegetable relish tray, and serve with your favorite dip.
- Tiny whole kohlrabis or thinly sliced rounds are delicious pickled.
- Prepare kohlrabi cream-style, and pair it with fried chicken and potato salad.
- Roast kohlrabis with other vegetables like carrots, potatoes, turnips, and rutabagas.
- Substitute kohlrabi for cauliflower in an Indian curry.
- Hollow out kohlrabis and prepare like stuffed peppers, filling them with a mixture of ground meat and tomato, or whatever you desire, and baking them in the oven.
- Shred kohlrabi and stir-fry or sauté in fresh herbs and butter.

KOHLRABI KEBABS

SERVES 4

12 small kohlrabi bulbs, peeled
1 tablespoon sesame oil
1 tablespoon honey
2 tablespoons sherry or rice wine
½ cup black bean paste (sold in Asian markets)
Water

1. Heat the broiler.

2. Bring a large pot of water to boil. Add the kohlrabis and boil 5 minutes; drain.

3. Place 3 bulbs on each of the 4 skewers and brush them with sesame oil. Broil the skewers until the kohlrabi becomes tender, about 8 minutes, rotating every 2 minutes.

4. Mix the honey, sherry, black bean paste, and 2 tablespoons water in a small bowl. Brush the kohlrabi liberally with the black bean mixture and broil until the paste is dry and has formed a glaze. Spoon the remaining sauce over the kohlrabi and serve.

— *MACSAC,* From Asparagus to Zucchini

PARMESAN-BAKED KOHLRABI

SERVES 3 TO 4

2 tablespoons breadcrumbs
3 cups of ¼-inch slices of kohlrabi
1 tablespoon melted butter

2 tablespoons grated Parmesan cheese
¼ teaspoon pepper

1. Preheat the oven to 350°F.

2. Butter an 8-inch round pan, and dust with ½ tablespoon of the breadcrumbs.

3. Boil the kohlrabi until they become just tender, about 7 minutes; drain. Toss with melted butter. Place the kohlrabi in the prepared pan, sprinkle with Parmesan cheese, the remaining breadcrumbs, and pepper.

4. Bake 1 hour until browned.

— *Barbara Hunt, mother of Margaret Trott, Featherstone Farm CSA member*

KOHLRABI STUFFED WITH PEPPERS

SERVES 4

The slightly sharp flavor of the peppers is an excellent foil to the more earthy flavor of the kohlrabi.

4 small kohlrabis, about 6 to 8 ounces each
About 1½ cups hot vegetable stock
1 tablespoon olive or sunflower oil
1 onion, chopped
1 small red bell pepper, seeded and sliced
1 small green bell pepper, seeded and sliced
Salt and freshly ground black pepper
Flat-leaf parsley, for garnish (optional)

1. Preheat the oven to 350°F.

2. Trim and remove the ends of the kohlrabis, and arrange on the bottom of a medium-sized ovenproof dish. Pour in the stock so it reaches about half way up the kohlrabis. Cover and braise in the oven for about 30 minutes, until tender. Transfer to a plate and allow to cool, reserving the stock.

3. Heat the oil in a saucepan and cook the onion for 3 to 4 minutes over low heat, stirring occasionally. Add the bell peppers and cook for another 2 to 3 minutes, until the onion is lightly browned. Add the remaining stock and season with salt and pepper. Simmer, uncovered, over medium heat until the stock has almost evaporated.

4. Scoop out the flesh from the kohlrabis and roughly chop. Stir the kohlrabi flesh into the onion and pepper mixture, and taste and adjust the seasoning. Arrange the kohlrabi shells in a shallow ovenproof dish.

5. Spoon the filling into the shells. Place them in the oven for 5 to 10 minutes to heat through and then serve, garnished with parsley, if desired.

— *Christine Ingram,* Cook's Encyclopedia of Vegetables

Leek

ALLIUM AMPELOPRASUM,
PORRUM GROUP

A member of the onion family, leeks are not popular in North America, which is most unfortunate, because they are a delicious, delicately-flavored vegetable.

More subtle than onions, leeks are widely used in France and the British Isles. In Wales, leeks are part of that country's national emblem. Bits of them are worn by Welshmen in their buttonholes on St. David's Day in memory of the victory of King Cadwallader over the Saxons in 640 C.E.

Unlike onions, leeks do not form bulbs but instead grow into thickened stems, from which sheaths of leaves emerge. The edible part is this stem, which is blanched white by piling soil high around it (trenching), and the light-green portion of the leaves.

In America, the most famous use of leeks is in vichyssoise, that creamy potato and leek soup made famous in the mid-1900s by New York City Ritz-Carlton chef Louis Diat, who recalled it from his French childhood. Leeks, however, are very versatile, lending their sophisticated, delicious character to any dish calling for onions.

HISTORY

The precise origin of leeks is a bit contentious. Many sources cite the Mediterranean, while the Irish and other British Isles natives like to claim them for their very own. Shakespeare mentioned leeks in *King Henry V.* On the other side of the globe, the Chinese and ancient Egyptians savored them as far back as recorded history allows. Leeks were described in the Bible as one of the foods that the Israelites missed most when they fled Egypt. Hippocrates prescribed leeks as a cure for nosebleeds, and Charlemagne had them cultivated in his gardens.

NUTRITION

Although not a storehouse of nutrients, leeks do contain manganese, vitamin C, iron, folate, and vitamin B6. Leeks and other members of the Allium family contain compounds that may reduce the risk of prostate and colon cancer when eaten three or more times a week.

SELECTION

Leeks should be firm and fresh-looking, with bright green leaves and long thick stalks (the edible part of the leek). Avoid leeks that are split, bruised, or overly large, which signal old age and toughness. Try to select leeks that are all the same size for more consistent cooking if you plan to prepare them whole.

STORAGE

Leeks should be stored unwashed and loosely wrapped in a perforated plastic bag in the refrigerator vegetable crisper. They will keep for up to 1 or 2 weeks this way.

TRIMMING & CLEANING

Leeks grow in sandy soil, which is piled high around their thick stems to make them turn white (and stay mild and tender). As a result, their layered foliage conceals a surprising amount of grit. Trim off the large greens (save them for making stock), and cut off the root end, but not so far up that the leek falls apart. Repeatedly rinse the stems under cold running water (cut them crosswise if necessary) until all of the sand is washed out.

STEAMING & BOILING

Leeks are particularly susceptible to overcooking, which makes them mushy and tasteless. They should be cooked just long enough to be tender but still offer a little resistance when a fork comes to call at their bases. Whole leeks can be steamed for 10 to 15 minutes; sliced leeks for 5 minutes. Leeks should be boiled for only about 10 to 12 minutes; overboiling makes them watery and less flavorful.

STIR-FRYING & SAUTÉING

Sauté thinly sliced leeks in a bit of oil or butter on medium heat for 3 to 5 minutes, or until tender. Leeks can be stir-fried over high heat for 2 to 3 minutes.

BAKING & ROASTING

Roasting leeks in the oven is one of the best ways to prepare this vegetable, as it concentrates their flavor and accentuates their sweetness. Preheat the oven to 400°F, trim and clean whole leeks, slice them in half lengthwise or leave them whole, and brush with olive oil or butter. Place the leeks in an oiled roasting pan with sides, sprinkle with salt and pepper, and roast for 35 to 45 minutes, occasionally basting them to keep them moist.

BRAISING & STEWING

To braise and stew leeks, arrange them in a shallow dish or pan and cover them with 2 to 3 cups of broth or water. Bring to a boil and simmer until done, about 20 to 30 minutes for whole leeks and 10 to 15 minutes for sliced or chopped leeks.

MICROWAVING

Whole leeks will not cook evenly in the microwave, so cut them into 1-inch pieces, put them in a microwavable dish, and add 2 tablespoons of water. Cook on High power for 5 to 8 minutes, stirring half way through.

BLANCHING & FREEZING

Leeks can be frozen, although freezing destroys some of their taste and texture. Blanch them for 2 minutes in rapidly boiling water, then place them in ice water for 2 more minutes to stop the cooking process. Cut them into ½-inch pieces so you can easily pour out what you need, and store them in zipper-lock freezer or vacuum food sealer-type bags. Squeeze out excess air (unless you are using the vacuum sealing method). Frozen leeks will keep for up to 3 months.

No Leeked Secrets

Growing leeks becomes serious business in the North East of England, where an unusual annual contest is held in late September.

No grower worth his leek will reveal the secret of his prizewinning vegetable, which can reach 3½ to 4 inches in diameter.

Rumors fly that the biggest leeks are fed brown sugar and wine. Leeks are marked weeks in advance to prevent cheating and vandalizing.

MEASURES & EQUIVALENTS

- 2 leeks = 1 side dish serving
- ½ cup cooked leeks = 1 serving
- 1 pound leeks = 2 cups chopped
- 1¼ pounds leeks = 2 large leeks or 3 medium leeks
- 2 pounds leeks = 1 pound cleaned = about 4 cups chopped = 2 cups cooked chopped

COMPLEMENTARY HERBS, SEASONINGS & FOODS

Bacon, basil, béchamel sauce, beets, breadcrumbs, butter, cheese, chervil, chicken, cream, fish, ham, hollandaise sauce, lemon, mustard, olive oil, Parmesan cheese, parsley, peas, potatoes, red wine, sage, thyme, tomatoes, veal, vinaigrette.

SERVING SUGGESTIONS

- Leeks become creamy and subtly sweet when baked. Serve them hot or cold with vinaigrette dressing, or layer them in a dish with ham and cheese and bake until they are hot and bubbling.
- Sprinkle thinly sliced raw leeks atop salads.
- Don't throw away the trimmed darker green tops: they make wonderful soup stock.
- Bake leeks and asparagus together and top with hollandaise sauce for a first-class dish worthy of royalty—or your family.
- Throw leeks on the grill along with tomatoes and peppers for a tasty summer treat.
- Braise leeks in chicken or meat stock until the leeks are glazed.
- Mix finely chopped raw leeks with sour cream, a little pepper, and Worchester sauce for a chip dip.
- For a delicious, hearty vegetable side dish, place leeks, sweet potato wedges, and whole garlic cloves in a casserole dish and drizzle with olive oil, seasoned salt or Old Bay seasoning, and pepper. Cover and bake in a 375°F oven for about 1 hour, or until the sweet potatoes are tender.
- Braised leeks make a sumptuous accompaniment to rich meats like roast pork, beef, and lamb.
- Sauté leeks with fennel for a tasty, surprise vegetable side dish.

ROAST CHICKEN WITH ROOT VEGETABLES

SERVES 2 TO 4

CHICKEN

4 branches fresh rosemary, bruised
6 cloves garlic, crushed and peeled
½ cup extra-virgin olive oil
1 3½- to 4-pound chicken
Salt and freshly ground white pepper

VEGETABLES

6 cloves garlic, peeled
6 small new potatoes, quartered
2 bell peppers, cored, seeded, and cut into 2-inch squares

½ small kabocha squash, seeded, peeled, and cut into 2-inch squares
2 to 3 celery hearts, cut in half lengthwise, then into thirds
2 to 3 leeks, white part only, trimmed, halved lengthwise, cleaned,
    blanched for 30 seconds, and cooled in ice water
1 red onion, peeled and halved crosswise, each half quartered
Salt and freshly ground white pepper

SAUCE

1 tablespoon olive oil
3 cloves garlic, peeled, blanched for 15 seconds, cooled in ice water,
    then sliced
1 sprig fresh rosemary
½ cup rich chicken stock
4 tablespoons butter, cut into pieces
Juice of ½ lemon
Salt and freshly ground white pepper
¼ bunch parsley, leaves chopped

FOR THE CHICKEN

1. Strip the leaves from 2 of the rosemary branches and finely chop.
   Finely chop 3 of the garlic cloves. Combine the chopped rosemary,
   garlic, and oil in a bowl and set aside. Generously season the chicken
   cavity with salt and pepper, then stuff with the remaining 2 rosemary
   branches and 3 garlic cloves. Tie the legs together with kitchen twine
   and rub all over with half of the prepared oil. Wrap in plastic and
   refrigerate overnight.

2. Preheat the oven to 400°F. Rub the chicken with half of the remaining prepared oil and generously season with salt and pepper. Put the
   chicken, breast side up, directly on an oven rack set in the middle of
   the oven. Then set a large roasting pan on an oven rack underneath
   the chicken. Roast until skin is deeply golden and the internal temperature reaches 165°F, about 50 to 60 minutes.

FOR THE VEGETABLES

1. While the chicken is roasting, put the garlic, potatoes, peppers, squash,
   celery hearts, leeks, and onions into a large bowl. Add the remaining
   prepared oil, season to taste with salt and pepper, and mix well.

2. After the chicken has roasted for 25 minutes, put the vegetables in a
   roasting pan under the chicken to roast until the chicken is cooked
   through and the vegetables are soft, another 25 to 35 minutes.

FOR THE SAUCE

1. Heat the oil, garlic, and rosemary in a small pan over medium heat until the garlic starts to brown, about 2 minutes. Add the stock and simmer until it is reduced by half, 8 to 10 minutes; discard the rosemary.

2. Whisk in the butter, a few pieces at a time, then add the lemon juice
   and season to taste with salt and pepper. Add the parsley just before
   serving.

"Just washed,
How chill
The white leeks!"

— *Basho,*
Japanese haiku poet

3. Transfer the vegetables and chicken to a deep platter, remove the kitchen twine, and then pour the sauce over the top. Serve immediately.

— Saveur, *May–June 2001*

POTATO AND LEEK GRATIN   SERVES 6

You should not count calories when you make a potato gratin, but this version really is relatively low-calorie. It contains only enough butter to grease the dish and considerably less cream than most. Nevertheless, it is remarkably creamy, the cream infused with the lovely sweet flavor of leeks. Enjoy it with a grilled leg of lamb or a fresh pork leg cooked on the grill.

1 clove garlic
1 teaspoon butter
1½ pounds red-skinned potatoes, peeled and sliced ⅛ inch thick
1½ cups minced leeks, white and pale green parts only
**   (2 to 3 medium leeks thinly sliced crosswise, then minced)**
Salt and freshly ground black pepper
½ cup heavy cream
½ cup chicken stock
3 ounces grated Gruyère cheese

1. Preheat the oven to 325°F.

2. Cut the unpeeled garlic clove in half. Rub the bottom and sides of an earthenware or ceramic oval gratin dish (approximately 13 × 8 × 2 inches) with the cut clove. Let the garlic juices dry, then grease the dish with the butter.

3. Arrange one-third of the potatoes in the dish, and top them with half of the leeks. Season with salt and pepper. Add another third of the potatoes, then the rest of the leeks. Season again with salt and pepper. Top with the remaining potatoes. Season with salt and pepper.

4. Whisk the cream and chicken stock together and pour them over the potatoes. Cover the dish with aluminum foil and bake 30 minutes.

5. Uncover the dish. Press the potatoes down lightly with a spoon and baste them with some of the liquid so that the surface is moist. Raise the oven temperature to 375°F. Sprinkle the surface of the potatoes evenly with cheese. Return the gratin to the oven uncovered and continue baking until it is well-browned, about 25 to 30 minutes.

— *Janet Fletcher*, More Vegetables, Please

BACON, HAM, AND LEEK QUICHE   SERVES 8

This is a low-fat version that is healthier for you but does not sacrifice flavor.

6 strips turkey bacon
12 leeks, thinly sliced
½ cup low-sodium ham, diced
1½ cups low-fat Swiss cheese, grated
1 tablespoon flour
1 cup egg substitute
1 cup fat-free half-and-half
1 cup skim milk
1 prepared 9-inch pie shell

1. Fry the bacon until it becomes crisp. Drain. Reserve 1 tablespoon of the drippings. Fry the leeks and ham in the bacon drippings until the leeks are tender, about 5 to 10 minutes. Drain.

2. Mix the Swiss cheese with the flour, and set aside.

3. Preheat the oven to 375°F.

4. Beat the egg substitute, and add the half-and-half and milk. Add the cheese and flour mixture. Mix well. Stir in the crumbled bacon, ham, and leeks. Mix well. Pour the mixture into a 9-inch pie shell. Bake for about 45 minutes, or until a knife inserted in the center comes out clean.

— *Produce for Better Health/Burma Farms, Inc.; Fruits and Veggies—More Matters; Centers for Disease Control & Prevention*

POTATO LEEK SOUP

SERVES 6

1 tablespoon extra-virgin olive oil
1 tablespoon unsalted butter
3 cups leeks, white and part of the green included, well-washed
    and chopped
½ cup chopped onions
6 cups cubed potatoes, skins on
1 carrot, diced
1 stalk celery, chopped
7 cups vegetable stock or water
1 teaspoon salt
1 teaspoon freshly ground pepper
1 cup milk or soy milk

1. Heat the oil and butter in a medium-sized soup pot. Stir in the leeks and onions. Cook on low heat, without browning, for 5 minutes.

2. Add the potatoes, carrot, celery, stock or water, and salt. Bring to a boil, decrease the heat and simmer for 40 minutes, or until the potatoes are fork-tender.

3. Let the soup cool slightly. Then purée it in a blender or run it through a food mill.

4. Add the milk. Return the soup to the pot and gently reheat. Do not let it boil, as this will scald the milk. Salt and pepper to taste and serve.

— *Tracy, Featherstone Farm CSA member*

VEGETABLE BOUILLON MAKES 1 QUART

¼ cup plus 1 tablespoon olive oil
3 large onions, halved
3 celery ribs, coarsely chopped
2 leeks, trimmed, washed, and coarsely chopped
2 large parsnips or turnips, scrubbed and coarsely chopped
2 large carrots, scrubbed and coarsely chopped
1 fennel bulb, coarsely chopped, including fronds
1 large tomato, diced
Water
Salt

1. Heat 1 tablespoon of the olive oil in a small sauté pan over high heat and cook the onions, flat sides down, until they are blackened on one side, about 5 minutes. Remove from the heat.

2. In a large stockpot, heat the remaining olive oil over medium heat, Add the celery, leeks, parsnips or turnips, carrots, and fennel; cook until the vegetables are softened but not browned, about 20 minutes. (Be careful not to caramelize the vegetables, unless a darker color and sweeter taste are desired.)

3. Add the onions and tomato, and cover the vegetables with 7 cups of water. Bring to a boil, decrease the heat, and simmer for 40 minutes. Season to taste with salt, and strain through a colander lined with cheesecloth into a large bowl. To maximize the yield, let the cheesecloth hang over the bowl for several hours.

— *Joel Patraker*, The Greenmarket Cookbook

CREAM OF LEEK SOUP 3½ CUPS (3 TO 4 SMALL SERVINGS)

This was sent in by Featherstone Farm CSA member Claire, who revised it from Cooking Basics for Dummies *by Bryan Miller and Marie Rama. Claire says, "Everyone seems to love this soup. I always use the 2% milk instead of cream, and also have gotten away with 3 instead of 4 leeks."*

3 to 4 medium leeks, cleaned and trimmed
1 tablespoon butter
2 teaspoons olive oil
1 clove garlic, finely minced
3 tablespoons flour
2⅔ cups chicken or vegetable broth

½ cup milk
Generous dash of nutmeg (optional)
Salt and freshly ground pepper
½ cup heavy cream or half-and-half or 2% milk
4 small chervil sprigs or 1 tablespoon chopped chives (optional)

1. Quarter the leeks lengthwise and cut into ½-inch-long pieces. (You should have about 2½ cups.)

2. In a large saucepan or pot, melt the butter with the olive oil over medium heat. Add the leeks and garlic. Cook for about 2 minutes, stirring often.

3. Add the flour, blending well with a wooden spoon or wire whisk. Add the chicken or vegetable broth, ½ cup milk, nutmeg (if desired), salt, and pepper. Stir well and bring to a simmer. Cook for about 15 to 20 minutes, stirring occasionally.

4. Cool the soup slightly. (Hot liquids in blenders could trap steam and explode.) Spoon and scrape the mixture into a blender or food processor container and purée well.

5. To serve hot, warm the cream or half-and-half or 2% milk. Just before serving, add it to the soup and stir well. To serve cold, chill the soup and add the cold cream or half-and-half or 2% milk before serving. Always check the seasonings before serving. Garnish each serving with a sprig of chervil or chopped chives, if desired.

— *Claire, Featherstone Farm CSA member*

The Tractor

by Jenni McHugh,
Featherstone Farm Partner
June 19, 2002

If there is one obvious difference between this year and last year here at the farm, it is the number of tractors cruising the fields. I just looked out the window for some inspiration and saw no fewer than three tractors putt-putting along.

One was cultivating; one was chisel-plowing; one was heading down the road. No wonder our two-year-old son Oscar is obsessed with big equipment. This morning I asked him if he had a favorite animal, and he answered most seriously, "Yes, a tractor!"

Mustard Green

BRASSICA JUNCEA,
GROUP CRISPIFOLIA

Mention "mustard greens" to different ethnic groups, and likely you will hear them talking about completely different plants. The mustard family is a diverse, confusing one, a single species called Brassica juncea *that evolved into nearly twenty different subgroups, all with distinct leaf characteristics and flavors, scattered across various continents.*

The mustard green that Featherstone grows is American or Southern (also sometimes called curled) mustard, which is distinguished by its large, heavily veined, very curly-edged leaves and potent, spicy taste. Munch a big leaf and you may think of horseradish, once your sinuses clear and your eyes stop watering.

HISTORY

Mustard greens probably originated in the Asian Himalayas, where they spread to India, China, and the Caucasus regions, and where they have been eaten for thousands of years. To this day, many of the mustard greens most commonly eaten are Asian varieties that are little known outside their home countries and in Asian markets.

American or curled mustard probably traveled to the New World on African slave ships, where it firmly established itself as an essential part of soul food, with its "mess o' greens" and accompanying pot liquor.

NUTRITION

Mustard greens are outstanding sources of vitamins A, B6, C, E, K, folate, manganese, dietary fiber, calcium, and tryptophan. They are also packed with phytonutrients and beta-carotenes that have antioxidant and possibly anticancer properties.

SELECTION

Look for fresh, crisp bunches with no wilted or yellowing leaves, which indicate mustard well past its prime. Larger, older leaves often pack more heat than very small, young ones, although size is not always a reliable indicator of taste and heat. The only sure way to know is to taste a leaf.

STORAGE

Mustard should be stored unwashed in a perforated plastic bag in the refrigerator vegetable crisper, where they will keep for up to 5 days or 1 week. They prefer high humidity, and benefit from a light misting before storing, or you can wrap them in moist paper towels. Avoid keeping it next to fruits that emit ethylene gas, such as apples, avocados, pears, and bananas, for the gas breaks down chlorophyll and can promote spoilage in green vegetables.

TRIMMING & CLEANING

Mustard should be thoroughly rinsed in several changes of tepid water to flush out hiding insects or lurking soil. Unless the leaves are young and small, the central stem is likely to be quite tough and should be cut away from the foliage and discarded before cooking. An easy way to trim mustard greens and other large flat leaves is to fold them in half along the stem, and cut away the leaf part.

STEAMING & BOILING

Steam mustard greens over rapidly boiling water for about 8 to 12 minutes, depending on their size and age. Mustard can also be slow-simmered as you would collards for southern-style greens. Or for faster preparation, cook them in rapidly boiling water for 2 to 4 minutes, depending on their size and age, then plunge them into ice water to halt the cooking process.

STIR-FRYING & SAUTÉING

Mustard greens can be stir-fried or sautéed in a little broth or oil over high heat for about 5 minutes, depending on their size and age, or until they are wilted.

MICROWAVING

Freshly washed mustard greens can be microwaved with just the water clinging to their leaves. Place them in a microwave-safe dish and cook on High power for 7 to 10 minutes, or until they become tender; stir half way through cooking.

BLANCHING & FREEZING

Freezing works well with mustard greens. After washing, trimming, and cutting them into 1-inch pieces, blanch the leaves first in rapidly boiling water for 3 minutes; then drain and plunge them into ice water to stop the cooking. Squeeze out the excess water and place them in zipper-lock freezer or vacuum food sealer-type bags, or freezer containers. Squeeze out excess air and leave ½ inch of headspace (unless you are using the vacuum sealing method). Mustard greens will keep for up to 1 year at 0°F this way.

EQUIVALENTS, MEASURES & SERVINGS

- 1 pound = 2 cups cooked

COMPLEMENTARY HERBS, SEASONINGS & FOODS

Bacon, butter, chiles, cream, coconut milk, curry, garlic, ginger, ham, lemon, mint, mustard, nuts, onions, salt pork, sausage, seafood, sesame oil, soy sauce, vinegar, walnuts.

SERVING SUGGESTIONS

- Mustard greens are wonderful in curries and other spicy concoctions, especially if tempered a bit with cream or coconut milk.
- Sauté mustard greens and sprinkle with a little lemon juice, walnuts, or pine nuts.
- The next time you make southern-style greens, try combinations of col-

"Most plants taste better when they've had to suffer a little."

— *Diana Kennedy, Mexican cooking authority*

lards, mustard greens, kale, and turnip and beet greens, slow-simmered with ham hocks or salt pork and seasoned with hot peppers and vinegar.

- When you feel yourself coming down with a cold or flu, stir young or finely shredded mustard greens into steaming miso or chicken broth, along with mushrooms and plenty of garlic for a healthful, sinus-clearing alternative to chicken soup.

- The next time you have a large holiday ham, make a most wondrous soup from the leftovers with chopped ham, potatoes, cream, and mustard greens. If you have a genuine country ham like a Smithfield, even better!

- For Chinese-style greens, sauté with fresh ginger, garlic, soy sauce, or oyster sauce. Finish with a little sesame oil or chili paste. Or stir-fry with scallion, garlic, and fermented black beans.

- Larger mustard greens make a piquant, sharp-tasting wrap. Lightly steam or braise the leaves, with or without filling, or wrap them around choice pieces of tuna, cod, or salmon.

- Chop raw or cooked mustard greens and mix them into pasta salads, rice, beans, and casseroles.

- Mix a few young mustard greens in with lettuces and spinach in your next green salad, to add a zesty kick.

. . . .

MUSTARD GREENS WITH PEPPER VINEGAR SERVES 6 TO 8

6 bunches mustard greens
Salt
4 or 5 slices salt-cured hog jowls or thick bacon
1 large clove garlic, minced
1 teaspoon sugar
Freshly ground black pepper
Pepper vinegar (see Note)

1. Wash the greens by stripping the leaves from the stems (discard the stems) and placing them in a sink filled with cold water. Sprinkle a tablespoon of salt over them and swish around. Allow the sediment to settle and lift out the greens, shaking off the excess water, but not drying.

2. In a heavy-bottomed pot over medium-low heat, fry the jowls or bacon until it becomes just translucent and curled, about 5 minutes. Add the garlic, being careful not to burn it. Add the wet greens and sugar, and cover. Stir and lift greens as they wilt during cooking. Cook 1 hour or until they are tender.

3. Taste the cooking liquid ("pot liquor") and add salt and pepper if necessary. Allow to drain slightly as the greens are served. Sprinkle with pepper vinegar.

Note

- Pepper vinegar is made in most places by pouring about one-fourth of the vinegar out of a cider-vinegar bottle and then filling it with hot peppers. The peppers are then marinated for several days.

— *Lee Bailey,* Lee Bailey's Southern Food

WILTED MUSTARD GREENS SALAD WITH BACON

SERVES 2

½ pound mustard greens, stems and center ribs cut out and
    discarded, and leaves cut crosswise into ½-inch-wide strips
3 tablespoons olive oil
1½ teaspoons mustard seeds
1 small onion, chopped fine
1½ tablespoons balsamic vinegar
2 slices bacon, cooked until crisp and crumbled
Salt and pepper

1. Wash the mustard greens, spin them dry, and put them in a large heatproof bowl.

2. In a skillet, heat the oil with the mustard seeds, taking care to partially cover the pan to keep the exploding seeds from flying out, over medium heat for 2 to 4 minutes, or until the popping subsides. Add the onion and cook the mixture, stirring constantly, until the onion softens.

3. Remove the skillet from the heat, stir in the vinegar, and then bring the mixture to a boil. Drizzle the dressing immediately over the mustard greens and toss the salad. Add the bacon and salt and pepper to taste, and toss the salad well.

— *Featherstone Farm*

CURRIED MUSTARD GREENS AND GARBANZO BEANS WITH SWEET POTATOES

SERVES 4

2 medium sweet potatoes, peeled and thinly sliced
1 medium onion, halved and thinly sliced
2 medium cloves garlic, sliced
½ cup plus 1 tablespoon chicken or vegetable broth
½ teaspoon curry powder
¼ teaspoon turmeric
2 cups mustard greens, rinsed and chopped
1 (15-ounce) can garbanzo beans, drained
1 (15-ounce) can sodium-free diced tomatoes
Salt and white pepper
2 tablespoons extra-virgin olive oil

1. Steam the sweet potatoes for approximately 5 to 8 minutes.

2. While steaming the potatoes, slice the onion and garlic. Heat 1 tablespoon of the broth in a 12-inch skillet. Sauté the onion in broth over medium heat for about 4 to 5 minutes, stirring frequently, until it turns translucent. Add the garlic, curry powder, turmeric, and mus-

tard greens. Cook, stirring occasionally until the mustard greens are wilted, about 5 minutes. Add the garbanzo beans, diced tomatoes, salt, and pepper. Cook for another 5 minutes.

3. Mash the steamed sweet potatoes with olive oil, salt, and pepper. If you need to thin the potatoes, add a little more broth. Serve the mustard greens with the mashed sweet potatoes.

— Fruits and Veggies—More Matters; Centers for Disease Control & Prevention

Harvesting broccoli.

Pumpkin

Few plants symbolize fall (and fun) in America as much as pumpkins, which are actually a type of gourd. Pumpkins belong in the same family as cucumbers, melons, and squashes, developing on rambling vines that demand huge amounts of water, fertilizer, and space.

In the United States, millions of pumpkins are carved every autumn into fanciful jack-o'-lanterns, their flesh baked to make pumpkin pie, their seeds roasted as a seasonal snack, and post-Halloweeners sent to feed livestock. In Europe, Latin America, the Caribbean, and parts of Asia, however, pumpkins are used more widely in cooking, especially as a vegetable or in stews. Shelled, roasted pumpkin seeds are commonly found in Latin American markets as pepitas.

Featherstone grows pie pumpkins, which are sometimes known as sugar pumpkins or sugar pie pumpkins. These fruits are especially bred for cooking and baking, with a higher sugar content and more convenient size than the larger pumpkin varieties.

HISTORY

The pumpkin probably originated in Central America; seeds from its ancestors have been found in Mexico and carbon-dated to 5500 B.C.E. American Indian peoples used pumpkin as a staple food along with other squashes, maize, and beans, and introduced the plant to European settlers in the seventeenth century. (Incidentally, throughout history, pumpkins have been constantly confused with and referred to interchangeably with other gourds and hard-skinned squashes.)

The tradition of jack-o'-lanterns began in the British Isles, when various hollowed-out vegetables like turnips, mangelwurzels, beets, and potatoes were used as lanterns. Irish folklore has it that a lazy, stingy farmer named Jack strikes a deal with the Devil to never let him into Hell. When Jack dies, he is refused admittance into Heaven, and the Devil keeps his promise, leaving Jack no choice but to forever wander the earth, carrying a carved-out turnip with a candle inside it to light his way.

Legend aside, the term jack-o'-lantern originally referred to a night watchman. When the Irish arrived to America in the 1800s, they presumably found pumpkins easier to carve out than turnips.

NUTRITION

Pumpkins are among the richest plant sources of vitamin A, in the form of beta-carotene. They also contain potassium and vitamin C. The seeds are even greater nutritional powerhouses, with a quarter cup containing half of the adult daily requirement for manganese, 45 percent of magnesium, 40 percent of phosphorus, and significant tryptophan, iron, copper, zinc, vitamin K, protein, and monounsaturated fat.

Cooking Tip

Freshly made pumpkin purée is much more watery than the commercially canned stuff.

You will need to drain or evaporate this moisture before using it for baking, either by spooning off the pooled liquid that forms on the top of the purée, or let the pumpkin drip overnight through a cheesecloth-covered strainer over a bowl in the refrigerator.

SELECTION

Choose heavy fruits that are uniformly hard, with no soft, shriveled, or bruised areas. Steer clear of pumpkins developing moldy patches, and check the undersides or spots on which they are resting for potential problem areas. Discoloration or scabbing is not necessarily a sign that the flavor is affected; just inspect for softening or rot.

STORAGE

Pumpkins are best stored in cool, dry places, such as a basement or a root cellar with the proper temperature and lack of humidity. (For more information, see "Preserving the Bounty" on page 331.)

The cooler the temperature, the longer pumpkins will keep. At room temperature they can last for several weeks, or at 40°F to 50°F for several months. They should remain unwashed until ready to use. Refrigerate after cutting.

TRIMMING & CLEANING

If you are carving a pumpkin, you will be cutting off its top and scooping out its seeds and flesh anyway. Scrape the flesh clear of seeds and their associated stringy pulp, and cut into 1½-inch chunks.

If you won't be making a jack-o'-lantern, then cut the entire pumpkin into wedges and remove the flesh in large sections with a heavy, sharp knife. Then boil the chunks until tender (see below under Steaming & Boiling).

STEAMING & BOILING

Steam 1½- to 2-inch chunks for 15 to 20 minutes. Or boil 1½-inch chunks in rapidly boiling salted water for 8 to 10 minutes, or until they become tender. This pumpkin is then ready to use as-is, or it can be puréed or mashed like potatoes. Because freshly made pumpkin tends to be quite watery, draining is a must; place mashed pumpkin in a colander suspended over a bowl and refrigerate for at least 1 hour.

STIR-FRYING & SAUTÉING

It may surprise you that pumpkin not only can be stir-fried, but it is a popular dish in Southeast Asia. Cut pumpkin into ½-inch or bite-sized pieces and stir-fry with mustard oil, red chiles, ginger, sugar, turmeric, coriander, cumin, and salt for 3 to 5 minutes, or until the pumpkin is tender but still slightly al dente.

BAKING & ROASTING

Large jack-o'-lantern pumpkins are not the best candidates for baking, as they are bred for large size rather than appetizing flavor and texture. Sugar or pie pumpkins are better for home baking, as they average about 4 to 8 pounds and their flesh is sweeter and far less stringy. Because hacking through the skin of a raw pumpkin sometimes requires tools like keyhole saws and wood gouges (according to Martha Stewart), baking the whole pumpkin to soften it first makes life far more pleasant (and safer).

To prepare, use a sharp chef's knife to make a shallow cut between the stem and blossom end on both sides. Penetrate slowly and carefully until the two halves start to separate, then cut all of the way through the blossom end and pull apart. Cut off the stem, scoop out the seeds, and cut the pumpkin halves crosswise in half again.

Arrange the pumpkin pieces in a shallow roasting pan or a baking sheet with a high rim. Pour in 1½ cups of water and roast at 375°F, uncovered for 1 to 1½ hours, or until very tender.

Sugar pumpkins can also be baked whole. Pierce the skin in several places with a sharp knife (exploding pumpkins are not much fun in the kitchen), then place the pumpkin on a baking sheet, and bake for about 2 hours at 350°F, or until the flesh can be easily pierced with a knife or fork.

MICROWAVING

Cut the pumpkin into sections and place, skin side up, on a microwavable dish or platter. Microwave on High power for 7 minutes per pound, turning the pieces every few minutes so they cook evenly.

BLANCHING & FREEZING

Pumpkin freezes well, but it requires a thorough cooking first, not just a regular blanching. Follow the above instructions to boil, steam, or bake; then cool and remove the seeds. Scoop out the flesh and run it through a food mill or processor to purée it. Then pack the puréed flesh in convenient amounts for preparing pie or other recipes into zipper-lock freezer or vacuum food sealer-type bags or freezer containers, leaving ½ inch of headspace.

Frozen pumpkin purée will keep for up to 5 months. Thaw it in the refrigerator the day before you plan to use it, and drain the excess moisture through a cheesecloth-covered sieve.

EQUIVALENTS, MEASURES & SERVINGS

- 1 4-pound sugar pie pumpkin = 1½ to 2 cups puréed

COMPLEMENTARY HERBS, SEASONINGS & FOODS

Apples, brown sugar, butter, cheese, cinnamon, cream, eggs, honey, maple syrup, molasses, nutmeg, salt, squash, walnuts.

SERVING SUGGESTIONS

- For a twist on tomato-basil soup, try adding puréed pumpkin for a smooth, creamy texture.
- Cook pie pumpkins in the half-shell until creamy, scoop out, season, bake in a pie shell, top with whipped cream, and call in the neighbors.
- Whip up a batch of pumpkin dip, using canned or fresh pumpkin purée, brown sugar, cinnamon, ginger, nutmeg, and cream cheese. Great with crackers, carrots, gingerbread, or molasses cookies.
- Use puréed pumpkin in your favorite pancake recipe.
- Substitute lightly sweetened, cooked pumpkin in recipes calling for sweet potatoes. Whip puréed pumpkin into mashed potatoes, or finely shred pumpkin and potatoes for a twist on hash browns.
- Combine pumpkins with other seasonal autumn fruits like apples, persimmons, and quinces to make thick, almost cakelike puddings.
- An unusual side dish is to sauté thin slices of pumpkin with onion rings and cooking apples, and top with freshly grated ginger, honey, or maple syrup.

The Greatest Pumpkin

The biggest pumpkin ever recorded tipped the scales at 1,502 pounds, grown in Rhode Island in 2006.

"What do you get if you divide the circumference of a pumpkin by its diameter? Pumpkin pi."

— *www.gardendigest.com*

- A very popular Argentinian dish is *carbonada en zapallo*, a savory beef stew cooked in a pumpkin shell, calling for beef cubes, potatoes, kabocha squash, onions, tomatoes, corn, sweet potatoes, and peaches.
- Use hollowed-out pumpkins as decorative containers for soups and stews, saving the stem end as a lid!

ROASTED PUMPKIN SEEDS

Unfortunately, this recipe involves that traumatic step immortalized in Charlie Brown's The Great Pumpkin: *Killing the pumpkin.*

1. Slice open one pumpkin, and scoop out the seeds. Separate the seeds from the pulp, rinsing thoroughly under running water to remove as much flesh as possible.

2. Preheat the oven to 350°F.

3. Place the seeds in a bowl and sprinkle them with lots of seasoned salt, a little flavored oil, soy or Worcestershire sauce, minced fresh garlic, or any other flavoring you prefer. (Garlic salt, a little pepper, Tabasco sauce, Old Bay, Tex-Mex, or cheese-flavored popcorn seasoning are good too.) Mix well.

4. Spread the seeds out in a single layer on a well-greased cookie sheet.

5. Bake the seeds for about 20 minutes. Then stir the seeds and sample them for doneness by taking out a few, letting them cool, and munching. Adjust the seasoning if necessary.

Tip

- The seeds will continue to roast for a little while after removing them from the oven, so take them out a little ahead of the time you think they will be done.

Variation

- For sweet pumpkin seeds, use sugar, cinnamon, nutmeg, ground cloves, salt, and a little honey for a sweet and salty treat.

— *Mi Ae Lipe, Featherstone Farm CSA member*

TWICE-ROASTED MINIATURE PUMPKINS SERVES 6

At Thanksgiving, these filled pumpkins make a nice vegan or vegetarian option for members of the party who don't enjoy turkey. Served with green beans, mashed potatoes, and whatever other side dishes are part of the feast, these miniature pumpkins provide a focal point. For people who do eat meat, they provide a whimsical side dish with turkey, pork, or chicken.

6 miniature pumpkins, about 8 ounces each
1 medium onion, peeled and finely chopped
¼ cup (½ stick) butter or 4 tablespoons canola oil

Black Gold

Austria commercially produces pumpkin seed oil, extracted from the seeds of the Styrian oil pumpkin; this dark, viscous oil is especially prized for its high levels of monounsaturated fat and vitamin E.

1 teaspoon fresh thyme leaves or ½ teaspoon dried thyme

1 teaspoon kosher salt, or to taste

½ teaspoon pepper, or to taste

¼ teaspoon nutmeg (optional)

1 cup fresh breadcrumbs

1 egg

1. Preheat the oven to 375°F. Roast the miniature pumpkins until fork-tender, about 30 minutes.

2. While the squash is roasting, sauté the chopped onion in butter or oil until it turns soft and translucent. Stir in the thyme, salt, pepper, and nutmeg and cool the sauté to room temperature.

3. When the pumpkins are tender, use a very sharp knife to cut a lid from each one. With a teaspoon, scoop out the seeds and the stringy fibers, but leave the thick walls of the little pumpkins intact.

4. Combine the breadcrumbs with the egg and the cooled sautéed onion. Fill each pumpkin with the prepared stuffing. (The pumpkins may be made ahead up to this point and refrigerated for up to a day in advance.)

5. Bake the filled pumpkins until they are heated through, about 20 minutes; serve hot.

— *Greg Atkinson*

. . . .

PUMPKIN PIE WITH SPICED WALNUT STREUSEL

SERVES 10

For a double-crust pie, double the ingredients, divide the dough in half, and form two disks. The pie crust dough can be made 2 days ahead; keep it chilled until you are ready to use it, and let it soften slightly at room temperature before using.

BUTTER PIE CRUST DOUGH

1¼ cups all-purpose flour

½ tablespoon sugar

½ teaspoon salt

½ cup (1 stick) chilled unsalted butter, cut into ½-inch cubes

3 tablespoons (or more) ice water

1. Blend the flour, sugar, and salt in a food processor. Add the butter and cut in, using on/off turns, until a coarse meal forms. Add 3 table-spoons water. Using on/off turns, blend just until moist clumps form, adding more water by half-tablespoonfuls if the dough is dry.

2. Gather the dough into a ball; flatten it into a disk. Wrap it in plastic and refrigerate 1 hour. Let it soften slightly at room temperature before rolling.

The Pumpkin Must Go On

The Circleville Pumpkin Show, held in Circleville, Ohio, is the largest annual U.S. festival dedicated to the pumpkin.

It has taken place every year since 1903, even during the 1918 influenza epidemic, with the exception of three years during World War II.

STREUSEL

⅓ cup all-purpose flour
¼ cup firmly packed brown sugar
1 tablespoon minced crystallized ginger
1 teaspoon ground cinnamon
¼ teaspoon ground nutmeg
2 tablespoons (¼ stick) chilled, unsalted butter, cut into cubes
⅓ cup walnuts, coarsely chopped

PUMPKIN FILLING

15 ounces cooked pumpkin
1 cup white sugar
½ cup firmly packed brown sugar
3 large eggs
½ cup (1 stick) unsalted butter, melted
1 teaspoon vanilla extract

Sweetened whipped cream

1. Roll out the butter pie crust dough on a lightly floured surface to create a 13-inch round. Transfer to a 9-inch-deep glass pie dish. Trim the overhang to ½ inch. Fold the overhang under; crimp the edges decoratively. Refrigerate 1 hour.

2. Preheat the oven to 375°F. Line the crust with aluminum foil and fill it with dried beans or pie weights. Bake until the edges begin to brown and the crust is set, about 17 minutes. Take it out from the oven, and remove the foil and beans. Then continue to bake until the crust turns golden brown, pressing it with the back of a fork if the crust bubbles, about 5 minutes longer. Transfer to the oven rack, and maintain the oven temperature.

FOR THE STREUSEL

Mix the flour, sugar, ginger, cinnamon, and nutmeg in a medium-sized bowl. Add the butter, rubbing it in with your fingertips until a coarse meal forms. Stir in the walnuts.

FOR THE PUMPKIN FILLING

Whisk the pumpkin and white and brown sugars together in a medium-sized bowl. Whisk in the eggs, one at a time. Whisk in the melted butter and vanilla. Pour the mixture into the prepared crust.

TO COMPLETE THE PIE

Sprinkle the streusel over the filling. Bake the pie until the streusel is golden and the filling is set, about 45 minutes. Cool on the oven rack for at least 2 hours. (The pie can be made up to 6 hours ahead). Let stand at room temperature. Serve with sweetened whipped cream.

— Bon Appétit, *November 2003, as appeared on www.epicurious.com*

Books

The Compleat Squash: A Passionate Grower's Guide to Pumpkins, Squashes, and Gourds
Amy Goldman; Artisan, 2004.

Pumpkin, a Super Food for All 12 Months of the Year
Dee Dee Stovel;
Storey Publishing, 2005.

Pumpkin, Butternut & Squash: 30 Sweet and Savory Recipes
Elsa Petersen-Schepelern;
Ryland Peters & Small, 2003.

The Perfect Pumpkin: Growing, Cooking, Carving
Gail Damerow;
Storey Publishing, 1997.

The Great Little Pumpkin Cookbook
Michael Krondl; Celestial Arts, 1999.

CHICKEN PUMPKIN CHILI

SERVES 6

For a peppier version, try this with the quantities of jalapeño, garlic, coriander, and cilantro doubled.

2 tablespoons olive oil
2 cups onion, chopped
2 cups red bell pepper, chopped
3 tablespoons jalapeño, minced
1 clove garlic, minced
1 cup beer
1 cup chicken broth
¼ cup ripe olives, sliced
3 tablespoons chili powder
1 teaspoon ground coriander
½ teaspoon salt
1 (29-ounce) can diced tomatoes, with juice
1 pound boneless, skinless chicken breasts, cubed
2 cups cooked pumpkin or butternut squash, peeled and cubed
2 tablespoons cilantro, chopped
1 tablespoon cocoa powder
1 (16-ounce) can pinto beans, drained
6 tablespoons scallions, sliced
1½ ounces Cheddar cheese, shredded
6 tablespoons sour cream

1. Heat the oil in a Dutch oven over medium heat. Sauté the onions until they are lightly browned, about 8 minutes. Add the bell pepper, jalapeño, and garlic. Sauté for 5 minutes more.

2. Add the beer, broth, olives, chili powder, coriander, salt, tomatoes, and chicken. Bring the mixture to a boil, decrease the heat, cover partially, and simmer for 15 minutes.

3. Stir in the pumpkin, cilantro, cocoa powder, and beans. Cook for 5 minutes.

4. Serve in individual bowls, topped with scallions, cheese, and sour cream.

— *Mimi Hiller, www.epicurean.com*

TURNIPS, PUMPKIN, AND POTATOES

SERVES 6

½ pumpkin, peeled and quartered
3 turnips, peeled and sliced
4 potatoes, peeled and quartered
1 cup milk, scalded
2 tablespoons butter

And You Should've Seen the Size of That Oven

The world-record pumpkin pie was baked by the New Bremen Giant Pumpkin Growers at New Bremen, Ohio, on October 8, 2005, and weighed 2,020 pounds (after baking).

For More Information

Pumpkin Nook
www.pumpkinnook.com

The Pumpkin Patch
www.pumpkin-patch.com

Seasonings to taste

1. Boil the pumpkin, turnips, and potatoes in salted water for about 30 minutes. Drain.

2. Mash with a potato masher. Add the milk, butter, and seasonings. Serve immediately.

— *LoveToKnow.com*

Radish

RAPHANUS SATIVUS

Most Americans associate radishes with their roots, but this is not necessarily so in other parts of the world. In fact, this vegetable has been cultivated for not only its nether regions but also its leaves, seeds (for oil), and seedpods (produced long after the root has ceased to be appetizing).

Anyone who has sampled the zippy leaves and roots of radishes will not be surprised that it is a close relative of the mustard and turnip. Radishes come in many different forms. In Europe and America, small red, white, pink, and purple globe-shaped table radishes are enjoyed as a snack on buttered bread or as a welcome addition to the hors d'oeuvres tray. But in Asia, huge, thick-rooted winter radishes may grow to three feet long and weigh up to sixty pounds, such as the Japanese daikon. Such radishes constitute a full-fledged food, used extensively raw, cooked, and pickled. Black radishes are yet another variety, very different from Asian or table radishes, with their dry, dense, assertively potent flesh. India grows the rat-tailed radish, a variety noted for its seedpods, which can grow eight to twelve inches long and are often pickled.

When they are at their best, table radishes can be irresistibly succulent and crunchy, with an appealing blend of both peppery and sweet flavors. Yet they are equally susceptible to becoming lifeless, pithy, wormy, potently bitter, and spicy in growing conditions that are too dry or hot. Thus these radishes are best enjoyed as either a late-spring or fall crop, but decidedly not during the height of summer.

As a result, Featherstone's fall table radishes tend to be much sweeter than its spring ones; the cool weather allows their sugars to develop slowly, giving them a sweet and mild flavor. Radish greens can also be a treat when they are young and tender. Older leaves tend to be tough and prickly, but they are still suitable for long, slow cooking, like turnip or mustard greens.

HISTORY

Humans have cultivated different species of radishes since antiquity, but they most likely originated in the Far East, possibly China. In ancient Egypt, radishes were so prized for their seeds, which yielded an extremely expensive oil, that the Roman author Pliny complained that farmers ceased to grow grain in favor of radishes.

The modest radishes most familiar to us today seem to be a relatively recent and historically insignificant edible. Huge, thick-rooted winter radishes (of which the Japanese daikon is one) were the most commonly eaten radishes in northern and southern Europe in medieval and Renaissance times, but they have disappeared from those cuisines in modern times. Radishes reached Great Britain in the mid-1500s, and the Spanish and Portuguese introduced the plant to the Americas around that time.

NUTRITION

Radishes are well-known as a diet food, with three radishes averaging just 8 calories. They also contain vitamin C, folate, riboflavin, potassium, calcium, magnesium, manganese, and dietary fiber. Like other Brassica crops, radishes have sulphurous compounds that may help fight cancer but also sometimes contribute to flatulence.

SELECTION

Selecting good radishes can be a challenge, for size (or the lack of it) does not necessarily indicate quality. More reliable factors include season (early spring and fall radishes taste the best) and whether fresh-looking greens are still attached. Choose radishes that are uniformly hard, with absolutely no signs of shriveling or give when firmly pressed. Their skins should be smooth and unbroken, with a slight sheen. Sampling is the only sure-fire way to tell a radish's true character.

STORAGE

Table radishes do not store well, even in the refrigerator. Keep them unwashed and unwrapped in a plastic bag in the refrigerator vegetable crisper for only a few days if you plan to eat them raw; if they are destined for the cooking pot, they will keep for up to 1 week.

TRIMMING & CLEANING

Given their proximity in their native environment, dirt tends to be a radish's best friend. Roots need a thorough scrubbing with a soft vegetable brush, and leaves must be submerged and vigorously swished in water as long as it takes to remove all traces of sand.

STEAMING & BOILING

Radishes transform into a surprisingly sweet and mild vegetable when cooked. Quarter or slice the roots, then steam, covered, over rapidly boiling water for 5 minutes or until they turn just tender.

STIR-FRYING & SAUTÉING

Radishes and their greens are delicious stir-fried or sautéed lightly in a little butter or olive oil, garlic, and salt. Cook radish roots on moderately high heat for about 10 to 12 minutes, or until crisp-tender; greens for about 5 minutes, or until wilted but still bright green.

BAKING & ROASTING

Baking or roasting radishes tames their pungency and makes a surprisingly good vegetable side dish. Toss sliced radishes with olive oil and seasoning, then spread them on a baking sheet or roasting pan, and roast for 30 to 45 minutes in a 425°F oven.

MICROWAVING

Place radishes in a covered microwave-safe container with 2 to 3 table-spoons of water, and microwave on High power for 8 minutes, or until they are tender when pierced with a fork.

BLANCHING & FREEZING

Radishes do not make good candidates for freezing, as they will lose their flavor and crispness upon thawing.

EQUIVALENTS, MEASURES & SERVINGS

½ pound = 1⅔ cups sliced

COMPLEMENTARY HERBS, SEASONINGS & FOODS

Asparagus, butter, chicken, crab, fish, garlic, ginger, greens, ham, lemons, mushrooms, oranges, pea shoots, prosciutto, salami, salmon, scallops, seafood, shrimp, snap peas, spinach, sweet onions, watercress.

SERVING SUGGESTIONS

- Try making radish soup with chicken stock, rice vinegar, sugar, cayenne pepper, ginger, shrimp, sliced radishes, spinach, and green onions.
- Serve braised, roasted, or grilled radishes with savory meats like roast pork, beef, lamb, or chicken.
- For a dainty hors d'oeuvres, serve tea sandwiches made with layers of very thinly sliced radishes and raw mint leaves on white bread spread with a mixture of mayonnaise, lemon juice, and sour cream.
- Add chopped radish to your favorite salsa recipe.
- Stir-fry radish greens with soy sauce, sesame seeds, and garlic.
- In Korea, daikon radishes and pears are combined to create a highly prized white kimchi, or pickled vegetable. Try this combination in an unusual salad with sliced table radishes, crisp Asian or Bartlett pears, watercress, shredded napa cabbage, ginger, and a touch of green onion or chives.
- Add chopped or sliced radishes to your favorite potato, egg, tuna, or ham salad recipe.
- Thinly slice radishes and pickle them in the refrigerator as you would cucumbers (see Barely Pickled Cucumbers on page 105).
- Toss lightly cooked or raw radishes in your favorite vinaigrette.
- Combine and purée radish tops with other spring greens like arugula, lettuce, and spinach; finish with cream and chicken stock for a lovely spring soup.

- -

RADISH, MANGO, AND APPLE SALAD   SERVES 4

With its crisp, clean tastes and mellow flavors, this salad goes well with smoked salmon, ham, or salami.

DRESSING

½ cup sour cream
2 teaspoons creamed horseradish
1 tablespoon chopped fresh dill
Salt and freshly ground black pepper
Sprig of dill, for garnish

10 to 15 radishes, ends removed
1 eating apple, peeled, cored, and thinly sliced
2 celery stalks, thinly sliced
1 small ripe mango, peeled and cut into small chunks

1. To prepare the dressing, blend together the sour cream, horseradish, and dill in a small jug or bowl and season with a little salt and pepper.

> "The first gatherings of the garden in May of salads, radishes, and herbs made me feel like a mother about her baby—how could anything so beautiful be mine. And this emotion of wonder filled me for each vegetable as it was gathered every year. There is nothing that is comparable to it, as satisfactory or as thrilling, as gathering the vegetables one has grown."
>
> — *Alice B. Toklas,*
> *life partner of Gertrude Stein*

2. Thinly slice the radishes. Place them in a bowl together with the apple and celery.

3. Cut through the mango lengthwise, on either side of the pit. Make even criss-cross cuts through each side section. Take each one and bend it back to separate the cubes. Remove the mango cubes with a small knife and add to the bowl.

4. Pour the dressing over the vegetables and fruit and stir gently so that all of the ingredients are coated in the dressing. When ready to serve, spoon the salad into an attractive bowl and garnish with a dill sprig.

— *Christine Ingram,* The Cook's Encyclopedia of Vegetables

SOUTHWESTERN RADISH SALAD   SERVES 4

6 cups lettuce (about ½ large head), cut into 1-inch strips
1½ cups sliced radishes
3 hard-boiled eggs, cut into wedges
1 (16-ounce) can red kidney beans, drained and rinsed
1 (7-ounce) can corn kernels, drained
1 cup Monterey Jack cheese, cut into 1-inch cubes
½ cup crumbled cooked bacon or bacon bits
¼ cup sliced green onions

ORANGE-SALSA DRESSING

1 cup prepared salsa
½ cup orange juice, preferably freshly squeezed
2 tablespoons cider vinegar
1 teaspoon grated orange zest

Combine everything and toss with dressing.

— *Featherstone Farm*

RADISHES WITH SALT AND BUTTER   SERVES 4

This is a popular snack in France, eagerly devoured by the young and old alike. Sometimes the radishes are sliced and eaten atop a thick slice of generously buttered French bread, open-faced, and finished with a shake of the salt grinder.

12 radishes, trimmed and washed
¼ pound sweet cream butter, unsalted
Coarsely ground sea salt and freshly cracked black pepper

To eat, dab each radish with a dollop of butter, sprinkle with sea salt and pepper, and enjoy.

— *Mi Ae Lipe, Featherstone Farm CSA member*

SAUTÉED RADISHES AND SUGAR SNAP PEAS WITH DILL
SERVES 6

This side dish pairs beautifully with roast lamb or salmon.

1 tablespoon butter
1 tablespoon olive oil
½ cup thinly sliced shallots
12 ounces sugar snap peas, trimmed and strings removed
2 cups thinly sliced radishes (about 1 large bunch)
¼ cup orange juice
1 teaspoon dill seeds
1 tablespoon chopped fresh dill

1. To remove the strings from the fresh peas, just snap off the stem end and pull the attached string lengthwise down each pod.

2. Melt the butter with the oil in a large nonstick skillet over medium heat. Add the shallots and sauté until golden, about 5 minutes. Add the sugar snap peas and radishes; sauté until crisp-tender, about 5 minutes.

3. Add the orange juice and dill seeds; stir 1 minute. Season with salt and pepper. Stir in the chopped dill. Transfer to a bowl, and serve.

— Bon Appétit, *April 2004, as appeared on www.epicurious.com*

ROASTED RADISHES AND ROOT VEGETABLES
SERVES 4

Serve as a side dish, or toss with pasta or rice if desired.

3 medium-sized sweet potatoes, peeled and cut into 2-inch chunks (3 cups)
4 medium-sized parsnips, peeled and cut into 2-inch chunks (about 2 cups)
2 medium-sized red onions, peeled and quartered
12 ounces radishes
3 tablespoons olive oil
1 garlic head, cut in half lengthwise
Salt and black pepper
1 tablespoon fresh thyme or 1 teaspoon dried thyme

1. Preheat the oven to 450°F.

2. Place the mushrooms, bell pepper, zucchini, and onion in a 13 × 9 × 2-inch nonstick baking pan. Toss with the olive oil, garlic, salt, pepper, and thyme.

3. Bake uncovered, until the mushrooms and vegetables are tender, about 20 minutes.

— *Courtesy of the Radish Council*

When Woodcarvers Get Bored

Every December 23rd, since 1897, the town of Oaxaca, Mexico, celebrates Noche de Rabanos (Night of the Radishes), a festival in which enormous daikon-like radishes are carved into unbelievably elaborate scenes and figures and displayed around a zocalo.

Often the intricate carvings depict saints, conquistadors, and nativity scenes.

Raspberry

Few fruits bring instant delight as do raspberries. These soft, delicate morsels, with their luscious perfume and melting texture, have been enjoyed by humans and animals alike throughout history, although mostly in their wild forms. Only relatively recently have raspberries been cultivated and new varieties developed.

Red and yellow raspberries taste similar, but black and purple ones have a stronger, often more tart flavor. Orange and yellow (often referred to as golden) raspberries tend to be sweeter and less acidic than their crimson counterparts. Raspberries are divided into two categories: everbearing, which produce fruit in both the summer and fall, and summer-bearing, which fruit only in the summer.

HISTORY

Raspberries are native to Asia, where more than two hundred known species grow, but the Rubus family is vast and complicated, with wild species growing throughout Asia, Europe, and North America. Wild raspberries have been eaten by humans since antiquity, but the plants have been cultivated only during the past few centuries. They were gathered on Mount Ida in Turkey and have been popular in spots in Europe, although until very recently they were almost unheard of in some countries such as Italy. Despite the New World's own native species, European colonists in America preferred to import their own raspberry. To this day, "wild" European canes still run rampant in some eastern U.S. states, having escaped from early colonial gardens.

NUTRITION

Like most berries, raspberries are antioxidant powerhouses, in particular containing anthocyanins (which give red and purple raspberries their color) and ellagic acid. A cup of raspberries contains over 60 percent of an adult's daily supply of manganese, as well as 50 percent of vitamin C, for only 60 calories. They are also very high in dietary fiber and contain B vitamins, potassium, and magnesium.

SELECTION

Choose firm, intact raspberries, with no signs of mold or sliminess, which can spread quickly among crowded fruits. When choosing raspberries packaged in those clear plastic boxes in the supermarket, check all sides of the box to make sure there are no crushed or moldy fruits.

STORAGE

Raspberries are among the most perishable of fruits, so great care must be taken to store them properly. They should remain unwashed in the refrigerator and kept as dry as possible. (Sunlight, moisture, and warm

Cooking Tip

Whole raspberries will stay firmer in a sauce if you add a tablespoon of brown sugar.

temperatures will all cause the berries to spoil quickly.) Moldy or soft raspberries tend to infect their companions, so be vigilant about promptly removing these specimens. Raspberries can be stored in their original container, or placed on a dish lined with dry paper towels. Use within 1 to 3 days.

TRIMMING & CLEANING

Raspberries should remain unwashed until right before serving. Because they are so delicate, place them in a colander and use the sink sprayer so as not to crush them. Then spread them out on a plate lined with paper towels, and pat very gently dry.

MICROWAVING

Place separated frozen berries in a single layer on a plate lined with a paper towel. They should be microwaved just long enough to defrost mostly but not completely, and when done, should still retain their shape and appear slightly frosted. Remove the berries immediately when they have finished microwaving, so they stop cooking.

- ¼ cup = Defrost 30 seconds
- ½ cup = 50 seconds
- 1 cup = 1 minute, 20 seconds

BLANCHING & FREEZING

Raspberries can be frozen as whole fruits or in a sugar syrup. To freeze whole, wash the berries, place them as a single layer on a tray, and freeze them until they are nearly solid. Then package them in zipper-lock freezer or vacuum food sealer-type bags, or freezer containers. Squeeze out excess air and leave ½ inch of headspace (unless you are using the vacuum sealing method). Frozen raspberries will keep for up to 1 year at 0°F.

To package raspberries for jam, wash the berries and put them in a syrup made with 3 cups of sugar to 1 quart of water, or 1 cup sugar to 7 or 8 cups of fruit. Pack in freezer containers, leaving at least 1 inch of headroom.

MEASURES & EQUIVALENTS

- ½ pint = scant 1½ cups
- 2 cups berries = 1 pint
- 4 cups berries = 1 quart

COMPLEMENTARY HERBS, SEASONINGS & FOODS

Almonds, apricots, bananas, brandy, brown sugar, buttermilk, caramel, Champagne, chocolate, cinnamon, cognac, cream, cream cheese, currants, fruits, Grand Marnier, honey, kirsch, lemon, mangoes, melons, mint, oranges, other berries, peaches, pears, peppers, pineapple, pistachios, red wine, sour cream, sugar, vanilla.

SERVING SUGGESTIONS

- Few dishes are as simply good as a big bowl of chilled raspberries sprinkled with sugar or drizzled with honey, and flooded with thick cream.
- Combine lightly crushed fresh raspberries with other berries, like blueber-

Books

Remarkable Red Raspberry Recipes
Sibyl Kile;
BCG Ltd., 1985.

Raspberry Delights Cookbook: A Collection of Raspberry Recipes
Karen Jean Matsko Hood;
Whispering Pines Press, 2007.

Berries: A Country Garden Cookbook
Sharon Kramis;
Collins Publishers, 1994.

The Very Special Raspberry Cookbook
Carrie Tingley Hospital Foundation and Very Special Cookbook Committee; Jumbo Jack's Cookbooks, 1993.

Cooking with Fruit
Rolce Redard Payne and Dorrit Speyer Senior; Crown Publishers, 1992.

ries, strawberries, and blackberries, as a topping for cold cereal, oatmeal, parfaits, ice cream, pudding, or chilled fruit soup.

- Sprinkle a few drops of high-quality balsamic vinegar over fresh, ripe raspberries. The taste combination is unusual but highly addictive.
- Liven up a raspberry sauce by adding a little Grand Marnier, apricot brandy, or cherry kirsch.
- Raspberries and sponge or pound cake were made for each other; garnish with whole berries, or lightly crush them with a little sugar or honey for a delicious topping.
- Scatter a handful of raspberries in a green tossed salad.
- Dip raspberries into warm, melted chocolate for a luxurious treat.

BAKED RHUBARB WITH RASPBERRIES   SERVES 4

1⅓ cups raspberries (about 6 ounces)
¾ cup firmly packed light brown sugar
¼ cup very hot water
2 tablespoons unsalted butter, cut into bits
¼ teaspoon vanilla
1 pound rhubarb, trimmed and cut into ½-inch pieces
    (about 4 cups)
8 small scoops low-fat frozen yogurt

1. Preheat the oven to 350°F.

2. In a blender, purée the raspberries with the brown sugar and hot water; strain the purée through a sieve into a bowl, pressing hard on the solids. Stir in the butter, vanilla, and the rhubarb.

3. Transfer the mixture to an 11 × 7 × 2-inch baking dish and bake in the middle of the oven for 30 minutes, stirring once very gently after 15 minutes.

4. Cook until the rhubarb is soft. Let the dessert cool for 10 minutes and serve it over frozen low-fat yogurt.

— Fruits and Veggies—More Matters; Centers for Disease Control & Prevention

RASPBERRY WHIP   SERVES 6

RASPBERRY WHIP

1 tablespoon unflavored gelatin
¼ cup ginger ale
¼ cup boiling water
1½ teaspoons grated lemon rind
2 tablespoons lemon juice
1 cup crushed raspberries
4 egg whites
¾ cup sugar

1. Sprinkle the gelatin over the ginger ale, and allow it to soften, about 3 to 5 minutes. Add the boiling water. Stir until dissolved. Add the lemon rind, juice, and berries.

2. Chill until the mixture begins to thicken. Using an electric mixer, mix on low speed until it becomes frothy. In another bowl, beat the egg whites and sugar until they stiffen. Add the whites to the gelatin mixture and continue to whip until it holds its form.

3. Pour into a decorative mold, and chill for at least 4 hours. Unmold and serve with Raspberry Creme (recipe below).

RASPBERRY CREME

¼ cup butter
1 cup sugar
2 whole eggs
2 egg yolks
1 cup milk
1 teaspoon vanilla
1 cup crushed raspberries

1. Cream the butter and sugar together until the mixture turns light and fluffy.

2. Beat in the whole eggs, one at a time, then the yolks. Slowly stir in the milk and vanilla. Heat the mixture over boiling water until it forms a thin custard.

3. Add the berries. Let cool, then serve it over the Raspberry Whip.

— *SandhillBerries.com*

CROCKPOT CHOCOLATE RASPBERRY STRATA   SERVES 6

This dessert is actually a type of bread pudding.

6 cups Hawaiian bread, challah, or brioche, cut into 1-inch cubes
1½ cups semisweet chocolate chips
½ pint fresh raspberries (do not use frozen), rinsed and drained
½ cup heavy cream
½ cup milk
4 eggs
¼ cup sugar
1 teaspoon vanilla extract
Whipped cream

1. Place half of the bread cubes in a well-buttered 3½-quart crockpot. Sprinkle on half of the chocolate chips and raspberries. Cover with the remaining bread cubes, then top with the remaining chocolate chips and raspberries.

2. In a medium-sized bowl, whisk together the cream, milk, eggs, sugar,

---

- **Make it a fun finger food.** Asparagus and green beans are delightful to eat with the fingers. And don't forget carrot sticks, bell pepper strips, pea pods, cherry tomatoes, radishes, broccoli and cauliflower florets, and corn on the cob.

- **Don't mix things up.** Young children often dislike their food all mixed together, as in a casserole, but instead prefer separate, identifiable items.

  I found that salad niçoise, the French salad of whole green beans, tomatoes, tuna, and hardboiled eggs served over lettuce leaves, was a big hit with my kids because its ingredients are arranged separately and not tossed together, with dressing served on the side. They loved being able to serve themselves buffet-style, which gave them a satisfactory sense of decisionmaking on their part.

- **Use bright or novel colors to attract and entice.** Try serving red, green, orange, and yellow bell peppers, carrots, green-and-red striped heirloom tomatoes, blue potatoes, purple broccoli, red and white-ringed slices of Chiogga beets, or the brilliantly colored stems of Rainbow Brights swiss chard.

- **Make it sweet.** Children tend to be attracted to sweet-tasting foods. Try red bell pepper strips, beets, carrots, heirloom and Sungold tomatoes, and sugar snap peas.

- **Don't cook them.** Many vegetables, such as broccoli and cauliflower, smell strong when cooked. Children also tend to be sensitive to certain textures. Try serving some commonly cooked vegetables raw instead. (A novel treat is a raw ear of corn on the cob!)

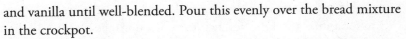

and vanilla until well-blended. Pour this evenly over the bread mixture in the crockpot.

3. Cover and cook over high heat about 1¾ to 2 hours, or until set. (Do not cook on low heat for a longer time.) Let stand for about 5 to 10 minutes before serving. Serve garnished with whipped cream.

— *www.razzledazzlerecipes.com*

For More Information

Sand Hill Berries
www.sandhillberries.com

Oregon Raspberry & Blackberry Commission
www.oregon-berries.com

PEA PODS WITH RASPBERRIES   SERVES 4 TO 6

This unusual pairing is visually spectacular with a refreshingly different flavor. A great color and taste accent for a chicken salad, this recipe works equally well with grilled fish or poultry.

½ pound snow pea pods
1 tablespoon balsamic vinegar
2 tablespoons olive oil
¼ teaspoon salt
Freshly ground pepper
¾ cup raspberries

1. Wash and remove the tips and strings from the pea pods.

2. Bring a large saucepan of water to a rapid boil and add the pea pods. After the water returns to a full boil, cook the pods for just 3 minutes. Drain them well in a colander, then toss them in a serving bowl with the vinegar, oil, salt, and pepper until they are well-coated. Gently stir in the raspberries, taking care not to mash them. Serve warm.

— *Rolce Redard Payne and Dorrit Speyer Senior,* Cooking with Fruit

POLKA DOT CLOUDS

A fun fruit dish for kids.

Red or golden raspberries
Blueberries
Whipped cream
Melba toast rounds
Honey (optional)

Arrange the melba toast rounds in a single layer on a big plate. Spray whipped cream on each round, then dot with the raspberries and blueberries to form "polka dots." Drizzle with a little honey, if desired.

— *Mi Ae Lipe, Featherstone Farm CSA member*

Squash (Winter)

CUCURBITA MAXIMA, C. MOSCHATA, AND C. PEPO

With so many members, variations, and lineages, the world of squashes is vast and frequently confusing. Cucurbita pepo *includes several varieties: the yellow-ivory-skinned Delicata, various gourds, and summer squash. These fruits are typically ribbed and available earlier in the season. They are also one of the oldest domesticated species (traces have been found in Mexican caves dating before 7000 B.C.E.).*

Cucurbita moschata represents such varieties as butternut, cushaw, winter crooknecks, Japanese pie, and large cheese pumpkins. Cucurbita maxima includes well-known varieties as hubbard, Delicious, marblehead, Boston marrow, and turban.

Literally hundreds of different varieties belong to these three species, representing fruits that weigh from one to fifty pounds and come in amazingly diverse shapes and colors. But they all share in common a thick, outer rind and dense, fairly dry flesh that allows them to store far longer than their summer squash cousins. All squashes prefer hot weather, and they are at their best in September and October. If properly stored, some winter squashes can last for as long as six months.

Featherstone grows several varieties of winter squash:

Acorn *(Cucurbita pepo)*
Acorn squash, with its distinctive shape and dark-green skin, has yellow flesh that is mildly sweet and slightly nutty in flavor. A smallish squash that measures about 4 to 6 inches long, it will keep in a cool, dark, well-ventilated place for months. Remember, however, that the Acorn is an early-ripening squash, so it will not last throughout the winter.

Buttercup *(C. maxima)*
This old classic has distinctive, dark-green roundish fruits that wear "beanies" as they mature. Averaging about 5 to 7 pounds, this is a superb squash with deliciously sweet orange flesh, which becomes dry and fine-textured when baked, creamy and smooth when steamed. Buttercups make wonderful soup or pie.

Butternut *(C. moschata)*
One of the most popular of the winter squashes, this is a pear-shaped, dependably good squash with an elongated neck, tan skin, and plenty of dense, sweet, orange flesh. This squash is best baked, used in soups, or sliced and made into casseroles. It also works well in custards and pies (try substituting it for pumpkin). One risk is that they can get too moist, so it is best to cook them dry. This squash can be stored for 3 to 6 months.

Carnival (C. pepo)

The Carnival is a striking, heart-shaped, smallish to medium-sized squash, whose diameter ranges from 5 to 7 inches and usually weighs 1 or 2 pounds. A cross between the Acorn and Delicata, the Carnival has ivory skin that is heavily splotched with green ribs and veins, but adds bright splashes of orange and yellow to its middle. Its somewhat coarse flesh is sweet, with pleasant, nuanced flavors. It is good baked, puréed to make soup, or carved out and stuffed.

Heart of Gold (C. pepo)

This beauty is a cross between the Acorn and Sweet Dumpling. It is the size and shape of the Acorn, but the fruit has the sweetness and dramatically striped skin of the Dumpling. Sweet and rich, this squash is excellent baked, steamed, or mashed. It is a good storage squash that should keep until January.

Kabocha (C. maxima and C. moschata)

The name of this roundish green squash is something of a misnomer, for *kabocha* is a generic term for all winter squash bred in Japan, but rarely is any distinction awarded to the several types available in America. Weighing an average of 3 pounds, kabochas, whatever the cultivar, all possess delicious, honey-sweet, deeply flavored flesh that is the texture of custard when cooked. It is superb steamed, and fantastic in recipes calling for sweet potatoes or pumpkin.

Red Kuri (C. maxima)

A kabocha-type squash that somewhat resembles an orange pumpkin without the ridges, it weighs from 5 to 10 pounds. Its firm, pale orange flesh tends to be firm, with a mellow flavor somewhat reminiscent of chestnuts. This is a good squash for baking, braising, steaming, or puréeing into soups.

Spaghetti (C. pepo)

Featherstone grows a unique variety of spaghetti squash called Small Wonder. Bred to be a single-serving squash, this compact, oblong-shaped squash has a solid orange skin and weighs only 1 to 2 pounds (in contrast to full-size varieties that average 4 to 8 pounds). When cooked, its pale, mild flesh can be fluffed into pleasantly crunchy strands with a fork, like spaghetti noodles. Topped with your favorite sauce, this squash is a filling, low-calorie alternative to pasta.

Sweet Dumpling (C. pepo)

This is a rather small, apple-shaped squash that averages only about 4 to 5 inches in diameter and weighs about 1 pound. The Sweet Dumpling is delicately colored, with tan skin and pale green stripes. Its pale yellow flesh is more starchy than some squashes but is quite sweet, with some corn undertones. This squash makes a fine dish steamed, baked, or stuffed.

Pie Pumpkin

See Pumpkin section on pages 261–268.

HISTORY

Winter squashes and pumpkins are native to South and Central America, ranging from Mexico to northern Argentina. These heat-loving plants tend to be popular in warm climates, and have never been commonly cultivated in northern Europe or places with short or cool summers. Winter squashes were unknown in the Old World until the 1500s, when European explorers imported them to their home countries. Later they introduced them to other continents, including Asia and Africa.

The earliest squash fruits were not valued so much for their flesh, which tended to be extremely bitter and sparse, but rather for their protein- and oil-rich seeds. As they were domesticated, humans began selectively breeding them for size, flavor, and proportion of flesh to seeds.

NUTRITION

Most winter squashes are packed with nutrients. Depending on the variety, a 1-cup serving may contain nearly 150 percent of the adult daily requirement for vitamin A, over 30 percent of vitamin C, over 20 percent of potassium, manganese, and dietary fiber. In addition, winter squashes contain significant folate, omega 3 fatty acids, vitamin B1, and copper. Squashes with darker shades of orange flesh contain more beta-carotene and phytonutrients, which may play a role in helping prevent certain cancers.

SELECTION

Winter squashes are hardy and sturdy by nature, so choosing a good specimen would not appear to be difficult. However, if you are seeking a squash with maximum flavor and storage potential, look for a specimen that is rock-hard, with absolutely no soft or moldy spots. Its stems should be intact, and its skins relatively dull (shiny skins may mean that the squash is immature or that it has been waxed to mask its true condition).

Winter squashes are at their best in the fall. Although they are often available year-round in the supermarket, they are likely to be tasteless at other times.

STORAGE

Winter squash are surprisingly prone to decay, and should be stored in a cool, dry, well-ventilated place, preferably with temperatures of 45°F to 50°F and 65 to 70 percent humidity. Many varieties will keep, properly stored, from 2 weeks to 6 months in a basement, root cellar, or other place with the proper cool temperature and lack of humidity (for more information, see "Preserving the Bounty" on page 331).

Mildew may become a problem if your storage area is not dry enough. If you suspect that your storage area is too damp, wipe your squash with a solution of 1 part chlorine to 9 parts water (or some hydrogen peroxide solution). Then air-dry the squash completely and rub its exterior with salad oil.

TRIMMING & CLEANING

Rarely are the tough outer rinds of winter squash edible, and thus they require removal before eating. Peeling or cutting them away, however,

> "Half the cookbooks tell you how to cook the food and the other half tell you how to avoid eating it."
>
> — *Andy Rooney, television curmudgeon*

can be quite challenging, requiring an implement akin to a machete or ax. Some people suggest using a rubber mallet to smash the squash open, while others recommend simply dropping larger specimens from a great height onto a paper-lined floor. Some of the smaller squashes have tender enough skins that they can be cut fairly easily with a knife, but you may be better off (and safer) by baking others whole in the oven until they soften.

Simply wash the outside of the squash, pierce it several times with a knife or fork to prevent explosions, and cut down the stem if it is too tall (I once nearly set a squash on fire because its stem was inadvertently touching my oven's upper heating element). Once cooked, you can then easily remove the seeds and their surrounding stringy pulp, and then scoop out the soft flesh from the collapsed shell.

STEAMING & BOILING

Squashes that are very hard or starchy make good candidates for steaming. Halve and seed the squash, set the pieces on a steamer rack or basket, cover, and steam over rapidly boiling water for 15 to 30 minutes, depending on the size and variety. Chunks cut into 2-inch pieces require only about 15 minutes, but test all squash for doneness by piercing it with a knife or fork.

STIR-FRYING & SAUTÉING

An unusual method for preparing winter squash is to stir-fry or sauté it. The key to making this work is to cut the squash into pieces small enough so that they will cook evenly and all the way through. Peel the skins from the squash, cut into pieces 1 inch long and ½ inch thick, and sauté over high heat for 7 to 10 minutes, or until they become tender.

BAKING & ROASTING

Baking and roasting are wonderful ways to prepare winter squash, as these methods caramelize their natural sugars and concentrate flavors. Follow the directions above for trimming and cleaning, and place the entire squash on a baking sheet or pan, if possible. If they are too big, you may halve them and place the halves on the sheet, cut sides down. Most squashes weighing 1 to 1½ pounds will take about 45 minutes in a 350°F to 375°F oven, with 3-pounders requiring about 1½ to 2 hours.

In the last third of the cooking time, check constantly for doneness by inserting the point of a sharp knife into the center of the squash. If the knife blade passes through easily with no resistance, then the squash is done. Halve it, extract the seeds and surrounding stringy pulp, and scoop out the flesh into another container. Season to taste and reheat if necessary.

MICROWAVING

Place halves or quarters, cut sides down, in a shallow, microwave-safe dish; add ¼ cup water or apple juice. ((If water is used in cooking, the amount should be kept minimal to avoid leaching out flavor and nutrients.) Or pierce whole squash several times with a fork and place in a microwave-safe dish. Cover tightly and microwave on High power for 6 minutes per pound, or until the flesh softens.

What's in That Can?

Most commercially canned pumpkin is not true pumpkin at all, but the richer, more full-flavored flesh of *C. maxima*, a type of winter squash. Delicious and Boston Marrow are two varieties often used in canning.

Non-spaghetti Types

- 1½ cups = 3 to 4 minutes
- 1 pound = 6 to 7 minutes
- 1 squash (4 to 5 pounds) = 15 to 20 minutes

Spaghetti Squash

- 1 whole Small Wonder squash (1 to 2 pounds) = 6 to 9 minutes on either side

BLANCHING & FREEZING

To properly freeze winter squash, it must first be thoroughly cooked, not just briefly blanched, as with most vegetables. Steam, boil, or bake the squash as described above, and then scoop out the flesh, discarding the seeds, stringy surrounding pulp, and skins. Mash the flesh, or run it through a food processor, or press it through a sieve.

Or cube, peel, and steam the flesh. Pack the puréed or cubed squash in zipper-lock freezer or vacuum food sealer-type bags, or freezer containers. Squeeze out excess air and leave ½ inch of headspace (unless you are using the vacuum sealing method).

MEASURES & EQUIVALENTS

- 1 pound peeled, trimmed squash = 2 cups cooked = 1½ cups mashed = 2 to 3 servings
- 2½ pounds whole squash = 1½ pounds, 10 ounces cut-up pieces = 2¾ to 3 cups puréed squash
- 1 pound trimmed squash = 2 cups cooked = 2 to 3 servings
- 12 ounces frozen squash = 1 to ½ cups
- Acorn squash: 1 medium squash = 1 pound = 2 cups cooked, mashed
- Spaghetti squash: 1 medium squash = 5 pounds = 6 to 6½ cups strands

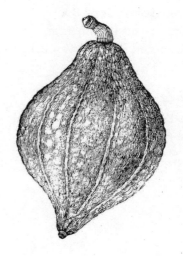

COMPLEMENTARY HERBS, SEASONINGS & FOODS

Ancho chiles, apples, bacon, brown sugar, butter, celery root, Cheddar cheese, cinnamon, cloves, curry powder, garlic, ginger, honey, maple syrup, marjoram, nutmeg, nuts, onion, oranges, Parmesan cheese, pears, pecans, pepper, rosemary, sage, sherry.

SERVING SUGGESTIONS

- Boil or mash winter squash just as you would potatoes.
- Add peeled squash cubes to your favorite soups, stews, beans, gratins, and vegetable ragouts.
- Steam cubes of winter squash and dress with olive oil, garlic, tamari, and ginger for a savory dish, or with apples and ginger for a sweeter dish.
- Bake squash, cut into halves, and stuff with seasoned meat, rice, breadcrumbs, or a favorite stir-fry recipe. Season and reheat as necessary.
- Make shredded strands of spaghetti squash into an au gratin, with butter and cheese.
- Very tender, sweet winter squashes can be finely shredded to make an unusual slaw, along with raisins, mayonnaise, vinegar, cream, and sugar.
- Prepare mashed or finely shredded squash into pancakes, much like potato

Books

The Compleat Squash: A Passionate Grower's Guide to Pumpkins, Squashes, and Gourds
Amy Goldman; Artisan, 2004.
Sibyl Kile; BCG Ltd., 1985.

The Classic Zucchini Cookbook: 225 Recipes for All Kinds of Squash
Nancy C. Ralston, Marynor Jordan, Andrea Chesman; Storey Publishing, 2002.

Squash Lovers Cook Book
Golden West Publishers and Lee Fischer; Golden West Publishers, 2003.

Pumpkin, Butternut & Squash: 30 Sweet and Savory Recipes
Elsa Petersen-Schepelern; Ryland Peters & Small, 2003.

pancakes, or deep-fry like hash browns.

- Purée cooked squash and blend with sugar, cinnamon, honey, nutmeg, maple syrup, and cream for a luscious dessert.
- Substitute sweet-flavored winter squash in any recipe calling for pumpkin.
- Dress cooked winter squash with butter and herbs, a cream sauce, cheese sauce, maple syrup and nuts, marinara sauce, or stewed fruit.
- Use cooked, mashed squash in breads (especially cornbread), muffins, custards, and pies. Be sure to compensate in the recipe for the squash's extra moisture.

. . . .

GINGER SQUASH SOUP   SERVES 4

This is the soup we sometimes make for tastings at the Seward Co-op in Minneapolis. Steaming allows the butternut squash flesh to stay moist while retaining the vitamins. The soup seems to go over well, but it is made with heavy cream, so how can it be bad?

1 butternut squash, split in half and de-seeded
1 tablespoon fresh ginger, finely grated
2 tablespoons unsalted butter, softened
4 cups chicken or vegetable stock
Salt and pepper
¼ cup heavy cream
¼ cup chopped, toasted pecans (optional)

1. Steam the butternut squash for 30 minutes until it is fork-tender (and you do want this tender). Scoop the flesh out into a food processor. (Or you may use a blender, but the processor works better.)

2. Add the ginger and butter, and process. The squash will be a bit thick, so add the stock until the soup reaches the desired consistency.

3. Place the soup in a large stockpot and heat. Add stock to thin as necessary. Salt and pepper to taste. (You can also add more ginger if you wish, but remember to go slowly—it is more difficult to take away a strong flavor than it is to add.)

4. Before serving, add the heavy cream and reheat, taking care not to let the soup boil. Top with toasted pecans.

— *Sarah Libertus, former Featherstone Farm CSA manager*

. . . .

STUFFED SQUASH   SERVES 2

2 acorn squash, halved and seeded
4 tablespoons butter or olive oil
1 cup chopped onion
2 stalks celery, chopped
½ cup walnuts
½ cup sunflower seeds

2 large cloves garlic, minced
1 teaspoon dried sage
1 teaspoon dried thyme
1 teaspoon dried marjoram
2 cups coarsely crumbled whole wheat bread
Juice of 1 lemon or orange
Salt and pepper
½ cup raisins or cranberries
1 cup grated Cheddar cheese

1. Preheat the oven to 375°F.

2. Oil a baking dish that can snugly fit the halved squash. Place the squash, flesh side down, on the dish and pour in 2 cups of water. Bake until it is fork-tender, about 20 minutes.

3. Meanwhile, heat the butter or oil in a frying pan and sauté the onions until they turn translucent. Add the celery, walnuts, seeds, and garlic. Cook over low heat until the nuts are browned. Add the sage, thyme, and marjoram. Stir in the breadcrumbs, juice, salt, pepper, and raisins or cranberries; then cook over low heat for 5 to 8 minutes. Remove from the pan and stir in the cheese.

4. Set the oven to 350°F. Pack the stuffing into the squash cavities and cover with aluminum foil. Bake, flesh side up, for 25 minutes. Then uncover and cook 5 to 8 minutes longer to brown.

— *Featherstone Farm*

. . . .

ROASTED SQUASH WITH POTATOES AND GARLIC

SERVES 8

The squash may be peeled if desired.

1 unpeeled acorn squash (about 1 to 1½ pounds), washed, halved, seeded, and cut into 12 equal pieces
4 to 5 medium-sized potatoes (about 2 pounds), unpeeled, washed, and quartered
4 cloves garlic, peeled and crushed
3 tablespoons olive oil
1 large sprig rosemary

1. Preheat oven to 425°F.

2. Combine the squash, potatoes, and garlic in a 9 × 13-inch shallow baking pan. Drizzle with the oil, and add salt and pepper to taste. Top with a rosemary sprig.

3. Bake 45 to 50 minutes, turning once after the vegetables are browned on one side.

— *Fruits and Veggies—More Matters; Centers for Disease Control & Prevention*

"Seventy years ago, farmers were seduced into going for mechanization and, later, the use of chemicals, because these practices gave good returns. No one could have foreseen the damage that this approach to growing food would wreak."

— *Bryan Lynas, science writer and farmer*

AUTUMN SQUASH AND CORN

SERVES 4

Butternut squash is good for this recipe because it is so sweet and easy to peel when raw. Roast chicken, pork chops, or a braised pork shoulder are excellent accompaniments.

1½ tablespoons butter
⅓ cup red bell pepper, minced
12 ounces hard-shelled squash, peeled and cut into ½-inch cubes
2 cups fresh corn kernels
Salt and freshly ground black pepper

1. Melt the butter in a heavy-bottomed 10-inch skillet over moderate heat. Add the bell pepper and sauté until it is slightly softened, about 5 minutes.

2. Add the squash and corn and toss to coat them with butter. Cover the skillet, decrease the heat to low, and cook until the squash and corn are tender, about 10 to 15 minutes. Shake the pan occasionally to keep the squash from sticking (lift the cover a few times to check). Season to taste with salt and pepper before serving.

— *Janet Fletcher*, More Vegetables, Please

BUTTERNUT SURPRISE

SERVES 4

1 butternut squash
3 tablespoons butter
1 cup small fresh or canned pineapple chunks
Parsley, finely chopped

1. Preheat the oven to 375°F.

2. Halve the butternut squash lengthwise. Scoop out the seeds and the stringy, surrounding pulp. Make several horizontal and vertical slits in the squash. Rub the butter into each squash half, place the pineapple chunks into the hollowed-out part of the squash, and sprinkle with parsley. Bake until soft (about 30 to 45 minutes). Serve immediately.

— *Nickolas Vassili*

SQUASH-APPLE CASSEROLE

SERVES 4

Besides being cholesterol-free and almost sodium-free, this dish is high in vitamin A and a good source of vitamin C.

2½ cups fresh winter squash, cut into ½-inch slices
1½ cups cooking apples, pared and cut into ½-inch slices
2 teaspoons cinnamon
1 teaspoon nutmeg

1. Preheat the oven to 350°F.

2. Alternate layers of squash and apples in an 8 × 8-inch pan, ending with apples on the top layer. Sprinkle the spices over the top layer. Cover the pan with aluminum foil and bake for approximately 45 to 60 minutes, or until the squash is tender.

3. Remove the foil and bake another 10 to 15 minutes to remove any excess liquid that might have accumulated. Cool slightly before serving.

— *Massachusetts Department of Agricultural Resources*

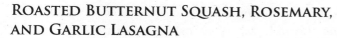

Roasted Butternut Squash, Rosemary, and Garlic Lasagna

Makes 6 main-course or 12 side-dish servings

3 pounds butternut squash, quartered, seeded, peeled, and cut into
⅓-inch dice (about 9½ cups)
3 tablespoons vegetable oil
Salt and pepper to taste
4 cups milk
2 tablespoons dried rosemary, crumbled
1 tablespoon minced garlic
½ stick (¼ cup) unsalted butter
4 tablespoons all-purpose flour
9 (7 × 3½-inch) sheets dry, no-boil lasagna pasta
1 cup heavy cream
½ teaspoon salt
1⅓ cups freshly grated Parmesan cheese (about 5 ounces)
Fresh rosemary sprigs, for garnish

1. Preheat the oven to 450°F. Oil two large shallow baking pans.

2. In a large bowl, toss the squash with oil until it is well-coated, and spread it in one layer in the pans. Roast the squash in the oven 10 minutes and season with salt and pepper. Stir the squash and roast 10 to 15 minutes more, or until it becomes tender and begins to turn golden.

3. While the squash is roasting, bring the milk to a simmer with the rosemary in a saucepan. Heat the milk mixture over low heat 10 minutes and pour through a sieve into a large pitcher or measuring cup. In a large, heavy-bottomed saucepan, cook the garlic in butter over moderately low heat, stirring, until it is softened. Stir in the flour and cook the resulting roux, constantly stirring, for 3 minutes. Remove the pan from the heat, and whisk in the milk mixture in a stream until the roux is smooth. Return the pan to the heat and simmer the sauce, whisking occasionally, about 10 minutes, or until it becomes thick. Stir in the squash and salt and pepper to taste. (The sauce may be made 3 days ahead and chilled.)

4. Lower the oven temperature to 375°F, and butter a 13 × 9 × 2-inch baking dish. Pour 1 cup of the sauce into the baking dish (note that the sauce

will not completely cover the bottom) and cover with three lasagna sheets, making sure they do not touch one another. Spread half of the remaining sauce over the pasta and sprinkle with ½ cup Parmesan cheese. Make one more layer in the same manner, beginning and ending with the pasta.

5. Place the cream in a bowl. Use an electric mixer to beat the cream with the salt until the mixture holds soft peaks. Spread the cream evenly over the top pasta layer, making sure that the pasta is completely covered. Sprinkle the remaining ⅓ cup Parmesan over the cream.

6. Cover the dish tightly with aluminum foil, tenting it slightly to prevent the foil from touching the top layer, and bake in the middle of the oven for 30 minutes. Remove the foil and bake the lasagna 10 minutes more, or until the top is bubbling and golden. Let the lasagna stand 5 minutes. Garnish each serving with a rosemary sprig.

— Gourmet, *December 1995, from Featherstone CSA member Robin Taylor*

JOHN'S WINTER SQUASH SOUP WITH VANILLA ICE CREAM

SERVES 6

8 cups winter squash (butternut or hubbard), peeled, seeded, cubed
4 tablespoons olive oil
2 cups onion, peeled and sliced
2 cups carrot, peeled and sliced
1 cup celery, sliced
1 garlic clove, minced
1 bay leaf
4 (14½-ounce) cans of chicken or vegetable stock
1 pint Ben & Jerry's vanilla ice cream
2 tablespoons chopped nuts (walnuts, almonds, pecans, etc.)
Salt and pepper to taste

1. Preheat the oven to 350°F.

2. In a large bowl, toss the squash with 2 tablespoons of the olive oil to coat. Place the squash in a roasting pan or on a sheet pan covered with foil. Place in the oven for 25 minutes.

3. Meanwhile, in a 3-quart soup pot, add the remaining olive oil and sauté the onions until translucent. Add the garlic and cook for 15 seconds more, stirring constantly to avoid burning. Add the carrots, celery, bay leaf, and chicken stock; bring to a simmer and cook uncovered for 45 minutes to 1 hour, until approximately half of the liquid has evaporated. Remove the bay leaf and discard.

4. In a blender or food processor, purée the vegetables and stock. Return the purée to the pot and add ½ pint of the ice cream. Simmer over low heat to warm the mixture thoroughly.

5. Season to taste with salt and pepper, and serve with a dollop of vanilla ice cream and some chopped nuts sprinkled over the top.

— *Ben & Jerry's Homemade Ice Cream*

Tatsoi

Tatsoi (pronounced "that-SOY") is a newcomer to the American gastronomical scene but a common fixture in Asian cuisine, especially in China, where it originated. It is a member of the cabbage family, closely related to bok choy, which it somewhat resembles in flavor and texture; it is occasionally called rosette bok choy. To add to the confusion, horticulturists sometimes classify it as a type of mustard green.

Whatever its true nomenclature, tatsoi is a most distinctive plant, with attractive, shiny, dark-green leaves that are spoon-shaped and grow in a beautifully shaped rosette. Its flavor is pleasantly vegetable, reminiscent of spinach, with a spicy hint of mustard. Its juicy leaves are usually eaten raw but can be used in stir-fries or added to soups and stews at the end of cooking.

Featherstone's tatsoi comes either whole or as small leaves added to its salad mixes.

HISTORY

Tatsoi is native to China, where it and legions of other Oriental Brassicas have been enjoyed for centuries as a cooked vegetable. The tatsoi that is gradually becoming available in the U.S. is a Japanese variant. Recently tatsoi has begun to show up in commercial prewashed salad mixes, as its sweet, mild, durable personality blends well with other greens.

NUTRITION

Like all Brassicas, tatsoi is an extremely nutritious green, an excellent source of vitamins C and E, fiber, folate, calcium, iron, magnesium, potassium, and B6.

SELECTION

Its leaves should be fresh and intact, with no signs of yellowing or wilting.

STORAGE

Tatsoi is not the most durable of vegetables and should be used within a few days. Store tightly wrapped and unwashed in the refrigerator vegetable crisper.

TRIMMING & CLEANING

Like all ground-level vegetables, tatsoi benefits from a thorough washing to remove dirt and insects. If the head is small enough, submerge the entire rosette in a sinkful of water, swish, and rinse. If the rosette is too large, first cut it into sections, or pull off and rinse individual leaves briefly.

STEAMING & BOILING

Steaming is a gentle way of cooking that brings out the best in tatsoi without making it too watery. Place detached leaves or small halved or quartered bunches in a vegetable steamer and cook for about 5 minutes. Or place a whole small head of tatsoi in a steamer basket or rack inside a larger pot filled with 1 inch of water brought to a boil.

Stir-Frying & Sautéing

Tatsoi should be added to stir-fries only near the very end of cooking (within the last 2 minutes or so) and sautéed only until it just wilts but is still crisp. Small bunches can be halved or quartered and stir-fried without detaching the leaves.

Microwaving

Nuking tatsoi is simplicity itself. Place the leaves in a microwave-safe dish or zipper-lock freezer bag and add about ½ inch of water. Either cover lightly with a paper towel or leave an opening in the bag and microwave on High power for 5 to 7 minutes, or until tender.

Blanching & Freezing

Because of its high water content, freezing is not recommended for tatsoi.

Complementary Herbs, Seasonings & Foods

Bok choy, chicken, chiles, fish, garlic, ginger, mushrooms, onions, oyster sauce, scallops, sesame, shallots, shrimp.

Serving Suggestions

- Serve the tender young leaves raw, tossed with a little vinaigrette dressing.
- Shred the leaves into fine strips and sprinkle them with finely diced mushrooms on top of miso soup.
- Stir-fry tatsoi with a bit of sesame oil and soy sauce.
- Tatsoi can be used as a substitute for baby or frozen spinach in many recipes. Try experimenting!
- Mushrooms and tatsoi make an irresistible combination, with their meaty textures and robust flavors. Try sliced portabellas, oyster mushrooms, or porcinis.
- Lightly stir-fry or steam tatsoi, toss in a reduced savory sauce, and use the leaves as a bed for roast chicken, pork loin, filet mignon, braised lamb, or a fine fish.

Tender Tatsoi with Sesame Oil Vinaigrette   SERVES 4

8 cups tender tatsoi leaves or other salad greens
2 scallions, including some of the greens, thinly sliced
1 tablespoon thinly sliced garlic chives or regular chives
1 tablespoon toasted sesame seeds

Sesame Oil Vinaigrette

2 teaspoons rice vinegar
2 tablespoons sesame oil
1 tablespoon dark sesame oil

Books

Local Flavors: Cooking and Eating from America's Farmers' Markets
Deborah Madison;
Broadway Books, 2002.

Greens Glorious Greens: More Than 140 Ways to Prepare All Those Great-Tasting, Super-Healthy, Beautiful Leafy Greens
Johnna Albi and Catherine Walthers; St. Martin's Griffin, 1996.

Vegetarian Cooking for Everyone
Deborah Madison;
Broadway Books, 1997.

½ teaspoon sea salt

1. Sort through the greens; then trim, wash, and dry them well. Toss the greens with the scallions and chives.

2. To make the vinaigrette: In another bowl, whisk together the vinegar, oils, and salt. Taste the dressing on a leaf and adjust the oil or vinegar if necessary.

3. Pour the dressing over the salad, toss well, add the sesame seeds, toss again, and serve.

— *Deborah Madison,* Vegetarian Cooking for Everyone

. . . .

FARMERS MARKET GREEN SALAD WITH FRIED SHALLOTS
SERVES 6

Although we used Asian greens and radish sprouts for our salad, we encourage you to explore your local farmers market and use whatever small young greens (baby spinach, arugula, or watercress, for example) and other fresh goodies you find. For more information about mizuna, see pages 131–134.

½ pound shallots
1½ cups vegetable oil for frying
6 ounces mizuna
6 ounces tatsoi (about 6 cups total of mixed greens, loosely packed)
⅓ cup radish sprouts
1 tablespoon white-wine vinegar
Sea salt to taste

1. Cut the shallots into ⅛-inch-thick slices. In a heavy-bottomed 10-inch skillet, cook the shallots in oil over moderate heat, stirring occasionally, until they turn golden, 15 to 20 minutes. With a slotted spoon, transfer the shallots to paper towels to drain and season with salt. Reserve 3 tablespoons of the oil for dressing the salad, and cool the shallots to room temperature. (The shallots may be fried 2 days ahead and kept in an airtight container at room temperature.)

2. Just before serving, toss together the greens, sprouts, reserved oil, vinegar, and sea salt in a large bowl. Sprinkle the shallots over the salad.

— Gourmet, *June 1999, as appeared on Epicurious.com*

. . . .

MISO BROTH WITH TATSOI-ENOKI SALAD
SERVES 4

A paste made from aged, fermented, salted soybeans, miso is one of the staple flavorings in Japanese cuisine. Shinshu or golden miso is a milder, lighter-colored variety that imparts a mellow, salty flavor.
Dashi is another essential ingredient in the Japanese kitchen—a soup

stock made from dried bonito tuna flakes and kombu, a variety of sea-weed. Wasabi, or Japanese horseradish, is powerfully pungent and comes either as a paste or in powdered form, to be combined with water and used much like dry mustard.

Enoki mushrooms grow in clumps, their tiny caps sprouting forth on long, delicate, sphaghetti-like stems. Unlike most fungi, enokis are appealingly crunchy when raw, with a somewhat fruity flavor, making them a wonderful last-minute addition to cooked dishes or salads.

Miso, dashi, wasabi, and enoki are all available in Asian markets and some gourmet supermarkets, or through online retailers.

¼ cup yellow miso (shinshu miso)
4 cups dashi
2 slices fresh ginger
1 tablespoon rice wine vinegar
½ tablespoon wasabi powder
½ tablespoon soy sauce
2 tablespoons sliced scallions, green parts only
½ teaspoon sugar
1 packet enoki mushrooms
2 cups tatsoi leaves
1 block of soft tofu, cut into ¼-inch slices

1. To make the broth, mix the miso with the dashi, and add the ginger. Bring the broth to a simmer over medium heat. Let simmer for 5 minutes, then remove the ginger.

2. In a small bowl, make a paste with the vinegar and wasabi. Whisk in the soy sauce, scallions, and sugar. Check for seasoning. Toss the vinaigrette with the enoki and tatsoi.

3. To serve, gently place one slice of the tofu into each soup bowl, and ladle the broth over the top. Place a small mound of salad on top of the tofu.

— www.fooddownunder.com

Winter

❄ DURING THE MIDWEST WINTER MONTHS OF DECEMBER THROUGH MARCH, A SURPRISING AMOUNT OF FARM PRODUCE IS AVAILABLE. IN ADDITION TO WHATEVER FRUITS OF SUMMER WE HAVE PRESERVED IN THE FREEZER, DEHYDRATOR, AND CANNER, A NUMBER OF CROPS STORE WELL. OTHERS CAN EVEN BE HARVESTED IN THE DEPTHS OF JANUARY AND FEBRUARY.

MANY SALAD CROPS—SPINACH, ARUGULA, AND EVEN SOME LETTUCES—ARE REMARKABLY TOLERANT TO COLD, PARTICULARLY WHEN THEY ARE YOUNG. IN A WELL-INSULATED, PROTECTED SITE INSIDE A LARGE GREENHOUSE, THE LIMITING FACTOR FOR GROWTH OF SUCH CROPS IS NOT COLD BUT LIGHT. THERE IS SIMPLY NOT ENOUGH SOLAR ENERGY DURING THE SHORT DAYS OF WINTER TO FUEL LIFE-SUSTAINING PHOTOSYNTHESIS. BUT A CLEVER SYSTEM CAN OVERCOME THIS.

Winter Crops Featured

Cabbage
Garlic
Onions
Turnips

At Featherstone, we plant lettuces, spinach, and other crops in beds on the greenhouse floors in late September. These crops grow slowly all fall and reach a harvestable size sometime in November, when they cease developing. At this point they are double-covered with floating row cover (imagine very thin bed sheets hundreds of feet long) and effectively "stored" in the ground for winter harvest. The well-known greenhouse effect keeps the ground from freezing in all but the very coldest weather, and a single sunny winter afternoon warms it up enough to pull off the row cover and harvest a wonderful salad.

Unfortunately our space for this kind of production is very limited, and crops cannot be replanted during the season. We know already on the first of November how much (or little!) we will harvest in this way all winter. For this reason, fresh Featherstone salads are available only through the special winter CSA program.

Winter storage crops can also provide wonderful sustenance well into early spring, if properly handled. In fact, the eating quality will actually improve in many cases, as starches are converted to sugars when fruits, bulbs, and tubers cure in storage. Cooking onions that in August were too acrid to cut without adequate ventilation become fantastically mellow by midwinter. *Cucurbita maxima*-type squashes (buttercup, kabocha, and the like) now have developed a deep sweetness and richness that is completely absent in the first harvest.

Featherstone grows lots of cabbage to store for sale to food co-ops right into January (large producers in the upper Midwest often store this crop into April). One year we were trimming up heads of cabbage from our storage cooler with a fellow from a local organic restaurant. We were munching on wedges of cut cabbages, months out of the field, commenting on their remarkable sweetness and vitality. "It's like a sugar snap pea in June!" Gionno remarked, and he was not overstating it.

The principle of storage crops—carrots and beets, squash and cabbage, leeks and onions and potatoes, and many others is the same—if the crop is harvested at peak quality and stored in the right conditions, it can be every bit as good months later … and even better!

FARMER'S TABLE MENU — WINTER
— UP TO MARCH 15 —

BY JACK HEDIN

SOUP
French Onion Soup

ENTRÉE
Pork Chops with Applesauce
Root Vegetable Medley

ON THE SIDE
Steamed Cabbage with Carrots

DESSERT
Shortcake with Frozen Strawberries

At this time of the year, making enough varied meals with the stored vegetables from fall is admittedly more difficult, and I find myself eating lots of frozen and California produce. Nevertheless, it is possible to make a fine supper with winter vegetables, even if you have not had the time to freeze and can back in the summer. This menu is an example.

Roasted root crops are a particular favorite around our house. Chop the potatoes and other roots (parsnips are the real star) in ¼-inch cubes, and toss with a bit of olive oil mixed with salt, pepper, and dried herbs (I prefer thyme and parsley) until everything is slightly coated. Spread the vegetables on a cookie sheet in a single layer and bake in the oven at 375°F to 400°F for 40 minutes, flipping them occasionally to avoid burning.

Winter Crops Available

Cabbage (late winter to February)
Green and Red Head, Napa, Savoy
Garlic
German Red, Porcelain White
Onions (Storage and cured)
Copra, Mars
Potatoes (Cured for storage through January)
All Blue, Bintje, Desiree Pink, Langlade White, Red Norland, Romance, Russian Fingerling, Yukon Gold
Squash (Winter)
Acorn, Butternut, Carnival, Heart of Gold, Kabocha/Buttercup, Red Kuri, Spaghetti, Sweet Dumpling
Turnips

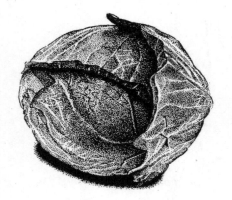

Cabbage

BRASSICA OLERACEA,
CAPITATA GROUP

Often disliked for its strong smell when cooking and regarded as a poor person's food, cabbage is one vegetable desperately in need of a public relations spin doctor. Despite its humble profile, cabbage is one of the most versatile vegetables around, eaten raw, cooked, and pickled in cuisines around the world.

Featherstone grows both the familiar head cabbage in red and green colors, and the napa cabbage, which resembles romaine lettuce with its oblong head and loosely packed, wrinkled, light-green leaves on wide, white stems. Napa cabbage (sometimes called Chinese cabbage) has a sweeter, milder flavor than its head cousins, making it a good alternative for diners who prefer a less potent cruciferous presence in their food.

HISTORY

Cabbage is one of humankind's earliest foods, but some skepticism exists as to where it originated. The ancient Romans enjoyed it, but it seems unlikely that such a cool-weather-loving plant would be native to the toasty Mediterranean climate. Perhaps the Celts introduced it from northern Europe to the southern portions of the continent around 600 B.C.E., and possibly to Asia about 300 years later. The savoy variety was developed in Italy in the 1500s. Cabbages were almost certainly brought to North America by the earliest European colonists.

NUTRITION

Cabbage is one of the most nutritious vegetables around, packing formidable amounts of vitamins C, K, and folate, as well as dietary fiber, vitamins B2 and B6, phosphorus, potassium, and manganese. Like other cruciferous vegetables, cabbage contains abundant phytonutrients, such as sulforaphane and indoles, which have proven in studies to fight cancer, especially prostate, colorectal, and lung.

SELECTION

With head cabbage, choose firm, tightly packed heads with uniform color and a heavy weight for their size. Large yellowish areas on the outer leaves may signal that the cabbage is old or has not been properly stored. Napa cabbage should have compact heads with tightly closed, crisp leaves with no signs of yellow or brown.

STORAGE

To help cabbage stay fresh longer, do not wash it until you are ready to use it. Store cabbage in the refrigerator vegetable crisper. Avoid slicing or shredding cabbage in advance as this will cause it to lose some of its vitamin C. Napa cabbage should be kept in a plastic bag as it tends to absorb odors; it will keep for 4 to 5 days. Most head cabbages will keep for 1 week to 10 days, but their flavor and aroma may increase as they become older.

If you must prepare cabbage an hour or more in advance before cooking, place it in a plastic bag, seal tightly, and refrigerate in the vegetable crisper until ready to use. If you do cut into the head, cover it with plastic for storage.

TRIMMING & CLEANING

For head cabbage, strip off the outer leaves if they are wilted or yellowing. If you are not shredding the cabbage, cut it into wedges, excluding the tough central core, which is often bitter. If you want to keep the outer leaves intact for wrapping or stuffing, first remove the central core and boil the entire head for 1 to 2 minutes to make it easier to peel off the leaves.

STEAMING & BOILING

Steaming cabbage leaves it less waterlogged than boiling. Head cabbage can be steamed for about 20 minutes, if you like it with a little crunch, or longer if you prefer it more tender. The more tender napa and savoy varieties do not need to steam as long as head cabbage, about 10 to 12 minutes.

Cabbage has a bad rap because it is often overcooked, which releases more of the vegetable's sulfurous compounds and makes it strong-smelling.

STIR-FRYING & SAUTÉING

Napa cabbage takes well to a quick stir-fry; just shred and cook it in a heated, oiled wok on medium heat for about 2 to 3 minutes, or until wilted but still crisp-tender. Green or red cabbages, cut into ½-inch ribbons, may need a little longer, depending on their toughness and age.

BAKING & ROASTING

Cabbage can be tasty sliced and combined in a casserole dish with other vegetables, bacon or other meat, seasonings, topped with butter, covered with aluminum foil, and baked for 30 to 40 minutes in a 325°F oven.

BLANCHING & FREEZING

As with almost all vegetables, cabbage must be blanched before freezing. Coarsely shred it, submerge in rapidly boiling water for 2 minutes, and then immediately chill it in an ice-water bath to stop the cooking. Drain and pack it tightly in zipper-lock freezer or vacuum food sealer-type bags, or freezer containers. Squeeze out excess air and leave ½ inch of headspace (unless you are using the vacuum sealing method). It will keep for up to 1 year.

MICROWAVING

Chop or shred, add 2 tablespoons water, place in a microwave-safe dish, and cook on High power.

- 2 cups = 5 to 7 minutes (chopped or shredded)
- 4 cups = 6 to 8 minutes (chopped or shredded)

MEASURES & EQUIVALENTS

Head or Savoy Cabbage
- 1 medium head cabbage = about 2 pounds = 4 servings

Cooking Tip

The cylindrical shape of Napa cabbage makes it naturally easy to cut up: Position the cabbage horizontally, cut off the top, then proceed to make thin cuts down the body of the cabbage.

This will produce a perfect shred for salads or stir-fries. Cut only the amount that you need and loosely wrap the rest in plastic wrap. This cabbage should stay fresh for up to 2 weeks in your crisper.

Cooking Tip

Red cabbage will often turn an unappetizing blue while cooking because the compound that gives it its characteristic hue, anthocyanin, reacts with akaline minerals in tap water.

To bring back its red color, add a little lemon juice or vinegar (a teaspoon may be enough), or cook the red cabbage with something acidic, like apples.

- 1 medium raw cabbage = 4 cups raw shredded
- 1 pound raw shredded = 9 to 10 servings raw
- 2 pounds head cabbage = about 10 cups shredded
- 1 pound raw cabbage = 2 cups cooked = 4 servings cooked
- ¼ pound cooked cabbage = 1 serving

Napa Cabbage
- 1 head = 6 cups shredded

Complementary Herbs, Seasonings & Foods

Apples, bacon, béchamel sauce, beef, beets, black pepper, butter, caraway seeds, carrots, celery root, celery seed, chervil, chicken, chiles, chives, coconut, corned beef, cream, dill weed, garlic, ginger, ham, horseradish, leeks, lemon, lime, mustard, nutmeg, olive oil, onions, parsley, pepper, pork, potatoes, sausage, savory, sesame, soy sauce, spinach, tarragon, thyme, tofu, vinegar.

Serving Suggestions

- Try cutting up small wedges of raw cabbage and serve with your favorite dip or salad dressing. Kids especially love eating cabbage (and many other raw veggies this way).
- Try baking cabbage with cheese at 350°F for 30 to 40 minutes for an unusual vegetable treat.
- Stuffed cabbage dishes abound around the world. Some delicious fillings include bacon and onions, ground beef, sausage, lamb, tomatoes, mushrooms, and sauerkraut.
- Braise red cabbage with apples, a little red wine, and cinnamon or cloves.
- Cabbage is one of the staples of the New England boiled dinner, where it is cooked with corned beef, potatoes, carrots, and onions.
- Napa cabbage is ideal for stir-fries; cut it into strips and toss in with garlic and ginger.
- Thinly shred napa cabbage and add to very hot, clear beef or chicken broth. Sprinkle with soy sauce and top with tofu, thinly sliced mushrooms, and scallions for a delicate soup.

PASTA WITH SAVOY CABBAGE AND GRUYÈRE
SERVES 4

An inexpensive and simple dish with a surprising texture and flavor. The cabbage is cooked so that it has plenty of "bite" to it, contrasting with the softness of the pasta.

1 ounce butter
1 small savoy or green cabbage, thinly sliced
1 small onion, chopped
12 ounces pasta (such as tagliatelle, fettucine, or penne)
1 tablespoon chopped fresh parsley
⅔ cup light cream
2 ounces Gruyère or Cheddar cheese, grated
About 1¼ cups hot vegetable or chicken stock
Salt and freshly ground black pepper

That's a Lot of Vinegar
Americans consume about 387 million pounds of sauerkraut annually.

1. Preheat the oven to 350°F and butter a large casserole. Place the cabbage in a mixing bowl.

2. Melt the butter in a small pan and fry the onion until it softens. Stir the onions into the cabbage in the bowl.

3. Cook the pasta according to the package instructions, until al dente. Drain well and stir into the bowl with the cabbage and onion. Add the parsley, mix well, and then pour the mixture into the prepared casserole.

4. Beat together the cream and Gruyère or Cheddar cheese, and then stir them into the hot stock. Season well and pour over the cabbage and pasta, so that the sauce comes about half way up the casserole. (If necessary, add a little more stock.)

5. Cover tightly and cook in the oven for 30 to 35 minutes, until the cabbage is tender and the stock is bubbling. Remove the lid during the last 5 minutes of the cooking time to brown the top.

— *Christine Ingram,* The Cook's Encyclopedia of Vegetables

ASIAN FUSION SLAW
SERVES 6 TO 8

This has become a staple in my potluck repertoire. It is easy and beautiful and offers a fresh twist to a classic.

DRESSING

½ cup vegetable oil
2 tablespoons toasted sesame oil
¼ cup rice vinegar
1½ tablespoons finely minced fresh ginger
2 teaspoons soy sauce

SLAW

6 cups shredded napa cabbage, thinly sliced
2 bell peppers, sliced into sticks
1 bunch green onions, finely chopped
Salt
1 cup chopped salted peanuts
1 cup minced cilantro

1. Mix the dressing ingredients in a small bowl.

2. In a big bowl, toss together the cabbages, peppers, and onions. Pour the dressing over the cabbage, and toss. Salt to taste.

3. Add the peanuts and cilantro right before serving. This salad tastes better the second day, but wait with sprinkling the peanuts on until just before serving, or else they will soak up the oil and get soft.

— *Sarah Libertus, former Featherstone CSA manager*

TACHIYAMA CHANKO-NABE (TACHIYAMA'S BEEF AND CHICKEN HOT POT)
SERVES 4

Nabe is Japanese for a hearty, one-dish meal traditionally made for sumo wrestlers to keep up their strength and need for lots of nourishing calories. Authentic nabe is cooked at the table on a portable stove and eaten communally. However, it can also be cooked entirely in the kitchen and then served at the table.

Daikon radish, mirin, abura-age, yaki-dofu, shiitake and shimeji mushrooms, burdock root, chrysanthemum greens, and udon noodles can all be found in Asian markets, some food co-ops or health food stores, or sometimes in the ethnic sections of larger American supermarkets. You can also find them through online retailers.

3 pounds chicken bones
1 (2.8-ounce) package abura-age (deep-fried tofu), cut into large pieces
1 clove garlic, peeled
¼ cup soy sauce
2 tablespoons mirin (sweet rice wine)
Salt
1 medium-sized waxy potato, peeled, quartered lengthwise, sliced crosswise, and blanched
2-inch piece daikon radish, peeled, quartered lengthwise, sliced crosswise, and blanched
1 small carrot, trimmed, peeled, sliced on the bias, and blanched
1 leek, white part only, trimmed, washed, and sliced on the bias
¼ head napa cabbage, cored and cut into large pieces
4 shiitake mushrooms, stemmed
4 ounces shimeji mushrooms, trimmed and separated
4 ounces fresh burdock root, trimmed, peeled, and shaved into long, thin strips

10 ounces yaki-dofu (grilled tofu), halved lengthwise and cut into
    ½-inch-thick pieces
½ pound boneless chicken thighs, cut into thin strips
½ bunch chrysanthemum greens, trimmed
½ pound very thinly sliced prime rib eye of beef
1 pound udon noodles
4 raw eggs (optional)

1. Bring a medium-sized pot of water to boil over high heat. Place the
   chicken bones and fried tofu in two separate colanders set in the sink.
   Pour two-thirds of the boiling water over the bones to rinse off any
   impurities, and the remaining boiling water over the tofu to rinse off
   excess oil. Transfer the bones to the medium-sized pot and set the
   tofu aside to drain.

2. Add the garlic and 14 cups of cold water to the pot with the bones.
   Bring to a boil over high heat, skimming away any foam that rises to
   the surface. Decrease the heat to medium-low and simmer until the
   broth has reduced by one-third, about 2½ hours. Strain the broth
   into a clean, wide, medium-sized pot, discarding the solids and skimming off the fat.

3. At the table, set the pot on a portable stove in the center of the table.
   Add the soy sauce and mirin, season to taste with salt, and bring the
   broth to a simmer over medium heat. Add about one-third of the
   potatoes, daikon, carrots, leeks, cabbage, mushrooms, burdock, grilled
   tofu, chicken, fried tofu, and chrysanthemum greens to the simmering
   broth, and cook until the vegetables begin to soften and the chicken
   is just cooked through, about 5 minutes. Add about one-third of the
   beef and simmer until it is just cooked through, about 1 minute.

4. The hot pot is now ready to be eaten "self-serve" style in small bowls.
   Add more of the remaining vegetables, tofu, chicken, greens, and beef
   to the pot of broth as it is depleted.

5. Once all of the vegetables, tofu, chicken, greens, and beef have been
   eaten, use a small sieve to pick out scraps. Bring the remaining broth
   in the pot back to a simmer; then add the noodles and simmer until
   they are cooked through, 6 to 8 minutes. Serve in individual bowls,
   with a raw egg cracked into the broth, if desired.

— Saveur, *December 2002*

- -

DILLED CABBAGE WITH HAM   SERVES 4 TO 6

2 smallish cabbages, about 2 pounds each
½ pound smoked ham, cooked and cut into julienne pieces
6 tablespoons butter
½ cup finely chopped fresh dill
½ teaspoon freshly ground pepper
Salt

in the hot sun!") But I would do it again in an instant. There is nothing quite like sleeping in a cabin without electricity, or riding in the back of a flatbed truck with seven Mexican guys and 1,678 ears of freshly picked sweet corn (I counted) to set one's priorities straight.

And although some days were hot and the labor could be hard, none of the days were long, despite many hours of cleaning onions and boxing tomatoes. It was during these times that could really think about my life goals. I was always shocked at the end of the day by how quickly time passed.

So now, after two weeks, I find it difficult to leave this land, these people, and this way of life that I find so comforting and rich. I have certainly learned something about organic farming, but maybe I have also learned something about myself, and not just that I am an avocado.

So if you feel the need to examine your life and reevaluate your goals, I recommend that you visit Featherstone Farm and while you are there, ask yourself: What kind of produce are you?

1. Wash and section the cabbages. Cook them in boiling salted water until they just crisp-tender. Drain, chop very finely, and combine with the ham, butter, and dill.

2. Season to taste and reheat if necessary. Serve in a heated serving dish.

— *James Beard,* James Beard's American Cookery

. . . .

ABIDJAN CABBAGE SALAD

SERVES 6

4 cups thinly sliced cabbage
1 cup shredded carrot
1 cup pineapple chunks

DRESSING

Juice of 1 lemon
Juice of 1 orange
¼ teaspoon salt
⅓ cup vegetable oil

1. Place the cabbage, carrot, and pineapple in a large bowl.

2. Mix the dressing by whisking all of the ingredients together until creamy, or by drizzling the oil and salt into the lemon and orange juices while mixing in a blender.

3. Thoroughly blend the dressing and the vegetables. Refrigerate or serve immediately.

— *www.fooddownunder.com*

. . . .

BEER-SIMMERED CABBAGE ROLLS

SERVES 6

1 head cabbage (large enough to provide 12 large leaves)
5 quarts boiling water
1 pound lean ground beef
1 cup cooked rice
¼ cup chopped onion
½ cup finely chopped celery
2 eggs, well-beaten
1 teaspoon salt
¼ teaspoon ground black pepper
8 ounces canned tomato sauce
¼ cup cider vinegar
½ cup firmly packed brown sugar
2 cups beer (or condensed beef broth)

1. Core the cabbage and carefully remove its large outer leaves, reserving 12 of them; wash the leaves. Place them in a large bowl, and pour

"Cabbages, whose heads, tightly folded see and hear nothing of this world, dreaming only on the yellow and green magnificence that is hardening within them."

— *John Haines,*
American poet

enough boiling water over them to cover. Let the leaves stand 5 minutes, or until they become flexible.

2. In a large bowl, combine the ground beef, rice, onion, celery, eggs, salt, and pepper. Mix well. Drain the cabbage leaves. Divide the meat mixture evenly to make 12 balls, using about ¼ cup meat mixture for each ball. Place 1 ball on each leaf. Wrap the leaf tightly around the meat to enclose it. Then fasten the ends with toothpicks.

3. In a large skillet, combine the tomato sauce, vinegar, brown sugar, and 1½ cups of the beer; mix well. Place the rolls in a skillet. Cover, and simmer them slowly for about 1 hour, adding more beer as needed.

— *www.fooddownunder.com*

. . . .

WARM RED CABBAGE BACON SALAD   SERVES 4

3 slices reduced-fat turkey bacon
1½ tablespoons olive oil
½ large onion, peeled and chopped
3 large stalks celery, sliced
⅓ cup cider vinegar
3 tablespoons sugar
½ teaspoon celery seed
½ large red cabbage, shredded to yield about 6 cups
Salt and pepper (optional)
2 tablespoons chopped parsley, for garnish

1. Cut the bacon slices into 1-inch pieces and sauté them over medium-low heat in a very large, deep skillet until they are crisp but not overdone. Remove them to absorbent paper and reserve. Drain off all of the bacon fat from the pan, wipe clean, and replace with olive oil.

2. Heat the oil in the skillet over high heat. Add the onion and celery and sauté briefly. Add the vinegar, sugar, and celery seed. Heat until the mixture boils, then immediately add the cabbage and bacon pieces all at once. Stir and toss for about 1 minute, or until the cabbage is warm but not cooked. Season with salt and pepper, if desired.

3. Serve the salad immediately while it is still very warm, with a garnish of chopped parsley.

— *Fruits and Veggies—More Matters; Centers for Disease Control & Prevention*

. . . .

SPICY CABBAGE   SERVES 16

I don't know what it is with me and pickles, but I love them. This recipe reminds me of a trip to Korea and all of the kimchi eaten there. Unlike that ubiquitous Korean accompaniment, this pickled cabbage is not

*"I wonder if the cabbage knows
He is less lovely than the Rose;
Or does he squat in smug content,
A source of noble nourishment;
Or if he pities for her sins
The Rose who has no vitamins;
Or if the one thing his green heart
knows—
That self-same fire that warms the
Rose?"*

— Anonymous

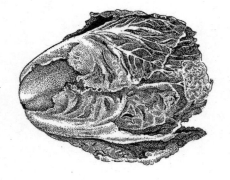

nearly as pungent, although the small Asian-style chiles do give this recipe a kick. You could expand the pickle by adding carrots, diakons (mild Asian radishes), and cucumbers.

1 head green head cabbage or napa cabbage (about 2 pounds)
2 to 3 red bird's-eye chiles, seeded and diced
1 (3-inch-long) piece of fresh ginger, peeled and julienned
1 tablespoon turmeric, ground
½ cup cilantro leaves, chopped
4 cloves garlic, chopped
2 teaspoons Thai fish sauce
1 cup rice vinegar
⅛ cup soy sauce

1. Cut the cabbage into eighths and remove the core. Place it in a 1-gallon glass or ceramic container with a nonmetallic lid. (If you use a plastic container, you will never get the smell of this pickle out of it, so be prepared to dedicate that container to this recipe.)

2. In a 4-cup saucepan, bring all of the other ingredients to a boil over medium heat, and simmer for 10 minutes. Pour this hot mixture over the cabbage.

3. Cover and store in the refrigerator for 3 days to 1 week before you start to enjoy it. It will last about 1 to 2 months.

— Richard Ruben, The Farmer's Market Cookbook

. . . .

COLESLAW   SERVES 6 TO 8

This is the coleslaw served at the famous Driesbach's Restaurant in Grand Island, Nebraska. Very tasty!

¾ cup Miracle Whip salad dressing
½ cup grated carrots
3 ounces half-and-half
3 tablespoons sugar
¾ head green cabbage, shredded
½ cup red cabbage, shredded
½ teaspoon celery seed
Salt and pepper to taste

Combine everything and toss well.

— Shirley Holt, The Schoenleber Family Cookbook

. . . .

COLCANNON   SERVES 3 TO 4

3 medium potatoes, peeled, cooked, and cubed
½ cup plain nonfat yogurt

4 cups chopped green cabbage, steamed until tender
3 to 4 leeks, cleaned, chopped, and steamed until tender
3 tablespoons chopped chives
¾ teaspoon salt
¼ teaspoon ground pepper
Pinch of ground nutmeg
2 teaspoons butter

1. Preheat the oven to 350°F. Spray a 1½-quart casserole with nonstick cooking spray.

2. In a large bowl, combine the potatoes and yogurt. With an electric mixer set at low speed, beat until the potatoes are fairly smooth; stir in the cabbage, leeks, chives, salt, pepper, and nutmeg, mixing well.

3. Transfer the mixture to the casserole and dot with butter. Bake until it is lightly browned, about 30 minutes.

— *Featherstone Farm*

Cabbage beds on the ridge.

Garlic

Few plants attract such polarizing opinions as garlic. Whether you consider it a delectable flavor or a rambunctious stink bomb, garlic is used almost universally in the world's cuisines. Garlic is the most pungent member of the large Allium family, which includes such kitchen favorites as onions, leeks, shallots, and chives.

Garlic, as most of us are familiar with, is actually the plant's mature bulb, which consists of numerous cloves. The very young and tender shoots, stems, and flower buds that emerge from the sprouting cloves in early spring can be eaten in season as the "green garlic," "scapes," or "whistles" that are such a fleeting favorite in farmers markets.

Garlic is classified as either hardneck or softneck, and literally hundreds of varieties exist, with bulbs whose personalities range from soft and mellow to very spicy and pungent. Hardnecks produce flower spikes, tend to be mild in flavor, grow well in northern climates, contain six to eleven cloves per bulb, and can be stored for three to six months. Softneck varieties (sometimes known as braiding garlic) usually lack flower spikes, have a spicier taste, thrive in warmer climates, contain twelve to twenty cloves per bulb, and can be stored up to a year.

Featherstone grows two hardneck varieties, German Red and Porcelain White. These are both picked in late July, then cured and sold dry in August to keep through the winter. Harvesting garlic calls for digging the bulb out of the ground, and Featherstone uses a tractor to cut the roots below the garlic bulbs. Then the crew pulls up each garlic plant, shakes out the dirt, and piles the garlic on a wagon for transport to the barn. The garlic then gets trimmed, cleaned, and bunched by hand, and hung to cure in a dark place.

HISTORY

Garlic's exact origin is unclear, although many sources list Asia as its homeland. References to it exist in so many ancient cultures and cuisines that it is impossible to be certain where it was first enjoyed by humans. (Not helping is the fact that it may have been confused with its Allium sibling, the leek.) Over the ages, garlic has been adored and shunned, and whether you were a garlic lover or hater often depended on your socio-economic and geographical status. Southern Europeans, especially in Italy and Provence, France, practically lived on it, while northern Europeans found it distasteful. The Greeks treated it as an important vegetable in its own right, and Egyptian pyramid builders ate it as part of their food rations. Garlic was probably brought to America from the Old World by the Spaniards, but American Indians likely had been consuming their own native wild garlic for centuries.

NUTRITION

Garlic is legendary for its nutritional and medicinal benefits, which hu-

306   WINTER — GARLIC   TASTES FROM VALLEY TO BLUFF

mans have been employing for centuries. The sulfurous compounds that give garlic its characteristic odor also have healthful benefits, especially allicin, which is released in greater amounts when the garlic is chopped or mashed rather than left whole. Regular garlic consumption may lower blood pressure and reduce the buildup of atherosclerotic plaques and the incidence of certain cancers. Both garlic and onions contain significant anti-inflammatory and antibacterial properties, even against antibiotic-resistant strains. Garlic is also a good source of manganese, vitamin B6, vitamin C, trytophan, and selenium.

Esteban trims and cleans garlic to prepare it for curing.

SELECTION

Choose bulbs that are fresh, dry, and plump, with unbroken skins. Squeeze the bulbs lightly to check that they are firm, with no large gaps beneath the skin, which could mean shriveled, dehydrated garlic well past its prime.

STORAGE

You can keep garlic in the refrigerator or continue to cure it by storing it in a dry, dark, well-ventilated place. Moisture and light will trigger the bulb to sprout. Although sprouting garlic is still edible, it tends to be bitter and less digestible. Whole garlic bulbs can keep from 2 weeks to several months, depending on the variety and storage conditions.

They will also keep quite well in a basement, root cellar, or other place with the proper cool temperature and lack of humidity (for more information, see "Preserving the Bounty" on page 331).

TRIMMING & CLEANING

Before you can use garlic, you must first separate and peel the cloves from the bulb, unless you plan to roast the bulbs whole. To do this, place the clove flat side down on a hard surface, then firmly press or rock the blade of a wide knife against the clove to split the skin. Then you can use either your fingers or a smaller knife to peel off the skin. Sometimes

Allicin Lives Here After All

The compound that gives garlic its pungency (and many of its health benefits) is allicin, which whole garlic does not actually contain. What forms it is alliin and the enzyme allinase, which garlic hoards in different cells. When the garlic clove is crushed, these compounds combine to form the allicin.

Waiting a few minutes after chopping, mashing, or crushing garlic before cooking with it increases the allicin production (and also its flavor).

peeling the cloves is easier if the very tips from both ends are sliced off.

STEAMING & BOILING

Peeled and sliced garlic cloves can be dropped into soups, stews, or other cooked dishes. The degree of garlic flavor you want dictates the cooking time and how finely sliced the cloves are; the longer garlic cooks, the more mellow and less pungent it will be in the finished dish. Finely chopped or mashed garlic will taste much stronger than unbroken cloves. Whole garlic cloves require about 20 to 25 minutes of rapid boiling to become a mild, sweet vegetable.

STIR-FRYING & SAUTÉING

Garlic is delicious stir-fried and sautéed, but care must be taken so it does not burn, or it turns unpleasantly bitter. Always use plenty of cooking oil or butter when stir-frying or sautéing garlic; chicken broth can also be used when the pan becomes too dry, or if you are watching calories. Warm up a wok or frying pan over medium-high heat, add 1 or 2 tablespoons of oil, add the chopped fresh garlic, and stir-fry for about a minute, or until it becomes fragrant, before adding the rest of your ingredients.

BAKING & ROASTING

Garlic responds wonderfully to slow roasting and baking in the oven, losing its pungency and becoming sweet and mellow. You can easily prepare a whole bulb by cutting off its top to expose the cloves and then placing the head in a baking dish or wrapping it in aluminum foil. Sprinkle with olive oil or butter, if desired, then bake at 350°F for about an hour. When done, gently squeeze the soft, roasted garlic directly over toasted French bread, or scoop out the flesh with a knife and spread over the food of your choice. Delicious!

MICROWAVING

Passable roasted garlic can be prepared in the microwave: Just cut off the tips from whole garlic heads, add the heads along with ⅓ cup of chicken broth and 3 tablespoons of olive oil in a microwave-safe dish (glass absorbs fewer odors than plastic), cover tightly with microwave plastic wrap, and cook on High power for 6 to 8 minutes. Let stand, covered, for 10 minutes, and peel the cloves after they have cooled.

To microwave peeled garlic, place cloves in a microwave-safe glass dish with enough chicken broth or water to submerge them. Cover the dish with plastic wrap and microwave on High power for about 5 to 10 minutes, or until the garlic is soft.

BLANCHING & FREEZING

Garlic can be frozen, although this method does affect its flavor. Since garlic is almost always available raw and its taste is far superior fresh, freezing garlic is not recommended. Still, you can freeze unpeeled whole cloves in a zipper-lock freezer or vacuum food sealer-type bags. Squeeze out excess air. Frozen garlic will keep for up to 3 months.

Then simply prepare the number of cloves you need by peeling them, then puréeing or chopping them in a food processor with a bit of oil. Use this garlic immediately; do not store it at room temperature because of the possibility of botulism contamination (see Safety Tip, opposite).

EQUIVALENTS, MEASURES & SERVINGS

- 1 small clove = 1 teaspoon minced

COMPLEMENTARY HERBS, SEASONINGS & FOODS

Beans, beef, beets, butter, cabbage, chicken, eggplant, eggs, fish, ginger, greens, hot pepper, lamb, lentils, mayonnaise, mushrooms, olive oil, onions, pasta, pesto, pork, potatoes, poultry, rice, rosemary, sesame, shellfish, soy sauce, spinach, tomatoes, vegetables, zucchini.

SERVING SUGGESTIONS

- Purée fresh garlic, canned garbanzo beans, tahini, olive oil, and lemon juice to make that Middle Eastern dip, hummus.
- Sauté thinly sliced or chopped cloves with steamed spinach and sprinkle with red pepper flakes.
- Add garlic to sauces, soups, stews, and casseroles.
- Insert thin slivers of garlic and sprigs of fresh herbs directly into meat or under the skin of poultry to be roasted.
- Top your favorite pizza with very thin slices of garlic. A must for garlic-lovers, not so for garlic-haters!
- Add garlic to your favorite pesto, marinade, and salsa recipes.
- Pickle whole garlic cloves in soy sauce.
- Add finely chopped garlic and fresh herbs to ground beef for out-of-this-world hamburgers and meatloaf.
- Roast whole garlic bulbs, then squeeze and spread the resulting paste onto slices of thick-cut French or sourdough bread like butter.
- Sprinkle vegetables that will be oven-roasted, like potatoes, sweet potatoes, turnips, onions, and carrots, with a combination of olive oil, chopped garlic, fresh herbs, and salt and pepper.

Safety Tip

Never store raw garlic in oil at room temperature; even in the refrigerator this is chancy, as the sulfurous compounds in garlic provide ideal conditions for breeding botulism, the most deadly form of natural toxin known to humans.

However, garlic can be safely stored in wine and vinegar if refrigerated; the high acid content of these mixtures prevents the formation of botulism.

CHICKEN WITH 40 CLOVES OF GARLIC   SERVES 4 TO 6

Do not be alarmed at the quantity of garlic in this traditional French dish. Baking the garlic in the oven along with the chicken softens and mellows it to a piquant, sumptuous sweetness, with none of the harsh pungency of the raw bulb. As you eat the chicken, squeeze the contents of the garlic cloves onto the chicken.

DRY HERB RUB

1½ tablespoons fresh thyme
1½ tablespoons rubbed fresh sage
1 tablespoon fresh rosemary, crushed
2 teaspoons garlic powder
2 teaspoons salt
1 teaspoon black pepper, freshly ground

CHICKEN

1 large frying or roasting chicken, 3½ pounds

Sources

The Pikled Garlic Company
www.pikledgarlik.com

The Garlic Store
www.thegarlicstore.com

Gilroy Garlic Festival
www.gilroygarlicfestival.com

The Aroma of the Windy City

The city of Chicago got its name from the American Indian word, "chicagaoua," for the wild garlic that grew on the shores of Lake Michigan.

¼ cup olive oil
1 medium lemon, cut into quarters
Sprigs of fresh rosemary or thyme (optional)
40 cloves garlic, separated but not peeled
1½ cups white wine
½ cup chicken stock
2 tablespoons fresh basil or parsley, minced, for garnish

1. Thoroughly mix the dry herb rub ingredients together.

2. Rinse the chicken thoroughly and pat it dry with paper towels. Rub the skin with 1 tablespoon of the olive oil. Apply the herb rub evenly over the chicken, including within the cavity. Place the lemon in the cavity along with the herb sprigs, if used. Refrigerate and allow to marinate for at least 2 hours.

3. Preheat the oven to 375°F.

4. In a saucepan, sauté the remaining olive oil and garlic cloves over medium heat for 3 to 4 minutes. Add the wine and stock and cook for 3 minutes longer.

5. In an oven-proof casserole dish large enough to hold the chicken, add the garlic-wine-stock mixture. Place the chicken in the casserole, cover, and bake for 25 minutes. Uncover, raise the oven temperature to 450°F, and bake for 40 to 50 minutes longer, or until the juices run clear when the thigh joint is pierced. (Be sure that some liquid always remains in the bottom of the casserole, to prevent scorching. If not, add a little more wine or stock.)

6. Remove the chicken and cut into serving pieces. Place them on a warm platter and spoon the pan juices over the top. Arrange the garlic cloves around the chicken, and garnish with minced basil or parsley.

— *www.fooddownunder.com*

POACHED GARLIC

1 garlic head
Milk

In a small saucepan, cut the ends from all of the garlic cloves. Set the cut sides down in a pan with enough milk to reach half way up the garlic head. Simmer for 20 to 30 minutes. Voila!

— *Featherstone Farm*

GARLIC COMPOUND BUTTER

Thinly slice 2 garlic cloves and sprinkle them with coarse sea salt. Using the flat side of a knife, squish the garlic into a fine paste. Mix the garlic with ½ stick of butter and other herbs (basil, cilantro, oregano, or thyme are good choices, either dried or fresh). Put into a dish, refrigerate, and serve with crusty bread. (It tastes great on corn, too.)

— Featherstone Farm

Books

Garlic Lovers' Greatest Hits
Gilroy Garlic Festival Association;
Celestial Arts, 1993.

Glorious Garlic: A Cookbook
Charlene A. Braida; Garden Way/
Storey Communications, 1986.

The Garlic Lover's Cookbook
Gilroy Garlic Festival;
Celestial Arts, 2005.

A Clove of Garlic: Garlic for Health
and Cookery: Recipes and Traditions
Katy Holder and Gail Duff;
Chartwell Books, 1997.

Garlic, Garlic, Garlic: More than 200
Exceptional Recipes for the World's
Most Indispensable Ingredient
Linda Griffith and Fred Griffith
Houghton Mifflin, 1998.

ROASTED GARLIC HUMMUS   SERVES 2 TO 3

The roasted garlic gives this hummus a subtler flavor than raw garlic. Even though it is time-consuming, removing the skins from the chickpeas makes the hummus smoother, especially if you are puréeing it with a mortar and pestle. Go easy on the tahini, and adjust the spices as you see fit. This hummus is delicious with baby carrots, pretzels, tortilla chips, warmed pita bread, pita chips, or celery.

1 garlic head
1 (20-ounce) can chickpeas (garbanzo beans) with liquid
Juice of 2 lemons
¼ cup tahini (sesame paste)
1 teaspoon ground cumin
1 teaspoon freshly ground black pepper
1 teaspoon salt
½ teaspoon cayenne pepper
1 tablespoon extra-virgin olive oil, plus more for garnish

1. Preheat the oven to 375°F. Cut the top off of the head of garlic. Roast for 45 minutes.

2. Meanwhile, drain the chickpea liquid into a small saucepan. Simmer over low heat for 5 minutes. Pour the chickpeas onto a plate, and pinch off and discard their skins, adding each chickpea to the saucepan.

3. When the garlic is done roasting, squeeze the pulp into a medium-sized mixing bowl and discard the skins.

4. Remove the chickpeas from their liquid and purée them with a mortar and pestle or in a food processor until they are smooth. Place them in a mixing bowl, add the remaining ingredients, and stir until combined. Use the remaining chickpea liquid to reach the desired consistency. Season to taste.

5. Serve the hummus at room temperature, garnishing with cayenne pepper and drizzling with extra-virgin olive oil.

— Justin Watt, www.justinsomnia.org

VEGETABLE BROTH   YIELDS 3½ TO 4 QUARTS

The distinction between broth and stock is slight—broth is salted to taste at the end of the cooking, whereas stock remains unsalted. It is easier to cook with broth because its flavors are more easily discerned once the salt

"There is no such thing as a little garlic."

— A. Baer

Restaurants in Korea serve raw garlic cloves in bowls for munching, like peanuts.

This habit may partly account for why Koreans have the highest garlic consumption per capita in the world (a whopping 22 pounds annually, compared to the U.S. average of about 2.5 pounds).

is added. But when using broth in a recipe, be sure that any additional salt is added to taste.

2 carrots
2 leeks
1 large onion
¼ small head cabbage
1 fennel bulb
4 cloves garlic
1 bunch parsley
4 sprigs fresh thyme
1 cup dried porcini mushrooms
4 quarts water
1 cup dry white wine
1 tablespoon black peppercorns
Salt (optional)

1. Quarter the carrots, leeks, onion, cabbage, fennel, and garlic. Combine with the parsley, thyme, and mushrooms in a large soup pot. Add the water. Cover, bring to a boil, then decrease the heat, and simmer for 30 minutes.

2. Add the wine and peppercorns and continue to simmer, covered, for 10 minutes. Strain and discard all of the solids.

3. Season to taste with salt, if desired, or leave unsalted and use as a base for soups and grain dishes. Use immediately, or cool and then refrigerate. This stock will keep for about 5 days in the refrigerator or 4 to 6 months in the freezer.

— *Andrea Chesman,* The Garden-Fresh Vegetable Cookbook

15-Minute Rosemary Lamb Chops   Serves 4

6 tablespoons fresh lemon juice
3 tablespoons fresh rosemary, chopped
3 medium cloves garlic, pressed
¼ teaspoon salt
¼ teaspoon black pepper
12 lamb chops

1. Mix together the lemon juice, rosemary, pressed garlic, salt, and pepper. Rub the lamb chops with this mixture. Set aside on a plate.

2. Preheat the broiler on high heat, and place a metal ovenproof pan big enough to hold the lamb chops under the heat to get hot, about 5 to 7 inches from the heat source. Heat the pan for about 10 minutes.

3. Once the pan is hot, place the lamb chops in the pan, and return it to the broiler for about 4 to 5 minutes, depending on the thickness of the lamb.

— *www.whfoods.com*

"If Leekes you like, but do their smell dislike,
Eat Onyons, and you shall not smell the Leeke;
If you of Onyons would the scent expell,
Eat Garlicke, that shall drowne the Onyons' smell."

— *Dr. William Kitchiner,*
The Cook's Oracle.

CARROT SALAD

SERVES 4

Make the vinaigrette no more than a couple of hours before serving. This salad keeps for 2 to 4 days in the refrigerator.

1 scant tablespoon balsamic vinegar
1 scant tablespoon white wine vinegar
1 small clove garlic, peeled
Salt
6 tablespoons extra-virgin olive oil
Pepper
1¼ pounds carrots (before trimming)

1. To make the vinaigrette, pour the vinegars into a small bowl. Crush the garlic clove and add it to the vinegar, along with ½ teaspoon salt. After 10 minutes or so, whisk in the olive oil and a little freshly milled pepper. Taste and adjust the seasoning.

2. Trim the tops off of the carrots and peel them. Finely shred the carrots using a grater or food processor.

3. Then pour the vinaigrette over the shredded carrots. Mix thoroughly. The salad should sit about 2 hours or more if possible for the flavors to blend.

— *Pam Garetto, Featherstone Farm CSA member*

AÏOLI

MAKES 1½ CUPS

Aïoli is a traditional Provençal dish, which can be eaten simply with a few raw vegetables or be made into a feast with chicken, snails, fish, boiled potatoes, and lightly cooked vegetables. Or you can use it as a simple garlic mayonnaise in sandwiches and salads. Aïoli keeps for a week in the refrigerator.

8 cloves garlic
1 cup olive oil
¼ teaspoon salt
2 egg yolks
Juice of ¼ lemon

1. Crush the garlic in a press or with a mortar and pestle. Add the oil very gradually, beating it in until a thick, heavy paste is formed.

2. Add the salt and egg yolks. Continue beating.

3. Add the lemon juice slowly while constantly beating.

— *www.fooddownunder.com*

Taking a Breather

To deal with the unpleasant breath that consuming garlic tends to cause, the easiest way is to simply associate with others who like garlic just as much.

Barring that, chlorophyll is quite effective in temporarily absorbing the distinctive odor; chew sprigs of raw parsley or mint for several minutes after eating a garlicky dish.

Onion

Like its Allium cousin the garlic, a gastronomic life without onions is nearly unimaginable. Few vegetables have so many versatile personalities and are equally good sautéed, baked, braised, stuffed, steamed, grilled, and of course, deep-fried. The pungent, distinctive flavor of onions melds well with so many ingredients, both meat and vegetable, that this bulb is truly a workhorse in the kitchen.

Onions come in many forms. Some are sweet and juicy, like Walla Walla and Vidalia, so mild that they can almost be eaten out of hand like an apple. These types are best for eating raw, as their delicate flavor dissipates when cooked too long. Others, like the large red (sometimes called Bermuda), yellow (sometimes called Spanish), and white storage varieties taste more pungent, with varying degrees of sweetness. These onions are ideal for long cooking. Immature onions— scallions, green onions, and bunching onions, in that order—tend to have delicate flavors and are best used raw or in dishes involving brief cooking.

Featherstone grows several varieties of onions:

Walla Walla
This variety, a regional favorite in Washington, is a type of sweet onion, juicy and mild. Their sweetness comes from their low sulfur content, which is about half that of an ordinary yellow onion, and the fact that they are about 90 percent water. They must be refrigerated and are not for storage. These onions taste best fresh, tossed in salads, on top of pizzas, or as a filling for quiches. If you keep them in a cool, dry, dark, ventilated location, they can be stored for up to 6 weeks.

Mars
These are beautiful red onions. Featherstone offers both cured and un-cured specimens, but these will taste better and last longer if you refrigerate them.

Copra
This a large yellow onion, one of the best keepers of all the storage onions (some say they will store for up to a year!). Blessed with a very high sugar content, they become even sweeter throughout the winter.

HISTORY
Precisely where humans ate their first onions remains a matter of some dispute. Several wild species exist, and these were probably foraged by ancient peoples long before domestication occurred. The first known record of them is in Mesopotamia, and it seems probable that onions originated in Asia or the Middle East.

The ancient Egyptians valued onions not only as food but as currency, for the pyramid builders were partially paid with these aromatic vegetables, along with garlic. Onions quickly spread throughout the rest of Europe and were often associated with the lower classes, who depended on them as a staple in their frugal diet.

Although the United States has several native wild species, nearly all of the onions eaten and cultivated today are descended from specimens brought from the Old World and planted in Massachusetts in the mid-1600s.

NUTRITION

A 1-ounce cup of onions contains 20 percent of an adult's daily requirement for chromium. Onions also have vitamins C and B6, dietary fiber, manganese, molybdenum, tryptophan, folate, and potassium. As with other members of the Allium family, the chromium and sulphurous compounds in onions may have beneficial effects against heart disease, diabetes, and high blood cholesterol.

SELECTION

When choosing all types of onions, look for fat, firm specimens with no signs of shriveling, sliminess, soft or dark spots, or moisture at the neck, which could signal decay. Onions past their prime also may be sprouting (although they are still edible, their flavor may be off). Green onions or scallions should be bright green and fresh-looking with firm, white roots, with no wilted, yellowing, or slimy tops.

STORAGE

Cured onions can be kept in a wire hanging basket or a perforated container with a raised base so air can circulate freely underneath. They keep best in an area like a basement, root cellar, or other place with the proper cool temperature and lack of humidity (for more information, see "Preserving the Bounty" on page 331).

Avoid storing onions next to potatoes, which emit ethylene gas and moisture, which can cause the onions to spoil more quickly. Also avoid storing them with apples, celery, and pears, as onions will absorb their odors.

Cut onions should be wrapped very tightly (aluminum foil is quite effective) or kept in an airtight container and used within a couple of days, as they oxidize quickly and tend to lose flavor and nutrients.

Scallions should be stored wrapped in a plastic bag in the refrigerator vegetable crisper, where they will keep for up to 1 week.

TRIMMING & CLEANING

To prepare onions, trim about ½ to ¾ inch from both ends (this should include the neck and the root stub). Cut a slit in the outer skin and peel off this first layer. Now your onion is ready for slicing into thin rounds, wedges, or chopping.

STEAMING & BOILING

Onions can be quickly steamed as a side dish on their own. Cut large onions into ½-inch-thick rounds or quarter them into wedges, place them over a steamer rack, add aromatics to the steaming water such as rosemary or oregano branches, and steam for 15 to 25 minutes, depending on the size of the onion, or until they become tender.

To boil onions, cut off the very ends, remove just enough of the outer layers to eliminate the tough skins but not so much that they fall apart, and place them in a pan, covering with water. Boiling times will vary

> "The onion is the truffle of the poor."
>
> — *Robert J. Courtine, French gourmet*

Cooking Tip

To help lessen or rid the scent of onions on your hands, try washing them with salt or lemon juice.

Rubbing your fingers on a stainless steel surface (like a spoon or even a soap-sized steel block made just for this purpose) also helps.

Cooking Tip

If you find yourself getting a bit sentimental and tearing up while chopping onions, try chilling them first before cutting into them.

The culprit is a chemical compound called propanethial-S-oxide, which is released when the onion is cut but converts to sulfuric acid upon contact with water.

A miniature food processor is terrific for chopping quantities of onions while saving time and tears.

widely, depending on the size of the onion, but it will be around 10 to 20 minutes. Avoid overcooking, and boil just until tender. Drain and serve with melted butter and seasonings.

STIR-FRYING & SAUTÉING

One of the most common ways to prepare onions is sautéing and stir-frying. (Indeed, many of the recipes in this book begin with sautéing onions.) Preheat oil or butter in a pan over medium-high heat, slice or chop the onions thinly, and sauté until the onions turn limp and begin to turn translucent, about 3 to 5 minutes. If you want to use the onions for a quiche or as a filling in another dish, cook them slowly on lower heat; they will caramelize and develop a much richer flavor.

BAKING & ROASTING

Onions take to baking like a duck takes to water. Keep their skins on, as they will prevent the onions from drying out. Cut the root ends down so that they have a flat surface to stand on, and rub the outside in a little oil. Prick them with a fork to allow steam to escape, and pour a little oil or butter on the bottom of a baking pan to prevent scorching. Bake in a 375°F oven for 50 minutes to 1½ hours, or until they become tender, depending on the size of the onions.

GRILLING

Both sweet onions and yellow and white storage onions turn out juicy and terrific when grilled whole. Peel the outer skin off each onion and slice just enough off one of the ends to create a flat surface for placing on the grill. Wrap each onion in aluminum foil, set them on the grill, and cook for about 20 to 30 minutes, depending on their size, or until they become tender. Then turn them over and roast the root side for another 20 minutes. Then peel and separate the onion layers, seasoning to taste.

(As a variation, some people carve out a hole within the onion, taking care not to pierce all of the way through, and fill the hole with butter, a little beer, or Coca-Cola to add flavor.)

BRAISING & STEWING

Small onions take very well to braising and stewing. One method is to braise white onions in broth, wine, or water into which butter, herbs, salt, and pepper have been added. Bring to a boil, cover, decrease the heat, and simmer over low heat for 15 to 25 minutes, or until the onions are tender.

An alternative recipe is to sauté the onions in butter first until they brown, then add the broth mixture and cook as described in the recipe above. These browned onions can then be added to a roast toward the end of the roast's cooking time.

MICROWAVING

To microwave, peel the onions, place them in a microwave-safe dish, add 1 tablespoon of water, cover, and cook on High power.

- 3 medium onions (about 1 pound) = 4 minutes (for stuffing) = 5 minutes (softened)
- 1 pound small white onions = 6 minutes

For More Information

National Onion Association
www.onions-usa.org

"Onion skins very thin,
Mild winter coming in.
Onion skins very tough,
Coming winter very rough."

— *Old English rhyme*

¼ pound scallions (24 to 30, about 6 inches long) = 2 minutes, softened

BLANCHING & FREEZING

Onions can be frozen without blanching. Simply peel and chop them into ½-inch pieces. Then package them in zipper-lock freezer or vacuum food sealer-type bags, or freezer containers. Squeeze out excess air and leave ½ inch of headspace (unless you are using the vacuum sealing method). They will keep for 3 to 6 months. They do not require thawing before using.

EQUIVALENTS, MEASURES & SERVINGS

- 1 large onion = 1 cup chopped
- 1 pound = 4 medium onions = 3 to 4 cups chopped
- 1 tablespoon dried minced onion = 1 medium chopped onion
- 1 teaspoon onion powder = 1 medium chopped onion

COMPLEMENTARY HERBS, SEASONINGS & FOODS

Apples, bacon, basil, beef, butter, cheese, chiles, cinnamon, cloves, cream, cucumbers, garlic, Mozzarella cheese, mushrooms, nutmeg, olive oil, paprika, Parmesan cheese, parsley, pepper, poultry, raisins, rice, sesame, sherry, soy sauce, taco mix, thyme, tomatoes, vegetables, vinegar, Worcestershire sauce.

SERVING SUGGESTIONS

- Try an unusual and tasty "coleslaw" made with thinly sliced red onion, fennel, and a tangy vinaigrette dressing.

- Try the quintessential Italian summer salad: vine-ripened tomatoes, sliced onion rings, cucumber slices, and mozzarella cheese, drizzled with olive oil, chopped fresh basil, and freshly ground sea salt and pepper (see recipe on page 192).

- The French slow-simmer very thinly sliced onions in butter and red wine to create a confit that is tasty with beef, pork, and lamb dishes.

- Chopped onions add flavor to just about any vegetable or side dish you can imagine.

- Make French onion soup. (Be sure to use a high-quality beef broth and cheese, or the soup may disappoint.)

- A simple but delicious lunch or snack idea: Roll up thinly sliced onions inside a slice of deli honey ham or honey turkey, along with a sprig of fresh herbs, if desired, like basil or dill. This is a delicious, nutritious treat that especially appeals to kids, especially if the onions are the sweet, mild kind, like Vidalias or Walla Wallas.

- Plain rice can be a delicious treat with a generous sprinkling of chopped scallions and sesame seeds.

DAL MAKHANI (INDIAN LENTILS AND BEANS)   SERVES 8

Garam masala is a blend of ground spices used in Indian cooking. Mixtures vary depending on the locale and type of dish in which it is used, but traditional mixes usually include cinnamon, roasted cumin, cloves,

I have read a couple of articles lately that have made me reflect upon our modern times. One commented on the fact that, one hundred years ago, everything was organic.

Of course. I think about my grandparents on their farm in the 1930s—what they grew each summer was what they had to eat, animal or vegetable or fruit. We have a picture of my mother as a teenager, dwarfed by a huge pile of squash, so you can guess what was on the table every day that winter! They certainly didn't have the luxury of choice, even in seeds, which they saved from year to year (our "heirloom" varieties). They ploughed the garden with a horse plough, and all they had for fertilizer was manure. Even if fertilizer or pesticides had been available, they would not have had the money to buy them.

The other article was about the Canadian version of "reality TV," in which two families spent a year living like they would have a century ago, except that they were filmed at every step of the way. The par-

nutmeg, and green cardamom seed or black cardamom pods. Commercial mixtures may contain less expensive spices such as dried red chile peppers, dried garlic, ginger powder, sesame, mustard seeds, turmeric, coriander, bay leaves, cumin, and fennel.

3 tablespoons vegetable oil
2 large onions, chopped
1 to 4 large cloves garlic, crushed
1 jalapeño pepper, diced small (optional)

Spice Mixture
1 teaspoon cumin seeds (optional)
2 tablespoons ground coriander
1 teaspoon ground cumin
1 teaspoon ground ginger or 1 tablespoon fresh ginger, minced
1 tablespoon turmeric
1 to 2 teaspoons curry powder
1 teaspoon commercial garam marsala (optional)

6 cups water (more if necessary)
2 cups lentils, sorted and washed
1 tablespoon bouillon
1 (15-ounce) can red kidney beans
1 can tomato paste
Salt
Cream or half-and-half (optional)
Chopped fresh cilantro, for garnish

1. Heat the oil on medium heat; add the onions, garlic, and jalapeño pepper (if desired) and sauté until wilted.

2. Stir in the spices and sauté until the mixture becomes fragrant. (Feel free to experiment with the spices, and don't hesitate to make the dish anyway if you are missing one or two of those suggested. Try something else instead!)

3. Add the water, lentils, and bouillon, and cook 20 minutes. Add the kidney beans and tomato paste and simmer for another 30 minutes, stirring occasionally and adding more water if necessary, so that the beans do not stick. Salt to taste.

4. For nonvegans, stir in 1 to 2 tablespoons of cream or half-and-half per serving, if desired, which makes this dish more like the original version. Garnish with chopped cilantro.

— *Robin Taylor, Featherstone Farm CSA member*

STUFFED AND BAKED SWEET ONIONS   SERVES 4

4 green bell peppers
4 medium-sized sweet onions

12 plum tomatoes, seeded and chopped
1 tablespoon capers
2 tablespoons chopped basil, fresh or dried
2 tablespoons chopped thyme, fresh or dried
¾ cup balsamic vinegar
1 teaspoon salt
1 teaspoon freshly ground pepper
Fresh thyme sprigs, for garnish

1. Preheat the oven to 400°F.

2. When the oven is ready, place the bell peppers on an aluminum foil-lined baking sheet, and with the oven door partially open, broil them 5 inches from the heat source for 5 minutes, or until their skins blister. Remove the peppers and let them cool slightly. Place them in a bag, close it, and let them stand 10 minutes to loosen their skins. Peel, seed, and chop them. Set them aside.

3. Cut a thin slice from the bottom of each onion, forming a base for the onions to stand on. Remove the onion centers, leaving ½-inch-thick shells. Reserve the centers for other uses.

4. Stir together the bell peppers, tomatoes, capers, basil, thyme, vinegar, salt, and pepper; spoon the mixture into the onion shells.

5. Place the onions in a baking dish and bake, covered, at 400°F for 50 minutes. Garnish with fresh thyme sprigs.

— *Barbara Hunt, mother of Featherstone Farm CSA member Margaret Trott*

· ·

SPICY PORK TENDERLOIN PITAS
SERVES 4

1 cucumber, peeled and diced
1 cup nonfat sour cream
1 teaspoon fresh dill or ½ teaspoon dried dill
8 ounces pork tenderloin
2 teaspoons Dijon mustard
1 tablespoon olive oil
1 tablespoon lemon juice
1 clove garlic, minced
1 teaspoon fresh oregano or ½ teaspoon dried oregano
1 green bell pepper, thinly sliced
1 red onion, thinly sliced into rings
1 cup spinach, shredded
4 pita breads, halved
8 cherry tomatoes, halved

1. In a small bowl, combine the cucumbers, sour cream, and dill. Refrigerate until needed.

2. Cut the pork across the grain into ½-inch cutlets, then slice each piece into thin strips. In a large bowl, combine the mustard, oil,

ticipants said that they had never been so tired in their lives.

On a personal level, every time I spend an hour weeding my garden and lawn (which has been daily this year because of the heat and the rain), I think about the labor that goes into every basket of food we receive. It is amazing in North America how little we value our food, or the work that goes into it. So thanks to Jack and Rhys and the Featherstone crew!

When I have traveled, I have always been struck by how other cultures seem to be more involved with their food. In France, you commonly see someone cycling by with a baguette or two; in Germany or Holland or any other European country, you see people going home from work on the bus or the tram with a shopping bag full of food. In Lesotho near South Africa, where food is not so plentiful, the market women make tidy little piles of their produce. It is only after you become a valued customer that they allow you to choose the pile. Otherwise it is their choice.

I know I am preaching to the choir, but I hope that what we are all involved in with this CSA spreads and becomes a bigger national trend.

Priorities First

During the Civil War,
General Ulysses S. Grant sent
an urgent message to the War
Department: "I will not move
my army without onions."
The very next day, three
trainloads were on their
way to the front.

lemon juice, garlic, and oregano. Add the pork and toss well to coat all of the pieces. Let stand about 10 minutes.

3. Coat a large nonstick frying pan with nonstick cooking spray and place over medium heat for 3 minutes. Working in bunches to avoid over-crowding in the pan, add the pork and sauté for about 3 minutes or until it is cooked through. Transfer to a plate, and wipe the pan clean.

4. Place the bell peppers and onions in a 9-inch glass pie plate. Cover the plate with vented plastic microwave wrap and microwave on High power for 3 minutes, or until the onions and peppers soften. Add them to the pan, and sauté them in oil for 3 minutes, or until they are lightly browned. Top the pork mixture with the peppers and onions.

5. Line the pita pockets with the spinach. Add the pork mixture. Top each sandwich half with a cherry tomato and some cucumber sauce.

— *Fruits and Veggies—More Matters; Centers for Disease Control & Prevention*

GREEN ONION PANCAKES   SERVES 4

These savoury little "pancakes" are easy to make. This one comes from chef Tom Douglas.

2 teaspoons sesame seeds
1 large egg
2 teaspoons sesame oil
4 (8-inch) flour tortillas
2 scallions (green onions), finely chopped
2 tablespoons vegetable oil, or more as required, for frying

1. In a small skillet over medium heat, toast the sesame seeds until golden, shaking the pan often. It should take less than 5 minutes; watch that they don't burn. Transfer the seeds to a small bowl or plate and set aside.

2. In a small bowl, lightly beat the egg with the sesame oil. Brush one side of each tortilla with the egg mixture to coat lightly—you will not use all the egg wash. Sprinkle each tortilla with the scallions (green onions) and the toasted sesame seeds. Fold the tortillas in half, press-ing down to seal.

3. Heat the vegetable oil in a 10-inch skillet over medium heat. Add 2 pancakes at a time and cook until lightly browned on both sides, about 2 minutes per side, using more oil as needed. Transfer the pan-cakes to a plate and cover to keep warm until ready to serve.

— *Kukla, adapted from chef Tom Douglas, as appeared on GroupRecipes.com*

FRENCH ONION SOUP   SERVES 8

This recipe calls for beef bones, but a perfectly respectable stock can be made with vegetarian beef-flavored soup base. However, the following recipe is richer than the vegetarian one. Either way, the real trick in this soup is to caramelize lots of onions.

5 pounds beef soup bones
8 cups water
¼ pound unsalted butter
1 tablespoon vegetable oil
1 tablespoon olive oil
3 pounds white or yellow onions, sliced into half-moon strips
     (use Vidalia or Walla Walla onions, if available)
1 tablespoon sugar
2 tablespoons flour
1 cup dry or semi-dry white wine (chenin blanc, chablis, dry
     vermouth, or white table wine)
½ teaspoon freshly ground black pepper
1½ teaspoons salt
1 loaf French bread, sliced into ¾-inch-thick rounds
Enough slices of Swiss or Gruyére cheese to cover each bowl of soup

1. In a roasting pan, roast the soup bones in a preheated 450°F oven for about 35 minutes. While roasting the bones, bring the water to a boil and maintain the boil, covered, until the bones are ready. Add the roasted bones to the boiling water, discarding the rendered fat that will have collected on the roasting pan. Simmer the bones, covered, for a minimum of 2 hours.

2. While the bones are simmering, melt the butter and both oils in a large frying pan or brazier. Brush the tops of the bread slices with the butter mixture, spread the slices on a baking sheet, and put them in a preheated 300°F oven to toast, for about 20 minutes. Set aside to cool.

3. In a large frying pan or heavy-bottomed pot, sauté the onions in the remaining butter-oil mixture over medium-high heat until they become soft and translucent. Add the sugar, and continue to cook until the onions caramelize (they will turn golden brown). This should take about 30 minutes. Do not leave the onions during this stage, but stir them steadily. When the onions turn a deep golden brown, stir in the flour until it disappears. Remove the pan from the heat and set it aside.

4. Remove the bones from the broth with a slotted spoon. Using a gravy separator or soup skimmer, strain out all of the fat from the broth. Transfer the onion mixture to the broth. Add the wine, pepper, and salt. Adjust the seasonings to taste.

5. Place 1 crouton on the bottom of each soup bowl. (This soup should be served in individual crock-style bowls, with a narrower width, rather than in a large serving bowl or wide-mouthed soup bowls.) Ladle the soup over the crouton, filling the bowl to ½ inch from the top. Float another crouton on top. Cover the bowl with sliced cheese. Place the bowl under the broiler or in a hot oven long enough for the cheese to melt over the top of the soup. Serve immediately.

— *Peter Reinhart,* Sacramental Magic in a Small-Town Café

"I crawled into the vegetable bin, settled on a giant onion and ate it, skin and all. It must have marked me for life for I have never ceased to love the hearty flavor of onions."

— *James Beard, American chef and food writer*

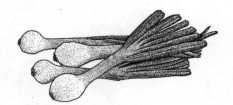

"An onion can make people cry, but there has never been a vegetable invented that can make people laugh."

— *Will Rogers,*
American comedian

BEEF BOURGUIGNON (FRENCH STEW)   SERVES 4

Bouquet garni (French for "garnished bouquet") is a little bundle of herbs that is tied with string or enclosed in a sachet. It is used to flavor soups, stews, and stock during cooking and is then removed before serving. Although there is no precise formula for bouquet garni, it usually includes parsley, peppercorns, thyme, and bay leaves. Basil, burnet, celery leaves, chervil, rosemary, savory, and tarragon may also be used.

MARINADE

1 large carrot, cut into ½-inch pieces
1 onion, cut into ½-inch pieces
1 stalk celery, cut into ½-inch pieces
2 cloves garlic
Bouquet garni
¼ cup brandy
10 black peppercorns
6 cups good red wine
2 tablespoons oil

2 pounds beef chuck steak, trimmed and cut into 1½-inch cubes
1 heaped tablespoon tomato paste
2 tablespoons all-purpose flour
1½ cups beef stock
32 small boiling onions, peeled
1 tablespoon unsalted butter
2 teaspoons sugar
5 ounces mushrooms, cut into quarters
2 tablespoons chopped garlic
8 ounces slab or sliced bacon, cut into cubes or short batons
2 slices white bread, crusts removed and cut into triangles
2 tablespoons chopped fresh parsley

1. Place all of the ingredients for the marinade in a bowl with the cubes of beef. Cover and refrigerate overnight.

2. Preheat the oven to 400°F. Strain the marinade into a saucepan, remove the beef, and set aside, and keep the vegetables and bouquet garni separate. Bring the marinade to a boil, skim off the foam, and cook for 6 to 8 minutes. Strain through a fine sieve.

3. In a large, heavy-bottomed flameproof casserole or Dutch oven, heat a little oil and butter. Pat dry the meat and brown it on all sides in batches; remove and keep to one side. Add the well-drained vegetables from the marinade, lower the heat slightly, and cook, stirring occasionally, until they are lightly browned.

4. Return the meat to the pan with the tomato paste and stir over medium heat for 3 minutes. Sprinkle the meat with the flour and place it in the oven for 6 to 8 minutes; then remove and mix in the flour. Place the meat over medium heat again, add the marinade, and bring

it to a boil, stirring constantly. Then add the stock and bouquet garni. Return it to a boil, cover, and cook in the oven for 1½ hours, or until the meat is tender.

5. Meanwhile, place the onions, butter, sugar, and some salt in a deep skillet and pour in enough water to cover. Cook over medium heat until the water has almost evaporated, and swirl the skillet until the onions are golden. Fry the mushrooms in some sizzling butter until they turn golden; season and drain them and add to the onions. Fry the garlic and bacon in a little oil, drain, and add to the onions and mushrooms.

6. Brush the bread with melted butter and toast in the oven for 3 to 5 minutes, or until brown.

7. Once the beef is cooked, skim off the excess fat. Remove the beef to a clean, flameproof casserole or serving dish, cover, and keep warm. Strain the sauce and return it to the pan, discarding the vegetables and bouquet garni.

8. Bring the sauce to a boil and simmer for 15 minutes, or until the sauce coats the back of a spoon, skimming frequently. Season, strain over the meat, and simmer or return to the oven for 5 minutes.

9. Add the onions, mushrooms, and bacon. Dip a corner of each bread crouton into the sauce, then into the parsley. Sprinkle the remaining parsley over the beef, and serve with the croutons on the edge of the dish or on the side.

— *Meryle, www.epicurean.com*

Books

The Elegant Onion: The Art of Allium Cookery
Betty Cavage; Storey Communications, 1987.

Onions, Onions, Onions: Delicious Recipes for the World's Favorite Secret Ingredient
Linda Griffith and Fred Griffith; Houghton Mifflin, 2002.

The Onion Cookbook
Jean Bothwell; Dover, 1976.

ONION LOVER'S DIP
MAKES 3 CUPS

Quark is a type of fresh, mild, unaged cheese, similar to cottage or ricotta cheese. The variety available in plastic tubs usually contains some whey and has the consistency of sour cream.

¼ cup olive oil, preferably extra-virgin
4 large shallots, peeled, halved, and thinly sliced
1 pound quark (or 8 ounces cream cheese at room temperature mixed with 8 ounces sour cream)
2 tablespoons fresh lime juice
1 teaspoon kosher salt
¼ teaspoon freshly ground pepper
Pinch of sugar
6 medium scallions, trimmed and thinly sliced
1 small red onion, peeled and finely diced
Chips and assorted cut-up raw vegetables, for serving

1. Heat the oil in a heavy-bottomed skillet over medium-high heat until hot but not smoking. Add the shallots and cook, stirring often, until they turn brown and crisp. Transfer them to paper towels to drain

and let cool.

2. In a large bowl, stir together the quark, lime juice, salt, pepper, and sugar until smooth. Stir in the scallions, red onion, and reserved shallots.

3. Cover and refrigerate for 1 hour to let the flavors blend. Serve with chips and raw vegetables.

— *Joel Patraker*, The Greenmarket Cookbook

MEATLOAF: YES, VIRGINIA THERE IS A GREAT MEATLOAF! 4 TO 5 SERVINGS

This is absolutely delicious meatloaf and sauce. Those who claim they don't believe there can be such a thing as a great meatloaf will love this. A second batch of sauce served hot is good to serve with the meatloaf.

1½ pounds ground beef (ground shoulder roast is good)
1 slice bread, broken or chopped finely
1 egg
1 small Vidalia onion or other type of sweet onion
       (such as Walla Walla), finely chopped
1 teaspoon salt
¼ teaspoon black pepper
4 tablespoons ketchup
½ to ⅔ cup milk or half-and-half

SAUCE
4 tablespoons apple cider vinegar
2 to 4 tablespoons firmly packed dark brown sugar, to taste
½ cup ketchup

1. Preheat the oven to 350°F.

2. Combine the meatloaf ingredients and place the mixture into a loaf baking dish. Smooth out the top.

3. Combine the sauce ingredients and pour over the top and sides of the meatloaf.

4. Bake for about 1 to 1¼ hours, or until done (the meatloaf should not be runny).

— *Nita Holleman, www.recipezaar.com*

SWEET ONION CASSEROLE SERVES 4 TO 6

4 to 5 sweet onions, like Walla Walla or Vidalia
¼ cup butter, softened
⅓ cup sour cream

²⁄₃ cup reduced-fat Parmesan cheese
10 Ritz crackers, crushed

1. Preheat the oven to 350°F.
2. Combine the onions, butter, and sour cream. Spoon half of this mixture into a lightly greased casserole baking dish.
3. Sprinkle the Parmesan cheese evenly over the top, and add the remaining onion mixture. Sprinkle the Ritz crackers evenly over the top.
4. Bake, uncovered, for 20 to 25 minutes.

— *Arlayne Fleming*

WARM ONION DIP

SERVES 4

The flavor in this dip is so subtle that you don't even know it is onion.

8 ounces cream cheese
1 tablespoon mayonnaise
¾ cup Parmesan cheese
½ tablespoon fresh dill or ½ teaspoon dried dill
1 sweet onion (like Walla Walla or Vidalia), finely chopped

1. Preheat the oven to 375°F.
2. Thoroughly combine the cream cheese, mayonnaise, ½ cup of the Parmesan cheese, and dill. Add the sweet onion and mix. Place in a casserole dish, and sprinkle the remaining Parmesan over the top.
3. Bake for 20 to 25 minutes, or until the dip is bubbly and the top is golden brown.

— *Arlayne Fleming*

food," Mitchell says. "By synthetically protecting the produce from these pests, we decrease their need to produce antioxidants. It suggests that maybe we are doing something to our food inadvertently."

Mitchell measured antioxidants found in corn, strawberries, and a type of blackberry called a marionberry. "We started with these three due to plant availability," Mitchell explains, "but we intend to include tomatoes, peppers, broccoli, and a variety of other vegetables. We expect these results to be transferable to most produce."

The investigation compared the total antioxidants found in food grown organically (using no herbicides, pesticides, or fertilizers) to foods grown sustainably (in this study fertilizers but no herbicides or pesticides were used) and conventionally (using synthetic chemicals to protect plants and increase yield).

The results showed a significant increase in antioxidants in organic and sustainably grown foods versus conventionally grown foods. The levels of antioxidants in sustainably grown corn were 58.5 percent higher than conventionally grown corn. Organically and sustainably grown marionberries had approximately 50 percent more antioxidants than conventionally grown berries. Organically and sustainably grown strawberries had approximately 19 percent more antioxidants than conventionally grown berries.

Antioxidant levels were the highest overall in sustainably grown produce, which indicates that a combination of organic and conventional practices yields the highest level of antioxidants. "Originally, the question was just really intriguing to me," says Mitchell, whose research grew naturally from a personal interest in organic foods. "I found that the higher level of antioxidants is enough to have a significant impact on health and nutrition, and it's definitely changed the way that I think about food."

Turnip

BRASSICA RAPA, RAPIFERA GROUP

Like their cruciferous cousins cabbage and rutabagas, turnips have a ways to go before they reach the gastronomical cachet of, say, artichokes or asparagus. Which is a shame, because they can make a fine root vegetable provided that they are not too tough or cooked too long, which tends to render them smelly, watery, and tasteless.

The turnips that are most familiar to Americans (and about the only ones commercially available in the U.S.) are the familiar white roots whose upper third portion is tinted a light purple. But heirloom turnips exist whose skins come in a multitude of festive colors, from gold and green to rose and nearly black.

Rutabagas and turnips are often confused with each other, for their roots may share nearly identical exterior coloring. Turnips, however, tend to be smaller and smoother, with flesh that usually cooks up pure white, whereas rutabagas are thicker, more elongated, with rough-textured skins and flesh that is golden yellow when cooked. Both are cool-growing vegetables that are at their best either in the spring or fall.

The root is not the only edible part of the turnip; its greens are a nutritional powerhouse and a proper vegetable in its own right. They are, however, a bit too fuzzy to eat raw and should be added to stir-fries or soups, or slow-cooked southern-style, like collards, along with products of the savory pig.

HISTORY

The turnip was believed to have originated in northern Europe over 4,000 years ago, and was soon relegated to the tables of the poor. In fact, around 1500 B.C.E., the Aryans passed a law that the turnip should never soil the lips of the noble classes (along with beans, garlic, onions, and mushrooms). Over the centuries Europeans used lowly turnips as livestock food, as weapons to be hurled at outcasts, and as sustenance food. But in India, China, and the Middle East, the vegetable was treated with far more respect, often pickled, sun-dried, and sautéed in savory dishes.

By the early 1600s turnips were already growing in Virginia and Massachusetts. Subsequently the American Indians took such a liking to them that an American general destroyed an extensive field of them in New York in 1779 as a tactical raid into Indian territory.

NUTRITION

Like other cruciferous vegetables, both turnip greens and roots are extremely nutritious, containing vitamin C, potassium, iron, thiamin, magnesium, folate, copper, and dietary fiber. Turnips also contain abundant phytonutrients such as sulforaphane and indoles, which have proven in studies to fight cancer, especially prostate, colorectal, and lung. Turnip greens are extremely rich in vitamins A, C, and K.

SELECTION

Choose turnips that are firm and evenly colored, with fresh green tops.

Avoid specimens that are shriveled, have wilted or yellowing leaves, or with cracked or blemished bulbs. Overly large specimens may be woody inside.

STORAGE

Turnip greens should be detached from their roots (if they come together) and stored separately, tightly wrapped in a plastic bag and stored in the refrigerator vegetable crisper. The greens will keep for a few days this way, whereas the roots may keep for up to 1 to 2 weeks.

The roots will also keep quite well in a basement, root cellar, or other place with the proper cool temperature and lack of humidity (for more information, see "Preserving the Bounty" on page 331).

TRIMMING & CLEANING

Turnips must be peeled before eating. Trim off the tops (save them for cooking later, if desired), then use a paring knife or a sharp vegetable peeler to cut off the thick outer skin. To remove traces of grit, sand, and insects lurking in turnip greens, the leaves must be thoroughly washed by submerging them in a sinkful of water and swishing well, then draining and rinsing again if necessary.

STEAMING & BOILING

Steam whole, peeled or unpeeled turnips for 15 to 20 minutes, depending on their size, and sliced turnips for 5 to 10 minutes, or until tender when pierced with a fork. Boil cubed, peeled turnips for 15 to 30 minutes, then drain.

STIR-FRYING & SAUTÉING

Stir-fry or sauté turnips, cut into ½-inch dice or cubes, in a well-oiled pan or wok over high heat for about 8 minutes, or until crisp-tender. Turnip greens can be sautéed after a quick parboiling for 2 to 7 minutes, depending on their size and thickness.

BAKING & BRAISING

Bake whole turnips in a 350°F oven for about 20 to 30 minutes, depending on their size. Or prepare like oven-roasted potatoes (see recipe on page 157). To braise turnips, trim and peel them, and cook them in butter or pan juices for 10 to 15 minutes over medium heat, or until they are lightly colored and tender.

MICROWAVING

Trim and peel 2 cups of turnip, cutting into ¼-inch-thick slices. Place them in a covered dish with ¼ cup water and microwave on High power until tender, about 10 to 15 minutes, while stirring every 5 minutes. Let stand 5 minutes before serving.

BLANCHING & FREEZING

Cube or slice the turnips into ½-inch-thick pieces, boil for 2 to 3 minutes, and then plunge into ice water to stop the cooking. Let cool, drain, and pack in zipper-lock freezer or vacuum food sealer-type bags, or freezer containers. Squeeze out excess air and leave ½ inch of headspace

Books

The Essential Root
Vegetable Cookbook
Martin Stone;
Clarkson Potter, 1991.

Roots: The Underground Cookbook
Barbara Grunes and Anne Elise Hunt;
Chicago Review Press, 1993.

EQUIVALENTS, MEASURES & SERVINGS

- 3 medium turnips = 1 pound = 2½ cups chopped

COMPLEMENTARY HERBS, SEASONINGS & FOODS

Apples, bacon, beef, butter, carrots, cheese, chicken, chives, cider, cinnamon, cream, cream sauces, duck, garlic, lamb, lemon, maple syrup, mushrooms, mustard, nuts, onions, paprika, parsley, peas, pork, potatoes, sausages, sherry, squash, sugar, sweet potatoes, tarragon, thyme, vinaigrette, vinegar.

SERVING SUGGESTIONS

- Turnips pair best with hearty meats and vegetables; they are especially good slow-cooked by braising, baking, stewing, or roasting (this last method caramelizes its natural sugars and best brings out its delicate flavors).
- Prepare turnip greens Southern-style (see recipe on page 235).
- Add a little variety to the traditional corned beef and cabbage or New England boiled dinner by adding turnips and celery root to the potatoes, carrots, and cabbage.
- For a twist, try preparing turnips cream-style.
- Prepare turnips as you would mashed potatoes, fixing them with plenty of butter, cream, and a touch of horseradish, cinnamon, or nutmeg if desired. Or mash turnips together with boiled pumpkin and potatoes (recipe on page 267).
- Pair turnips with beets and potatoes, drizzle with olive oil mixed with garlic and fresh herbs, and bake them slowly in a 375° oven for 45 minutes to 1 hour.
- Add cubes of turnips to beef and lamb stews.
- Slice very young, tender, raw turnips into thin rounds or sticks to add to the vegetable relish tray.
- Grate raw turnip into salads or slaws.

POTATO AND TURNIP AU GRATIN WITH LEEKS   SERVES 6

1 cup whole milk
1 cup heavy cream
3 large cloves garlic, minced
Salt and pepper to taste
2 tablespoons butter
3 leeks (white section only), thoroughly washed and thinly sliced
1 pound russet potatoes, peeled and thinly sliced
1 pound turnips, peeled and thinly sliced
2 cups shredded Gruyère cheese

1. Preheat the oven to 365°F.

2. In a saucepan, combine the milk, cream, garlic, salt, and pepper. Do

---

not boil. Decrease the heat and simmer for another 5 minutes, then set aside. (Do not be shy on the salt—it will help flavor the potatoes and turnips.)

3. In a small pan, melt 1 tablespoon of the butter and add the leeks. Cook for 7 to 8 minutes, until the leeks start to brown, stirring frequently; then set aside.

4. Spread the remaining butter around a 9 × 12-inch baking dish, covering all sides. Assemble the potatoes and turnips in a dish, alternating each vegetable. Season each layer with salt and pepper. Add 1 cup of the Gruyère cheese and cooked leeks on top of the first layer.

5. Pour enough of the cream mixture over the top to just barely cover it. Layer the remaining vegetables and season with salt and pepper. Top the last layer with the remaining cheese, and cover with the remaining cream mixture.

6. Bake for 40 to 45 minutes, until the top is golden brown and the potatoes can be pierced easily with a sharp knife.

— *David Cannata, Yolo Catering; Davis Farmers Market*

. . . .

TURNIP "FRIES"   SERVES 4

An adaptation of Deborah Madison's version with rutabagas.

4 medium turnips, peeled, trimmed, and cut into ½-inch sticks
¼ cup olive oil
¼ cup grated parmigiano-reggiano cheese
2 pinches grated nutmeg
Salt and freshly ground black pepper

1. Preheat the oven to 450°F.

2. Place the turnips in a bowl and toss them with the olive oil, cheese, nutmeg, salt, and pepper. Spread the turnips out on an oiled sheet pan.

3. Bake until they become golden, 18 to 20 minutes.

— Saveur, *March 2002*

. . . .

TURNIP-POTATO PURÉE   SERVES 4 TO 6

This dish goes well with pork sausages, a crisp green salad, and apple tart.

4 medium turnips, halved, peeled, and trimmed
2 russet potatoes, halved and peeled
4 tablespoons butter
Salt
Chopped chives

your exposure to cancer-causing pesticides. Also, certain types of outbreaks, such as E. coli, are far less likely to occur because of the different growing setups of organic farming.

(7) *Having a CSA share saves time,* with convenient pick-up sites and prepacked boxes—no more constant running to the grocery store and trying to decide what to bring home for dinner.

(8) *Visiting a real working farm is fun and educational* for children and adults alike. Most CSA farms have open houses, socials, festivals, harvest suppers, and other events when you and your family can visit and actually see how your food is grown and processed.

(9) *Having a CSA share cements the farmer-to-consumer connection.* Urban CSAers especially can forge closer relationships with the rural farm, seeing the origins of their food and sharing in the process.

(10) *Organic fruits, vegetables, and herbs simply taste better!* That is why discriminating chefs prefer organic foods for their recipes. In turn, the richer flavor of organic produce helps encourage you to eat your veggies. And that is always a good thing!

1. Boil the turnips and potatoes in a pot of salted water over medium heat until they become soft, 35 to 40 minutes. Drain, return the vegetables to the pot, and cook, stirring, until all of the moisture evaporates, 4 to 6 minutes.

2. Stir in the butter and salt to taste, and garnish with chopped chives.

— Saveur, *March 2002*

TURNIPS WITH TOMATOES AND MINT   SERVES 6

1½ pounds turnips
4 tablespoons ghee (clarified butter) or vegetable oil
12 ounces tomatoes, skinned and roughly chopped
1 (1-inch long) piece of fresh ginger, peeled and finely grated
1 tablespoon ground coriander
½ teaspoon ground turmeric
¼ teaspoon cayenne pepper
2 cups water
3 tablespoons chopped fresh cilantro leaves
2 tablespoons chopped fresh mint leaves
1 teaspoon salt

1. Peel the turnips and cut them in half lengthways, then into ¼-inch-thick slices. Heat the ghee or oil in a wok or frying pan over medium-high heat. Add the tomatoes and stir-fry for 2 minutes.

2. Add the ginger, coriander, turmeric, and cayenne pepper. Stir-fry for another 2 minutes, or until the sauce is thick. Add the turnips, water, cilantro, mint, and salt. Partially cover and cook over a moderately low heat for 20 minutes, stirring occasionally.

3. Cover tightly and cook for another 10 minutes over a low heat until the turnips are tender.

— *Robert Budwig,* The Vegetable Market Cookbook

"Let us be many-sided! Turnips are good, but they are best mixed with chestnuts. And these two noble products of the earth grow far apart."

— *Johann Wolfgang von Goethe,*
German polymath

Preserving the Bounty

This section is by Larisa Walk, Featherstone Farm bookkeeper and wholesale sales coordinator. She is the author of A Pantry Full of Sunshine—Energy-Efficient Food Preservation Methods, *and the inventor of the Walk Solar Food Dryer. Her website is at www.GeoPathfinder.com.*

Frost, freeze, snow—all elements of the cycle of seasons here in Minnesota. But they do not have to signal the end of eating our locally grown delectables. By using a few tricks to mimic nature's goal of reproduction and survival, you can have fresh produce in winter that isn't trucked in from warmer climes.

Root cellaring is an age-old food preservation method that holds foods in a state of suspended animation or hibernation. For some veggies, this dormancy is part of their biennial life cycle, in which their second summer triggers seed production after wintering over in the ground, as long as the soil does not freeze hard. This is the case with carrots, beets, cabbage, celery, and onions, among others. For crops like potatoes, the dormant spuds remain viable, as this plant's strategy is to reproduce as clones from the tubers themselves. Squashes remain intact containers for their clusters of seeds until they are opened and dispersed by humans or other critters. If you understand a bit of botany, you can help the plant preserve itself.

Most people picture a root cellar as a structure set into a north-facing hillside, maybe with stone masonry work and a heavy, oak-plank door. While this would be an ideal set-up, how many of us have the location, space, materials, and building know-how to take advantage of the earth's natural coolness? While almost nobody has this resource available, most Americans already own a root cellaring device—an ordinary picnic cooler works wonderfully for temporary, portable, versatile, and flexible food storage options. Most coolers aren't used over the winter months anyway, and if you don't already own one, they are relatively inexpensive or can be found at garage sales. (If you get into this, you may want more than one—I have eight.)

Here is how to operate a cooler as a root cellar: For potatoes, carrots, beets, and other root crops (or apples), place your produce in the cooler and set it outside in the fall in a cool, shady spot, like the north side of your house, in a porch, or an unheated garage. This will work even when the nights are below freezing but are getting above 32°F during the day. When winter really starts to take hold, move the cooler to a less cold spot. An unheated entryway, outside cellar stairs, buried in a hole in the ground and covered with leaves, or an unheated basement—you may have to get creative to make use of the resources at hand. You can monitor the conditions inside your cooler by sticking an indoor/outdoor thermometer probe into the drain plug (stick some crumpled paper or fabric into the gap around the wire). Ideally the temperature should be 32°F to 40°F with a humidity level of 80 to 90 percent.

By shuffling your cooler to various positions around your abode, you can keep potatoes and other roots all winter (it is early June as I write this and I still have a few beets left). If things aren't spoiling, shriveling from lack of moisture, or sprouting from being too warm, then you are doing things right.

I use the term root cellaring loosely, as some fall veggies are not strictly roots, nor do they store well under cellar conditions. Squash do best in a warmer and drier setting, about 50°F to 60°F, with 60 percent humidity. These conditions can often be found in a spare room that is closed off from the rest of the house—a guestroom with some squash under the bed works well for some folks. Onions and garlic require the same humidity as squash, but prefer a bit cooler temperatures.

Do not worry if your conditions are not ideal—even fair conditions are going to extend your harvest longer than doing nothing. Go through your bins regularly and use veggies before they spoil. The point of this exercise is to eat the food, not horde it. So remember to have fun with your food and let nature be the guide on your food storage trip. Here's wishing you the best on your squirrelly endeavor.

SOLAR FOOD DRYING

Using the sun to preserve foods that its energy provided is a great way to increase your use of local foods year-round. Although I have "invented" a solar food dryer that works well in the humid Midwest and written a book on the subject, you do not need to invest in any special equipment to do solar drying on a small scale.

In fact, I would like to encourage you to use the solar food dryer that, like most Americans, you already own—your car. Here is how to use your dryer on wheels: Park the car in the sun with the largest sloped pane of glass facing south (this may be the front windshield or rear window of the car, depending on the model). You will need something on which to place the food—cookie sheets, dryer screens from an electric dryer, baskets, or cotton dish towels will work. Just make sure that whatever you use is material that is safe for contact with food.

Arrange your veggies on the food tray and place it in the south-facing window if possible (or it could be elevated above the seats with some kind of spacer—books, boxes—be creative). Since you are trying to remove the water from food, you will need adequate airflow around, if not through, your trays to accomplish this task.

Next, put a dark piece of fabric, kitchen towel, or even a bandanna (black, navy blue, brown, or another dark color) on top of the food to keep the sunlight from bleaching out its nutrients and to help it heat up. Lastly, open your car windows about one inch, more or less depending on the air temperature outside and wind conditions. You will want your car to be at 100°F to 140°F, depending on what you are drying (you can use a thermometer to monitor conditions if you want). If things have not completed drying by day's end, they can be left in the car overnight to finish the next day.

This way, you can have your "dryer" and drive it too! I have a friend who would drive her car to work and set up the trays of food. Maybe with the rising cost of gas, more cars will be used as food dryers on sunny days and people will take to the streets on their bikes instead. That would be the healthier option in terms of fitness and nutrition. Cutting-edge new trend? We will see.

For more information on food drying techniques, check out my book, *A Pantry Full of Sunshine*, available on my website: www.GeoPathfinder.com.

Bibliography and Resources

This list includes not only the sources of this book's recipes but also many related websites, publications, and blogs about a vast range of food-related topics. The recent resurgence in ethnic cuisines and gourmet cooking in America has happily resulted in many wonderful recipe websites on the Internet, many of which are searchable by ingredient, and a few of them appear below. Besides offering literally thousands of recipe ideas with a few clicks of the mouse, some of these sites also provide invaluable cooking tips, baking info, and canning, preserving, and freezing guidelines, with step-by-step instructions and accompanying photos.

For those of us who do not use computers or the Internet, plenty of books and magazines abound, as the overflowing shelves in the food and cooking section in your local bookstore demonstrate. A book seems to have been written on just about every conceivable aspect of cuisine, and don't forget used, out-of-print volumes too—many terrific classics lurk in used bookstores and antique shops across the country, like gastronomic time capsules.

Also included here are a few favorites from my own library, some of which are not cookbooks *per se* but offer glimpses of food-related history and social commentary for the curious, inquiring mind. Happy reading!

About.com
www.about.com/food

Aki's Kitchen
www.akiskitchen.ca

Ahaar: Pleasure & Sustenance
www.ahaar.blogspot.com

All Around the World Cookbook
Sheila Lukins, Workman Publishing, 1994.

The All-Purpose Joy of Cooking
Irma S. Rombauer, Ethan Becker, and Marion Rombauer Becker, Scribner Book Company, 1998.

Allrecipes
www.allrecipes.com

Angela's Oregano
www.oreganofromitaly.com

Ani's Raw Food Kitchen: Easy, Delectable Living Foods Recipes
Ani Phyo, Marlowe & Company, 2007.

The Art of Eating
M. F. K. Fisher, John Wiley and Sons, 2004.

The Art of Eating magazine
www.artofeating.com

The Artful Eater: A Gourmet Investigates the Ingredients of Great Food
Edward Behr, Art of Eating, 2004.

The Asian Grocery Store Demystified
Linda Bladholm, Renaissance Books, 1999.

The Asparagus Festival Cookbook
Jan Moore, Barbara Hafly, and Glenda Hushaw; Celestial Arts, 2003.

AZcentral.com
www.azcentral.com/home

B's Cucumber Pages
www.lpl.arizona.edu/~bcohen/cucumbers/info.html

Ballymaloe Cookery School
www.cookingisfun.ie

Ben & Jerry's Homemade Ice Cream
www.ben andjerrys.com

Berries: A Country Garden Cookbook
Sharon Kramis, Collins Publishers, 1994.

The Best 50 Salad Dressings
Stacey Printz, Bristol Publishing Enterprises, 1999.

Beyond Bok Choy: A Cook's Guide to Asian Vegetables
Rosa Lo San Ross and Martin Jacobs, Artisan, 1996.

The Big Broccoli Book
Georgia Downard, Random House, 1992.

Blue Heron Coffeehouse
www.blueheroncoffeehouse.com

Bluff Country Co-op
www.bluff.coop

The Bluff Country Co-op Cookbook
Bluff Country Food Co-op, 2002.

Bon Appétit magazine
www.epicurious.com/bonappetit

The Breath of a Wok: Unlocking the Spirit of Chinese Wok Cooking Through Recipes and Lore
Grace Young, Simon & Schuster, 2004.

Brilliant Food Tips and Cooking Tricks: 5000 Ingenious Kitchen Hints, Secrets, Shortcuts, and Solutions
David Joachim, Rodale Inc., 2001.

Broccoli and Company
Audra Hendrickson and Jack Hendrickson, Storey Communications, 1989.

Brownie Points: A Good Girl's Notebook of Her Culinary World
www.browniepointsblog.com

California Strawberry Commission
www.calstrawberry.com

California Tomato Growers Association, Inc.
www.ctga.org

CDkitchen
www.cdkitchen.com

Centers for Disease Control and Prevention
www.fruitsandveggiesmatter.gov

Chachi's Kitchen
www.chachiskitchen.blogspot.com

The Chamomile Times and Herbal News
www.chamomiletimes.com

Chicago's Green City Market
www.chicagogreencitymarket.org

The Chile Man
www.thechileman.org

The Chile Pepper Encyclopedia: Everything You'll Ever Need to Know About Hot Peppers, With More Than 100 Recipes
Dave DeWitt, Diane Publishing, 2003.

Chow (CNet Networks)
www.chow.com

The Classic Zucchini Cookbook: 225 Recipes for All Kinds of Squash
Nancy C. Ralston, Marynor Jordan, and Andrea Chesman, Storey Publishing, 2002.

Chanterelle Catering
www.saucemagazine.com

A Clove of Garlic: Garlic for Health and Cookery: Recipes and Traditions
Katy Holder and Gail Duff, Chartwell Books, 1997.

Collard Greens Festival
www.epa.net/collardgreens

The Collard Patch
Mary Lou Cheatham and Paul Elliott, Blue Moon Books Louisiana, 2006.

The Complete Medicinal Herbal
Penelope Ody, Dorling Kindersley, 1993.

The Compleat Squash: A Passionate Grower's Guide to Pumpkins, Squashes, and Gourds
Amy Goldman, Artisan, 2004. Sibyl Kile, BCG Ltd., 1985.

Cooking Basics for Dummies
Bryan Miller and Marie Rama, 3rd Edition, IDG Books Worldwide, 2004.

Cooking with Fruit
Rolce Redard Payne and Dorrit Speyer Senior, Crown Publishers, Inc., 1992.

The Cook and the Gardener: A Year of Recipes and Writings for the French Countryside
Amanda Hesser, W. W. Norton & Company, 2000.

The Cook's Encyclopedia of Vegetables
Christine Ingram, Lorenz Books, 2001.

Cook's Illustrated magazine
www.cooksillustrated.com

Cooksrecipes
www.cooksrecipes.com

Cookwise: The Secrets of Cooking Revealed
Shirley O. Corriher, HarperCollins, 1997.

Daisies Do Tell … A Recipe Book
Betty Culp, 1979 (family cookbook).

Davis Farmers Market
www.davisfarmersmarket.org

Delicious Organics, Inc.
www.deliciousorganics.com

Diet for a Small Planet
Frances Moore Lappé, Ballantine Books, 1991.

Do It Yourself Home Improvement
www.doityourself.com/scat/homecanningandpreser

Eater's Digest: 400 Delectable Readings about Food and Drink
Lorraine Bodger, 2006.

The Eggplant Cookbook: Classic and Contemporary Recipes for Today's Healthy Diet
Rosemary Moon; Book Sales, 1998.

The eGullet Society for Culinary Arts & Letters
www.forums.egullet.org

The Elegant Onion: The Art of Allium Cookery
Betty Cavage, Storey Communications, 1987.

The Encyclopedia of Healing Foods
Michael T. Murray, Joseph Pizzorno, and Lara Pizzorno, Atria, 2005.

Epicentre
www.theepicentre.com

Epicurean.com for Food and Wine Lovers
www.epicurean.com

Epicurious for People Who Love To Eat
www.epicurious.com

Essentially Eggplant
Nina Kehayan, Fisher Books, 1996.

Essentials of Classic Italian Cooking
Marcella Hazan, Knopf, 1992.

The Essential Root Vegetable Cookbook
Martin Stone, Clarkson Potter, 1991.

Essortment: Information & Advice You Want To Know
www.essortment.com/food.html

The Farmer's Market Cookbook
Richard Ruben, Lyons Press, 2000.

Fast Food Nation: The Dark Side of the All-American Meal
Eric Schlosser, Houghton Mifflin Company, 2002.

The Fearless Frying Cookbook
John Martin Taylor, Workman Publishing Company, 1997.

Featherstone Fruits & Vegetables
www.featherstonefarm.com

Fields of Greens
Annie Somerville, Bantam, 1993.

Fire and Ice Café
www.fireandicecafe.ie

First Meals, Annabel Karmel, DK Publishing, 1999.

Florida Tomatoes
www.floridatomatoes.org

Food by Waverley Root: An Authoritative and Visual History and Dictionary of the Foods of the World
Waverly Root, Simon and Schuster, 1980.

Food Down Under
www.fooddownunder.com

The Food Network
www.foodnetwork.com

The Food Reference Website
www.foodreference.com

Food & Wine magazine
www.foodandwine.com

Food & Wine Annual Cookbook Series
American Express Publishing Corporation.

Florida Strawberry Growers Association
www.straw-berry.org

From Asparagus to Zucchini: A Guide to Cooking Farm-Fresh, Seasonal Produce
Madison Area Community Supported Agriculture Coalition (MACSAC), 2003.

The Garden-Fresh Vegetable Cookbook
Andrea Chesman, Storey Publishing, 2005.

Garlic Acres
www.garlic-acres.com

Garlic Central
www.garlic-central.com

Garlic, Garlic, Garlic: More than 200 Exceptional Recipes for the World's Most Indispensable Ingredient
Linda Griffith and Fred Griffith, Houghton Mifflin, 1998.

The Garlic Lover's Cookbook
Gilroy Garlic Festival, Celestial Arts, 2005.

Garlic Lovers' Greatest Hits
Gilroy Garlic Festival Association, Celestial Arts, 1993.

The Garlic Store
www.thegarlicstore.com

Gastronomica magazine
www.gastronomica.org

Gernot Katzer's Spice Pages
www.uni-graz.at/~katzer/engl/index.html

Gilroy Garlic Festival
www.gilroygarlicfestival.com

Glorious Garlic: A Cookbook
Charlene A. Braida, Garden Way/Storey Communications, 1986.

The Good Cook: Vegetables
Time Life Books, 1979.

The Good Food Store Co-op
www.rochestergoodfood.com

Good Things (Revised)
Jane Grigson, Bison Books, 2006.

Gourmet **magazine**
www.epicurious.com/gourmet

Gourmetsleuth: The Gourmet Food & Cooking Resource
www.gourmetsleuth.com

Grandma's Favorite Strawberry Recipes
Lanette Coalson, Father & Son Publishing, 2004.

The Great Chile Book
Mark Miller, Ten Speed Press, 1991.

The Great Food Almanac: A Feast of Facts from A to Z,
Irena Chalmers, Collins Publishers San Francisco, 1994.

The Great Little Pumpkin Cookbook
Michael Krondl, Celestial Arts, 1999.

Green Earth Institute
www.greenearthinstitute.org

Greene on Greens
Bert Greene, Workman Publishing Co., 1984.

The Greenmarket Cookbook
Joel Patraker, Viking Penguin, 2000.

Greens Glorious Greens: More Than 140 Ways to Prepare All Those Great-Tasting, Super-Healthy, Beautiful Leafy Greens
Johnna Albi and Catherine Walthers, St. Martin's Griffin, 1996.

Greg Atkinson
www.northwestessentials.com

Group Recipes
www.grouprecipes.com

The Harrowsmith Salad Garden
Turid Forsyth and Merilyn Simond Mohr, Camden House, 1992.

The Heirloom Tomato Cookbook
Mimi Luebbermann, Chronicle Books, 2006.

The Herbfarm Cookbook
Jerry Traunfeld, Scribner, 2000.

Herbs & Spices: The Cook's Reference
Jill Norman, DK Adult, 2002.

Home Cooking: A Writer in the Kitchen
Laurie Colwin, Harper Perennial, 2000.

Hot Spots
David DeWitt, Prima Publishing, 1992.

Idaho-Eastern Oregon Onions
www.ieoonions.com

Idaho Potato Commission
www.idahopotato.com

I Love Spinach Cookbook
Burgundy L. Olivier, 2003. www.ilovespinach.com

Immigration … The Great American Potluck, The Library of Congress, American Memory
www.memory.loc.gov/learn/features/immig/ckbk/index.html

In Celebration of Chives
Guy Cooper and Gordon Taylor, The Herb Society, 1981.

In Praise of Tomatoes: Tasty Recipes, Garden Secrets, Legends & Lore
Ronni Lundy, Lark Books, 2006.

In Search of the Perfect Meal: A Collection of the Best Food Writing of Roy Andries De Groot
Roy Andries De Groot, St. Martins Press, 1986.

James Beard's American Cookery
James Beard, Little, Brown and Company, 1972.

www.justinsomnia.org

Kalyn's Kitchen
Kalynskitchen.blogspot.com

Keep the Beat: Heart Healthy Recipes
National Institutes of Health

Lakewinds Natural Foods
www.lakewinds.com

Lee Bailey's Southern Food & Plantation Houses: Favorite Natchez Recipes
Lee Bailey and the Pilgrimage Garden Club, Clarkson N. Potter, Inc., 1990.

Lee Bailey's Tomatoes
Lee Bailey, Clarkson Potter, 1992.

Linden Hills Co-op
www.lindenhills.coop

Local Flavors: Cooking and Eating from America's Farmers' Markets
Deborah Madison, Broadway Books, 2002.

LoveToKnowRecipes
www.recipes.lovetoknow.com/wiki/Main_Page

Lu's Recipe Extravaganza
www.recipelu.com

Madison Area Community Supported
Agriculture Coalition (MACSAC)
www.macsac.org

Madison Herb Society Cookbook
Madison Herb Society, 1995.

The Man Who Ate Everything
Jeffrey Steingarten, Vintage Books, 1998.

Mariquita Farm
www.mariquita.com

Massachussets Department of Agricultural Resources
www.mass.gov/agr/markets/farmersmarkets/index.htm

McCormick & Company
www.mccormick.com

*Mediterranean Vegetables: A Cook's ABC of Vegetables and
Their Preparation in Spain, France, Italy, Greece, Turkey,
the Middle East, and North Africa, with More than 200
Authentic Recipes for the Home Cook*
Clifford A. Wright, The Harvard Common Press, 2001.

Mexican Family Cooking
Aída Gabilondo, Ballantine Books, 1992.

Michigan Asparagus Advisory Board
www.asparagus.org

Mississippi Market Natural Foods Co-op
www.msmarket.coop

*Mommy Made and Daddy Too! Home Cooking for a
Healthy Baby & Toddler*
Martha and David Kimmel, Bantam Books, 2000.

More Vegetables, Please
Janet Fletcher, Harlow & Ratner, 1992.

National Center for Home Food Preservation
www.uga.edu/nchfp/index.html

National Onion Association
www.onions-usa.org

National Watermelon Promotion Board
www.watermelon.org

The New Enchanted Broccoli Forest
Mollie Katzen, Ten Speed Press, 2000.

The New Moosewood Cookbook
Mollie Katzen, Ten Speed Press, 2000.

New England Herb Company
www.newenglandherbcompany.com

New Seasons Market
www.newseasonsmarket.com

*The New Soy Cookbook: Tempting Recipes for Soybeans, Soy
Milk, Tofu, Tempeh, Miso and Soy Sauce*
Lorna Sass, Chronicle Books, 1998.

The New Zucchini Cookbook
Nancy C. Ralston and Jordan Marynor, Storey Publishing,
1990.

Old Fashioned Living
www.oldfashionedliving.com

The Omnivore's Dilemma: A Natural History of Four Meals
Michael Pollan, Penguin Press, 2006.

One Hundred One Strawberry Recipes
Carole Eberly, Eberly Press, 1987.

On Food and Cooking: The Science and Lore of the Kitchen
Harold McGee, Scribner, 2004.

One Bite Won't Kill You
Ann Hodgman, Houghton Mifflin Company, 1999.

*Onion: The Essential Cook's Guide to Onions, Garlic, Leeks,
Spring Onions, Shallots and Chives*
Brian Glover, Lorenz Books, 2001.

The Onion Cookbook
Jean Bothwell, Dover, 1976.

*Onions, Onions, Onions: Delicious Recipes for the World's
Favorite Secret Ingredient*
Linda Griffith and Fred Griffith, Houghton Mifflin, 2002.

Oregon Raspberry & Blackberry Commission
www.oregon-berries.com

*A Pantry Full of Sunshine—Energy-Efficient
Food Preservation Methods*
Larisa Walk, www.geopathfinder.com

A Passion for Potatoes
Lydie Marshall, HarperPerennial, 1992.

PCC Natural Markets
www.pccnaturalmarkets.com

Peppers: A Story of Hot Pursuits
Amal Naj, Knopf, 1992.

*The Peppers Cookbook: 200 Recipes from the Pepper Lady's
Kitchen*
Jean Andrews, University of North Texas Press, 2005.

The Perfect Pumpkin: Growing, Cooking, Carving
Gail Damerow, Storey Publishing, 1997.

PickYourOwn
www.pickyourown.org

The Potato: How the Humble Spud Rescued the Western World
Larry Zuckerman, North Point Press, 1999.

Potatoes: A Country Garden Cookbook
Maggie Waldron, Collins Publishers, 1993.

PracticallyEdible, the Web's Biggest Food Encyclopaedia
www.practicallyedible.com

Pumpkin, a Super Food for All 12 Months of the Year
Dee Dee Stovel, Storey Publishing, 2005.

Pumpkin Nook
www.pumpkinnook.com

The Pumpkin Patch
www.pumpkin-patch.com

Pumpkin, Butternut & Squash: 30 Sweet and Savory Recipes
Elsa Petersen-Schepelern, Ryland Peters & Small, 2003.

The Quote Garden
www.quotegarden.com

Raspberry Delights Cookbook: A Collection of Raspberry Recipes
Karen Jean Matsko Hood, Whispering Pines Press, 2007.

Razzle Dazzle Recipes
www.razzledazzlerecipes.com

Recipe Encyclopedia: A Complete A–Z of Good Food and Cooking
Random House Publishing, 1997.

Recipes for a Small Planet
Ellen Buchwald Ewald, Ballantine Books, 1985

Recipes from a Kitchen Garden
Renee Shepherd and Fran Raboff, Ten Speed Press, 1993.

Recipes from an American Herb Garden
Maggie Oster, Macmillan, 1993.

The Recipe Link: Your Guide to What Is Cooking on the Net
www.recipelink.com

Recipe Lu
www.recipelu.com

Recipe Tips
www.recipetips.com

RecipeZaar
www.recipezaar.com

Remarkable Red Raspberry Recipes
Sibyl Kile, BCG Ltd., 1985.

The Rhubarb Compendium
www.rhubarbinfo.com

Rodale's Illustrated Encyclopedia of Herbs
Rodale Press, 2000.

Roots: The Underground Cookbook
Barbara Grunes and Anne Elise Hunt, Chicago Review Press, 1993.

Sacramental Magic in a Small-Town Café: Recipes and Stories from Brother Juniper's Café
Peter Reinhart, Addison-Wesley Publishing, 1994.

Sally's Place
www.sallys-place.com

Salads
Leonard Schwartz, HarperCollins, 1992.

Salsa, Sambals, Chutneys and Chow-Chows
Christopher Schlesinger, Morrow Cookbooks, 1995.

Sand Hill Berries
www.sandhillberries.com

Saveur magazine
www.saveur.com

The Schoenleber Family Cookbook
Lura Schoenleber Looper, 1993.

Seabreeze Organic Farm
www.seabreezed.com

Seasonal Chef: Buying and Using Produce from Farmers Markets
www.seasonalchef.com

Seed Savers Exchange
www.seedsavers.org

Serious Pig: An American Cook in Search of His Roots
John Thorne and Matt Lewis Thorne, North Point Press, 2000.

Seward Co-op
www.seward.coop

Share Organics
www.shareorganics.bc.ca

Shenandoah Growers
www.freshherbs.com

Shepherd's Garden Seeds
www.reneesgarden.com

Simply Salads: More than 100 Delicious Creative Recipes

Made from Prepackaged Greens and a Few Easy-to-Find Ingredients
Jennifer Chandler, Thomas Nelson, 2007.

Simply Strawberries
Sara Pitzer, Storey Communications, 1985.

Soupsong
www.soupsong.com

South Wind Through the Kitchen: The Best of Elizabeth David
Elizabeth David, Penguin Books Ltd., 1998.

The Splendid Table
splendidtable.publicradio.org

The Spice House:
Merchants of Exquisite Spices, Herbs & Seasonings
www.thespicehouse.com

Spinach and Beyond: Loving Life and Dark Green Leafy Vegetables
Linda Diane Feldt, Moon Field Press, 2003.

Squash Lovers Cook Book
Golden West Publishers and Lee Fischer, Golden West Publishers, 2003.

www.stephencooks.com

Stalking the Green Fairy and Other Fantastic Adventures in Food and Drink
James Villas, John Wiley & Sons, 2004.

Summer Squash & Squash Blossoms: From Seed to Supper
Jack W. Hazelton, Seed to Supper, 2000.

The Tabasco Cookbook
McIlhenny Company with Barbara Hunter, Clarkson Potter, 1993.

Talk of Tomatoes
www.talkoftomatoes.com

Tarragon Central (Cherry Creek Herbs)
www.tarragoncentral.com

A Taste of the Far East
Madhur Jaffrey, BBC Books, 1993.

Terhune Orchards
www.terhuneorchards.com

Thrifty Fun
www.thriftyfun.com

Tigers and Strawberries: A Food Blog by Barbara Fisher
www.tigersandstrawberries.com

The Tomato Festival Cookbook: 150 Recipes that Make the Most of Your Crop of Lush, Vine-Ripened, Sun-Warmed, Fat, Juicy, Ready-to-Burst Heirloom Tomatoes
Lawrence Davis-Hollander, Storey Publishing, 2004.

The Ultimate Potato Book: Hundreds of Ways To Turn America's Favorite Side Dish into a Meal
Bruce Weinstein and Mark Scarbrough, William Morrow Cookbooks, 2003.

Uncommon Fruits & Vegetables
Elizabeth Schneider, Harper & Row Publishers, Inc., 1986.

The United States of Arugula: The Sun-Dried, Cold-Pressed, Dark-Roasted, Extra Virgin Story of the American Food Revolution
David Kamp, Broadway, 2007.

University of Illinois Extension
www.urbanext.uiuc.edu/nutrition

University of Minnesota Extension
www.extension.umn.edu

United States Department of Agriculture (USDA)
recipefinder.nal.usda.gov

Valley Natural Foods
www.valleynaturalfoods.com

The Vegetable Market Cookbook
Robert Budwig, Ten Speed Press, 1993.

The Victory Garden Cookbook
Morene Morash, Alfred A. Knopf, 1982.

Vegetables from Amaranth to Zucchini: The Essential Reference
Elizabeth Schneider, William Morrow & Co., 2001.

Vegetarian Classics
Jeanne Lemlin, HarperCollins Publishers, Inc., 2001.

Vegetarian Cooking for Everyone
Deborah Madison, Broadway Books, 1997.

Vegetarian Journal
The Vegetarian Resource Group, www.vrg.org/journal

Vegetarians in Paradise
www.vegparadise.com

The Very Special Raspberry Cookbook
Carrie Tingley Hospital Foundation and Very Special Cookbook Committee, Jumbo Jack's Cookbooks, 1993.

Washington State Potato Commission
www.potatoes.com

The Wedge Natural Foods Co-op
www.wedge.coop

What's Cooking America
www.whatscookingamerica.net

Whole Food Facts: The Complete Reference Guide
Evelyn Roehl, Healing Arts Press, 1996.

Whole Foods Market
www.wholefoodsmarket.com

World's Healthiest Foods
www.whfoods.com

The Worldwide Gourmet
www.theworldwidegourmet.com

Zucchini: You Can Never Have Enough
John Butler, The University of Alberta Press, 2001.

Lettuce washday.

Recipes by Type of Dish

APPETIZERS

Asian Turkey Lettuce Wraps
Cherry Tomato Shish Kebobs
Deviled Eggs with Salmon and Basil
Fried Squash Blossoms
Mylar's Lettuce Wraps
Radishes with Salt and Butter
Watermelon Bits

BEVERAGES

Agua de Pepino (Cucumber Limeade)
Fruit Shake
Iced Green Tea with Lemongrass and Ginger
Watermelon Smoothie

CASSEROLES

Corn-Mac Casserole
Eggplant, Tomato, and Red Potato Casserole
Layered Vegetable Casserole
Midi-Poche (Eggplant Bake)
Squash-Apple Casserole
Summer Squash Casserole
Sweet Onion Casserole
Zucchini Casserole

CONDIMENTS, MARINADES & SALSAS

Abba's African Hot Sauce
Aïoli
Aïoli (for Beets and Their Greens)
Chili Oil
Corn Salsa
Crème Fraîche
Dry Herb Rub
Garlic Compound Butter
Herb Butter
Homemade Salsa
Pepper Vinegar
Pesto
Poached Garlic
Rhubarb Chutney
Rosemary- or Basil-Infused Oil

Salsa Marinade
Spicy Cantaloupe Salsa
Tarragon Chicken Marinade
Tarragon Vinegar
Watermelon Bits
Watermelon Strawberry Mint Salsa

DESSERTS

Baked Rhubarb with Raspberries
Balsamic Rhubarb Compote
Beet-Chocolate Cake
Butter Pie Crust Dough
Cantaloupe Pie
Crockpot Chocolate Raspberry Strata
Iced Honeydew and Gewürztraminer Soup
LaVerne's Potato Candy
John's Winter Squash Soup with Vanilla Ice Cream
Pumpkin Pie with Spiced Walnut Streusel
Raspberry-Honeydew Parfaits
Raspberry Creme
Raspberry Whip
Real Basil Cheesecake
Rhubarb Crisp
Rhubarb Pie
Strawberry Breakfast Pizza
Strawberry Nachos
Strawberry Shortcake
Summer Fruit in Wine Dessert
Summer Squash Muffins
Sweet-Tart Fresh Strawberries
Watermelon Bits

DIPS

Baba Ghanoush (Eggplant Dip)
Boursin Dip
Low-Fat Ranch Dip
Onion Lover's Dip
Roasted Garlic Hummus
Warm Onion Dip

DRESSINGS

Aïoli
Cilantro Lime Vinaigrette

Citrus Vinaigrette
Creamy Dill Dressing
Cumin-Yogurt Dressing
Greek Salad Dressing
Herb Vinaigrette
Jonno's Caesar Dressing
Orange-Salsa Dressing
Raspberry Crème
Rosemary- or Basil-Infused Oil
Salad Niçoise Vinaigrette
Sesame Oil Vinaigrette
Sweet-and-Sour Ginger Dressing
White Truffle Vinaigrette

EGG DISHES

Bacon, Ham, and Leek Quiche
Chard and Cheddar Omelet
Deviled Eggs with Salmon and Basil
Grandma's Spinach Soufflé
Poached Eggs with Pancetta and Tossed Mesclun
Vegetable Frittata

JAMS & PRESERVES

Rhubarb Chutney
Watermelon Pineapple Preserves

MAIN DISHES

15-Minute Rosemary Lamb Chops
Bacon, Ham, and Leek Quiche
Baked Chicken and Zucchini
Basic Lo Mein
Beef Bourguignon (French Stew)
Beer-Simmered Cabbage Rolls
Braised Lamb with Olives and Mushrooms
Chard and Cheddar Omelet
Cherry Tomato Shish Kebobs
Chicken Stir-Fry with Basil
Chicken with 40 Cloves of Garlic
Eggplant, Tomato, and Red Potato Casserole
Enchiladas Verdes
Garlic Scape Pizza
Green Curry Chicken with Broccoli and Cauliflower
Jesse's Chicken Stew
Meatloaf: Yes, Virginia There IS a Great Meatloaf!
Midi-Poche (Eggplant Bake)
Millet Garden Medley
Poached Eggs with Pancetta and Tossed Mesclun
Roast Chicken with Root Vegetables
Roasted Butternut Squash, Rosemary, and Garlic Lasagne
Rosemary Crockpot Chicken
Salmon Poached with Tomatoes and Swiss Chard
Spaghetti with Cilantro, Corn, and Tomatoes

Spaghetti with Spring Vegetables
Spicy Pork Tenderloin Pitas
Spicy Veal Roast
Stir-Fried Dungeness Crab with Sweet Sauce
    and Bok Choy
Sunflower Meatloaf
Tachiyama Chanko-Nabe (Tachiyama's Beef
    and Chicken Hot Pot)
Ten-Minute Zucchini Pizza
Trina's Green Salmon
Vegetable Cornmeal Crepes
Vegetable Frittata
Vegetable Lasagna
Vegetarian Paella
Zucchini Casserole

MUSHROOM DISHES

Asparagus and Morels
Basmati Rice with Mushrooms, Broccoli, and Onion
Braised Lamb with Olives and Mushrooms
Creamy Green Bean and Mushroom Soup
Miso Broth with Tatsoi-Enoki Salad
Mushroom, Snow Pea, and Spinach Salad
Sautéed Mushrooms on Tricolore Salad
Thyme and Mushroom Gravy
Wild Mushroom and Mizuna Salad

PASTA DISHES

Basic Lo Mein
Corn-Mac Casserole
Oregano and Zucchini Pasta
Pasta with Arugula
Pasta with Savoy Cabbage and Gruyère
Pasta with Veggies and Cheese
Roasted Butternut Squash, Rosemary, and Garlic Lasagna
S. Nardecchia's Spaghetti Sauce
Spaghetti with Cilantro, Corn, and Tomatoes
Spaghetti with Spring Vegetables
Vegetable Lasagne

PICKLES

Barely Pickled Cucumbers
Marinated Zucchini
Moen Creek Pickled Beets
Pickled Green Beans
Zucchini Pickles

POTATO DISHES

Baby Green Garlic Mashed Potatoes
Baby Potatoes with Lemon and Chives
Barbecued Potatoes

Potato dishes, continued

Creamy Spinach Soup
Eggplant, Tomato, and Red Potato Casserole
Jesse's Chicken Stew
Kale Mashed Potatoes
LaVerne's Potato Candy
Millet Garden Medley
Mylar's Rosemary Potato Wedges
Peppery Potato and Zucchini Packets on the Grill
Peter Rabbit's Birthday Soup
Potato and Leek Gratin
Potato and Turnip Au Gratin with Leeks
Potato Leek Soup
Roast Chicken with Root Vegetables
Roasted Squash with Potatoes and Garlic
Sour Cream Potato Salad
Sunflower Meatloaf
Turnip-Potato Purée
Turnips, Pumpkin, and Potatoes
Ultimate Root Soup
Vegetable Cornmeal Crêpes
Yukon Gold Potato Soup

POULTRY DISHES

Asian Turkey Lettuce Wraps
Baked Chicken and Zucchini
Chicken Coconut Soup
Chicken Pumpkin Chili
Chicken Stir-Fry with Basil
Chicken with 40 Cloves of Garlic
Green Curry Chicken with Broccoli and Cauliflower
Jesse's Chicken Stew
Roast Chicken with Root Vegetables
Rosemary Crockpot Chicken
Tachiyama Chanko-Nabe
    (Tachiyama's Beef and Chicken Hot Pot)
Watermelon and Chicken Salad

RICE DISHES

Arroz Verde (Green Rice)
Basmati Rice with Mushrooms, Broccoli, and Onion
Congri (Cuban Beans and Rice)
Enchanted Broccoli Forest, The
Rice with Lemongrass and Green Onion
Vegetarian Paella

SALADS

Abidjan Cabbage Salad
Arugula and Grilled Goat Cheese Salad
Asian Fusion Slaw
Asparagus and Shrimp Salad
Blackberry-Walnut Mesclun Salad

Broccoli Stem Salad
Carrot Salad
Citrus Butter Salad
Coleslaw
Eggplant Salad with Sesame Seeds (Khaji Namul)
Farmer's Market Green Salad with Fried Shallots
Greek Salad
Grilled Summer Corn and Sugar Snap Pea Salad
Honeydew and Cucumber Salad with Sesame
Khaji Namul (Eggplant Salad with Sesame Seeds)
Marinated Bean Salad
Mesclun with Maple Mustard Tofu Points
Mexican Black Bean & Tomato Salad
Minty Melon Salad
Miso Broth with Tatsoi-Enoki Salad
Mushroom, Snow Pea, and Spinach Salad
Radish, Mango, and Apple Salad
Raw Kale Salad
Roasted Baby Beet Salad
Roasted Eggplant Salad with Beans & Cashews
Sabzi (Herb Salad)
Salad Niçoise
Salmon, Cucumber, and Dill Salad
Sautéed Mushrooms on Tricolore Salad
Seasonal Salad with Herb Vinaigrette
Seedless Cucumbers, Yogurt, Mint, and Garlic Salad
Sheila Lukins's Summer Succotash Salad
Simple Romaine Salad
Sour Cream Potato Salad
Southwestern Radish Salad
Spinach, Rocket, and Mizuna Salad
Spinach and Warm Sungold Tomato Salad
Sungold Salad with Feta and Cumin-Yogurt Dressing
Tomato, Onion, and Cucumber Salad
Tossed Mesclun Salad
Warm Red Cabbage Bacon Salad
Watermelon and Chicken Salad
White Bean & Basil Salad
Wild Mushroom and Mizuna Salad
Wilted Mustard Greens Salad with Bacon
Wrigley-Marco's Caesar Salad
Zucchini Salad

SALSAS

Corn Salsa
Homemade Salsa
Salsa Marinade
Spicy Cantaloupe Salsa
Watermelon Strawberry Mint Salsa

SANDWICHES

Bacon, Lettuce, and Cantaloupe Sandwich
Spicy Pork Tenderloin Pitas
Vegetable Subs

SAUCES & GRAVIES

Abba's African Hot Sauce
Oven-Roasted Tomato Sauce
Pesto
Quick Tomato Sauce for the Freezer
    for Roast Chicken with Root Vegetables
Roasted Chiles in Sauce with Pine Nuts and Cream
S. Nardecchia's Sphagetti Sauce
Thyme and Mushroom Gravy

SEAFOOD DISHES

Asparagus and Shrimp Salad
Deviled Eggs with Salmon and Basil
Maine Lobster Chowder
    with Coconut, Corn, and Lemongrass
Salmon, Cucumber, and Dill Salad
Salmon Poached with Tomatoes and Swiss Chard
Stir-Fried Dungeness Crab
    with Sweet Chili Sauce and Bok Choy
Trina's Green Salmon

SIDE DISHES

Arroz Verde (Green Rice)
Asparagus with Morels
Autumn Squash and Corn
Aviyal (Mixed Vegetables with Coconut and Tamarind)
Ayib be Gomen (Collards with Cottage Cheese)
Baby Green Garlic Mashed Potatoes
Baby Potatoes with Lemon and Chives
Baked Honey Tomatoes
Baked Tomatoes with Feta
Ballistic Baby Bok Choy and Fried Tofu
Barbecued Potatoes
Basmati Rice with Mushrooms, Broccoli, and Onion
Beer-Simmered Cabbage Rolls
Beets and Their Greens with Aïoli
Big Jim Chiles Stuffed with Corn and Jack Cheese
Blasted Broccoli
Bok Choy Provençale
Braised Lettuces
Butternut Surprise
Chard and Cheddar Omelet
Chard with Raisins and Almonds
Cherry Tomato Shish Kebobs
Colcannon
Congri (Cuban Beans and Rice)
Corn Pudding
Corn-Mac Casserole
Curried Mustard Greens & Garbanzo Beans
    with Sweet Potatoes
Dilled Cabbage with Ham
Fried Squash Blossoms
Garlic Spinach

Ginger Kale
Gomae (Sesame Spinach)
Grandma's Spinach Souffle
Green Curry Chicken with Broccoli and Cauliflower
Green Onion Pancakes
Grilled Eggplant Quesadillas
Kale Mashed Potatoes
Kohlrabi Kebabs
Kohlrabi Stuffed with Peppers
Layered Vegetable Casserole
Lemon-Walnut Green Beans
Marinated Tofu with Mizuna or Swiss Chard
Mexican-Style Corn on the Cob
Midi-Poche (Eggplant Bake)
Mizuna and Summer Squash
Mother Africa's Spicy Kale and Yam
Mustard Greens with Pepper Vinegar
Mylar's Rosemary Potato Wedges
Oregano and Zucchini Pasta
Parmesan-Baked Kohlrabi
Pasta with Arugula
Pasta with Savoy Cabbage and Gruyère
Pasta with Veggies and Cheese
Pea Pods with Raspberries
Peppery Potato and Zucchini Packets on the Grill
Poached Garlic
Potato and Leek Gratin
Potato and Turnip Au Gratin with Leeks
Ratatouille Niçoise
Rice with Lemongrass and Onion
Roasted Bacon-Wrapped Asparagus
Roasted Cauliflower
Roasted Green Beans
Roasted Radishes and Root Vegetables
Roasted Squash with Potatoes and Garlic
Sautéed Radishes and Sugar Snap Peas with Dill
Simple Kale
Southern-Style Greens with Slab Bacon
Spicy Cabbage
Spinach, Nuts, and Cheese
Spinach Superballs
Squash-Apple Casserole
Stuffed and Baked Sweet Onions
Stuffed Squash
Stuffed Squash with Basil and Honey
Summer Squash Casserole
Summer Vegetable Medley
Sweet Onion Casserole
Swiss Chard Wonton Raviolis
Tender Tatsoi with Sesame Oil Vinaigrette
The Enchanted Broccoli Forest
Tomatoes Stuffed with Blue Cheese and Walnuts
Turnip "Fries"
Turnip-Potato Purée
Turnips with Tomatoes and Mint
Turnips, Pumpkin, and Potatoes
Twice-Roasted Miniature Pumpkins

Recipes by Ingredient

BROCCOLI

Basic Lo Mein
Basmati Rice with Mushrooms, Broccoli and Onion
Blasted Broccoli
Broccoli Soup
Broccoli Stem Salad
Chicken Stir-Fry with Basil
Enchanted Broccoli Forest
Green Curry Chicken with Broccoli and Cauliflower
Millet Garden Medley
Pasta with Veggies and Cheese
Summer Vegetable Medley
Vegetable Cornmeal Crepes

CABBAGE (GREEN OR RED HEAD)

Abidjan Cabbage Salad
Basic Lo Mein
Beer-Simmered Cabbage Rolls
Colcannon
Coleslaw
Dilled Cabbage with Ham
Mother Africa's Spicy Kale and Yam
Spicy Cabbage
Summer Savory Soup
Ultimate Root Soup
Vegetable Broth
Warm Red Cabbage Bacon Salad

CABBAGE (NAPA)

Asian Fusion Slaw
Tachiyama Chanko-Nabe (Tachiyama's Beef
   and Chicken Hot Pot)

CABBAGE (SAVOY)

Pasta with Savoy Cabbage and Gruyère

CANTALOUPE

Bacon, Lettuce, and Cantaloupe Sandwich
Minty Melon Salad
Cantaloupe Pie
Spicy Cantaloupe Salsa

CAULIFLOWER

Green Curry Chicken with Broccoli and Cauliflower
Pasta with Veggies and Cheese
Roasted Cauliflower
Summer Savory Soup
Summer Vegetable Medley

Vichyssoise (with Cauliflower)
Zucchini Salad

CHIVES

Baby Potatoes with Lemon and Chives
Boursin Dip
Chive and Parmesan Popcorn
Cream of Leek Soup
Herb Butter
Low-Fat Ranch Dip
Salmon, Cucumber, and Dill Salad
Tarragon Chicken Marinade
Tender Tatsoi with Sesame Oil Vinaigrette
Turnip-Potato Purée

CILANTRO

Arroz Verde (Green Rice)
Asian Fusion Slaw
Chicken Coconut Soup with Lemongrass
Chicken Pumpkin Chili
Cilantro Lime Vinaigrette
Dal Makhani (Indian Lentils and Beans)
Garlic Compound Butter
Homemade Salsa
Maine Lobster Chowder with Coconut, Corn,
   and Lemongrass
Mexican Black Bean and Tomato Salad
Mylar's Lettuce Wraps
Roasted Chiles in Sauce with Pine Nuts and Cream
Roasted Eggplant Salad with Beans and Cashews
Sabzi (Herb Salad)
Sheila Lukins's Summer Succotash Salad
Spaghetti with Cilantro, Corn, and Tomatoes
Spicy Cabbage
Spicy Cantaloupe Salsa
Turnips with Tomatoes and Mint
Vegetarian Stir-Fry

COLLARDS

Ayib be Gomen (Collards with Cottage Cheese)
Millet Garden Medley
Southern-Style Greens with Slab Bacon

CORN

Autumn Squash and Corn
Basic Lo Mein
Big Jim Chiles Stuffed with Corn and Jack Cheese
Corn Chowder
Corn Oysters
Corn Pudding
Corn Salsa

- Corn Soup with Basil
- Corn-Mac Casserole
- Grilled Summer Corn and Sugar Snap Pea Salad
- Maine Lobster Chowder with Coconut, Corn, and Lemongrass
- Mexican-Style Corn on the Cob
- Millet Garden Medley
- Sheila Lukins's Summer Succotash Salad
- Spaghetti with Cilantro, Corn, and Tomatoes

CUCUMBERS

- Agua de Pepino (Cucumber Limeade)
- Aviyal (Mixed Vegetables with Coconut and Tamarind)
- Barely Pickled Cucumbers
- Cherry Tomato Shish Kebobs
- Golden Gazpacho
- Greek Salad
- Honeydew and Cucumber Salad with Sesame
- Salmon, Cucumber, and Dill Salad
- Seedless Cucumbers, Yogurt, Mint and Garlic Salad
- Sheila Lukins's Summer Succotash Salad
- Sour Cream Potato Salad
- Spicy Pork Tenderloin Pitas
- Tomato, Onion, and Cucumber Salad
- Tossed Mesclun Salad
- Vegetable Subs
- Watermelon and Chicken Salad
- White Bean and Basil Salad

DILL

- Barely Pickled Cucumbers
- Borscht
- Creamy Dill Dressing
- Dilled Cabbage with Ham
- Dilled Vegetable-Barley Soup
- Pickled Green Beans
- Radish, Mango, and Apple Salad
- Sabzi (Herb Salad)
- Salmon, Cucumber, and Dill Salad
- Sautéed Radishes and Sugar Snap Peas with Dill
- The Enchanted Broccoli Forest
- Ultimate Root Soup
- Warm Onion Dip

EGGPLANT

- Aviyal (Mixed Vegetables with Coconut and Tamarind)
- Baba Ghanoush (Eggplant Dip)
- Grilled Eggplant Quesadillas
- Layered Vegetable Casserole
- Midi-Poche (Eggplant Bake)
- Eggplant, Tomato, and Red Potato Casserole
- Pasta with Veggies and Cheese

- Ratatouille Niçoise
- Roasted Eggplant Salad with Beans and Cashews
- Spicy Roasted Vegetable Soup

GARLIC (GREEN)

- Baby Green Garlic Mashed Potatoes
- Citrus Butter Salad
- Garlic Scape Pizza
- Garlic Scape Soup
- Marinated Zucchini
- Simple Kale
- Spinach, Nuts, and Cheese
- Tarragon Vinegar
- Ultimate Root Soup

GARLIC

- 15-Minute Rosemary Lamb Chops
- Aïoli
- Arroz Verde (Green Rice)
- Asian Turkey Lettuce Wraps
- Asparagus and Morels
- Baba Ghanoush (Eggplant Dip)
- Ballistic Baby Bok Choy and Fried Tofu
- Barbecued Potatoes
- Basic Lo Mein
- Basmati Rice with Mushrooms, Broccoli, and Onion
- Beef Bourguignon (French Stew)
- Beets and Their Greens with Aïoli
- Big Jim Chiles Stuffed with Corn and Jack Cheese
- Black Bean Soup with Garlic and Summer Savory
- Blackberry-Walnut Mesclun Salad
- Bok Choy Provençale
- Borscht
- Braised Lettuces
- Carrot Salad
- Chard and Cheddar Omelet
- Chicken Pumpkin Chili
- Chicken with 40 Cloves of Garlic
- Cilantro Lime Vinaigrette
- Congri (Cuban Beans and Rice)
- Corn Soup with Basil
- Cream of Leek Soup
- Curried Mustard Greens and Garbanzo Beans with Sweet Potatoes
- Dilled Vegetable-Barley Soup
- Eggplant, Tomato, and Red Potato Casserole
- Enchiladas Verdes
- French Cream of Lettuce Soup
- Garlic Compound Butter
- Garlic Scape Pizza
- Garlic Spinach
- Ginger Kale
- Golden Gazpacho
- Greek Salad and Dressing

Homemade Salsa
🖛 Jesse's Chicken Stew
John's Winter Squash Soup with Vanilla Ice Cream
Khaji Namul (Eggplant Salad with Sesame Seeds)
🖛 Maine Lobster Chowder with Coconut, Corn,
  and Lemongrass
Marinated Bean Salad
Mexican Black Bean and Tomato Salad
Midi-Poche (Eggplant Bake)
Millet Garden Medley
Mizuna and Summer Squash
🖛 Mother Africa's Spicy Kale and Yam
Mustard Greens with Pepper Vinegar
🖛 Mylar's Rosemary Potato Wedges
🖛 Oregano and Zucchini Pasta
Oven-Roasted Tomato Sauce
Pasta with Arugula
Pesto
Peter Rabbit's Birthday Soup
🖛 Pickled Green Beans
🖛 Poached Garlic
Potato and Leek Gratin
🖛 Potato and Turnip Au Gratin with Leeks
Quick Tomato Sauce for the Freezer
🖛 Ratatouille Niçoise
Raw Kale Salad
🖛 Roast Chicken with Root Vegetables
Roasted Butternut Squash, Rosemary,
  and Garlic Lasagne
🖛 Roasted Garlic Hummus
🖛 Roasted Radishes and Root Vegetables
Roasted Squash with Potatoes and Garlic
🖛 Rosemary Crockpot Chicken
Sautéed Mushrooms on Tricolore Salad
Seasonal Salad with Herb Vinaigrette
🖛 Seedless Cucumbers, Yogurt, Mint, and Garlic Salad
Sheila Lukins's Summer Succotash Salad
Soupe au Pistou (French Vegetable Soup with Pesto)
Spaghetti with Cilantro, Corn, and Tomatoes
Spaghetti with Spring Vegetables
🖛 Spicy Cabbage
Spicy Pork Tenderloin Pitas
🖛 Spicy Roasted Vegetable Soup
Spicy Veal Roast
Spinach and Warm Sungold Tomato Salad
Spinach Superballs
Spinach, Nuts, and Cheese
Stir-Fried Dungeness Crab with Sweet Chili Sauce
  and Bok Choy
Summer Savory Soup
Summer Vegetable Medley
Sunflower Meatloaf
Sungold Salad with Feta and Cumin-Yogurt Dressing
Swiss Chard Wonton Raviolis

Tachiyama Chanko-Nabe (Tachiyama's Beef
  and Chicken Hot Pot)
The Enchanted Broccoli Forest
🖛 Vegetable Broth
Vegetable Lasagna
🖛 Vegetarian Stir-Fry
🖛 Vegetarian Stuffed Peppers
White Bean and Basil Salad
Wild Mushroom and Mizuna Salad
Wrigley-Marco's Caesar Salad
Zucchini Salad

KALE

Basic Lo Mein
🖛 Ginger Kale
🖛 Kale Mashed Potatoes
🖛 Millet Garden Medley
🖛 Mother Africa's Spicy Kale and Yam
  (Abba's African Hot Sauce)
🖛 Raw Kale Salad
🖛 Simple Kale

KOHLRABI

🖛 Kohlrabi Kebabs
🖛 Kohlrabi Stuffed with Peppers
🖛 Parmesan-Baked Kohlrabi

LEEKS

🖛 Bacon, Ham, and Leek Quiche
🖛 Cream of Leek Soup
🖛 Potato and Leek Gratin
🖛 Potato and Turnip Au Gratin with Leeks
🖛 Potato Leek Soup
🖛 Roast Chicken with Root Vegetables
Soupe au Pistou (French Vegetable Soup with Pesto)
Tachiyama Chanko-Nabe (Tachiyama's Beef
  and Chicken Hot Pot)
🖛 Ultimate Root Soup
🖛 Vegetable Bouillon
🖛 Vegetable Broth
🖛 Vichyssoise (with Cauliflower)
🖛 Yukon Gold Potato Soup

LEMONGRASS

🖛 Chicken Coconut Soup with Lemongrass
🖛 Iced Green Tea with Lemongrass and Ginger
🖛 Maine Lobster Chowder with Coconut, Corn,
  and Lemongrass
🖛 Rice with Lemongrass and Onion
🖛 Summer Fruit in Wine Dessert

LETTUCE (BUTTER AND LEAF)

- Asian Turkey Lettuce Wraps
- Bacon, Lettuce, and Cantaloupe Sandwich
- Braised Lettuces
- Citrus Butter Salad
- French Cream of Lettuce Soup
- Greek Salad and Dressing
- Mylar's Lettuce Wraps
- Pamela's Fresh Pea Soup
- Roasted Baby Beet Salad
- Salad Niçoise
- Southwestern Radish Salad
- Stir-Fried Dungeness Crab with Sweet Chili Sauce and Bok Choy
- Tossed Mesclun Salad
- Vegetable Subs

LETTUCE (ROMAINE)

- Greek Salad and Dressing
- Jonno's Caesar Dressing
- Tossed Mesclun Salad
- Wrigley-Marco's Caesar Salad

MELON (HONEYDEW)

- Honeydew and Cucumber Salad with Sesame
- Iced Honeydew and Gewurztraminer Soup
- Raspberry-Honeydew Parfaits
- Summer Fruit in Wine Dessert

MIZUNA

- Farmer's Market Green Salad with Fried Shallots
- Marinated Tofu with Mizuna or Swiss Chard
- Mizuna and Summer Squash
- Spinach, Rocket and Mizuna Salad
- Wild Mushroom and Mizuna Salad with White Truffle Vinaigrette and Sage

MUSTARD GREENS

- Curried Mustard Greens and Garbanzo Beans with Sweet Potatoes
- Mustard Greens with Pepper Vinegar
- Wilted Mustard Greens Salad with Bacon

ONIONS (GREEN)

- Asian Fusion Slaw
- Asian Turkey Lettuce Wraps
- Asparagus and Spinach Soup
- Ballistic Baby Bok Choy and Fried Tofu
  Golden Gazpacho

- Green Onion Pancakes
  Honeydew and Cucumber Salad with Sesame
  Khaji Namul (Eggplant Salad with Sesame Seeds)
- Lemon-Walnut Green Beans
  Mexican Black Bean and Tomato Salad
  Millet Garden Medley
  Miso Broth with Tatsoi-Enoki Salad
  Mother Africa's Spicy Kale and Yam
  Onion Lover's Dip
- Rice with Lemongrass and Green Onion
  Sabzi (Herb Salad)
  Sour Cream Potato Salad
  Southwestern Radish Salad
  Stir-Fried Dungeness Crab with Sweet Chili Sauce and Bok Choy
- Sungold Salad with Feta and Cumin-Yogurt Dressing
  Tarragon Chicken Marinade
  Tender Tatsoi with Sesame Oil Vinaigrette
  Tossed Mesclun Salad
  Watermelon and Chicken Salad
  White Bean and Basil Salad

ONIONS

  Arroz Verde (Green Rice)
  Aviyal (Mixed Vegetables with Coconut and Tamarind)
  Baba Ghanoush (Eggplant Dip)
- Basmati Rice with Mushrooms, Broccoli, and Onion
- Beef Bourguignon (French Stew)
  Beer-Simmered Cabbage Rolls
  Big Jim Chiles Stuffed with Corn and Jack Cheese
  Black Bean Soup with Garlic and Summer Savory
- Bok Choy Provençale
- Borscht
  Broccoli Soup
  Broccoli Stem Salad
  Chicken Pumpkin Chili
- Congri (Cuban Beans and Rice)
- Corn Chowder
  Corn Soup with Basil
- Creamy Green Bean and Mushroom Soup
- Curried Mustard Greens and Garbanzo Beans with Sweet Potatoes
- Dal Makhani (Indian Lentils and Beans)
  Deviled Eggs with Salmon and Basil
- Dilled Vegetable-Barley Soup
- Eggplant, Tomato, and Red Potato Casserole
- Enchiladas Verdes
- French Cream of Lettuce Soup
- French Onion Soup
- Garlic Scape Pizza
  Garlic Scape Soup
  Ginger Kale
  Greek Salad
- Green Onion Pancakes

Mesclun with Maple Mustard Tofu Points
Mylar's Lettuce Wraps
Oven-Roasted Tomato Sauce
Ratatouille Niçoise
Roast Chicken with Root Vegetables
Roasted Chiles in Sauce with Pine Nuts and Cream
S. Nardecchia's Spaghetti Sauce
Salad Niçoise
Salsa Marinade
Spaghetti with Spring Vegetables
Spicy Cantaloupe Salsa
Spicy Pork Tenderloin Pitas
Spicy Roasted Vegetable Soup
Stuffed and Baked Sweet Onions
Summer Squash Casserole
Summer Vegetable Medley
Terhune Orchards Vegetable Soup
Tossed Mesclun Salad
Vegetable Cornmeal Crepes
Vegetarian Paella
Vegetarian Stir-Fry
Vegetarian Stuffed Peppers
Watermelon Gazpacho
White Bean and Basil Salad
Zucchini Salad

PEPPERS (HOT)

Aviyal (Mixed Vegetables with Coconut and Tamarind)
Ballistic Baby Bok Choy and Fried Tofu
Big Jim Chiles Stuffed with Corn and Jack Cheese
    (Poblano)
Black Bean Soup with Garlic and Summer Savory
    (Jalapeño)
Chicken Coconut Soup with Lemongrass
    (Green or red chiles)
Chicken Pumpkin Chili (Jalapeño)
Chili Oil
Corn Salsa (Serrano)
Dal Makhani (Indian Lentils and Beans) (Jalapeño)
Enchiladas Verdes
Grilled Summer Corn and Sugar Snap Pea Salad
    (Serrano, jalapeño, habañero)
Homemade Salsa (Jalapeño)
Mother Africa's Spicy Kale and Yam
    (Serrano, jalapeño, habañero)
Salsa Marinade
Spicy Cabbage
Spicy Cantaloupe Salsa
Vegetable Subs
Watermelon Strawberry Mint Salsa (Jalapeño)

POTATOES (RUSSET OR BAKING)

Aviyal (Mixed Vegetables with Coconut and Tamarind)
Baby Green Garlic Mashed Potatoes

Baby Potatoes with Lemon and Chives
Borscht
Creamy Spinach Soup
Kale Mashed Potatoes
LaVerne's Potato Candy
Millet Garden Medley
Mylar's Rosemary Potato Wedges
Peppery Potato and Zucchini Packets on the Grill
Peter Rabbit's Birthday Soup
Potato and Turnip Au Gratin with Leeks
Potato Leek Soup
Roasted Squash with Potatoes and Garlic
Salad Niçoise
Sour Cream Potato Salad
Sunflower Meatloaf
Tachiyama Chanko-Nabe (Tachiyama's Beef
    and Chicken Hot Pot)
Turnip-Potato Purée
Turnips, Pumpkin, and Potatoes
Ultimate Root Soup
Vegetable Cornmeal Crepes
Vichyssoise (with Cauliflower)

POTATOES
(YUKON GOLD, RED, OR NEW)

Baby Potatoes with Lemon and Chives
Barbecued Potatoes
Eggplant, Tomato, and Red Potato Casserole
Jesse's Chicken Stew
Kale Mashed Potatoes
Millet Garden Medley
Potato and Leek Gratin
Roast Chicken with Root Vegetables
Salad Niçoise
Soupe au Pistou (French Vegetable Soup with Pesto)
Yukon Gold Potato Soup

PUMPKIN

Chicken Pumpkin Chili
Pumpkin Pie with Spiced Walnut Streusel
Roasted Pumpkin Seeds
Turnips, Pumpkin, and Potatoes
Twice-Roasted Miniature Pumpkins

RASPBERRIES

Baked Rhubarb with Raspberries
Crockpot Chocolate Raspberry Strata
Fruit Shake
Pea Pods with Raspberries
Polka Dot Clouds
Raspberry Creme
Raspberry-Honeydew Parfaits

- Raspberry Whip
- Summer Fruit in Wine Dessert

RADISHES

Mushroom, Snow Pea, and Spinach Salad
- Radish, Mango, and Apple Salad
- Radishes with Salt and Butter
- Roasted Radishes and Root Vegetables
- Sautéed Radishes and Sugar Snap Peas with Dill
- Southwestern Radish Salad
Zucchini Salad

RHUBARB

- Baked Rhubarb with Raspberries
- Balsamic Rhubarb Compote
- Rhubarb Chutney
- Rhubarb Crisp
- Rhubarb Pie

ROSEMARY

- 15-Minute Rosemary Lamb Chops
- Braised Lamb with Olives and Mushrooms
Braised Lettuces
Chicken with 40 Cloves of Garlic
- Mylar's Rosemary Potato Wedges
- Roast Chicken with Root Vegetables
- Roasted Butternut Squash, Rosemary, and Garlic Lasagne
Roasted Squash with Potatoes and Garlic
- Rosemary Crockpot Chicken
- Rosemary- or Basil-Infused Oil
- S. Nardecchia's Spaghetti Sauce
Sautéed Mushrooms on Tricolore Salad

SALAD MIX

- Blackberry-Walnut Mesclun Salad
- Greek Salad
- Mesclun with Maple Mustard Tofu Points
- Poached Eggs with Pancetta and Tossed Mesclun
- Seasonal Salad with Herb Vinaigrette
- Tossed Mesclun Salad

SAVORY

- Black Bean Soup with Garlic and Summer Savory
- Summer Savory Soup
- Sunflower Meat Loaf

SPINACH

- Asparagus and Spinach Soup
- Creamy Spinach Soup
Garlic Scape Pizza
- Garlic Spinach
- Gomae (Sesame Spinach)
- Grandma's Spinach Soufflé
- Mushroom, Snow Pea, and Spinach Salad
- Pamela's Fresh Pea Soup
- Pasta with Veggies and Cheese
- Sabzi (Herb Salad)
Spicy Pork Tenderloin Pitas
- Spinach and Warm Sungold Tomato Salad
- Spinach Superballs
- Spinach, Nuts, and Cheese
- Spinach, Rocket, and Mizuna Salad
Summer Savory Soup
- Trina's Green Salmon
Vegetable Frittata
- Wilted Greens with Coconut

SQUASH (SUMMER)

- Fried Squash Blossoms (blossoms only)
- Mizuna and Summer Squash
- Stuffed Squash with Basil and Honey
- Summer Squash Casserole
- Summer Squash Muffins
- Vegetable Frittata

SQUASH (WINTER, INCLUDING ACORN AND BUTTERNUT)

- Autumn Squash and Corn
- Butternut Surprise
- Ginger Squash Soup
- John's Winter Squash Soup with Vanilla Ice Cream
- Roast Chicken with Root Vegetables
- Roasted Butternut Squash, Rosemary, and Garlic Lasagne
- Roasted Squash with Potatoes and Garlic
- Squash-Apple Casserole
- Stuffed Squash

STRAWBERRIES

- Fruit Shake
- Strawberry Breakfast Pizza
- Strawberry Nachos
- Strawberry Shortcake
- Summer Fruit in Wine Dessert
- Sweet-Tart Fresh Strawberries
- Watermelon Strawberry Mint Salsa

SWISS CHARD

Basic Lo Mein
- Chard and Cheddar Omelet
- Chard with Raisins and Almonds
- Marinated Tofu with Mizuna or Swiss Chard
- Salmon Poached with Tomatoes and Swiss Chard
- Swiss Chard Wonton Raviolis

TARRAGON

- French Cream of Lettuce Soup
- Low-Fat Ranch Dip
- Mushroom, Snow Pea, and Spinach Salad
- Poached Eggs with Pancetta and Tossed Mesclun
- Spicy Veal Roast
- Tarragon Chicken Marinade
- Tarragon Vinegar
Vegetarian Paella

TATSOI

- Farmer's Market Green Salad with Fried Shallots
- Miso Broth with Tatsoi-Enoki Salad
- Tender Tatsoi with Sesame Oil Vinaigrette

THYME

Braised Lettuces
Broccoli Soup
- Chicken with 40 Cloves of Garlic
- Garlic Compound Butter
Garlic Scape Soup
- Jesse's Chicken Stew
- Layered Vegetable Casserole
Midi-Poche (Eggplant Bake)
- Peppery Potato and Zucchini Packets on the Grill
- Roasted Radishes and Root Vegetables
- Spicy Veal Roast
- Stuffed and Baked Sweet Onions
- Terhune Orchards Vegetable Soup
- Thyme and Mushroom Gravy
Twice-Roasted Miniature Pumpkins
- Vegetable Broth
- Vegetable Cornmeal Crepes

TOMATOES (CHERRY)

- Cherry Tomato Shish Kebobs
- Garlic Scape Pizza
- Golden Gazpacho
- Maine Lobster Chowder with Coconut, Corn, and Lemongrass
- Spicy Pork Tenderloin Pitas

Spicy Roasted Vegetable Soup
- Spinach and Warm Sungold Salad
- Sungold Salad with Feta and Cumin-Yogurt Dressing
- Vegetarian Stuffed Peppers

TOMATOES

Baba Ghanoush (Eggplant Dip)
- Baked Chicken and Zucchini
- Baked Honey Tomatoes
- Baked Tomatoes with Feta
- Corn Salsa
Corn Soup with Basil
- Eggplant, Tomato, and Red Potato Casserole
- Enchiladas Verdes
- Greek Salad
- Grilled Eggplant Quesadillas
- Homemade Salsa
Layered Vegetable Casserole
- Marinated Bean Salad
- Mexican Black Bean and Tomato Salad
- Midi-Poche (Eggplant Bake)
- Millet Garden Medley
- Oven-Roasted Tomato Sauce
- Pasta with Arugula
Pasta with Veggies and Cheese
- Quick Tomato Sauce for the Freezer
- Ratatouille Niçoise
- Salad Niçoise
- Salmon Poached with Tomatoes and Swiss Chard
Salmon, Cucumber, and Dill Salad
- Salsa Marinade
Sheila Lukins's Summer Succotash Salad
- Spaghetti with Cilantro, Corn, and Tomatoes
- Spaghetti with Spring Vegetables
Spicy Roasted Vegetable Soup
- Stuffed and Baked Sweet Onions
- Terhune Orchards Vegetable Soup
- Tomato, Onion, and Cucumber Salad
- Tomatoes Stuffed with Blue Cheese and Walnuts
- Turnips with Tomatoes and Mint
Vegetable Bouillon
- Vegetable Lasagna
Vegetable Subs
Zucchini Salad

TURNIPS

- Potato and Turnip Au Gratin with Leeks
- Turnip "Fries"
- Turnip-Potato Purée
- Turnips with Tomatoes and Mint
- Turnips, Pumpkin, and Potatoes
Ultimate Root Soup
- Vegetable Bouillon

WATERMELON

- Watermelon and Chicken Salad
- Watermelon Bits
- Watermelon Gazpacho
- Watermelon Pineapple Preserves
- Watermelon Smoothie
- Watermelon Strawberry Mint Salsa

ZUCCHINI

- Baked Chicken and Zucchini
- Fried Squash Blossoms (blossoms only)
  Layered Vegetable Casserole
- Marinated Zucchini
- Oregano and Zucchini Pasta
- Peppery Potato and Zucchini Packets on the Grill
- Ratatouille Niçoise
- Soupe au Pistou (French Vegetable Soup with Pesto)
  Spaghetti with Spring Vegetables
- Spicy Roasted Vegetable Soup
- Summer Squash Muffins
- Ten-Minute Zucchini Pizza
- Terhune Orchards Vegetable Soup
- Vegetable Cornmeal Crepes
- Vegetable Lasagna
- Zucchini Casserole
- Zucchini Pickles
- Zucchini Salad

Vegetarian and Vegan Recipes

None of the vegetarian recipes listed here contain meat, seafood, or poultry, but they may contain eggs and dairy. Many of the recipes in this book may be altered to be vegetarian by omitting meat, chicken, and seafood, and substituting vegetable stock for chicken or beef broth.

VEGETARIAN

Abba's African Hot Sauce
Abidjan Cabbage Salad
Agua de Pepino (Cucumber Limeade)
Aïoli
Arugula and Grilled Goat Cheese Salad
Asian Fusion Slaw
Autumn Squash and Corn
Aviyal (Mixed Vegetables with Coconut and Tamarind)
Ayib be Gomen (Collards with Cottage Cheese)
Baba Ghanoush (Eggplant Dip)
Baby Green Garlic Mashed Potatoes
Baby Potatoes with Lemon and Chives
Baked Honey Tomatoes
Baked Rhubarb with Raspberries
Baked Tomatoes with Feta
Ballistic Baby Bok Choy and Fried Tofu
Balsamic Rhubarb Compote
Barely Pickled Cucumbers
Basmati Rice with Mushrooms, Broccoli, and Onion
Beet-Chocolate Cake
Beets and Their Greens with Aïoli
Big Jim Chiles Stuffed with Corn and Jack Cheese
Black Bean Soup with Garlic and Summer Savory
Blackberry-Walnut Mesclun Salad
Blasted Broccoli
Bok Choy Provençale
Borscht
Boursin Dip
Braised Lettuces
Broccoli Stem Salad
Butternut Surprise
Carrot Salad
Chard and Cheddar Omelet
Chard with Raisins and Almonds
Cherry Tomato Shish Kebobs
Chili Oil
Chive and Parmesan Popcorn
Cilantro Lime Vinaigrette

Citrus Butter Salad
Colcannon
Coleslaw
Congri (Cuban Beans and Rice)
Corn Chowder
Corn Oysters
Corn Pudding
Corn Salsa
Corn Soup with Basil
Corn-Mac Casserole
Cream of Leek Soup
Creamy Dill Dressing
Creamy Green Bean and Mushroom Soup
Crockpot Chocolate Raspberry Strata
Cumin-Yogurt Dressing
Curried Mustard Greens and Garbanzo Beans
    with Sweet Potatoes
Dal Makhani (Indian Lentils and Beans)
Dilled Vegetable-Barley Soup
Eggplant, Tomato, and Red Potato Casserole
Farmer's Market Green Salad with Fried Shallots
French Cream of Lettuce Soup
Garlic Compound Butter
Garlic Spinach
Ginger Kale
Ginger Squash Soup
Golden Gazpacho
Gomae (Sesame Spinach)
Grandma's Spinach Soufflé
Greek Salad
Greek Salad Dressing
Green Onion Pancakes
Grilled Eggplant Quesadillas
Grilled Summer Corn and Sugar Snap Pea Salad
Herb Butter
Herb Vinaigrette
Homemade Salsa
Honeydew and Cucumber Salad with Sesame
Iced Green Tea with Lemongrass and Ginger
Iced Honeydew and Gewurztraminer Soup
John's Winter Squash Soup with Vanilla Ice Cream
Kale Mashed Potatoes
Khaji Namul (Eggplant Salad with Sesame Seeds)
Kohlrabi Kebabs
Kohlrabi Stuffed with Peppers
LaVerne's Potato Candy
Layered Vegetable Casserole
Lemon-Walnut Green Beans

Vegetarian Paella
Vegetarian Stir-Fry
Vegetarian Stuffed Peppers
Warm Onion Dip
Watermelon Bits
Watermelon Gazpacho
Watermelon Pineapple Preserves
Watermelon Smoothie
Watermelon Strawberry Mint Salsa
White Bean and Basil Salad
White Truffle Vinaigrette
Wild Mushroom and Mizuna Salad
Wilted Greens with Coconut
Yukon Gold Potato Soup
Zucchini Pickles
Zucchini Salad

VEGAN

None of the vegan recipes listed here contain meat, seafood, poultry, eggs, or dairy. Many of the recipes in this book may be altered to be vegan by omitting meat, chicken, and seafood; substituting vegetable stock for chicken or beef broth; and using dairy substitutes, like rice-, tofu-, or soy-based products.

Abba's African Hot Sauce
Abidjan Cabbage Salad
Agua de Pepino (Cucumber Limeade)
Asian Fusion Slaw
Aviyal (Mixed Vegetables with Coconut and Tamarind)
Baked Honey Tomatoes
Ballistic Baby Bok Choy and Fried Tofu
Balsamic Rhubarb Compote
Barely Pickled Cucumbers
Basil- or Rosemary-Infused Oil
Black Bean Soup with Garlic and Summer Savory
Blasted Broccoli
Borscht
Carrot Salad
Chili Oil
Cilantro Lime Vinaigrette
Citrus Butter Salad
Citrus Vinaigrette
Congri (Cuban Beans and Rice)
Corn Chowder
Cream of Leek Soup
Creamy Dill Dressing
Curried Mustard Greens and Garbanzo Beans
    with Sweet Potatoes
Dal Makhani (Indian Lentils and Beans)
Dilled Vegetable-Barley Soup
Eggplant, Tomato, and Red Potato Casserole
Farmer's Market Green Salad with Fried Shallots

Garlic Spinach
Golden Gazpacho
Gomae (Sesame Spinach)
Green Onion Pancakes
Grilled Summer Corn and Sugar Snap Pea Salad
Herb Vinaigrette
Homemade Salsa
Honeydew and Cucumber Salad with Sesame
Iced Green Tea with Lemongrass and Ginger
Kale Mashed Potatoes
Khaji Namul (Eggplant Salad with Sesame Seeds)
Kohlrabi Kebabs
Kohlrabi Stuffed with Peppers
Lemon-Walnut Green Beans
Low-Fat Ranch Dip
Marinated Bean Salad
Marinated Tofu with Mizuna or Swiss Chard
Marinated Zucchini
Mesclun with Maple Mustard Tofu Points
Mexican Black Bean and Tomato Salad
Millet Garden Medley
Minty Melon Salad
Miso Broth with Tatsoi-Enoki Salad
Moen Creek Pickled Beets
Mother Africa's Spicy Kale and Yam
Mushroom, Snow Pea, and Spinach Salad
Mylar's Rosemary Potato Wedges
Orange-Salsa Dressing
Oven-Roasted Tomato Sauce
Pea Pods with Raspberries
Peppery Potato and Zucchini Packets on the Grill
Pickled Green Beans
Potato Leek Soup
Quick Tomato Sauce for the Freezer
Raspberry-Honeydew Parfaits
Ratatouille Niçoise
Raw Kale Salad
Rhubarb Chutney
Rice with Lemongrass and Green Onion
Roasted Baby Beet Salad
Roasted Cauliflower
Roasted Eggplant Salad with Beans and Cashews
Roasted Garlic Hummus
Roasted Green Beans
Roasted Pumpkin Seeds
Roasted Radishes and Root Vegetables
Roasted Squash with Potatoes and Garlic
Rosemary- or Basil-Infused Oil
Sabzi (Herb Salad)
Salad Niçoise Vinaigrette
Salsa Marinade
Seasonal Salad with Herb Vinaigrette
Sesame Oil Vinaigrette
Sheila Lukins's Summer Succotash Salad
Soupe au Pistou (French Vegetable Soup with Pesto)
Spaghetti with Cilantro, Corn, and Tomatoes
Spaghetti with Spring Vegetables

General Index

Items in **boldface** indicate fruits and vegetables with their own sections in the book. Items in *italics* indicate book and magazine titles. Recipe titles are in initial-caps.

Permissions and Additional Credits

Grateful acknowledgment is made to all those who granted permission to reprint their material in this book. Every effort has been made to properly credit, trace, and contact copyright holders; if any error or omission has been made, please contact me, and I will be glad to remedy the situation in future editions of this book.

- "Arugula and Grilled Goat Cheese Salad"; "Kohlrabi Stuffed with Peppers"; "Radish, Mango, and Apple Salad"; and "Pasta with Savoy Cabbage and Gruyère" from *The Cook's Encyclopedia of Vegetables* by Christine Ingram. Copyright © 2001 by Christine Ingram. Used by permission of Lorenz Books, New York, New York.

- "Agua de Pepino (Cucumber Limeade)" by Fire & Ice Café. Reprinted from www.fireandicecafe.ie. Used by permission of Gary Masterson, Fire & Ice Café, Midleton, County Cork, Ireland.

- "Poached Eggs with Pancetta and Tossed Mesclun" by Julie Ridlon. Copyright © 2005 by Julie Ridlon, chef/owner, Chanterelle Catering and Clayton Farmer's Market, St. Louis, Missouri.

- "John's Winter Squash Soup with Vanilla Ice Cream" by Ben & Jerry's. Copyright © 2006 by Ben and Jerry's Homemade Holdings, Inc. Reprinted from www.benandjerrys.com. Used by permission of Ben & Jerry's Homemade Holdings, Inc., South Burlington, Vermont.

- "The Enchanted Broccoli Forest" and "Dilled Vegetable-Barley Soup" from *The New Enchanted Broccoli Forest* by Mollie Katzen. Copyright © 1982, 1995, 2000 by Tante Malka, Inc., and Ten Speed Press. Reprinted with permission from Mollie Katzen and Ten Speed Press, Berkeley, California.

- "Wilted Greens with Coconut"; "Grilled Summer Corn and Sugar Snap Pea Salad"; "Spicy Cabbage"; and "Swiss Chard Wonton Raviolis" from *The Farmer's Market Cookbook* by Richard Ruben. Copyright © 2000 by Richard Ruben. Used by permission of The Lyons Press, Guilford, Connecticut.

- "Basic Lo Mein" and "Vegetable Broth" from *The Garden Fresh Vegetable Cookbook* by Andrea Chesman. Copyright © 2005 by Andrea Chesman. Used by permission of Storey Publishing LLC, North Adams, Massachusetts.

- "Marinated Tofu with Mizuna or Swiss Chard" by Seabreeze Organic Farm. Reprinted from www.seabreezed.com. Used by permission of Seabreeze Organic Farm, San Diego, California.

- "Pumpkin Pie with Spiced Walnut Streusel"; "Sautéed Radishes and Sugar Snap Peas with Dill"; and "Farmer's Market Green Salad with Fried Shallots" by Epicurious.com. Reprinted from www.epicurious.com. Used by permission of Epicurious.com.

- "Minty Melon Salad"; "Millet Garden Medley"; and "Chicken Stir-Fry with Basil" by Whole Foods Market. Reprinted from www.wholefoodsmarket.com. Recipes courtesy of and used by permission of Whole Foods Market, Austin, Texas.

- "Strawberry Nachos" by Roz Kelmig and "Strawberry Breakfast Pizza" from the California Strawberry Commission. Reprinted from www.calstrawberry.com. Used by permission of the California Strawberry Commission.

- "Summer Savory Soup" and "Black Bean Soup with Garlic and Summer Savory" from Brenda Hyde. Reprinted from www.oldfashionedliving.com. Copyright © 2005 by Brenda Hyde. Used by permission of Brenda Hyde.

- "Turnip-Potato Puree" and "Turnip 'Fries'" by *Saveur* Editors. Both published in *Saveur*, December 2002, Issue #63. Reprinted by permission. ✒ "Big Jim Chiles Stuffed with Corn and Jack Cheese" by Eugenia Bone. Published in *Saveur*, July/August 2001, Issue #52. Reprinted by permission. ✒ "Aviyal (Mixed Vegetables with Coconut and Tamarind)" by Maya Kaimal. Published in *Saveur*, September/October 2000, Issue #45. Reprinted by permission. ✒ Roast Chicken with Root Vegetables" by John Anderson. Published in *Saveur*, May/June 2001, Issue #51. Reprinted by permission. ✒ "Beets and Their Greens with Aïoli" by Prune Restaurant. Published in *Saveur*, September/October 2002, Issue #61. Reprinted by permission. ✒ "Tachiyama Chanko-Nabe (Tachiyama's Beef & Chicken Hot Pot)" by Tomoegata Restaurant. Published in *Saveur*, November 2002, Issue #62. Reprinted by permission. ✒ "Arroz Verde (Green Rice)" by Saveur Editors. Published in *Saveur*, April 1998, Issue #26. Reprinted by permission. ✒ "Sheila Lukins's Summer Succotash Salad" by Sheila Lukins. Published in *Saveur*, May/June 1995, Issue #6. Reprinted by permission.

✒ "Greek Salad"; "Greek Salad Dressing"; and "French Onion Soup" from *Sacramental Magic in a Small-Town Café* by Peter Reinhart, Addison Wesley. Copyright © 1994 by Peter Reinhart. Used by permission of the author.

✒ "Watermelon Pineapple Preserves"; "Watermelon and Chicken Salad"; and "Watermelon Gazpacho" from the National Watermelon Promotion Board. "Watermelon Strawberry Mint Salsa" by Chef Marty Blitz, Mise En Place, Tampa, Florida. All recipes reprinted from www.watermelon.org and used by permission of the National Watermelon Promotion Board.

✒ "Spaghetti with Cilantro, Corn, and Tomatoes" from *Uncommon Fruits & Vegetables* by Elizabeth Schneider, Harper & Row Publishers, Inc. Copyright © 1986 by Elizabeth Schneider. Used by permission of the author.

✒ "Borscht" from *Vegetarian Journal*, September 2000, by Debra Daniels-Zeller. Copyright © 2000 by The Vegetarian Resource Group/Vegetarian Journal. Used by permission of The Vegetarian Resource Group/Vegetarian Journal, Baltimore, Maryland.

✒ "Yukon Gold Potato Soup"; "Blasted Broccoli"; "Corn Pudding"; "Twice-Roasted Miniature Pumpkins"; and "Soupe au Pistou (French Vegetable Soup with Pesto)" by Greg Atkinson. Reprinted from www.northwestessentials.com. Copyright © 2005, 2006, by Greg Atkinson. Used by permission of the author.

✒ "Chili Oil" and "Sweet-Tart Fresh Strawberries" from *Cookwise* by Shirley Corriher. Copyright © 1997 by Shirley Corriher. Reprinted by permission of HarperCollins Publishers, William Morrow, New York, New York.

✒ "Onion Lover's Dip"; "Asparagus with Morels"; and "Vegetable Bouillon" from *The Greenmarket Cookbook*, by Joel Patraker, Viking Penguin. Copyright © 2000 by Joel Patraker. Used by permission of the author.

✒ "Midi-Poche (Eggplant Bake)"; "Asparagus and Spinach Soup"; "Asparagus and Shrimp Salad"; and "Zucchini Pickles" from *Greene on Greens* by Bert Greene, Workman Publishing Company, Inc., New York, New York. Copyright © 1984 by Bert Greene. Used by permission of the Estate of Bert Greene, represented by Sobel Weber Associates, Inc.

✒ "Turnips with Tomatoes and Mint" and "Corn Soup with Basil" from *The Vegetable Market Cookbook* by Robert Budwig. Copyright © 1993 by Robert Budwig and Ten Speed Press, Berkeley, California. Reprinted with permission by Robert Budwig.

✒ "Mizuna and Summer Squash" and "Baked Chicken and Zucchini" by Mariquita Farm. Reprinted from www.mariquita.com. Used by permission from Mariquita Farm, Watsonville, California.

✒ "Spicy Cantaloupe Salsa"; "Grilled Eggplant Quesadillas" by Marc Casale of Dos Coyotes Border Cafe, Davis, California; "Vegetable Frittata"; and "Potato and Turnip Au Gratin with Leeks" by David Cannata of Yolo Catering. All recipes from Davis Farmers Market, Davis, California; reprinted from www.davisfarmersmarket.org, and used under the Creative Commons Attribution License.

✒ "Mexican-Style Corn on the Cob"; "Autumn Squash and Corn"; "Potato and Leek Gratin"; "Southern-Style Greens with Slab Bacon"; and "Baked Tomatoes with Feta" from *More Vegetables, Please*, by Janet Fletcher. Copyright © 1992 by Janet Fletcher. Reprinted by permission of Harlow & Ratner, Berkeley, California.

✒ "Creamy Green Bean and Mushroom Soup"; "Spicy Roasted Vegetable Soup"; "Golden Gazpacho"; "Spinach and Warm Sungold Salad"; and "Sungold Salad with Feta & Cumin-Yogurt Dressing" by Coleen Wolner, Chef, Blue Heron Coffeehouse, Winona, Minnesota. "Creamy Green Bean and Mushroom Soup" and "Spicy Roasted Vegetable Soup" reprinted from the *Bluff Country Co-op Cookbook*. Recipes used by permission of Colleen Wolner and the Bluff Country Co-op, Winona, Minnesota.

✒ "Fruit Shake" by Kathy Delano. Reprinted from the *Bluff Country Co-op Cookbook*. Recipe used by permission of Kathy Delano.

✒ "Boursin Dip"; "Wrigley-Marco's Caesar Salad"; "Salsa Marinade"; "Peter Rabbit's Birthday Soup"; and "S. Nardecchia's Spaghetti Sauce" by Maureen Cooney. Reprinted from the *Bluff Country Co-op Cookbook*. Recipe used by permission of Maureen Cooney and the Bluff Country Co-op, Winona, Minnesota.

. . . .

The following Featherstone CSA members generously donated recipes for the farm's CSA newsletters and this cookbook.

- Amy Chen—"Corn Salsa."
- Emily—"Herb Butter."
- Claire—"Cream of Leek Soup" (adapted from *Cooking for Dummies*, by Bryan Miller and Marie Rama, 2004, IDG Books Worldwide, Foster City, California).
- Jonno—"Jonno's Caesar Dressing."
- Judy—"Spinach, Nuts, and Cheese."
- Margaret Houston—"Simple Romaine Salad"; "Grandma's Spinach Soufflé"; and "Ratatouille Niçoise."
- Margaret Trott—"Cherry Tomato Shish Kebobs"; "Pasta wth Veggies and Cheese"; and "Parmesan-Baked Kohlrabi" and "Stuffed and Baked Sweet Onions" [by Barbara Hunt]).
- Mi Ae Lipe—"Roasted Bacon-Wrapped Asparagus"; "Deviled Eggs with Salmon and Basil"; "Mylar's Lettuce Wraps"; "Garlic Spinach"; "Barely Pickled Cucumbers"; "Mylar's Rosemary Potato Wedges"; "Tomato, Onion, and Cucumber Salad"; "Oregano and Zucchini Pasta"; "Roasted Pumpkin Seeds"; "Radishes with Salt and Butter"; and "Polka Dot Clouds."
- Pam Garetto—"Seasonal Salad with Herb Vinaigrette"; "Roasted Cauliflower"; and "Carrot Salad."
- Robin Taylor—"Rhubarb Crisp"; "Mexican Black Bean and Tomato Salad"; "White Bean and Basil Salad"; "Raw Kale Salad"; and "Dal Makhani (Indian Lentils and Beans)."
- Ruth Charles—"Pasta with Arugula"; "Bok Choy Provençale"; and "Chard with Raisins and Almonds."
- Susan Roehl—"Broccoli Stem Salad."
- Tracy—"Potato Leek Soup."

The following recipes are courtesy of Featherstone Farm (reprinted from its CSA newsletters).

- "Ultimate Root Soup"; "Citrus Butter Salad"; "Gomae (Sesame Spinach)"; "Roasted Eggplant Salad with Beans and Cashews"; "Peppery Potato and Zucchini Packets on the Grill" "Stuffed Squash with Basil and Honey"; "Tarragon Chicken Marinade" by Jan Taylor; "Quick Tomato Sauce for the Freezer"; "Marinated Zucchini"; "Trina's Green Salmon" by Trina; "Simple Kale" by Sarah Libertus; "Kale Mashed Potatoes" by Sarah Libertus; "Wilted Mustard Greens Salad with Bacon"; "Southwestern Radish Salad"; "Ginger Squash Soup" by Sarah Libertus; "Stuffed Squash"; "Asian Fusion Slaw" by Sarah Libertus; "Colcannon"; "Poached Garlic"; and "Garlic Compound Butter."

- "Eggplant, Tomato, and Red Potato Casserole" by Nelda Danz. Courtesy of Nelda Danz.

- "Summer Fruit in Wine Dessert" by Melinda McBride. Courtesy of Melinda McBride.

- "Rhubarb Pie" by Rich Hoyle. Courtesy of Rich Hoyle.

- "Fried Squash Blossoms" and "Butternut Surprise" by Nickolas Vassili. Courtesy of Nickolas Vassili.

- "Braised Lamb with Olives and Mushrooms" by Jacob Wittenberg. Courtesy of Jacob Wittenberg.

- "Tomatoes Stuffed with Blue Cheese and Walnuts"; "Zucchini Casserole"; "Sweet Onion Casserole"; and "Warm Onion Dip" by Arlayne Fleming. Courtesy of Arlayne Fleming.

- "Oven-Roasted Tomato Sauce" by Maria Runde. Courtesy of Maria Runde.

- "Roasted Garlic Hummus" by Justin Watt. Reprinted from www.justinsomnia.org, and used under the Creative Commons Attribution License.

- "Zucchini Salad" from *Daisies Do Tell ... A Recipe Book* by Betty Culp. Date, publisher, and location of publication unknown.

- "Corn-Mac Casserole" by Donna Kaliff; "Layered Vegetable Casserole" by Aria Boydston; "Sour Cream Potato Salad" by Matthew George Looper; and "Coleslaw" by Shirley Holt, from *The Schoenleber Family Cookbook*, edited by Lura Looper. Copyright © 1993. Used courtesy of family.

The following recipes were reprinted from federal and state government websites and are assumed to be in the public domain.

- "Spaghetti with Spring Vegetables" by Jeanette Mettler Cappello; "Lemon-Walnut Green Beans"; "Vegetarian Stuffed Peppers"; "Broccoli Soup"; "Warm Red Cabbage Bacon Salad"; "Corn Chowder"; "Baba Ghanoush (Eggplant Dip)"; "Spicy Pork Tenderloin Pitas"; "Vegetarian Paella"; "Roasted Radishes and Root Vegetables," courtesy of the Radish Council; "Baked Rhubarb with Raspberries"; "Balsamic Rhubarb Compote"; "Creamy Spinach Soup"; "Homemade Salsa"; "Watermelon Bits"; "Watermelon Smoothie"; "Roasted Squash with Potatoes and Garlic"; "Summer Squash Muffins"; "Vegetable Cornmeal Crêpes"; "Curried Mustard Greens & Garbanzo Beans with Sweet Potatoes"; "Low-Fat Ranch Dip"; "Bacon, Ham & Leek Quiche" by Burma Farms, Inc., and "Seedless Cucumbers, Yogurt, Mint, and Garlic Salad" from Produce for Better Health Foundation. All recipes reprinted from the Centers for Disease Control & Prevention's Fruits and Veggies—More Matters website at www.fruitsandveggiesmatter.gov.

- "Spicy Veal Roast" from *Keep the Beat: Heart Healthy Recipes* by the National Institutes of Health, 2003. Reprinted from www.nhlbi.nih.gov/health/public/heart/other/ktb_recipebk.

- "LaVerne's Potato Candy" from American Memory Project's *Immigration ... The Great American Potluck*, Library of Congress, 2006. Reprinted from www.memory.loc.gov/learn/features/immig/ckbk/.

- "Vegetable Lasagna"; "Squash-Apple Casserole"; and "Summer Vegetable Medley" by the Massachussetts Department of Agricultural Resources. Reprinted from www.mass.gov/agr/markets/farmersmarkets/resources_consumers_recipes.htm.

The following entities were contacted for permission, but a reply was never received.

- "Salmon Poached with Tomatoes and Swiss Chard" and "Eggplant Salad with Sesame Seeds (Khaji Namul)" from A Taste

- Information on drying tomatoes on pages 189–190 adapted from "Drying Tomatoes" article by Shila Patel; excerpted from www.doityourself.com.

- Information on freezing rosemary on page 165 adapted from Kalyn's Kitchen website, by Kalyn Denny; excerpted from www.kalynskitchen.blogspot.com.

- Information on microwaving vegetables adapted and reprinted from the National Cancer Institute (www.dccps.nci.nih.gov), A to Z Central (www.azcentral.com), and the Michigan Asparagus Advisory Board (www.asparagus.org/maab).

- Information on freezing and blanching adapted and reprinted from Pick Your Own (www.pickyourown.org) and the University of Illinois Extension (www.urbanext.uiuc.edu).

- Nutritional information adapted from World's Healthiest Foods at www.whfoods.com.

- Partial information on chives adapted from article by Susan Mahr, the Department of Horticulture, the University of Wisconsin-Madison.

- Information on food weights, equivalents, conversions, and measurements adapted and reprinted from About.com (www.about.com); RecipeZaar (www.recipezaar.com); GourmetSleuth.com (www.gourmetsleuth.com), and *The Victory Garden Cookbook* by Morene Morash, Alfred A. Knopf, 1982.

Graphics credits:

- **Front Cover:** Background photo by Featherstone Farm. Clockwise from far left: Stir-fry by Paul Cowan, represented by Dreamstime.com; stuffed peppers by Pawel Strykowski, represented by Dreamstime.com; strawberries, lettuce seedlings, and squash seedlings by Featherstone Farm; and salad by Ingrid Balabanova, represented by Dreamstime.com.

- **Back Cover:** Background photo by Featherstone Farm. Clockwise from far left: Tomatoes by Irina Ponomarenko, represented by Dreamstime.com; shrimp pasta by David Smith, represented by Dreamstime.com; cabbage by Featherstone Farm; melon balls by Olga Lyubkina, represented by Dreamstime.com; and lettuce washing by Featherstone Farm.

- **Book Interior:** All illustrations from Clipart.com; all photographs courtesy of Featherstone Farm and its members, except arugula on page 4: Joanna Wnuk, represented by iStockphoto.com; bok choy on page 19: Sandra Caldwell, represented by iStockphoto.com; green garlic on page 27: iStockphoto.com; salad mix on page 46: Suzannah Skelton, represented by iStockphoto.com; rhubarb on page 69: "Dirkr," represented by iStockphoto.com; tomatoes on page 73: Irina Ponomarenko, represented by Dreamstime.com; lemongrass on page 125: "Floortje," represented by iStockphoto.com; mizuna on page 131: John Shepherd, represented by iStockphoto.com; leek on page 248: Clipart.com; tatsoi on page 289: Laurel, from Roux.vox.com; and Minnesota winter landscape on page 293: Lawrence Sawyer, represented by iStockphoto.com.

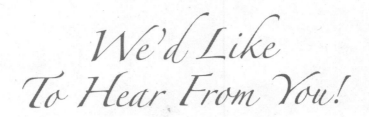

We'd Like To Hear From You!

We would love to know what you think about this book.
Thoughts? Questions? Feedback?

Please let us know!

We are also looking for recipe contributions and cooking tips
for future editions of this cookbook.

Please send us your comments and ideas:

Mi Ae Lipe
What Now Design
206-349-2038
miae@whatnowdesign.com
www.whatnowdesign.com

Featherstone Fruits and Vegetables
30997 Zephyr Valley Lane
Rushford, Minnesota 55971
507-452-4244
info@featherstonefarm.com
www.featherstonefarm.com

Thank you so very much ... we *really* appreciate your input!